C000089951

Transforming National Holidays

Discourse Approaches to Politics, Society and Culture (DAPSAC)

The editors invite contributions that investigate political, social and cultural processes from a linguistic/discourse-analytic point of view. The aim is to publish monographs and edited volumes which combine language-based approaches with disciplines concerned essentially with human interaction – disciplines such as political science, international relations, social psychology, social anthropology, sociology, economics, and gender studies.

For an overview of all books published in this series, please see
http://benjamins.com/catalog/dapsac

General Editors

Ruth Wodak, Greg Myers and Johann Unger
University of Lancaster

Editorial address:
Department of Linguistics and English Language
Lancaster University
Lancaster LA1 4YL, United Kingdom
r.wodak@lancaster.ac.uk; g.myers@lancaster.ac.uk and j.unger@lancaster.ac.uk

Advisory Board

Volume 47

Transforming National Holidays. Identity discourse in the West and South Slavic countries, 1985-2010
Edited by Ljiljana Šarić, Karen Gammelgaard and Kjetil Rå Hauge

Transforming National Holidays

Identity discourse in the West and South Slavic
countries, 1985-2010

Edited by

Ljiljana Šarić
Karen Gammelgaard
Kjetil Rå Hauge
University of Oslo

John Benjamins Publishing Company

Amsterdam / Philadelphia

The paper used in this publication meets the minimum requirements of the American National Standard for Information Sciences – Permanence of Paper for Printed Library Materials, ANSI z39.48-1984.

Library of Congress Cataloging-in-Publication Data

Transforming national holidays : identity discourse in the west and south Slavic
      countries, 1985-2010 / edited by Ljiljana Šarić, Karen Gammelgaard,
      Kjetil Rå Hauge.
   p. cm. (Discourse Approaches to Politics, Society and Culture, ISSN 1569-9463 ; v. 47)
Includes bibliographical references and index.
1. Slavic languages--Political aspects. 2. Slavs--Ethnic identity. 3. Discourse
      analysis--Political aspects--Slavic countries. 4. Holidays--Slavic countries.
      5. Nationalism--Slavic countries. 6. Nationalism and literature--Slavic
      countries. 7. Sociolinguistics--Slavic countries. 8. Slavic countries--Social life
      and customs--20th century. 9. Slavic countries--Social life and customs--21st.
      century. I. Šarić, Ljiljana. II. Gammelgaard, Karen. III. Hauge, Kjetil Rå, 1945-
PG44.73.T73   2012
394.269496--dc23   2012034477
ISBN 978 90 272 0638 1   (Hb ; alk. paper)
ISBN 978 90 272 7297 3   (Eb)

John Benjamins Publishing Co. · P.O. Box 36224 · 1020 ME Amsterdam · The Netherlands
John Benjamins North America · P.O. Box 27519 · Philadelphia PA 19118-0519 · USA

Table of contents

Contributors

Alexander Bielicki is currently a PhD research fellow at the Faculty of Humanities at the University of Oslo. He studied at the Central European University (MA thesis *Religious Pilgrimage in Slovakia: Catholic Sentiment, National Identity*) and University of Pittsburgh (BA). Bielicki focuses on topics of religious and national identity, especially identity construction and pilgrimage in Slovakia. In his PhD dissertation *A Nation in Worship? Identity Construction Processes in the Slovak National Pilgrimage to Šaštín-Stráže* he analyzes homiletics and uses ethnographic approaches to determine how pilgrimage participants navigate these religious events in response to the material delivered in the homilies.

Titus Ensink is a senior lecturer in discourse studies at the University of Groningen. He is the founder and editor of a Dutch-language book series for Thela Thesis Publishers in Amsterdam on perspectives in language use. His research interests include political rhetoric in relation to commemorations and frame analysis of text and media messages. His relevant publications pertaining to the first topic include "The Footing of a Royal Address: An Analysis of Representativeness in Political Speech, Exemplified in Queen Beatrix's Address to the Knesset" (in *Current Issues in Language and Society* 3(3): 205–232, 1996); *The Art of Commemoration. Fifty Years after the Warsaw Uprising* (Amsterdam: Benjamins, 2003, coedited with Christoph Sauer); and "Resolving Antagonistic Tensions. Some Discourse Analytic Reflections on Verbal Commemorative Practices" (in Ruth Wodak and Gertraud Auer Borea, eds., *Justice and Memory: Confronting Traumatic Pasts*, Vienna: Passagen, 2009: 169–193). His publications pertaining to the second topic include *Framing and Perspectivising in Discourse* (Amsterdam: Benjamins, 2003, coedited with Christoph Sauer) and "Pragmatic Aspects of Televised Texts: A Single Case Study of the Intervention of a Televised Documentary Program in Party Politics" (in *Journal of Pragmatics* 38(2): 230–249, 2006).

Karen Gammelgaard is a professor of Czech language and literature at the Department of Literature, Area Studies, and European Languages, University of Oslo. Throughout her academic career, Gammelgaard has taken a broad interest in language and text as social phenomena. Her interest in Prague School semiotics is reflected in her *Tekstens mening: En introduktion til Pragerskolen* (The Meaning of the Text: An Introduction to the Prague School; Copenhagen: Roskilde University Press, 2003). She has participated in several joint research projects dealing with texts in context. She coauthored and coedited *Tekst og Historie: Å lese tekster historisk* (Text and History: Reading Texts Historically, Oslo: Universitetsforlaget, 2008), and she contributed the chapter "Were the Czechs More Western than Slavic? Nineteenth-Century Travel Literature from Russia by Disillusioned Czechs" to *Imagining the West in Eastern Europe and the Soviet Union* (University of Pittsburgh Press, 2010). Since 2006, she has headed the project *The Upheaval of Czech Textual Culture* ("Coping with Stalinist Panegyrics: A Semantic and Pragmatic Analysis of a Czech Text," in *Journal of Historical Pragmatics* 9(1): 48–70, 2008; "Czech Classified Advertising under Stalinism: Transformation of a Genre," in *Slavonica* 16(2): 79–95, 2010). In 2009, she headed the project *Red-Letter Days in Transition* at the University of Oslo.

Knut Andreas Grimstad is an associate professor of Polish at the Department of Literature, Area Studies, and European Languages, University of Oslo. He has published works on Russian and on Polish literature and culture. He is the author of *Styling Russia: Multiculture in the Prose of Nikolai Leskov* (2007) and the coeditor of *Gender and Sexuality in Ethical Context: Ten Essays on Polish Prose* (2005). He is currently working on a volume about Witold Gombrowicz, whose plays he has also translated into Norwegian. Among Grimstad's main interests are popular culture and Jewish-Polish relations in independent Poland since 1918. His publications include "The Rhetoric of Absence: Representing Jewishness in Post-Totalitarian Poland" (in *Contesting Europe's Rim: Cultural Identities in Public Discourse*, Bristol, 2010), "Polsko-żydowskie gry kabaretowe, czyli Juliana Tuwima próba akulturacji" (Polish-Jewish Cabaret Acts, or Julian Tuwim's Attempted Acculturation; in *Polonistyka bez granic. Wiedza o literaturze i kulturze*, Cracow, 2010), and "Transcending the East-West? The Jewish Part in Polish Cabaret in the Interwar-Period" (in *Jahrbuch des Simon-Dubnow-Instiuts* 7, Ruprecht, 2008).

Elżbieta Hałas is a professor of humanities and sociology at the University of Warsaw, Poland. Her research interests focus on cultural sociology, social symbolism and collective memory, interpretive social theory, and history of sociology. Hałas received her PhD in sociology from the Catholic University of Lublin in 1986 and was appointed a professor in 1993. She received a Fulbright Award and fellowships from the American Council of Learned Societies (United States) and the Institute for Human Sciences (Vienna, Austria). She has served two terms on the Executive Council of the European Sociological Association. Her recent books include *Towards the World Culture Society: Florian Znaniecki's Culturalism* (Frankfurt am Main: Peter Lang, 2010), *Symbole i społeczeństwo* (Symbols and Society; Warsaw: Wydawnictwa Uniwersytetu Warszawskiego, 2007), and

Interakcjonizm symboliczny. Społeczny kontekst znaczeń (Symbolic Interaction-ism. The Social Context of Meanings; Warsaw: Wydawnictwo Naukowe PWN, 2006), and she edited *Symbols, Power and Politics* (Frankfurt am Main: Peter Lang, 2002). She is the founder and coeditor of the book series *Studies in Sociology: Symbols, Theory and Society* (Frankfurt am Main: Peter Lang).

Kjetil Rå Hauge is an associate professor of Bulgarian at the University of Oslo. He received his *cand. philol.* at the University of Oslo in 1974. His recent publications include "The Word Order of Predicate Clitics in Bulgarian" (in *Journal of Slavic Linguistics* 7: 91–139, 1999); *A Short Grammar of Contemporary Bulgarian* (Columbus, OH: Slavica, 1999), "At the Boundaries of the Balkan Sprachbund: Pragmatic and Paralinguistic Isomorphisms in the Balkans and Beyond" (in *Mediterranean Language Review* 14: 21–40, 2002); "Compiling a Dictionary of Turkisms" (in *Turkic Languages* 6(2): 275–283, 2002); and *Colloquial Bulgarian. The Complete Course for Beginners* (London: Routledge, 2006). He participated in several research projects including *Red-Letter Days in Transition* (2008–2010) and *Slavic-Romance-Germanic Parallel Corpus* (2010) (a subproject of *Russian Meets Norwegian*, http://www.hf.uio.no/ilos/forskning/forskningsprosjekter/run/).

Svein Mønnesland is a professor of Slavic studies at the Department of Literature, Area Studies, and European Languages at the Faculty of Humanities, University of Oslo. He has written extensively on the languages, history, and culture of the Balkans, especially Yugoslavia; for example, *Land ohne Wiederkehr. Ex-Jugoslawien: Die Wurzeln des Krieges* (Land of No Return. Former Yugoslavia: The Roots of the War; Klagenfurt: Wieser, 1997). His more recent publications in English include "Bosnia – Religion and Identity" (Stig Jarle Hansen et al., eds., *The Borders of Islam*, London: Hurst & Co, 2009); "The Sociolinguistic Situation in Bosnia-Herzegovina" (in *Language, Society, History: The Balkans*, Thessaloniki: Centre for the Greek Language, 2007); and "Turkey Seen from Europe's Near East, the Balkans" (in Edgeir Benum et al., eds., *Are We Captives of History?*, Oslo: Uniped, 2007).

Vjeran Pavlaković is an assistant professor in the Department of Cultural Studies at the University of Rijeka, Croatia. He received his PhD in history in 2005 from the University of Washington. He has published articles on the politics of memory, World War II commemorations, war criminals and war crime tribunals, and democratization in Croatia, and coedited the book *Serbia since 1989: Politics and Society under Milošević and After* (2005), published by the University of Washington Press. His recent publications include "Flirting with Fascism: The Ustaša Legacy and Croatian Politics in the 1990s" (in *Una storia balcanica: Fascismo, comunismo e nazionalismo nella Jugoslavia del Novecento*, 2008); "Red Stars, Black Shirts: Symbols, Commemorations, and Contested Histories of World War Two in Croatia" (an *NCEEER Working Paper*, 2008); and "The Commemorative Culture of Bleiburg, 1990–2009" (in *Kultura sjećanja: 1945*, 2009).

Tatjana Radanović Felberg is an associate professor of interpreting at Oslo University College. She is particularly interested in discourse analysis of political media texts. Her master's thesis and PhD dissertation (University of Oslo, 1992 and 2008, respectively) both dealt with identity constructions, analyzed through media texts, of former Yugoslav countries. Her relevant works include *Brothers in Arms? Discourse Analysis of Serbian and Montenegrin Identities and Relations as Constructed in Politika and Pobjeda Front Page Articles during the NATO Bombing of Yugoslavia in 1999* (dissertation, University of Oslo, 2008); "Semiotička konstrukcija vođe na naslovnim stranicama Politike i Pobjede" (The Semiotic Construction of the Leader on *Politika* and *Pobjeda* Front Pages; in *Njegoševi dani, zbornik radova*, University of Montenegro, 2008); "Inhabiting the Theatre of War: The Discourse Models of the NATO Bombing of Yugoslavia in Milošević's Address to the Nation and Đukanović's Address to the Citizens of Montenegro" (in *CADAAD journal* 1(1): 124–147, 2007); and "Construction of Serbian and Montenegrin Identities through Layout and Photographs of Leading Politicians in Official Newspapers" (in *Contesting Europe's Rim: Cultural Identities in Public Discourse*, Bristol: Multilingual Matters, 2010).

Christoph Sauer has been a senior lecturer in discourse studies and media communication at the University of Groningen since 1992. He has authored many publications on pragmatics, linguistics, and media influences in institutional discourse, and on rhetoric and problem-solving in political discourse, representative political speeches and their role concerning collective memory. Other topics include media semiotics and corpus studies in institutional settings, such as press photographs, documentary films, and their "audience design." His publications include editing *The Art of Commemoration. Fifty Years after the Warsaw Uprising* (Amsterdam: Benjamins, 2003, in collaboration with Titus Ensink); "Echoes from Abroad: Speeches for the Domestic Audience: Queen Beatrix's Address to the Israeli Parliament" (in *Current Issues in Language and Society* 3(3): 233–267, special issue: *Analysing Political Speeches*, ed. by Christina Schäffner); "Ceremonial Text and Talk: A Functional-Pragmatic Approach" (in Paul Chilton and Christina Schäffner, eds., *Politics as Talk and Text: Analytic Approaches to Political Discourse*, Amsterdam: Benjamins, 2002: 111–142); and "Christmas Messages by Heads of State: Multimodality and Media Adaptations" (in Anita Fetzer and Gerda Lauerbach, eds., *Political Discourse in the Media*, Amsterdam: Benjamins, 2007: 227–273).

Ljiljana Šarić is a professor of Bosnian, Croatian, and Serbian at the Department of Literature, Area Studies, and European Languages at the University of Oslo. Her research areas are discourse analysis (specifically, discursive construction of cultural identity), cognitive linguistics, and South Slavic languages, literatures, and cultures. As a coordinator and participant, she has been and is engaged in several international research projects (e.g., *Media Constructions of Images of the Self and the Other*, and *Intercultural Identities – Cross-National Discourses in Europe*). In 2010, she coordinated the project *Red-Letter Days in Transition* at the University of Oslo. She has authored, coauthored, and edited several books, including *Contesting Europe's Eastern Rim: Cultural Identities in Public Discourse* (Multilingual Matters, 2010) and *Discourses of Intercultural Identity in Britain, Germany and Eastern Europe* (special issue of the *Journal of Multilingual and Multicultural Development,* 2004). Her publications include "Balkan Identity: Changing Self-Images of the South Slavs" (in *Discourses of Intercultural Identity in Britain, Germany and Eastern Europe,* 2004); "*Metaphorical Models in EU Discourse in the Croatian Media*" (in *Jezikoslovlje* 6(2), 2005); and "Foreign and Domestic Media Images of the Balkans" (in *Contesting Europe's Eastern Rim,* 2010).

Marko Soldić studied Balkan history and politics as well as cultural anthropology at the University of Oslo. He wrote his master's thesis on veterans of the Croatian war of independence. While working on his thesis, Soldić was employed as a research assistant on the *Red-Letter Days in Transition* project. In 2009 he worked at the Norwegian embassy in Skopje, where among other things he conducted research on ethnic, political, and economic issues in Macedonia, and reported his findings to the Norwegian Ministry of Foreign Affairs. He also acted as an election observer with the OSCE/ODIHR during the 2009 Macedonian presidential and local elections. Soldić is currently working with issues related to Turkey, Cyprus, and Greece for the Norwegian Ministry of Foreign Affairs in Oslo while awaiting his first posting abroad.

Acknowledgements

The idea for this book originated in the project *Red-Letter Days in Transition: Calendric Public Rituals and the Articulation of Identities in Central Europe and the Balkans 1985 to Present*, funded by the Faculty of Humanities, University of Oslo, 2008–2010. Some initial ideas were discussed at a workshop held at the University of Oslo in November 2009. Adding new inspiration, Biljana Dragišić, Betine Huflåtten, and Irfan Turković wrote their master's theses as part of the project.

We are grateful to the Faculty of Humanities for funding the *Red-Letter Days* project, the workshop, and all other activities related to this book.

We would also like to thank the project's research assistants engaged in various activities directly and indirectly related to this book at different stages: Biljana Dragišić, Dragana Kovačević, Hanna Maria Heggem Holmene, Agnes Banach, Aleksandra Bartoszko, Marko Soldić, and Kristina Tanasković.

Many thanks are due to the authors for their cooperation during the compilation process, and to the copyeditor of the final manuscript, Frank Azevedo, for his work and comments to improve the manuscript.

Draft chapters were commented on by our colleagues Kristian Gerner, Christina Schäffner, Ulrich Schmid, and Stefan Troebst. Special thanks go to them for the time invested in this book project, and all the valuable suggestions and advice at various stages of the book's development.

We are indebted to the two anonymous reviewers, whose insightful comments and suggestions helped the authors improve their chapters, and to the series editors at Benjamins, who agreed to include this edited volume in the DAPSAC series.

We would like to thank the following copyright holders:

- The Montenegrin newspaper *Pobjeda* for permission to reproduce the illustrations in Chapter 4.
- The Croatian newspapers *Novi list, Slobodna Dalmacija*, and *Vjesnik* for permission to reproduce the illustrations in Chapter 5.
- The Czech News Agency (CTK) for permission to reproduce the illustrations in Chapter 10.
- The Polish newspaper *Gazeta Wyborcza* for permission to reproduce the illustrations in Chapter 12.

Preface

Kjetil Rå Hauge

This book and the research project that produced it stem from a fascination with calendric events – dates charged with more meaning, be it related to religion, politics, or folklore, than other days, including Sundays, and on which people partake in or attend certain public rituals. National holidays constitute a subset of such days. They have an intrinsic relation to a country's history, and at times of radical changes in that history, they may have to be reconsidered or reinterpreted. Radical changes in Central and South Eastern Europe during the twentieth century's last decade engendered considerable reconsideration and reinterpretation of national holidays, much of it still ongoing. This volume's chapters deal with these transformation features in the Slavic-speaking countries of Central and South Eastern Europe.

The introduction by Karen Gammelgaard and Ljiljana Šarić following this preface reviews the volume's theoretical background. It discusses aspects of transformations related to national holidays, holiday-specific terminology in the countries examined, factors relevant for the discursive construction of national holidays, and how discourse is related to creating collective memory and historical narratives.

In Poland, two holidays coincide on a single day: the state holiday celebrating Poland's first constitution, and the church holiday Feast of Our Lady, Queen of Poland. Both holidays are closely related to Polish identity, but to different sides of it: to civil society and the Polish Catholic church, respectively. Elżbieta Hałas shows, employing the elements of Kenneth Burke's dramatistic pentad, how three Polish presidents have chosen different rhetorical strategies in their speeches on the occasion of this combined celebration, and compares their discourse with ecclesial discourse on the same occasion.

In Serbia, such constellations of holidays are deliberately aimed for: after Yugoslavia's breakup, a new Statehood Day was assigned to the date of the religious holiday of Candlemas, a date on which an uprising against the Ottoman Empire took place in the early 19th century, and some years after that, the ratification of

Serbia's first constitution. The date is also Army Day, providing an occasion for celebration of state, army, and church on the same day. In one of her two chapters in this volume, Ljiljana Šarić examines the various ways, through different media genres, in which new instances of collective memory connected with this holiday were constructed in the media. Examining material from a wide variety of print and online media as well as radio and TV transcripts, she identifies central actors and specific genres, such as the short "history reader."

A very specific religious holiday is the subject of Alexander Bielicki's chapter: Our Lady of Seven Sorrows Day, celebrated by Catholics worldwide, has been elevated to the status of an official state holiday in Slovakia, and a national pilgrimage to a Marian shrine takes place. Bielicki studies how the homilies on this occasion over the years, before and after communism's fall, have involved more than religious matters and have even used religious motives for building national consciousness.

The Macedonians have been inclined through the years, like the Serbians, towards a national holiday that celebrates several underlying events on one date. The Macedonian example is St. Elijah's Day, on which occurred an uprising against the Ottoman Empire, including the proclamation of a republic that was very short-lived. Moreover, the Socialist Republic of Macedonia (within Yugoslavia) was proclaimed on that day. Macedonia's declaration of independence from Yugoslavia missed the date by weeks, but public debate before this event was full of references to the prospect of a third St. Elijah's Day. These factors, as well as the role played by the myth of St. Elijah's Day in building and confirming national consciousness while Macedonia was surrounded by countries contesting that national consciousness, are the topics of Marko Soldić's chapter.

Commemoration of events in recent wars with one's neighbors, with both the victors and the defeated participating, is bound to be a sensitive issue. Titus Ensink and Christoph Sauer's chapter deals with two commemorations, ten years apart, of the Warszaw Uprising of 1944. Poland's interpretation of this event is complex, especially as regards Russia, the Soviet Union's successor state. On one hand, the Soviet Union was, together with Poland, among the victors of World War II; on the other hand, the Red Army failed to militarily support the uprising, and Soviet domination following the war is regarded as a kind of occupation. Poland itself suffered a defeat in the uprising, but ultimately won a moral victory by being on the victorious Allied side. And Germany, Poland's wartime occupier, had become Poland's close political and economic partner a few months before the second of these commemorations. Through analysis of speeches from the two events, the authors find that one of Aleida Assmann's proposed solutions for dealing with a traumatic past, the strategy of joint dialogic remembering, best describes Poland's attitude towards this commemoration.

The collective memories of World War II are also the subject of Vjeran Pavlaković's chapter. The scene is Croatia, and the focus is less on official holidays than on the ways in which some groups in speeches at rallies contest them. The conflict is rooted in diametrically opposed conceptions of the narratives about the short-lived fascist Croatian state during World War II and about the role of the Croat partisans. Pavlaković finds the debates passionate and highly polemical, with few instances of the spirit of reconciliation that Ensink and Sauer notice in Poland.

Three chapters analyze aspects of national holidays that appear on newspapers' front pages. Tatjana Radanović Felberg analyzes textual, visual, and typographic elements in a dominant Montenegrin daily's web edition published on Montenegro's Independence Day or days close to it. From these pages she points out *discourse models*, in the sense in which the term is used by James Paul Gee, for different perceptions of Montenegro as a nation. The analyses of the front pages are supplemented by analyses of interviews with the dominant political figure Milo Đukanović.

Knut Andreas Grimstad's contribution is also based on a prominent daily, but one that achieved its status from a start early in the transformation period. The analyzed material is taken from its print editions. The holiday in question is Poland's National Holiday of Independence, and Grimstad focuses on the paper's efforts in constructing a Polish identity compatible with a European orientation. Drawing on Ruth Wodak's theory of argumentation, and analyzing textual elements as well as elements of newspaper layout, Grimstad discovers a tendency to advocate a European supranationalism that is compatible with Polish nationalism.

Ljiljana Šarić's other chapter deals with the front pages of three major Croatian newspapers, two state-owned and one independent, and three national holidays: Republic Day during the time of Yugoslav unity; the first Statehood Day introduced after Croatia's secession, commemorating the first multi-party parliament, which was constituted during Yugoslav unity; and the second Statehood Day, celebrating Croatia's declaration of independence. Opinions about whether events like forming the first multi-party parliament and declaring independence are suitable as reference points of the two new Statehood Days have differed in Croatian public discourse, and these differences are reflected on the front pages. Šarić's analysis is based on the semiotic theory of Gunther Kress and Theo van Leeuwen.

Karen Gammelgaard's chapter focuses on speeches given at Prague Castle by presidents on the occasion of the most prominent state holiday. One president addresses the citizens of socialist Czechoslovakia; two other presidents speak to the citizens of a democratic Czech Republic separated from Slovakia. Gammelgaard focuses on the verbal aspect of these addresses as well as on the pomp and circumstance surrounding the event – including its staging. Their textual part is analyzed with respect to genre, "us" vs. "them" categorization, and modalities, as well as to the fixed point in history that they accentuate.

In some countries debate continues about what event or events merit being the reference point for the country's official state holiday. The most striking example is the newly formed state of Bosnia and Herzegovina, where ethnic differences underlie the debate. A federative state, it has been unable to reach consensus on a common state holiday for the Serb-dominated and the Bosniak/Croat-dominated parts, or "entities," which is the official term for them. Svein Mønnesland scrutinizes the argumentation of leading politicians in the two entities within the framework of Paul Chilton's concept of modalities of discourse.

Bulgaria has existed longer than Bosnia and Herzegovina as a polity, but it won its independence gradually through a series of events. The debate in Bulgaria, as Kjetil Rå Hauge shows in his chapter, is characterized by the search for an event that can produce a narrative portraying Bulgaria and/or Bulgarians in the semantic role of acting subject, as opposed to showing foreign powers in this role.

Organization of this volume

In this volume, not all chapters focus on a single national holiday. Therefore, we have simply decided to order chapters by the calendar, according to the dates most in focus: 15 February (Serbia), 3 March (Bulgaria), 3 May (Poland), 21 May (Montenegro), 22 June (Croatia), 25 June (Croatia), 1 August (Poland), 2 August (Macedonia), 15 September (Slovakia), 28 October (the Czech Republic), 11 November (Poland), and 25 November (Bosnia and Herzegovina).

Primary sources used in individual chapters are listed at the end of the chapters. References to secondary literature are merged into a common Reference list on pages 297–309. Appendix (pages 311–312) provides a survey of current laws on national holidays in the countries under scrutiny.

The overarching idea of this volume is that identity is formed and transformed in spoken and written discourse. Therefore, all analyzed quotations are given in the original language or script. The translations into English are by the authors unless indicated otherwise. Official translations are used in some cases (e.g., presidential speeches). Most material analyzed in the volume does not exist in translation. The intention of the translations is to illustrate the structure and the meaning of the originals. Translations closely follow the originals, sometimes sacrificing idiomaticity.

Discursive construction of national holidays in West and South Slavic countries after the fall of communism

Introductory thoughts

Karen Gammelgaard and Ljiljana Šarić
University of Oslo

1. National holidays as sites of transformation

National holidays provide a yearly recurrent opportunity for people to reflect upon the identity of the collective they belong to. When people talk and write about those reflections, they contribute to constructing the collective identity, that is, they contribute to answering the question "Who are we?" In this volume, authors analyze how in the period from the mid 1980s to 2010 people reflected upon and constructed collective identity by talking and writing about national holidays in nine Central and Southeastern European countries: Bosnia and Herzegovina, Bulgaria, Croatia, the Czech Republic, Macedonia, Montenegro, Poland, Serbia, and Slovakia.

In the period under scrutiny, people in all nine countries experienced profound societal transformations. The fall of communism during 1989–1990 was followed by democratization, marketization, state-institution building, and civic nation-building. Therefore, scholars speak of triple or even quadruple transformations and emphasize the extraordinarily thorough character of transformations taking place in all post-communist countries (see, e.g., Bunce 1995; Linz and Stepan 1996; Kuzio 2001). In Central and Southeastern Europe, transformations included the splits of Czechoslovakia and Yugoslavia (with the wars following the split of the latter) and new states emerging in their places: Slovenia (1991), Macedonia (1991), Croatia (1992), Bosnia and Herzegovina (1992), the Czech Republic (1993), Slovakia (1993), Montenegro (2006), Serbia (2006), and Kosovo (2008). Among the countries addressed here, only Poland and Bulgaria remained stable constitutional entities. The peoples of all these countries have shared the experience of totalitarian communism. Its fall and the subsequent transformations brought to the fore the question "Who are we?" Under communism, public debates on collective identity had been impeded due to general restrictions on debate under totalitarian rule. A specific obstacle to debates on national identity consisted of the communist ideology's professing itself internationalist and, particularly in Yugoslavia, supranational.

Focusing in this volume on specific kinds of cultural transformations, namely those transforming collective identity, we would like to highlight two points originally made by political sociologist Claus Offe (1997) about how cultural transformations relate to other post-communist transformation processes. First, although happening simultaneously with those other processes, cultural transformations are "indispensable cement" for the success of them. Participants in political and economic life must gain the confidence that all other members of the relevant collective act with trust, solidarity, and inclusive self-recognition towards that collective. Second, whereas models for transformation of economic and political institutions may be imported from abroad – models were indeed imported to the Central and Southeastern European countries from abroad, namely from West Europe and North America, as demonstrated by the countries' admission (or prospects for admission) into the North Atlantic Treaty Organization and/or the European Union – the "mental software" of such institutions cannot be provided from the outside. Its successful implementation depends on the collective self-understanding of people living in the countries under transformation.

What this volume offers, therefore, is analyses of collective self-understanding during transformation processes in Central and Southeastern Europe. Authors seek to understand how people living in this region conceived of themselves during post-communist transformation and how they actively participated in specific kinds of cultural transformations, namely those of transforming collective identities. These transformations took place mainly in discourse, as we will discuss in more detail below.

To analyze processes of collective identity transformation, national holidays are chosen as a shared focus. We define "national holiday" provisionally as a day regarded as referring to a significant event in the past of the collective (national or other) that observes the holiday.[1] The term "national holiday" normally does not refer to religious holidays and international holidays. However, as several analyses in this volume show, an originally religious holiday may become a national holiday, or a religious holiday and a national holiday may merge on the same date. In addition, religious holidays may obtain features from nation-oriented discourse and vice versa. International holidays less often lend features to national holidays, but overlaps exist, since some national holidays are regarded as instances of

---

1.   English-language scholarly publications also use the term "national days" for this subgroup of holidays (e.g., McCrone and McPherson 2009; Fuller 2004).

international movements (e.g., constitutionalism) or international events (e.g., World War II).

None of the year's days has any inherent meaning. Their meaning first comes into being when people begin to assign meaning to them, when they begin to regard days as symbols of something. This assignment of meaning takes place in discourse. As are all symbols, national holidays are subject to editing, overwriting, and erasure. National holidays are far less stable than other collective symbols – flags, currency, monuments, language(s), and anthems. They are, in Michael Geisler's words (2009: 10), "unstable signifiers." Moreover, national holidays are less capable of being materialized in the ways that most other national symbols can be, for example, as replicas or miniatures. Furthermore, national holidays are less ubiquitous than other collective symbols to which people are often exposed daily (Billig 2005). People encounter the single national holidays only once yearly and therefore tend to notice them more than other, more ubiquitous symbols (e.g., flags). However, national holidays compete for meaning with holidays that are based on the religious demarcation of the calendar and with international secular holidays, such as May Day and New Year's Day.

Under communism, sets of ideologically loaded national holidays existed in all Central and Southeastern European countries. These holidays included celebrations of communist takeovers and other events important for the ruling communist parties. For example in Czechoslovakia, 25 February, the day in 1948 when the communists seized power, was observed as *Den vítězství pracujícího lidu* (Day of the Working People's Victory). In Yugoslavia, 25 May was celebrated as *Dan mladosti* (Youth Day), with celebrations including adoration of the communist leader Josip Broz Tito; 25 May was Tito's symbolic birthday (see Slavnić 2010). Bulgaria had 9 September, *Ден на свободата* (Freedom Day), to mark the communist takeover in 1944. Poland observed 22 July as *Rocznica ogłoszenia Manifestu PKWN* (Anniversary of the Manifest of the Polish Committee of National Liberation) to commemorate the beginnings of communist rule in 1944. All communist countries grandiosely celebrated May Day.

As unstable signifiers, national holidays lend themselves easily to analysis of change over time. Recurring every year, the single holiday prompts people to resume discourse about specific events in the past and about their legacy. This discourse is linear in the sense that new contributions relate to previous discourse on the same topic and to discourse used on previous celebrations, and use these previous discourses as a resource (Krzyżanowski and Wodak 2009). Accordingly, when focusing on discourse connected with national holidays, analysts of identity discourse find ample evidence of resumed discourse. In countries under profound and rapid transformations, such as those countries included here, changes in identity-shaping discourse are particularly noticeable and frequent.

Regard for discourse as the main means of transforming collective identity governed our selection of countries. Aware of their political, economic, cultural, and religious diversity, we delimit our area linguistically. We use this linguistic delimitation to circumvent the often too sharply defined borderline between Eastern and Western Europe (on the discursive construction of this border see, e.g., Eger and Langer 1996; Langer 1999; Péteri 2010; Šarić et al. 2010; and Wolff 1994). This too sharply defined borderline easily leads to placing in the East the countries dealt with here, so that their societal changes are seen as more or less successful attempts to live up to Western standards (Todorova 2005).

Cases analyzed in this volume cover countries where the majority of people speak languages classified as West and South Slavic (see, e.g., Sussex and Cubberley 2006).[2] The major West Slavic languages are Polish, Czech, and Slovak. The major South Slavic languages are Bosnian,[3] Bulgarian, Croatian, Macedonian, Montenegrin, Serbian, and Slovenian (see below on the difficult delimitation of the languages of the former Yugoslavia). The structures and vocabularies of these languages are similar enough to provide their speakers with comparable means of expression. Alphabets differ because Cyrillic is used in Bulgaria, Macedonia, and to a lesser degree in Serbia (although the constitution defines Cyrillic as the only alphabet of Serbian "in its official use") and Montenegro (the constitution defines both alphabets as equal), whereas the Latin alphabet is used in the other countries (and increasingly in Serbia and Montenegro). All West and South Slavic languages have the grammatical category of aspect and rich verb inflections capable of specifying stages and states of processes. Also, they use word order as the main means to signal given and new information; only Bulgarian and Macedonian have articles that may be used for the same purpose. Due to their similarities, the West and South Slavic languages provide similar means for discursive identity construction. For example, generally, the tendency towards dropping non-emphasized subject pronouns forces the analyst to detect construction of Us and Them groups in verbal endings rather than in these two pronouns. However, the languages do have personal pronouns that may be used for explicit contrast. Furthermore, there is a widespread use of the possessive pronoun *naš*, 'our' and

---

2. East Slavic languages, the third main group in this classification, are used in Belarus, Russia, and Ukraine. East Slavic languages all use the Cyrillic alphabet. Post-communist developments in these countries differ considerably from developments in the countries of Central and Southeastern Europe.

3. The name "Bosnian" has emerged as the official name of the language of the Bosniac people. However, there are some controversies regarding this name: Many Croatian and Serbian linguists reject the term "Bosnian (language)," preferring the attribute *bošnjački*, 'Bosniac' (see Greenberg 2004: 139–142).

prepositional phrases with the personal pronoun *mi/my/nie*, 'we' (e.g., *u nas*, 'here, in our country') in these languages in contexts where other languages use the name of the country, the nationality, or the national language: for example Polish: *Że każdy może zostać u nas prezydentem?* 'That everybody may become president in Poland?'; Bulgarian: *у нас*, 'in Bulgaria,' *нашите*, 'the Bulgarian team,' *нашенски*, 'Bulgarian language or dialect'; Slovak: *u nášho obyvateľstva*, 'in the Slovak population.' Sometimes, speakers of the language formerly called Serbo-Croatian name their mother tongue *naš jezik*, 'our language,' instead of naming it with an expression denoting a specific nation. In addition, all West and South Slavic languages may use the dative case to express ownership and belonging. Last but not least, due to shared genesis and mutual borrowings, the West and South Slavic languages exhibit many common words central to the subject discussed here. Cases in point are *dan/den/deň/dzień*, 'day,' *narod/národ/naród*, (meaning both 'nation' and 'people'), and their derivations. Croatian, Czech, and for most cases Polish, use Slavic names for months, not names inherited from the Julian calendar.

The splits of Czechoslovakia and Yugoslavia affected languages. Influences were minor in the Czechoslovak case because already before the split, Czech and Slovak were established as two distinct languages used in the territories of what became the two independent states, the Czech Republic and Slovakia. Until 1990, the primary language of the former Yugoslav republics of Bosnia and Herzegovina, Croatia, Montenegro, and Serbia was commonly referred to as Serbo-Croatian. Its slightly different varieties in the Yugoslav republics stemmed from individual traditions and dialectal differences. Differences were primarily observable in vocabulary. The states that arose from the dissolution of Yugoslavia have seen language as a primary marker of national identity. Consequently, Serbo-Croatian was given ethnic names (Bosnian in Bosnia, Croatian in Croatia, and Serbian in Serbia); recently, there have also been attempts to differentiate Montenegrin from Serbian in Montenegro. Since the 1990s, there have been both moderate and extreme attempts in all former Yugoslav republics to further differentiate the former varieties. This differentiation has primarily affected vocabulary (on the language issue in Yugoslavia and its successor states, see Greenberg 2008; on language and nationalism, see Kordić 2010).

Since the national revivals in the 19th century, national identities in the West and South Slavic countries are based heavily on language and literature (see, e.g., Wachtel 2006). Arguably, this practice stems from the fact that the people of these countries all struggled against the German and Russian hegemonic threats to their cultures; in the southern and easternmost countries, the threat also came from the Ottoman Empire (Cornis-Pope and Neubauer 2004). Several of the countries' national holidays are connected with literacy. Bulgaria celebrates on 24 May, The

Day of Bulgarian Enlightenment and Culture and of Slavonic Literacy. Macedonia, the Czech Republic, and Slovakia observe one day in common for Saints Cyril and Methodius commemorating the "Apostles to the Slavs," the brothers credited with devising the first Slavic alphabet (observed in Macedonia on 24 May, in the Czech Republic and in Slovakia on 5 July). Slovenia marks Reformation Day on 31 October, with its accent on the historical efforts to create a Slovenian literary language, as well as the Day of Slovenian Culture (8 February), also called Prešeren's Day after the Romantic poet.

Significant social changes are usually followed by changes in the entire inventory of national symbols, including national holidays.[4] When entities and identities change, national holidays change. A newly independent state will observe or celebrate its newly acquired independence. The set of national holidays is an important framework of collective identity. Therefore, a radical change in the political system can lead to changes in the selection of national holidays and in their meaning. Moreover, social changes affect the temporal order of a collective and its shared memory of the past, which are registered by inaugurating a new calendar (Hałas 2002b). In other words, changes in the way the past is viewed correspond to major social transformations that affect entire communities. These processes can be clearly traced in the countries examined in this volume.

The chapters concentrate on different phases in the life cycles of national holidays: the inception phase and the period immediately after (their birth), the period of their (relative) acceptance and contestation, the end phase of a national holiday, and its death. The case studies show that especially the first and third phases are rich in discourses that shape the holiday's identity and thereby contribute to shaping the identity of the relevant collective. Also, many of the countries in the area have initiated the re-birth of specific national holidays. Some of those re-born holidays had been banned from the official communist calendar; others had been interpreted in manners too closely linked with the ideology of the ruling parties to survive in those interpretations the fall of communism. Since these national holidays reached back to events in the pre-communist period, their rebirth contributed to expanding the time span the collectives may claim as part of their collective identity.

All aspects of national holidays in the West and South Slavic countries are generally under-explored in international scholarship. Recent investigations of national holidays (e.g., McCrone and McPherson 2009; Fuller 2004) do not cover the countries discussed in this volume. Therefore, this volume fills a gap with its

---

4. See contributions to the special issue of *Osteuropa* 53 (7) (2003) on state symbolism and the historical culture.

focus on countries where rapid and profound transformations provide preeminent opportunities to study changes in collective identity.

The focus on West and South Slavic countries entails some terminological problems that we pinpoint in Section 2. In Sections 3 to 5, we discuss some of the patterns that analyses in this volume enable us to identify, patterns concerning national holidays and official discourse, national holidays and collective memory, and the underlying historical events that national holidays refer to. We close this introductory chapter in Section 6 by briefly surveying the methods used by authors of this volume.

2. Terminology

English-language research on national holidays evidences that these days may function as symbols of a collective's past (see contributions in McCrone and McPherson 2009). Prototypically, national holidays mark dates related to political history and nationhood, or to the formation or disintegration of a state; therefore, they are called, for example, independence days, constitution days, and statehood days (see also Fuller 2004). Sometimes national holidays mark separation, and sometimes union. They may also mark the beginning of a revolution, the fall, or the beginning of a regime. They may be patron saints' days, rulers' birthdays and so on, and countries may have more than one national holiday.

This volume deals with a number of national holidays, but not exclusively with this category as it is established in English-language research. Our understanding of the term "national holiday" is influenced by how speakers of West and South Slavic linguistically categorize days observed for their symbolic relation to the past. Our understanding is influenced by the lexical items speakers use in their respective languages.[5]

Generally, for "holiday" the West Slavic languages use lexical items based on a root meaning 'holy': Czech uses *svátek*, Polish *święto*, and Slovak *sviatok*. Czech and Slovak use these same lexical items for 'saint's day' and 'name day.' The South Slavic languages base their lexical items for "holiday" on a root meaning 'vacant,' implying 'free from labor': *praznik/празник*. However, this root is not used in all South Slavic expressions within this domain. For example, in Croatian everyday language, *praznik* usually refers to all secular non-working holidays, whereas *svetak* or *svetac* (both also from the root meaning 'holy') refer to the religious holidays, if individual names are not used. The word *blagdan* has been favored

---

5.   Information on everyday lexical items for "holiday" and "national holiday" below is based on dictionaries, national corpora, and a wide range of journalistic texts.

in official Croatian usage instead of *praznik* since 1990, an instance of language politics seeking to distance Croatian from Serbian.

Regarding compounds, in some South Slavic languages, *nacionalni praznik* functions as an equivalent to "national holiday."[6] In Slovenian, *nacionalni praznik* occurs as a synonym for *državni praznik* (literally, 'state holiday'), thus referring to any day related to state formation or with symbolic value for a state. In Croatian, *nacionalni praznik* is used mostly for foreign national holidays. Single occurrences can be found referring to Croatia as well. *Hrvatski nacionalni praznik* (Croatian National Holiday) occurs in media and (official) political contexts as a synonym for *Dan državnosti* (Statehood Day). *Državni blagdan* and *državni praznik* (both meaning 'state holiday') are also used. Serbian speakers use *nacionalni praznik* to convey two meanings: a day related to an ethnic group (e.g., *Nacionalni praznik Slovaka u Srbiji* (National Holiday for Slovaks living in Serbia)) and a day related to a state's formation. The latter meaning relates to all holidays celebrating historical matters related to Serbia as a state or to states Serbia was part of. Examples of this usage are *Dan državnosti* (Statehood Day), *Dan kraljevine* (Kingdom Day), and *Dan ujedinjenja* (Unification Day). For its part, *državni praznik*, 'state holiday,' comprises, for example, May Day and other international holidays. Yet also Serbian Statehood Day (*Sretenje*, 'Candlemas') is sometimes referred to as a *državni praznik* (state holiday). In Bulgarian and Macedonian, the compound национален ден, 'national day,' occurs. In Bulgarian, it may refer to various days, for example, *Национален ден на природните паркове* (National Nature Reserve Day), or *Национален ден на ромите* (National Roma Day). In Macedonian, национален ден, 'national day,' refers to a day dedicated to an ethnic group. Additionally, it may refer to days linked with transnational groups or campaigns, for example, *Национален ден на преживеаните од рак* (National Cancer Survivors' Day).

Also in everyday usage in West Slavic languages, qualifiers meaning 'national' or 'state' are used in compounds related to holidays. In Polish, both *święto narodowe*, 'national holiday,' and *święto państwowe*, 'state holiday,' are used, often interchangeably. Also *dzień narodowy/narodowy dzień*, 'national day,' occurs, but seldom about the central Polish holidays. In Czech, *státní svátek*, 'state holiday,' is more frequently used than *národní svátek*, 'national holiday,' both for Czech national holidays and foreign national holidays. The same tendency applies to

---

6. In South Slavic languages, the adjectives *nacionalan* and национален mean 'pertaining to a nation/state/country'; for example, in Bosnian, Croatian and Serbian, *nacionalni simboli* means 'national/state symbols,' but also means 'pertaining to ethnic groups' as, for example, in *nacionalne manjine,* 'ethnic minorities.'

Slovak: *štátny sviatok*, 'state holiday,' is more frequent for both Slovak and foreign national days than is *narodny sviatok*, 'national day.' Presumably, the frequent occurrences of compounds with a literal meaning of 'state holidays' and not 'national holidays' in the West and South Slavic languages reflect the discontinuity of the nation-based states in the region.

While in everyday language lexical items are permanently negotiated and therefore lack precise, fixed meaning, legislative language comes closer to providing terms, that is, lexical items with fixed usage and unambiguous meaning. Most national holidays dealt with in this volume are "legal holidays" in US terminology: They are established by law.[7] As several chapters point out, collective identity construction includes parliamentarians' debating the selection and the meaning of national days. The resulting national legislation differs considerably between the individual West and South Slavic countries. Differences attest to how fluid the concept of national holidays is and to how intimately linked national holidays are with ideas of identity for each collective.

Bulgarian legislation has no separate law regulating national holidays. Instead, they are defined in Article 154 of the Labor Code, which gives a list of eleven fixed-date holidays and four moveable Easter holidays (not counting Easter Sunday). The date of 3 March is given the additional qualification of *национален празник*, 'national holiday,' and it and the rest are collectively termed *официални празници*, 'official holidays.' Curiously, a 2010 amendment to the Labor Code introduced two more holidays around Easter and also changed the wording allowing the government to declare other days as once-only official holidays. These once-only holiday days now have the double-barreled qualifier "national official holidays."[8]

Poland's law on non-working days was first passed under communism in 1951 and has been amended after 1990. The most important amendments concern 3 May and 11 November. The law states that in addition to Sundays, thirteen religious and secular holidays are non-working. The secular holidays are New Years Day, May Day, 3 May, and 11 November (Independence Day).[9] Also, in single acts, the Polish Parliament has focused on specific dates. For example, in 1998, Parliament declared 27 September *Dzień Polskiego Państwa Podziemnego* (Day of Polish Underground State, referring to activities during World War II).

---

7. A list of current laws on national holidays in the West and South Slavic countries is provided in Appendix.

8. http://balans.bg/78-kodeks-na-truda/.

9. Regarding the names of 3 May, see Hałas in this volume.

The rest of the countries have specific laws on national holidays, deemed necessary by these countries' new constitutional status. National legislation establishes hierarchies of the days in question. Their classification as working or non-working is an important means in establishing hierarchies.

Most national legislation has two categories of holidays. In Montenegro, the Law on Holidays distinguishes between *državni praznici*, 'state holidays' and *praznici*, 'holidays.' State holidays are *Dan nezavisnosti* (Independence Day) and *Dan državnosti* (Statehood Day). The other category of holidays comprises New Year's Day and May Day. A separate law regulates religious holidays. It states that the government observes Orthodox Christmas and Easter as national holidays, that Orthodox believers may also celebrate patron saints' days at their own discretion, that Catholics have the right to observe their Christmas, Easter, and All Saints' Day, that Jews have the right to observe Passover and Yom Kippur, and that Muslims have the right to observe Eid and Ramadan.

Serbian legislation distinguishes between *verski praznici*, 'religious holidays,' and *državni praznici*, 'state holidays,' the later comprising *Dan državnosti* (Statehood Day), *Dan pobede* (Victory Day), *Praznik rada* (Labor Day), and *Nova godina* (New Year's Day). According to the law, a *državni praznik*, 'state holiday,' can be a working holiday (*Dan pobede*) or a non-working holiday (the rest).

Croatian law defines *blagdani*, 'holidays,' as all political and religious holidays that are non-working days. In addition to Catholic holidays, the term *blagdani* comprises six holidays: *Nova godina* (New Year's Day), *Praznik rada* (Labor Day), *Dan antifašističke borbe* (Antifascist Struggle Day), *Dan državnosti* (Statehood Day), *Dan pobjede i domovinske zahvalnosti* (Victory and Homeland Thanksgiving Day), and *Dan neovisnosti* (Independence Day). Also, the category non-working days includes Sundays. *Spomendani*, 'memorial days,' are working holidays, for example, *Dan hrvatskoga sabora* (Day of the Croatian Parliament).

Slovenia distinguishes *prazniki*, 'holidays,' from *dela prosti dnevi* (literally 'days off work'). There are ten holidays, seven of which are also days off work. Seven holidays commemorate historical events and persons (e.g., Slovenia's independence from Yugoslavia, Resistance Day, and Slovenian poet France Prešeren). The law defines *Prešernov dan* (Prešeren Day) as *slovenski kulturni praznik*, 'Slovenian culture holiday.' The remaining holidays are New Year's Day, May Day, and All Saints' Day. Presumably, the inclusion of All Saints' Day in the category of holidays signals this day's specific status as compared with five other religious holidays categorized as days off work. In addition to four Catholic holidays, this group includes *dan reformacije* (Reformation Day).

Concerning countries with a tripartite distinction, Czech legislation differentiates between *státní svátky*, 'state holidays,' *ostatní svátky*, 'other holidays,' and *významné dny*, 'significant days.' Holidays in the first two categories are non-working holidays. The category "state holidays" comprises seven days of great national significance, for example, *Den vítězství* (Victory Day), *Den upálení mistra Jana Husa* (Day of Master Jan Hus' Burning at the Stake), and *Den vzniku samostatného československého státu* (Day of the Establishment of the Independent Czechoslovak State). The category "other holidays" includes religious and international holidays. After the most recent amendments (2006), the category of "significant days" contains ten days, most of them connected with events of the twentieth century.

Slovakia has a similar system that differentiates *štátne sviatky*, 'state holidays,' *dni pracovného pokoja* (literally, 'days of work quiet') and *pamätné dni*, 'memorable days.' The prominent category of state holidays comprises *Deň vzniku Slovenskej republiky* (Day of Establishment of the Slovak Republic), *Sviatok svätého Cyrila a svätého Metoda* (Holiday of St. Cyril and St. Methodius), *Výročie Slovenského národného povstania* (Anniversary of the Slovak National Uprising), *Deň Ústavy Slovenskej republiky* (Day of the Constitution of the Slovak Republic), and *Deň boja za slobodu a demokraciu* (Day of Fight for Freedom and Democracy). The category "days of work quiet" refers to religious (Catholic) holidays, including *Sedembolestná Panna Mária* (Our Lady of the Seven Sorrows Day), May Day, and *Deň víťazstva nad fašizmom* (Day of Victory over Fascism). The category of "memorable days" comprises no less than sixteen days, most of them connected with Slovak history.

Macedonian holidays are regulated by the 1998 Law on Holidays, amended in 2007. Legislation defines three groups of holidays: *државни празници*, 'state holidays,' *празници*, 'holidays,' and *нераборни денови*, 'non-working days.' The category "state holidays" relates to Macedonian history and comprises six days: *Св. Кирил и Методиј – Ден на сесловенските просветители* (Saints Cyril and Methodius Day: Day of the Slavic Enlighteners), *Ден на Републиката* (Republic Day), *Ден на независноста* (Independence Day), *Ден на народното востание* (People's Uprising Day), *Ден на македонската револуционерна борба* (Day of the Macedonian Revolutionary Struggle), and *Св. Климент Охридски* (Saint Clement of Ohrid Day). The category "holidays" comprises New Year's Day, Christmas, and Easter according to the Orthodox calendar, May Day, and Eid ul-Fitr. The category "non-working days" comprises a number of days celebrated either by religious communities or by ethnic groups in Macedonia, for example, *Свети Сава* (Saint Sava's Day) celebrated by Serbs, *Ден на албанската азбука* (Day of the Albanian Alphabet) celebrated by Albanians, and *Национален ден на Власите* (Vlach National Day) celebrated by the Vlach minority.

In Bosnia and Herzegovina, the legislative situation is complex. A law on holidays exists on the state level, but it is contested, and holidays regarded as too closely related to specific ethnic groups are boycotted by other groups. Moreover, on the territories of Republika Srpska and Brčko District within the state of Bosnia and Herzegovina, local political bodies have established their own holiday legislation. Particularly the holiday legislation of Republika Srpska challenges the set of holidays established on the state level.

3. National holidays in official discourse

More than previous research on national holidays does (e.g., Geisler 2009), this volume highlights their dependence on discourse. People claim ownership over national holidays in and through discourse, and they distance themselves from national holidays via discourse. People use holidays' references to historical events to struggle for their specific version of collective memory. This struggle, which is often politically motivated and seeks to achieve a certain political outcome, also takes place in discourse. National holidays spur negotiations of collective belonging to political, religious, social, ethnic, and cultural entities, and of the meaning of the past for these entities' present and future. National holidays are an outlet for negotiations of collective identity. The platform for all these negotiations is also discourse. In short, the meaning of national holidays is created and negotiated through discourse. Discourse is the medium in which national holidays come into being.

For these reasons, the authors of this volume have chosen discourse as their main research topic. These authors' understanding of discourse follows that of Ruth Wodak and Martin Reisigl (2001:36) who define discourse as "a complex bundle of simultaneous and sequential interrelated linguistic acts that manifest themselves within and across the social fields of action as thematically interrelated semiotic, oral and written tokens, very often as 'texts,' that belong to specific semiotic types, i.e., genres." We emphasize that when people speak and write about a specific theme of national holidays, they use discourse as a means to shape and reshape collective identity. Texts about national holidays do not merely contribute to building up knowledge and beliefs about the shared theme; they have important pragmatic aspects, too.

So far, research on national holidays has neglected their discursive construction (see, e.g., McCrone and McPherson 2009; Fuller 2004). This is surprising, given the central role of discourse to establish, maintain, and challenge those events of the past that national holidays mark. (For a general discussion of discourse as a collectively shaped means to categorize extra-discursive realities and to provide them with meaning, see, e.g., Teubert 2010). The selection of underlying events of national holidays and the meaning of the holidays depend on discursive negotiations in the collective that observes them. Most people in a particular collective may not have lived when the events took place, and they may not have participated directly. They know about the events only because they have been told about them or read about them. And even direct participants may disagree regarding which dimensions of the events were most important, and they may have different interpretations of the events' causes and outcomes.

Most of the following chapters concentrate on official discourse, that is, on how people in office – politicians, church dignitaries, and military leaders – and influential intellectuals discursively create national holidays. Typical genres include presidential addresses, commemorative speeches, interviews, homilies, and newspaper commentaries. Almost all discourse analyzed here is produced by men, a predominance reflecting the weak position of women in the public sphere in the West and South Slavic countries. Not until 2009 could any of them boast female prime ministers, Slovakia's Iveta Radičová and Croatia's Jadranka Kosor.[10] Before the fall of communism, all the countries officially celebrated International Women's Day, 8 March. Today, however, only reminiscences of those celebrations remain.

Official discourse is largely mediated communication. Spoken or written, accompanied or unaccompanied by pictures and/or music, this discourse is disseminated by means of print and/or electronic media. Via the media, discourse on national holidays may reach potentially vast audiences. The media do not passively describe or record news events; they are not neutral agents, but actively reconstruct events (see e.g., Oktar 2001). Therefore, they shape and influence the ideological structure of the society in which they act. To paraphrase Thompson (1990: 226), they are sites for production and diffusion of ideology. Many readers and viewers tend to adopt media representations as their own. The influential power of the media is the key for explaining their specific role in ideology reproduction (van Dijk 1989: 203–204). When social groups compete for power, the media discourse is shaped by that competition and influences its course.

Therefore, analysis of discourse about national holidays must include activities by media workers: Journalists and commentators, who contribute their own texts, and those doing layout, who together with editors frame others' messages. Media workers influence discourse about national holidays and therefore

---

10. Croatia's Vesna Pusić ran unsuccessfully for president of her country in 2009–2010. Blaga Dimitrova was Bulgaria's vice president 1992–1993. The Republika Srpska, the entity within Bosnia and Herzegovina, had Biljana Plavšić as its second president; she was in office 1996–1998.

influence the transformation of collective identity. Moreover, particularly in the 1990s, the media presented people in the region analyzed with many newly available political and cultural options, including identity options (see, e.g., Melegh 2006; Mihelj 2011; Petrović 2009). Rather than communicating collective identities that were already largely agreed upon, media presented options that could serve as bases for establishing new collective identities.

Chapters in this volume portray different media attitudes, from that of a liberal-democratic platform (Poland's *Gazeta Wyborcza*; see Grimstad in this volume) to that of a loyal mediator of the president's worldview (Montenegro's *Pobjeda online*; see Radanović Felberg in this volume). In other cases, media contribute to strengthening the orientations of specific reader groups. Some media maintain relatively stable attitudes throughout the analyzed period, but the transformation of media attitudes is also evidenced, perhaps most conspicuously in the Croatian dailies after the fall of Franjo Tuđman's regime in 2000 (see Šarić on Croatia in this volume). Therefore, analyses in this volume confirm what media scholars have seen as a conspicuous feature of media in post-communist countries, namely that as the media were contributing to identity transformation, they simultaneously were being transformed by events and were also transforming themselves (Jakubowicz 2007). In the case of national holidays, the problems of the region's media after 1989 – their over-politicization and partisanship and their lack of fact-based journalism (Gross 2002; see also Splichal 1994) – turn into an advantage for analysts because the media frequently display partisan views on historical events underlying national holidays. They thereby lay bare national holidays as sites for debate and dispute.

Paradoxically, the power of the media in the West and South Slavic countries testifies to these countries' democracy. According to Teun A. van Dijk, power in democratic societies is discursive in its nature, and the media in these societies have "nearly exclusive control over the symbolic resources needed to manufacture popular consent, especially in the domain of ethnic relations" (1991: 43). In communist Europe, popular consent was often achieved also by coercion (or consent was simply falsified in the state monopoly media); so, the use of symbolic resources in post-communist Europe is indisputably progress. However, the use of symbolic resources once again testifies to the media's central role. Just as in other democratic societies, mass media in the West and South Slavic countries gain a central role in how participants in public discourse may proliferate, topicalize, detopicalize, and create facts and beliefs (see also KhosraviNik 2009: 478).

Elites who have access to mass media, and who thereby control the production and reproduction, creation, and recreation of narratives, acquire more power (van Dijk 2005). Elites may consist of politicians, journalists, scholars, writers, or policy-setting editorial boards of international media. Their contributions to media discourse are perhaps particularly critical, and particularly important to scrutinize, in post-communist countries because the profound societal transformations lead to new constellations of social groups, and those constellations must be explained and legitimized (Erjavec 2001: 721).

Analyzing how elites assign meaning to national holidays, this volume provides insights into transformations in media discourse of the respective countries, and provides examples of their "national filters" (Krzyżanowski, Triandafyllidou, and Wodak 2009: 265) that are applied when in discourse people construct, categorize, and negotiate the aspects of reality concerning national holidays. In their analyses, some authors chose to exclude considerations of the media's role, and instead to focus more on how elite members use discourse about national holidays to communicate their ideology, often in dispute with other elite members: for example, the rival main political parties of Macedonia (see Soldić in this volume); the leaders of ethnic groups in Bosnia and Herzegovina (see Mønnesland in this volume); the consecutive presidents of the Czech Republic (see Gammelgaard in this volume); and Polish journalist Adam Michnik vis-à-vis his country's politicians (see Grimstad in this volume). In most West and South Slavic countries, a divide exists between participants advocating civic-democratic values (conceived of as typical of Europe and the West) and those advocating national particularities, an advocacy that is often coupled with condemnation of the West's influences, conceived of as universalist, secular, and pluralistic (see Šarić on Serbia in this volume).

In official discourses about national holidays in the West and South Slavic countries, the four macro-strategies of discursive construction of national identities identified by Ruth Wodak (2006) can be discerned: constructive strategies, strategies of perpetuation and justification, strategies of transformation, and destructive strategies. Not surprisingly, the new nation states established after 1989/1990 show many examples of the constructive strategies whereby participants seek to establish particular national identities. Discourses about Montenegro's Independence Day (see Radanović Felberg in this volume), and Croatia's Statehood Day (see Šarić on Croatia in this volume) may serve as particularly clear instances of such strategies. However, the most widespread strategies appear to be those of transformation whereby the meaning of already established (or re-established) national holidays is changed into new meanings. Discourses about Macedonia's *Ilinden* (see Soldić in this volume), about Poland's national holidays celebrated on 3 May (see Hałas in this volume) and on 11 November (see Grimstad in this volume), and about the Day of the Establishment of the Independent Czechoslovak State (observed in the Czech Republic; see Gammelgaard in this volume) demonstrate these transformation strategies, but most other discourses analyzed also demonstrate some elements of these transformation strategies. When national identities are perceived to be under threat, strategies of perpetuation and justification are used. These strategies, or elements of them, occur only seldom in the cases analyzed here. However, had the authors of the chapters about countries of the former Yugoslavia focused on the 1990s, they would have identified many uses of these strategies (see Kolstø 2009). Destructive strategies are described in this volume concerning discourses about days commemorating World War II in Croatia (see Pavlaković in this volume), and those discourses are particularly forceful in Bosnia and Herzegovina, where leaders of ethnic groups attempt to demolish national holidays of other ethnic groups (see Mønnesland in this volume). Again, a focus on the 1990s could have provoked authors to analyze cases of the destructive strategies because communist national holidays and Czechoslovakia's and Yugoslavia's national holidays provided opportunities to demolish the identities linked with those entities.

The reception of discourse about national holidays involves an active process in which the receiver's attitudes and beliefs mediate how the discourse will be received and responded to. Groups and individuals interpret discourse about national holidays differently, and may come up with contrasting responses. As this volume concentrates on only official discourse produced by elites, it implies a need to investigate in future research the attitude of the receivers of such discourse, and to include the everyday nation-making discourse and activities also of those who do not listen to and do not read official discourse (see the methodology proposed by Fox and Miller-Idriss 2008).

Official discourse carries societal weight already due to the social position of those who produce it. Disseminated via the media, it is also easy for analysts to access. However, official discourse constitutes only one way of how members of a collective construe national holidays. Concentrating on unofficial discourse is equally interesting as a subject for future analyses. Those talking and writing outside the official channels contribute, too. Instances of their unofficial and semi-official discourse on national holidays may be collected from thematically relevant Internet forums and sites, in interviews, or by setting up focus groups to discuss national holidays (see De Cillia, Reisigl, and Wodak 1999). Other sources of unofficial discourse are the large collections of linguistic data created in national corpora.

4. National holidays and collective memory

The samples of discourse discussed in this volume are strongly related to collective memory. The term "collective memory" applies to the conception that memory is inter-subjectively constituted (see Misztal 2003). Individuals remember, but their memory exists and is shaped by relations with what has been shared with other people. Moreover, individuals' memory is of an inter-subjective past. For participants in discourses dealing with the past, the discourses create an image of selected past events and highlight some of their features. Simultaneously, they neglect certain other events and features of the selected events.

The volume thus contributes to research into how discourse constructs collective memory.

Collective memory in post-communist Europe has been the subject of many analyses dealing with a wide range of topics (see, e.g., Jedlicki 2005; Kubiš 2005; Kuzmanić 2008; Roudometof 2002; Szacka 1997). Scholars of discursive psychology (Billig 1999; Middleton and Edwards 1990) and of cultural psychology (Wertsch 2002; White 1997) have shown an intense interest in collective memory. Yet, few scholars have focused on the discursive practices of collective memory in the post-communist European countries and on how these practices relate to transformations of collective identity (some examples are Luczynski 1997; Tulviste and Wertsch 1994; and Wertsch 2002). The study of collective memory, transformation, and change in post-communist European countries has usually been concerned with macro processes of societal transformation placed within diverse historical and political explanatory frameworks. Less attention has been given to discourse approaches. Only a few studies show how discourse analysis may shed light on the production and dissemination of collective memory (see, e.g., Tileagă 2008).

Collective memory is partly about historical facts that may be contested and that are open to revision. Historical facts may be contested because, as described briefly and aptly by John Walton (2001: 289), they "acquire their credibility from social consensus fashioned by time, negotiation, and corroboration." The border between what occurred and what has been said to occur is unclear. Nevertheless, it is ethically important to identify that border in many situations (Achugar 2008; Medgill 1998). In line with that claim, Ruth Wodak and Gertraud Auer Borea d'Olmo (2009: 15–16) emphasize that "history written with hindsight and instilled with meaning like a 'narrative' must be invariably perceived as a construction […]. It is not the facts per se that are called into question, but the interpretations of facts – the context they are embedded in, the causes attributed to them and who is named as being responsible for which events." Interpretation of historical facts *for* the relevant collectives is precisely what happens regularly on national holidays. Celebrating national holidays is a mode of coming to terms with the past, in addition to modes like erecting monuments, making documentary films, and setting up exhibitions (Wodak and Borea d'Olmo 2009).

When people speak and write about the past, they rearrange, delete, add, and substitute the elements of past social practices (see, e.g., papers in Heer et al. 2008). When in their discourse they represent these elements, they must recontextualize them so that they are appropriate to the given discourse; they must implement elements – such as a topic, an argument, a genre, or a discursive practice – in a new context. Recontextualization happens after an element is taken out of context (see Van Leeuwen and Wodak 1999). Therefore, representing social practices implies recontextualizing them (Heer and Wodak 2008). When people speak and write about national holidays, they select and arrange certain aspects of past events in a meaningful structure, but the arrangements of the selected elements in their discourse may differ substantially from the arrangements of the elements in the past they refer to. Also, their recontextualized elements always (explicitly or implicitly) manifest themselves as relations to other texts and discourse patterns (Wodak and Fairclough 2010).

When producing discourse about national holidays, people contribute to larger narratives about the past. These narratives influence the experience and knowledge of the people that are exposed to them. Therefore, in addition to historical facts, meaning-making activities influence the experience and knowledge of a collective's members (Berger and Luckman 1967). Discourse forms a prominent part of meaning-making activities related to national holidays. Other meaning-making activities are celebratory activities and public rituals such as concerts, laying wreaths, planting trees, presenting medals, and singing national anthems (that often also rest on discourse). The construction of collective memory that takes place through these activities is an active and dynamic process. In this process, "issues of power and social positioning contribute to the creation of different or contesting narratives of the same event" (Achugar 2008: 13). Predominantly, such issues of power and social positioning are channeled via discourse. For example, in this volume, analysis of homilies given on a religious and national holiday in Slovakia shows how the national narrative may be expanded and contracted (see Bielicki in this volume). What is included and what is excluded contribute to somewhat different images of the past. Moreover, discursive devices are what enable constructions of the past. Discourse (understood as linguistic means with co-occurring non-linguistic audio-visual means) is the most important means that people use to objectify experiences, and through discourse they access historical facts (see also Castoriadis 1987). So, discourse is a means for a collective's members to access their shared past and to come to terms with it. The case of Poland's 1 August commemorations of the Warsaw Uprising shows how jointly addressing the past in commemorative practices may relieve burdens of the past and reinforce the present relationship between different collectives (see Ensink and Sauer in this volume).

In previous research, scholars have approached the relation between discourse and collective memory somewhat differently. Discursive psychology approaches collective remembering as an activity in which remembered material blends with personal reactions (see Edwards and Potter 2001; Edwards 2003). Tileagă (2008) uses a critical discursive psychological approach to analyze commemorative addresses in the Romanian parliament. Action theory (e.g., Bangerter, von Cranach, and Arn 1997) applies conversation analysis in studying collective memory. Critical discourse analysis (see, e.g., De Cillia, Reisigl, and Wodak 1999; Wodak 2007) approaches discourse and collective memory by focusing on identity, discourse strategies, topics, linguistic means, and their respective roles in identity construction. Some studies integrate critical discourse studies and systemic functional linguistics in exploring the re-readings of the past, and follow how different historical genres and contexts interact in interpreting the past (e.g., Martin and Wodak 2003). Studies devoted to discourse and human rights violations focus on the ways language mediates in various social and political processes of remembering and forgetting (see Anthonissen and Blommaert 2007). In a study of the construction of memory in military discourse in Uruguay, Achugar (2008) examines discursive aspects, such as intertextuality, that relate to continuities in discourse, as well as genre, and lexical-grammatical and discursive semantic devices.

Specific genres related to collective memory, such as commemorative political speeches and commemorative addresses, have frequently been the focus of critical discourse analysis (e.g., Ensink 1996, 2009; Ensink and Sauer 1995; Sauer 1996; Schäffner 1996; Reisigl 2009). As Tileagă (2008: 363) shows, these speeches and addresses are often used to build or rebuild political legitimacy, and to authorize the preferred version of specific events. The cases analyzed in this volume demonstrate many instances where political actors clearly build their own legitimacy while simultaneously promoting their versions of events: the Polish presidents on the Warsaw Uprising (see Ensink and Sauer in this volume), Croatian politicians on the course of World War II (see Pavlaković in this volume), Czech and Slovak heads of state on events leading to the establishment of Czechoslovakia (see Gammelgaard in this volume), and Serbian politicians on the Serbian uprisings in 1804 and 1815 (see Šarić on Serbia in this volume), to mention just a few.

Chapters in this volume approach collective memory as a social and discursive practice constructed on the occasion of national holidays. This practice mediates and represents other social practices, namely those (allegedly) having taken place in the past of the relevant collective. Authors concentrate on the dynamic aspects of this practice and on linguistic and other discursive means used (for example, the audial means of music and voice pitch, the visual means of text segmentation, layout, pictures, and participants' clothes). The focus on a period of profound societal transformations enables the authors of this volume to capture the dynamic and linear character of discourse. Particularly those cases where discourse participants have produced new texts within the same genres (presidential addresses, homilies, commemorative addresses) show how discourse is structured and restructured over time, what has been more stable, and what is subject to change.

Language and other semiotic systems, both audial and visual ones, construct social context and are simultaneously constructed by it (Martin 1997). Along similar lines, James Wertsch (2002) argues that collective memory is not a stable attribute of individuals or groups (see also Halbwachs 1992). Instead, collective memory is a dynamic process that involves an array of complex relationships between active agents and the narrative tools they employ (e.g., newspapers and newspaper genres, speeches, addresses, etc.): "narrative tools" are primarily discourse-based, and therefore analysts cannot approach collective memory without studying discourse.

According to Pennebaker and Banasik (1997), members of a society create and maintain collective memory in their ongoing reflections and when talking about events that are objects of memory. These processes have political, ideological, and discursive dimensions. In addition to public rituals and individual acts of recollection, commemorations of events include public debates on the meaning and significance of historical events (Turner 2006). The meaning of the commemorated event might be justified or criticized (Billig 1996). The meaning-making of commemorated events takes place through the discourse used at commemorations. For that reason, Tileagă (2008) places commemorative discourses at the center of transformation discourses in post-communist countries.

The presentist approach to collective memory (Hobsbawm and Ranger 1983) stresses that groups in power are responsible for memory's selectiveness. Groups in power control or impose the content of social memories, and "invented" memories serve their current purposes.

National holidays and the memories they imply are also selective, and more or less controlled by those in power. Paul Connerton (1989) also emphasizes that collective memory is a dimension of political power: control of a society's memory largely conditions the hierarchy of power. Also, regarding the collective memory occasioned by national holidays, those in power (the elites with power to control and impose collective memory) decide on national holidays. All states are engaged in creating an official account of the past, highlighting some historical periods, and forgetting others. The choice of underlying events for national holidays, the introduction of a new holiday, or the revival of an old one is also part of this effort, and the same institutional force involved in the production of official history is involved in the "production" of national holidays.

Collective memory comes into being and is controlled through the production of texts and other semiotic products. Their planned production by the state can promote one account and discount alternative accounts of the past (see Wertsch 2002). Societies produce a variety of semiotic products thematizing the past, and the rise of collective memory is related to their consumption. As several chapters in this volume show, the media employ various genres and contribute to shaping collective memory by featuring parts of the historical narrative related to national holidays before, during, and after their yearly observances. However, the past narrative is employed for present purposes, and is adapted in accordance with the present needs of those that reproduce it and their audiences.

5. Underlying events

On national holidays, people celebrate historical events that they consider relevant for their collective's political or cultural history. Which events are considered relevant and why must be discursively negotiated. Participants in those processes of selection and negotiation may stress different aspects when they argue in favor or against the importance of historical events. The national holidays of countries relate to very diverse events. Sometimes, underlying events relate to widely accepted historical truths, and sometimes they relate to myths. In other cases, events are partly or entirely invented. Many national and other holidays do not even relate to an underlying event. For example, in Bulgaria, *Баба Марта* (Granny March) on 1 March celebrates the coming of spring. The Czech Republic has seen right-wing politicians attempt to de-historicize May Day by changing it into *Den lásky* (Day of Love).[11] Moreover, the underlying event of a national holiday, even if historically traceable, may not be among the most significant events in a nation's history. The significance and authenticity of events are not decisive for the success of national holidays.

Remembering significant historical events relevant for statehood or independence establishes a sense of the state's continuity and its people's collective belonging. Celebratory activities related to national holidays simultaneously serve several functions: among others, they reflect a nation's cohesion, show the government's ability to mobilize the people, and foster collective memory. However, national holidays may also be a platform for quite the opposite tendencies, and

---

11. This attempt was unsuccessful. Valentine's Day, which has the same connotations, is gaining popularity in the Czech Republic just as elsewhere in the region.

may be contested in various ways that can be followed in discourse. The inception of national holidays is based on a historical narrative related to a past event considered to be crucially important for a state. Some community members may contest events underlying national holidays and related historical narratives. The importance of the historical – or invented – event is emphasized by an individual or by a group with power at a specific time. Groups with power select national holidays, and usually no public plebiscite is involved in their selection. In that respect, the many laws on national holidays and the amendments to them in the West and South Slavic countries deserve attention because they result from parliamentary debates. Consensus about holidays may be lacking among a community's members. Various attitudes towards national holidays may relate to individuals' political orientation or to their attitude towards their own history. The underlying events should be significant and remarkable enough in the prevailing collective memory to be widely accepted. To be uncontroversial, or minimally controversial, a national holiday should be at least tolerable for all members of the relevant collective, and it should not insult a group, coincide with the date of any group's historical tragedy, or relate to contested contemporary events. Such features may undermine the acceptability of national holidays.

Focusing on the potential of flags and coats of arms to create symbolic unity, Pål Kolstø (2006: 676) concludes that "there are […] no inherent qualities in state symbols that prevent them from being accepted, and likewise, no particular design will in and of itself guarantee their success." Nonetheless, precisely the linkage to the past that is so characteristic of national holidays makes them different from other national symbols. People's understandings of underlying events may prevent national holidays from being accepted. For example, Bulgaria's 3 March is connected to a problematic and never realized territorial claim, and Bulgarians may be conceived as active participants in the past event only if focus is put on its sub-events. Therefore, parts of the public do not accept 3 March as the most important Bulgarian national holiday (see Hauge in this volume). Also, the two Croatian statehood days observed since 1990 illustrate the problem of acceptability. The underlying events took place in the relatively recent past. They are subject to critical reflections by contemporaries who witnessed them, if only through the media, or who took an active role in them. These contemporaries developed very different understandings of "what really happened," and these disparate understandings make the statehood days unstable symbols (see Šarić on Croatia in this volume). A particularly palpable case of unacceptability is discussed in this volume's chapter on Bosnia and Herzegovina. There, the political leaders of an entity within Bosnia and Herzegovina, the Republika Srpska, observe 9 January as *Dan republike* (Republic Day). This holiday is completely unacceptable to the majority of the population in Bosnia and Herzegovina because they see it as a symbol of preparations for civil war (see Mønnesland in this volume).

If a distant historical event is chosen, nobody can reflect upon "what really happened" on the basis of their own experience. Yet, also in those cases, collective ideas of the underlying events may be considerably altered because of professional historians' findings. Their authority is frequently called upon in discourses on national holidays. In the region under scrutiny here, particularly national holidays connected with World War II have been subject to re-interpretations in recent years. Those re-interpretations include placing historical actors in roles such as the besieged, the winner, the victim, or the culprit. Croatian discourse on World War II is rich in such debate on how to place historical actors in narrative roles (see Pavlaković in this volume). Another example is that of Czech parliamentarians transforming *Den osvobození* (Liberation Day – the holiday marking the end of World War II) into *Den vítězství* (Victory Day). Cases in which a day connected to World War II is successfully used to re-establish international relations, as is the case of 1 August, when Poles and Germans (and in the future hopefully also Russians) commemorate the Warsaw Uprising, are still exceptions (see Ensink and Sauer in this volume). Concerning events of the wars following the split-up of the former Yugoslavia, such relational work is not yet done.

This volume deals with a few contested national holidays. A national holiday may be contested from the very day of its inception, and how it is contested may vary over time. One example is the Croatian case. In the relatively short period since Yugoslavia's breakup, Croatia has had two national holidays. The first one was strongly related to Croatia's first president in the 1990s and to his party's rule. It was abolished and replaced by a new one in 2001. The replacement created negative reactions among the public, sparked polemics in the media, and gave the impression that every newly elected government would launch its own national holiday. Croatian public discussions reflect a belief that symbols such as national holidays should be stable and endure longer than present governments (see Šarić on Croatia in this volume).

Changes in the official holiday calendar are unpopular. They are interpreted as signs of a state's political immaturity, indicate arbitrariness in making important decisions at the state level, and carry negative connotations. State and national symbols should convey stability and fulfill their function as promoters of national unity, but they often fail to do so in new, insecure nations (Kolstø 2006: 679).

In multiethnic states, the situation is especially complex because each ethnic group has its own memory, and they all struggle over ownership of the dominant memory. Again, Bosnia and Herzegovina evidences these struggles (see Mønnesland in this volume), but they occur also in discourse on national holidays in multiethnic Macedonia (see Soldić in this volume). In Montenegro, contemporary official discourse builds up a specific Montenegrin identity as different from the Serbian one (see Radanović Felberg in this volume).

For a national holiday to achieve success as a unifying symbol, perhaps the most important quality is that it must relate to a historical event that may be interpreted as complying with contemporary wishes and visions of the collective observing it. Hence, the many attempts to interpret events as instances of general European or Western tendencies evidenced in discourse in the selected countries during their attempts to enter into EU and other Western organizations. Important to note is that during those pre-accession and accession periods and later as members of the formerly exclusively Western organizations, the new member states' interpretations of Western ideals affected those ideals. The ideals were discursively challenged and re-constructed by both new and old member states. Similar processes of re-interpretation were and are taking place on other transnational levels. Therefore, the transformations in the West and South Slavic countries cannot be treated as isolated from those occurring elsewhere in Europe and the world (see Krzyżanowski and Galasińska 2009).

Some national holidays analyzed in this volume are closely linked with religion and therefore also relate to the transnational and supranational religious communities. To observe them as *national* holidays, discursive work must be done to allow interpretations of those holidays as relating to the particular national collective in question. Therefore, on the Slovak holiday of 15 September (see Bielecki in this volume) and on the Polish holiday of 3 May (see Hałas in this volume), the Virgin Mary is symbolically linked to Slovakia and Poland, respectively. Similarly, Serbian politicians have used the symbolic value of the Orthodox holiday *Sretenje* (Candlemas) to reinforce Serbian national identity (see Šarić on Serbia in this volume), and Macedonian politicians and religious leaders have exploited the religious connotations of *Ilinden* (St. Elijah's Day) to reinforce Macedonian self-consciousness (see Soldić in this volume).

Another feature that seems to be crucial to a national holiday's success is how it relates to persons and agency. In many cases, national holidays refer to historical persons functioning as national heroes: Tomáš Garrigue Masaryk and 28 October in the Czech Republic (see Gammelgaard in this volume), Józef Piłsudski and 11 November in Poland (see Grimstad in this volume), and Đorđe Petrović and 15 February in Serbia (see Šarić on Serbia in this volume). In discourses about national holidays, the names of these persons regularly occur. As discussed in the Bulgarian case, to establish such positive linkage between historical persons and a holiday, the selected person, or group of persons, must reflect agency (see Hauge in this volume). If actions failed to reach their goals, focus may be put on the aspects of actions as instances of struggle for elevated ideals, as is successfully done in Polish commemorative speeches about the Warsaw Uprising of 1 August 1944 (see Ensink and Sauer in this volume).

In sum, the material national holidays are made of is more complex than that of flags or coats of arms. To establish and maintain national holidays involve very complex discursive activities, particularly because of the complex references to the past. Moreover, because of their immaterial nature, and because of the linear character of discourse, national holidays are subject to change by every new discursive act.

6.   Methodologies

From various backgrounds, including anthropology, history, linguistics, literature, and sociology, the authors in this volume focus on how identity is constructed, reconstructed, or invented in discourse. They focus on discourse from somewhat differing viewpoints, which gives this volume an interesting interdisciplinary dimension. The individual analyses reveal the plurality of factors that play a role in discursive identity negotiations.

The following chapters focus on the role of discourse in the processes of memory construction and of remembering, specifically concentrating on the following:

1. How do the relevant actors construct a discourse about a usable past (Wertsch 2002: 35) on the occasion of holidays?
2. What role do linguistic patterns and other audio-visual discursive practices play in the construction of holidays?
3. How do individuals or groups use national holidays to construct inside and outside groups and to maintain or change power relations, and what role does discourse play in these processes?
4. How do discourse participants use *topoi* on the occasion of national holidays – that is, explicit or implied elements of argumentation (Wodak et al. 2009) – and what does this use reveal about their discursive strategy and the identity pattern they try to mediate?

The chapters are inspired by, or rely upon, various approaches within discourse analysis, and they link these approaches to research on collective memory. These approaches are explained in detail in each chapter. Here we provide only brief remarks about some of them to illustrate the scope of the book:

1. Critical discourse analysis (CDA), which considers discourse to be not only a container of ideologies but also a social action on its own. It maintains that language use is socially constitutive and socially conditioned (Fairclough and Wodak 1997:258), seeing the relation of discourse and ideology as dialectic (Fairclough 2001), and acknowledging that changes in discourses shape ideologies. Ideology and power manifest themselves in language through micro-linguistic choices within a text, but also through the choice of genre for a text (Weiss and Wodak 2003:13), its topics, and its argumentative strategies. This approach makes it possible to identify strategies in the construction of collective memory and how that construction is used, and to identify selective constructions of historical events in discursive identity formation. As an approach that is not interested in linguistic units per se, but rather in their role in shaping social phenomena, CDA accounts not only for the presence of some elements in the data but also for their absence (Kress and van Leeuwen 2001). CDA has also developed useful categories that can account for the presentation of the Self and Other in discourse, a topic that several chapters in this volume deal with (see, e.g., Mønnesland; Soldić in this volume).

2. Analysis of political discourse that makes it possible to analyze legitimization and othering strategies and the linguistic units they rely on. Among other things, particular attention in individual chapters is paid to lexical choices used in strategies of legitimization (e.g., adjectives, adverbs, and verbs used in the characterizations of holidays, celebratory activities, or of the main actors in celebrations). As the chapters indicate positive characterizations of the Self are regularly accompanied by negative characterizations of the Other (the category of the Other may drastically change and be redefined in a short time span), and national holidays serve as a platform for these characterizations (see, e.g., Mønnesland, Pavlaković, and Šarić in this volume).

3. Systemic functional linguistics and social semiotics (Halliday and Hassan 1989; van Leeuwen 2005) that enable analyses of "multimodal texts," that is, that enable integrating into an analysis semiotic resources besides the verbal text, such as photographs, drawings, and layout. Approaches to multimodal realms examine how semiotic resources interact and how their interaction contributes to meaning (see, e.g., Grimstad; Radanović Felberg in this volume). They make it possible to develop methods for analyzing text in various forms (print, electronic, and handwritten), internet pages, and other realms in which various semiotic resources combine to fulfill particular objectives (for the challenges that such approaches imply, see O'Halloran 2008).

4. Approaches to commemorations and collective memory: Assmann's (2009) model for approaches to dealing with the past (see Sauer and Ensink in this volume); Wertsch's (2002, 2008) semiotic approach to collective memory that

pays particular attention to various text types and other semiotic tools that shape collective memory (see Šarić on Serbia in this volume). Along with systemic-functional linguistics and social semiotics, this approach shares an interest in exploring the ways in which semiotic resources are used to fulfill particular objectives. It particularly concentrates on resources aimed at constructing knowledge and shaping collective memory (e.g., schoolbooks), and on the national mechanisms engaged in their production. The emphasis in this book is on printed texts of particular genres, and newspapers, and their respective roles in shaping collective memory and identity on the occasion of national holidays. Hauge (this volume) concentrates on semantic roles and how they contribute to shaping discourses about collective identity and memory.

5. Genre analysis that permits studies of social and discursive changes (see Bielicki; Gammelgaard in this volume). Discourse participants are restricted by the genres they use, and the genres help them realize their intents. In discourse on national holidays, on the one hand the analysts come across genres (e.g., presidents' and prime ministers' addresses on holidays) that exhibit some relatively stable features. On the other hand, the analysts encounter new features relating to transformations in the society and to the changing needs of the communities the genres are directed towards. For example, analyses of differences in newspaper genres employed on holiday occasions reveal shifting attitudes toward holidays over time.

6. Burke's (1989) rhetorical concepts that make possible a discourse typology that relies on the categories of act, scene, agent, agency, and purpose (see Hałas this volume). The five terms that Burke marks as a "dramatistic pentad" are applicable to analysis of all kinds of texts and discourse – for instance, they help determine pragmatic or idealistic orientation in a discourse – but also are applicable to broader analyses of philosophical systems, for example, in which different categories of the "pentad" are emphasized (Makaryk 1993: 268).

Most chapters show that scholars require a combination of approaches when analyzing an interdisciplinary phenomenon such as national holidays. We believe that the chapters in this book show the advantages of approaches that strongly focus on text and talk in analyzing national holidays, and that these chapters will promote further research in this field.

Analyses

CHAPTER 1

Collective memory and media genres

Serbian Statehood Day 2002–2010

Ljiljana Šarić
University of Oslo, ILOS
ljiljana.saric@ilos.uio.no

This chapter analyzes Serbian media discourse related to Serbia's Statehood Day (*Dan državnosti*) since its introduction, and how the discourse has shaped and reinforced collective memory. Statehood Day is celebrated on 15 February, the same day as a religious holiday and an army holiday. The analysis concerns how Statehood Day discourse relates to collective memory and to the two identity models observable in Serbian public discourse: the civic-democratic model and the national-liberation model. The material analyzed is primarily from well-known newspapers that are representative of the Serbian media landscape. Using Wertsch's (2002) definition of "remembering" as a mediated action that entails the involvement of active agents and cultural tools, and applying the main categories of political discourse analysis (Chilton 2004), I examine how various genres employed in the media contribute to shaping and reinforcing collective memory, building patriotism, and constructing national identity.

Keywords: Serbia, Serbian Statehood Day, collective memory, cultural tools, identity construction, identity models, media discourse, newspaper discourse, media genres, evaluation, legitimization

1. Introduction and background

This chapter focuses on Serbian media discourse, primarily newspaper discourse, produced on the occasion of Statehood Day and that relates to the creation and reinforcement of collective memory. In this section, I provide introductory remarks on collective memory, which is my main theoretical notion. Furthermore, after a brief sketch of the contemporary context for the holiday, I reflect upon its two underlying events that are objects of collective memory and how they relate to the two identity models observable in Serbian public discourse. Collective memory is revisited in Section 2. An analysis of media texts follows in Section 3, and a conclusion in Section 4.

1.1   Collective memory, remembering, and cultural tools

Collective memory is commonly defined as "the representation of the past, both that shared by a group, and that which is collectively commemorated, that enacts and gives substance to the group's identity, its present conditions and its vision of the future" (Misztal 2003: 25).

When referring to historical events, red-letter days (as state symbols) activate collective memory. According to the historian Holm Sundhaussen (2003: 354), the two Serbian uprisings against the Ottomans in the nineteenth century are among the five decisive wars in Serbian collective memory crucial for Serbs' self-image and for how others see them. Misztal's definition of collective memory suggests that it links three time axes: past, present, and future. A society's "memory" is a metaphorical concept referring to the society's active work on creating an image of its past. In the case of Serbian Statehood Day, each yearly observance contributes to creating that image, and all factors of observances are relevant: historical sites of the First Serbian Uprising, the central celebration that usually takes place in Orašac,[1] speeches delivered and interviews given on Statehood Day, book promotions and exhibitions for the occasion, and so on. The phenomena that create collective memory include rituals, commemorative practices, and the choice of memory sites, but first and foremost language. In addition to being itself a cultural tool (language "accumulates" the entire cultural heritage of the community of its speakers), language is the crucial medium in collective memory transmission and creation. Language is also employed in other cultural tools (e.g., commemorations) for various purposes. In this analysis, I use the term "cultural tool," as does James Wertsch (2002, 2008), who uses it synonymously with "mediational means" and "semiotic means." These cultural tools are provided by a particular sociocultural setting, and may include traditional textual resources (e.g., books and various documents) as well as the internet, knotted ropes in ancient Peru, and all kinds of narratives (Wertsch 2002: 11–13). Wertsch's definition of *remembering* is also crucial for this analysis: Wertsch defines "remembering" as a mediated action that entails the involvement of active agents and cultural tools, for example,

---

1. Serbian prime ministers usually attend the Orašac celebration together with high-ranking state, military, and church officials, and the president lays a wreath at the Monument to the Unknown Hero atop Mt. Avala in Belgrade.

narrative texts associated with various voices.[2] Remembering is thus an action of an active agent who masters a relevant cultural tool.

1.2   Statehood Day: Contextualization

Serbian Statehood Day relates to identity tensions in Serbia in both the late 1980s and the 1990s, as well as to developments after 2000. The following brief sketch seeks to contextualize the holiday.

The Socialist Republic of Serbia was a constituent republic of the Socialist Federal Republic of Yugoslavia from 1945 to 1991. Slobodan Milošević rose to power in the League of Communists of Serbia in 1989 and soon reduced the autonomy rights of the autonomous Serbian provinces of Kosovo and Vojvodina. Tensions with the communist leadership of the other republics followed, which eventually resulted in the secession of Slovenia, Croatia, Bosnia-Herzegovina, and Macedonia from Yugoslavia. In 1992, the governments of Serbia and Montenegro agreed to establish a federation, the Federal Republic of Yugoslavia (FRY). The FRY was reconstituted in 2003 as the State Union of Serbia and Montenegro. In May 2006, Montenegro held a referendum to determine whether to end this union. The required percentage of voters voted in favor of Montenegrin independence. Montenegro was the last entity that left one of the "incarnations of Yugoslavia" (Ramet 2006: 1), and Serbia was left alone. After Serbia and Montenegro separated, intense attempts by both to create a new identity could be expected.

Earlier, street protests and rallies throughout Serbia beginning in September 2000 eventually forced Milošević to surrender power to a broad coalition of anti-Milošević parties on 5 October 2000. His fall ended the international isolation of Serbia. Serbia's new leaders declared that Serbia would seek to join the European Union. Zoran Đinđić played a prominent role in the 5 October 2000 uprising that overthrew the Milošević regime and led the coalition to its victory in the Serbian elections in December 2000. Đinđić served as Serbian prime minister from 2001 until he was assassinated on 12 March 2003. Vojislav Koštunica (president of the Federal Republic of Yugoslavia from 2000 to 2003) was prime minister of Serbia from 2004 to 2008. He has been known for his opposition to Kosovo's independence, basing his opposition on the province's religious and cultural significance for Serbia. Koštunica was succeeded by Mirko Cvetković, an economist who

---

2.   Voice is the distinctive style of an author. In media texts, journalists seem to adopt a neutral, objective voice and to "simply report," but what most often happens is that they use, are influenced by, rely upon, or oppose the voices of the people they report about.

served as the Deputy Minister of Economy and Privatization in Đinđić's government, and as the Minister of Finance in Koštunica's government.

After Milošević was ousted in October 2000, one of the new coalition government's promises in the election campaign that followed was a new constitution (the previous Serbian constitution was adopted in 1990). This promise was not fulfilled because the coalition soon fell apart following disputes between president of the Federal Republic of Yugoslavia, Koštunica, and Serbian Prime Minister Đinđić. The issue was revisited in 2005 in Serbia, when teams selected by President Boris Tadić and Koštunica's government presented their drafts of the constitution to the public. In June 2006, Serbia became independent and a new constitution became urgent. The Kosovo status talks necessitated quick adoption of a new constitution to affirm Serbia's desire to keep the province under its sovereignty.[3]

1.3   Sretenje: Underlying events

Certain moves towards creating a new Serbian identity had already started some years before Montenegro's 2006 independence, such as the choice of Serbian Statehood Day in July 2001,[4] when a traditional religious holiday of the Serbian Orthodox Church, *Sretenje* (Candlemas),[5] observed on 15 February, was selected to celebrate Serbian statehood. The literal meaning of *sretenje* is 'meeting.' This religious holiday has a long history of observances. The Serbian Orthodox church categorizes holidays into six groups, with *Sretenje* in the most important group.[6] *Sretenje* relates to the biblical event when the Holy Family took Jesus to the temple

---

3.   For details related to the political developments in Serbia up to 2005, see Ramet and Pavlaković (2005).

4.   See *Zakon o državnim i drugim praznicima u Republici Srbiji* (The Law on State and Other Holidays in the Republic of Serbia), *Službeni glasnik RS* 43 (2001), 101 (2007). Available online at *propisi.com*. http://www.propisi.com/zakon-o-drzavnim-i-drugim-praznicima-u-republici-srbiji.html, accessed 30 June 2010. Former Yugoslav Republic Day, 29 November, was celebrated in Serbia until 2002. Two national days were celebrated from 2002 to 2006, when Serbia was in the state union with Montenegro: the Day of the Federal Republic of Yugoslavia, 27 April, and 15 February. Only 15 February has been celebrated since 2007.

5.   In some Christian churches, this holiday is known under various names, for example, the Presentation of the Lord, the Meeting of the Lord, and the Purification of the Virgin. In this text, I use the name "Candlemas," the most commonly used term in English. The historical constitution I discuss in this chapter is commonly referred to as the "Candlemas Constitution" in English-language scholarship.

6.   Kuburić, M. 2001. "Danas je Sretenje." *Politika*, 12.

in Jerusalem forty days after his birth to complete Mary's ritual purification after childbirth, and to perform the redemption of the firstborn. The Serbian Army has also been celebrating 15 February as its day, *Dan vojske* (Army Day), since 2007.

Statehood Day commemorates two historical events: the First Serbian Uprising (1804), and the ratification of the first Serbian constitution, on Candlemas in 1835. Scheduling important political events, such as the proclamations of constitutions, on religious holidays is a Serbian tradition,[7] as well as a tradition of many other countries (see Soldić, this volume). Geisler (2009: 18), speaking of Greece, emphasizes that some nations intentionally foreground the intersection of religion and "civil religion."[8]

The First Serbian Uprising against the Ottoman Empire began on Candlemas in 1804 in the village of Orašac. Đorđe Petrović (commonly known under the name Karađorđe, 'Black George') was elected leader of the uprising. This uprising, which lasted less than a decade,

> sparked the Second Serbian Uprising in 1815 which led to Serbia's semi-independence from the Ottomans in 1817, formalized in 1829 by the Peace of Adrianople and hatti-sherifs[9] in 1829, 1830 and 1833.   (Trbovich 2006: 196)

Some historians refer to 1804 as "the dawn of modern Serbia" (Pappas 1994), implying that it marks the beginning of Serbian liberation from Ottoman rule. They connect this date to the beginning of modern Serbian history and to Serbia's "desire for national emancipation" (e.g., Trbovich 2006: 196).

Statehood Day also commemorates Candlemas of 1835 and the ratification of the first Serbian constitution at the People's Assembly in the city of Kragujevac that took place on that day. Dimitrije Davidović, an educated Serb from Austria, a journalist, writer, politician, and historian, drafted the constitution. Miloš

---

7. On 28 June 1921 (St. Vitus Day), Serbian King Alexander I proclaimed the new *Vidovdan* Constitution of the Kingdom of Serbs, Croats, and Slovenes. On 8 November 2006, Serbia passed its first constitution in a multiparty parliament on the Orthodox feast of Saint Dimitrius (*Mitrovdan*), and thereafter named the constitution the *Mitrovdanski ustav* (St. Dimitrius Day Constitution).

8. In Serbian public discussions (e.g., online comments on media texts), many voices oppose the blending of the secular state and religion reflected in Statehood Day's choice, and oppose the mingling of high-ranking state, religious, and military officials at its central celebrations (e.g., http://www.b92.net/info/komentari.php?nav_id=162266#hrono, accessed 3 July 2010). Critical comments on the blending of state and religion can also be found among sociologists and historians (e.g., Kostić, S. "Državno-verski praznici," 'State-religious holidays' in *Danas*, 15 Feb. 2007).

9. An irrevocable Turkish decree countersigned by the sultan.

Obrenović (1783–1860), prince of Serbia, links the two underlying events: he participated in the First Uprising in 1804 and led the Serbs in the Second Uprising in 1815. Following one rebellion against his autocratic rule, Obrenović agreed to adopt˙the Candlemas Constitution in 1835. The Constitution lasted only a few weeks.[10]

The importance of the two historical events (the First Uprising and the ratification of the first constitution) is open to question. In his history of Serbia, Stevan Pawlowitch (2002:29) devotes little space to the First Serbian Uprising. According to him, the First Uprising

> was hardly the outcome of revolutionary ideological thinking or political planning […] the armed men of Karageorge had sparked off the rising with the typical gesture of outlaws – setting fire to a janissary commander's quarters and killing all the Turks they could lay their hands on.

The main figure of the First Uprising and his followers are characterized ambiguously, as both "outlaws" and "the first revolutionaries in the Balkans." Pawlowitch does not mention the Candlemas Constitution. Historian Sima Ćirković devotes only two pages to the context of the First Uprising. He characterizes Karađorđe as "an experienced soldier and former *Freikorps* and *hajduk*,"[11] and the Candlemas Constitution as "liberal for its time," but "more important for proclaiming civil rights and the principle of separation of powers than for the degree to which it restricted the prince [Obrenović]" (Ćirković 2004:195).

Indeed, the two underlying historical events of Serbian Statehood Day are not widely accepted as the most important events in Serbian history. For example, in informal public discussions such as online comments on newspaper articles, they compete with other events. In the media discourse occasioned by the Statehood Day observances from 2008 to 2010, several alternative events and periods significant for Serbian statehood have been discussed as being either equally important or more important, for example: the proclamation of the Serbian Kingdom of Raška in 1219, the establishment of the Serbian Empire under Stefan Dušan in 1346, and the recognition of Serbia as an independent principality at the Congress of Berlin in 1878. Serbia's independence from Montenegro in 2006 is not a favored date in public discourse, probably because it indicates that Serbia is among the youngest states in the Balkans.

---

10. Šarkić (2006:209) mentions a month, newspaper sources mention fifty-five days (e.g., *Politika* online, 15 Feb. 2010; http://www.politika.rs/rubrike/Srbija/Sretenjski-prvi-ustav-moderne-Srbije.lt.html, accessed 20 May 2010), and Ćirković (2004:195) mentions two weeks.

11. *Freikorps* – rebels and volunteer units; *hajduk* – a rural brigand in the European part of the Ottoman Empire.

The historian Radoš Ljušić has been one of the key figures in the discursive creation of the new Serbian identity. His texts, or texts inspired by his publications, or both, were frequently present in the material analyzed in this chapter (see Section 3). According to Ljušić (1995, 2008), Serbia was founded on the results of the two Serbian uprisings in 1804 and 1815. He also emphasizes the importance of the Candlemas Constitution for the reestablishment of statehood. In spite of its short existence, the Constitution functions as the keystone of Serbian statehood in Ljušić's origins-of-the-state narrative.

February 15 as Army Day also refers to the First Serbian Uprising. The Uprising marks the emergence of the first organized forms of armed forces that led to the creation of the Serbian military (Ejdus 2008: 17). Media discourses comment on the date's choice as "unifying the army and state identity."[12] The identity creation associated with February 15 is threefold – blending church, state, and military symbols – and thus the holiday is a multifaceted and complex symbol.

I will clarify this complexity with reference to political scientist Filip Ejdus (2007: 45–47), who argues for two "ideal discursive models" of what he terms current Serbian "political and strategic culture":[13] the civic-democratic and national-liberation models. The civic-democratic model's premise is that Europe and the West represent the cultural, political, and civilizational homeland of Serbia. The corresponding strategic culture pushes Serbia towards internal social emancipation and international integration. Among several formative historical moments relevant for this model are the adoption of the liberal Candlemas Constitution in 1835, student protests in 1968, and the anti-Milošević demonstrations in 1990. The national-liberation model relies on the Serbian people's long struggle for emancipation from foreign conquerors. The formative moments in this model include the rise of the Serbian state in the fourteenth century, the First Serbian Uprising in 1804, and the Balkan wars of 1912 and 1913. This model relies on three axiomatic beliefs: (1) great powers are a threat to Serbia's independence, which is priceless and should be pursued at any cost, (2) Serbia is important in the European context, and (3) civilizational ambivalence: the East and the West are two fundamentally different worlds in permanent conflict, between which Serbia should remain neutral.

---

12. *Dnevnik*, 15 Feb. 2007.

13. Political culture consists of assumptions about the political world; it is a product of and an interpretation of history, which provides us with axiomatic beliefs of who we are, and what we value. The term "strategic culture" is used in security studies. Strategic culture is a part of political culture, consisting of axiomatic beliefs about the usefulness and appropriateness of using military force in international relations (Ejdus 2007: 41–42).

2.   Collective memory and Serbian Statehood Day

Collective memory of any significant event in a community emerges in two situations. The prototypical situation is the one occurring when members of a group have all participated in an event and hence have individual memories. The second situation applies to Serbia: the community engaged in collective remembering did not directly experience the remembered events. In this case, memory is distributed between agents and the cultural tools they employ (Wertsch 2002: 25). Most cultural tools are language-based, or combine language with visual representations (e.g., illustrated history books). Collective memory is thus inevitably linked with language and discourse. All texts produced on the occasion of Statehood Day in Serbia can contribute to shaping collective memory if they deal with the past. Their importance and effect in the memory-shaping process depend on the standing of their producers, the channels they use, and the effectiveness of their rhetorical strategies. Serbian media, a "cultural tool" in Wertsch's sense of the term, may have contributed to shaping collective memory by featuring parts of the historical narrative related to Statehood Day before, during, and after its yearly observances.

The date of Statehood Day is somewhat controversial: it refers to distant, not necessarily very well-known historical events, and so it is necessary to distribute and share texts telling the "story" of Statehood Day within the community. A community can develop and share a representation of a past that community members never witnessed only if the members share cultural tools that help them create that representation.

Media help shape collective memory because they are sites of text production and channels of text dissemination. The Serbian media texts analyzed in the next section were thus important means for developing a shared representation of the past among their readers and listeners. Media texts are multimodal. In addition to language, photographs in the media also reinforce collective memory. Their task is to bring the historical persons of the underlying events closer to the audience. For example, in addition to photographs from celebrations, images of historical persons, documents, and buildings regularly appeared in relevant Serbian media. The portrait of Karađorđe was among regular motifs.[14] A painting of Miloš Obrenović was also featured,[15] as well as images of the Candlemas Constitution text and its author.[16]

---

14. For example, *Dnevnik*, 15 Feb. 2004, front page.

15. *Borba*, 17 Feb. 2004, p. 14.

16. For example, *Politika online*, 15 Feb. 2010.

3.   Analysis of media texts

3.1   Material and method

The analyzed material stems primarily from the newspapers *Politika* (Politics), *Večernje novosti* (Evening News), *Danas* (Today), and *Dnevnik* (Daily) 2002–2010.[17] My aim was to include well-known newspapers of various profiles and orientations that are representative of the Serbian media landscape.[18] I also collected texts from other media available online at the site *naslovi.net*, which can search a great volume of Serbian newspapers, and radio and television programs. Most material collected from this source dates from 2008 to 2010.[19] The texts analyzed all thematize Statehood Day and come from pre-holiday, holiday, and post-holiday print or online editions.

In what follows, I pay attention to media genres and to the thematic focus of the texts within single genres. By the term "genre" we may name sets of texts as a whole (e.g., a novel or editorial) based on a dominant generic feature. However, Kress (2003:119) uses the same term to name an aspect of the text's organization. How one defines genre depends on one's purposes. Typical definitions stress that genres constitute shared particular conventions of content and/or form, including structure and style. Distinctions between journalistic genres (e.g., feature articles, news articles, op-eds) are less relevant for this analysis. Instead, the temporal and thematic foci of the texts are much more important for this analysis, and so I base the analysis on examining those foci and their implications.

---

17. *Politika's* daily circulation is 135,000. *Večernje novosti* is the most popular Serbian newspaper, with a circulation between 210,000 and 270,000, and has continuously practiced nationalistic journalism (Erjavec and Volčič 2007:70). *Danas* is a liberal Belgrade daily and *Dnevnik* is a Vojvodina daily.

18. The material analyzed consisted of thirty-four front pages and 111 inside pages of five newspapers (the material contained some texts from *Borba* 'Struggle' in addition to the four newspapers mentioned). The material was collected in newspaper archives in Serbia. The material from the archives, comprising many more pages than selected for and cited in this analysis, is available in the project archive of the Red-Letter Days project group at the University of Oslo. A selection of material for this analysis was made in two steps, on the basis of thematic relevance and quantity/quality of holiday-related content: First, all the material thematizing the holiday in headlines, sub-heads, leads, and/or in photographs was selected and photographed. Next, the collected material was reviewed, and some material was ignored if the holiday received very little attention: Texts merely mentioning the holiday and discussing another, non-related topic were ignored.

19. Internet sources consisted of sixty-one texts from thirteen sources (newspapers, TV, radio).

The material contained three types of temporal foci: past, present, and how the past blends with the present and future. If the focus was on one temporal dimension only, I speak of "texts with a single focus" (Section 3.2). These texts are characterized by a distinct formal structure and purpose, and they all focus on the past. They narrated different aspects of past events, which may have served to shape or reinforce collective memory. The focus on how the past blends with the present and future resulted in "texts with multiple temporal foci" (Section 3.3) that were most frequent in the material analyzed. They reflected on present celebrations and underlying events of Statehood Day, and how they affect Serbia's present and future. A second subtype within the texts with multiple foci is the thematically mixed subtype, that is, texts reflecting on both the religious and the secular holiday. A separate subtype reported on current celebrations and their participants. These texts may have contributed to reinforcing collective memory by mentioning sites of memory where celebrations took place. However, I exclude them from my analysis because these texts did not concentrate on past events, and hence did not directly relate to creating a memory of the past.

The media seemed to be very engaged in educating their audience about history. Almost all long texts narrated underlying events. The amount of information and its interpretation varied. Below I concentrate on genres that provided details about history. Specifically, I analyze the dominant topics of the Statehood Day narrative, the most frequent voices in shaping collective memory and Statehood Day's identity, and how media discourse constructed collective memory by blending past, present, and future. As a rule, I concentrate on typical genre instances within texts with a single focus, and within texts with multiple (mixed) temporal foci.

In the analysis of the text types and how they constructed collective memory, I pay particular attention to evaluative lexis (e.g., adjectives and nouns), evaluative syntactic structures (e.g., certain existential constructions), and evaluative grammatical forms (e.g., superlatives) because these categories used within a particular text contribute to shaping collective memory. In addition, evaluative elements are used in legitimization strategies; for example, in legitimizing the choice of the specific date for Statehood Day, that is, in explaining the relevance of the holiday's underlying events.

3.2   Texts with a single temporal focus

Immediately after the inception of Statehood Day, temporally homogenous texts could be found: the "historical reader," interviews with historians, reports on cultural tools, biographies of historical persons, and quizzes. They strongly or exclusively focused on the past, reproducing parts of the historical narrative and neglecting current observances.

The term "historical reader" (*istorijska čitanka*) was coined by several newspapers and was used in them in the analyzed period. Texts in this genre provided an abridged story of a sequence of underlying sub-events of Statehood Day. This genre was typical of the first years after Statehood Day's inception. The genre informed readers of the holiday's importance, and thus had a didactic function. For instance, the author Dragić Lazić described the events of 1835 in the article[20] "Vatromet u čast ustava," 'Fireworks to Honor Constitution' in *Politika* (14–15 Feb. 2002, p. 9).[21] The last column of the article contained a framed[22] news item: a congratulation from a high-ranking military official to Prime Minister Đinđić. The congratulation established a link to the main article through a reference to the Candlemas Constitution. A historical reader also appeared in several issues of *Večernje novosti* in 2002, detailing the First Uprising's events. The same newspaper in 2003 (24 Aug.–11 Sept.) ran an eighteen-part series of articles by the historian Ljušić titled "Karađorđe: Istina i mit," 'Karađorđe: Truths and Myths' to mark the upcoming bicentennial of the 1804 Uprising. In another article titled "Novovekovna srpska državnost," 'Modern Serbian Statehood' in *Politika* (15 Feb. 2003), Ljušić focused on the end of the Uprising and on the numbers of Serbian victims. He also emphasized that Obrenović had renewed the state and had continued building its institutions on Karađorđe's foundations.

In 2004, the bicentennial of the Uprising,[23] there were numerous historical reminders of the Uprising and the Candlemas Constitution. In a typical article "Nepodmitljiv kao sudbina," 'Incorruptible like Destiny,' the author reflected on Karađorđe's life and his stormy personality: "zbog gluvoće na nepravdu znao je stolicom izudarati i sudiju i ministra inostranih poslova," 'he would beat the judge and the foreign minister with a chair because they were indifferent to injustice' (*Večernje novosti*, 15 Feb. 2004, p. 20).

The historical reader has remained a frequent genre. Even in 2010, when few articles have thematized Statehood Day, the journalist Brane Kartalović in *Politika online*[24] dedicated almost two pages to the Candlemas Constitution ("Sretenjski

---

20. All translations of headlines, quotes from the texts, and so on are by the author.

21. Kicker: "Sretenje u Kragujevcu, pre 167 godina," 'Candlemas in Kragujevac 167 Years Ago.'

22. A framed newspaper text is a text in a frame box. It can be incorporated into another text.

23. On 15 February, a monument to Karađorđe was unveiled in Orašac and fifteen thousand people attended the celebration. Three-day celebrations were organized across Serbia that year.

24. 15 Feb. 2010.

ustav – prvi ustav moderne Srbije," 'Candlemas Constitution: First Constitution of Modern Serbia') and to the participants and events of 14–16 February 1835. He emphasized the Constitution's author, Davidović, and Obrenović's comments on the Constitution.

Interviews with historians were also typical of the post-inception phase of Statehood Day. A representative example is the interview with the historian and Serbian Academy of Arts and Sciences member, Jovanka Kalić, titled "Praznik vere i države," 'Holiday of Faith and State' in *Večernje novosti*.[25] Kalić was the president of the committee for new Serbian holidays. The interview justified the choice of 15 February. Kalić claimed that the commemorated events represent a demarcation between the Turkish period and modern Serbia, in which the enslaved *rayah*, 'lower class' became a *narod*, 'nation.' Furthermore, she linked the Candlemas Constitution to European values: "uneo [je] evropska načela u Srbiju," '[it] brought European principles to Serbia.' Kalić strengthened this claim by citing Serbian historian and politician, Stojan Novaković (1842–1915), who referred to the era of the Uprising and the Candlemas Constitution as "vaskrs države Srbije," 'resurrection of the Serbian State.' *Vaskrs*, 'resurrection' is one of the two key terms of the Serbian post-Ottoman origins-of-the-state mythos (Sundhaussen 2003). Kalić claimed that all the committee members (including university professors, historians, and minority representatives), when asked about the most important date in Serbian history, answered, "15 February." In her unrealistic claim, Kalić used a legitimizing strategy. Legitimizing strategies are positive constructions, of the self and of somebody's own actions or decisions, that often occur simultaneously with delegitimization of the other through negative evaluations of their actions (Chilton 2004).

Reports on other cultural tools were prominent in 2004, the bicentennial of the Uprising. In a full-page article in *Dnevnik*,[26] "Srbi za slobodu, Evropa za računicu," 'Serbs for Freedom, Europeans for Calculations,' the journalist and writer, Đorđe Randelj, summarized and commented on the multiauthored book *Evropa i Srpska revolucija 1804–1815* (Europe and Serbian Revolution 1804–1815). A comment on the book and project *Hronologija – moderna srpska država 1804–2004* (The Modern Serbian State: A Chronology 1804–2004), by the Belgrade Historical Archive, appeared in *Politika* (15 Feb. 2004, p. A7). On the same day, an article about the first Serbian feature film, *Karađorđe, ili život i dela besmrtnog vožda Karađorđa*

---

25. Kicker: "Srbija sutra prvi put slavi Sretenje kao Dan svoje državnosti," 'Tomorrow Serbia Celebrates Candlemas as its Statehood Day for First Time,' 14–15 Feb. 2002, p. 5.

26. 15 Feb. 2004, p. 9.

(The Life and Works of the Eternal Leader Karađorđe) (from 1911), found in an Austrian archive in 2003, appeared in *Večernje novosti* (p. 4).

In addition, biographies of historical persons appeared, for example, a biography of Karađorđe ("Vožd ustanka," 'Leader of the Uprising') by Jovan Nikolić in *Politika* 2004.[27] The biography's descriptions reminded of descriptions in heroic literature. The biography followed the life of *svetao lik velikog srpskog vožda*, 'the bright figure of the great Serbian leader' and concluded with the story of his death: Karađorđe was murdered by his godfather at the order of Miloš Obrenović.[28] His death is presented as a sacrifice for Serbian liberation.

Finally, there was an interesting case of a quiz in *Danas* (16 Feb. 2001, p. 20). The quiz appeared before The Serbian Assembly ratified the Law on Holidays in July 2001. The quiz, "Prvi srpski ustanak," 'First Serbian Uprising,' concentrated on the Uprising only. Its five questions concerned the village where the Uprising began, the name of the duke that killed four Belgrade *dahias* in July 1804, the place of the insurgent victory of 1806, the Serbian leader that sacrificed his own and his soldiers' lives in the Battle of Čegar Hill in 1809, and the year when the Ottomans retook Belgrade and many Uprising leaders fled to Austria. The quiz was accompanied by a popular painting of Karađorđe and the framed comment "Vožd Karađorđe vrlo uspešno predvodio ustanike u boju sa turskom vojskom pod komandom Kulin kapetana," 'Vožd [leader] Karađorđe led the insurgents with great success in battle with the Ottoman Army under Captain Kulin.'

The quiz characterized the Uprising as "istorijski skup najviđenijih Srba," 'a historical meeting of the most significant Serbs.' The key motif of the narrative is self-sacrifices by the insurgents: "posle četiri odbijena juriša mnogo brojnijih Turaka, pucao je u burad s barutom, žrtvujući tako sebe i svoje momke," 'after four attacks by the much more numerous Turks, [Sinđelić] shot into the powder barrels, sacrificing himself and his men.'

To sum up, texts with a single temporal focus informed readers about historical events, their participants, and their significance. Historical readers and biographies functioned as simplified history texts for mass consumption. The term "historical reader" implies a reliable text, an official account of the past. Indeed, the authors of these texts often included historians (notably, Radoš Ljušić). The interviews informed the readers about historical events and their relevance to the present. They also legitimized the importance of historical events and persons. In legitimizing strategies, choosing a reliable source of information is important:

---

27. 15 Feb. 2004, p. A13.

28. Obrenović had his head stuffed and sent to Istanbul as a present for the sultan (Singleton 1985:85).

interviewees were well-known historians that cited other reliable sources in their argumentation, as Jovanka Kalić did, to explain the choice of date for Statehood Day. She emphasized the identical opinion of all the members of the appointed committee regarding the best date for Statehood Day, and quoted a Serbian historian valued for his account of the First Serbian Uprising. Reports on other cultural tools also referred to reliable sources that provide extensive information on Statehood Day's underlying events and their participants. Interestingly, the quiz tested readers' knowledge of historical events. It asked the average reader detailed questions; if readers could not answer, they might have been motivated to seek information elsewhere. The quiz suggested, by implication, which historical information is considered important for public knowledge. Noticeably, the 1836 constitution is absent. The general impression is that the text types analyzed in this sub-section provided more details about the Uprising than they did about the Candlemas Constitution. Therefore, they prioritized the national-liberation model. This prioritization partly relates to the Uprising's complexity (participants, duration, and the relation to the events that followed).

3.3   Texts with mixed topics and multiple temporal foci

A few text types that mixed topics and temporal foci relevant for shaping collective memory regularly occurred throughout the period analyzed.

In some texts, a short historical narrative was embedded in the church holiday narrative. This combination indicated unity of church and state. For example, an article headlined "Danas je Sretenje," 'Today is Candlemas' opened with the information that Patriarch Pavle would hold a requiem for the Uprising's insurgents (*Politika,* 15 Feb. 2001, p. 12). One paragraph explained why 15 February was chosen as Statehood Day and told about Karađorđe's role in the Uprising. The date is defined as *značajni datum iz srpske nacionalne istorije,* 'an important date of Serbian national history.' Four-fifths of the article is devoted to the church holiday; that is, the religious narrative was dominant. The same pattern is repeated elsewhere.[29]

In the second text type, which blended comments on current celebrations with the historical narrative, historical narrative was embedded in commentary on Statehood Day celebrations at relevant sites of memory.[30] The front-page headline "Sretenje, najvažniji srpski datum," 'Candlemas, Most Important Serbian Date' (*Politika,* 15 Feb. 2001) was evaluative: the date is qualified as *najvažniji,*

29. For example, in *Politika,* 15 Feb. 2005, p. 9.

30. Before 2002, in commentaries related to Uprising anniversary celebrations.

'most important.' The article's continuation was titled *Najvažniji srpski datum*, 'Most Important Serbian Date.' It repeatedly evaluated the date. This chapter gave an overview of events organized for the Uprising's anniversary by the authorities in Orašac. The events included a history lesson, awarding a prize for patriotic poetry, a festive program, and a memorial service for Karađorđe and the insurgents. The First Serbian Uprising Society, from the town of Aranđelovac, issued a request that 15 February be a state holiday. This request was reprinted in the middle of the article, reading: "Srpski narod nema značajnijeg datuma u svojoj istoriji od ovog prelomnog događaja, niti država Srbija ima važnijeg datuma od svog nastanka," 'The Serbian people have no date more important in their history than this watershed event, nor does the Serbian state have a date more important than its date of origin.' To strengthen this claim, the article made the same claim again. The lead qualified the date as *veliki datum nacionalne istorije*, 'a great date of our national history' and the site of memory as *znamenit*, 'significant.' It also provided arguments in favor of the date's importance: "[Srpskim ustankom je] […] posle vekova ropstva, obnovljena srpska državnost," 'after centuries of slavery, [the Serbian Uprising] renewed Serbian statehood' (*Politika,* 15 Feb. 2001, p. 14).

The historical reader occasionally occurred as a separate text with a single temporal focus (see Section 3.2). However, it was regularly incorporated into other, more complex structures, for example, articles containing several texts, all of which concentrated on various Statehood Day activities. The historical reader frequently occupied a significant space as part of complex structures such as comments on current celebrations.

For example, Milenko Pešić authored the first part of a historical reader titled "Temelj moderne Srbije," 'Foundation of Modern Serbia' (*Politika,* 14–15 Feb. 2002). Its lead located in time the two underlying events of Statehood Day. The first two introductory sentences dealt with the staging of the Assembly held in Kragujevac in 1835. Then, Pešić defined Candlemas as the "ugaoni kamen moderne Srbije," 'cornerstone of modern Serbia.' His voice blended with the supporting voice, cited by Pešić, of the deputy speaker of Serbia's National Assembly, who qualified the date as "nesporan datum," 'a non-controversial date' and "nepravedno zapostavljen dan […] kad je [srpski narod] počeo da se bori za slobodu," 'an unjustly neglected day […] on which [Serbs] started to fight for their freedom.' The last part of this front-page article mentioned celebratory events to be held at historical sites of memory in Orašac. Much of the rest of the article was dedicated to historical facts about the Candlemas Constitution.

Also in 2010, the historical reader dominated some articles.

Some texts focused on how the past blends with the present and future, that is, how the symbolic past should help modern society master its challenges.

Typically, the journalists used historical analogies and their voices blended with the voices they cited.

In comments on the first official observance in 2002, historical analogies dominated articles. Journalists asked what the Uprising and the first Serbian constitution meant for the present. For instance, quotes from Đinđić dominated the text "Temelji moderne građanske države," 'Foundations of the Modern Civil State' (*Borba*, 16–17 Feb. 2002). Đinđić was quoted as saying: "Naš zadatak je da slobodu koju imamo krunišemo jednim ustavom koji će dovršiti misiju naših predaka, a to je moderna srpska država," 'Our task is to crown our freedom with a constitution that will fulfill our ancestors' mission: a modern Serbian state.'

The comment "Srbija okrenuta budućnosti," 'Serbia Looking towards the Future,' embedded in the text "Foundations of the Modern Civil State" (*Borba*, 16–17 Feb. 2002, p. 3), contained evidence of authorial endorsement in which "the reported value position is framed or projected by formulations which simultaneously align the authorial voice with that value position and, by implication, construe it as true or otherwise warrantable" (White 2006: 59): the Uprising and Candlemas Constitution were characterized as "prelomni trenuci za srpsku istoriju, kada su postavljeni temelji moderne države, a Srbija svrstana u red malobrojnih uređenih evropskih država," 'the key moments of Serbian history when a modern state was founded, and Serbia joined the small number of orderly European states.' The comment reported on the present staging of the historical event, the Assembly in Kragujevac, that ratified the Candlemas Constitution in 1835.

A report on the central celebration in Orašac, titled "Srbija se vraća sebi i svetu," 'Serbia Returns to Itself and World,' also linked the past, present, and future (*Dnevnik* 14–15 Feb. 2002, p. 3). It summarized parts of historical events, concentrating on the present and on Đinđić's voice and his message, both of which suggested that an idealized, heroic past should serve to better master the present and future.

References to the Candlemas Constitution were particularly relevant in the years leading up to 2006, because a referendum on the draft of the new Serbian constitution was to be held in October 2006.

In reports on celebrations, some of which combined reporting and reflections on history, various language devices linked the past, the present, and the future. In the article "Dovršiti misiju predaka," 'To Complete the Mission of Our Ancestors' (*Politika*, 16 Feb. 2002), the verb *dovršiti*, 'to complete' linked something that had allegedly begun in the past with an imperative for the present. Đinđić's voice in the text reminded the audience that Statehood Day commemorates the beginning of Serbia's constitutional tradition. Đinđić linked the Candlemas Constitution and its human rights concerns with Serbs' forefathers' wishes for a country governed by the rule of law that respects citizens' rights and private property.

The article quoted Đinđić's remark: "Ideali slobode, pravde i jednakosti koji su pokretali sve srpske bune i ustanke ostaju naša trajna inspiracija i obaveza," 'The ideals of freedom, justice, and equality that drove all Serbian revolts and uprisings will remain our eternal inspiration and duty.' Đinđić's voice and the verb *ostati,* 'to remain' linked the past with the present and future.

In speeches[31] on Statehood Day, speakers blended the past, present, and future. The speeches had in common the message that the Uprising and the Constitution should inspire modern Serbia in its present economic, national, and moral crises. One example was the speech by Serbia's acting president, Dragan Marišćanin, at the celebration in Orašac in 2004.[32]

In the front-page article "Srbija prvi put obeležava dan vojske," 'Serbia Marks Army Day for First Time' (*Danas,* 15 Feb. 2007), the author established a connection between the Serbian Uprising in 1804 and all later times in which Serbia aimed at implementing European principles: "Srbija se od tada konstantno trudila da uđe u Evropu," 'Since then, Serbia has been constantly trying to enter Europe.' Similarly, in a report on the celebration in Orašac (*Danas,* 16 February 2007, p. 5), the voice of Koštunica linked the insurgents' policy with present-day Serbia's attitude of not giving up Kosovo. Koštunica said that the insurgents "nisu ni pomislili da odustanu od svoje državnosti i svetog prava da žive slobodno [...] tako i mi s punim uverenjem ponavljamo da se nikada nećemo odreći nijednog dela naše države," 'never thought of giving up their statehood and right to live in freedom [...] we also repeat with full conviction that we will never give up any part of our country.' A similar historical analogy by Koštunica appeared in *Politika* (16 Feb.)[33] in 2007 in a front-page report on the celebration in Orašac: "kao i pre više od dva veka [Srbija se] bori za očuvanje teritorijalne celovitosti i suvereniteta," 'as over two centuries ago, [Serbia] is fighting to keep its integrity and sovereignty.'

In 2009, media texts frequently quoted President Tadić's Statehood Day speech.[34] His speech concentrated on both historical events and actual issues, for example, on Kosovo's independence and on the EU. He strongly emphasized the Candlemas Constitution, using it as evidence of the long tradition of Serbia's devotion to democracy, and to prove that Serbia has traditionally been part of modern and advanced Europe. Tadić explicitly highlighted the role of the Constitution's author, Dimitrije Davidović, who "ostavio mu je u zadatak da uvek mora

---

31. I reflect on parts of speeches or quotes from speeches incorporated into, for example, media reports on celebratory activities. I do not analyze speeches in their entirety.

32. Quoted in *Večernje novosti,* 16 Feb. 2004, p. 2.

33. And in *Dnevnik* (15 Feb. 2007, p. 7).

34. For example, *Politika online* 15 Feb. 2009. Accessed 16 Aug. 2010.

da prednjači u ostvarenju sloboda i ljudskih prava," 'left [to the Serbian people] a great task to always be the first in securing freedom and human rights.' Tadić emphasized the Constitution's concern with human rights in its Section 11, which states that all people – without exception – are equal before the law. Tadić linked the past and present: He presented the Constitution as aiming at Serbia's Euro-peanization, at protecting human rights, and at transforming Serbia into a state governed by the rule of law. Statehood Day should recall these three aims. The Constitution's section on the equality of all people is mapped onto the principle of respecting all minorities in modern Serbia. Thus, Statehood Day was an op-portunity to stress efforts in promoting human rights and in respecting different traditions, religions, and identities as part of Serbian tradition.

By blending topics, texts in this group typically reflected on the meaning of the religious holiday (Candlemas) *and* on the meaning of the secular holiday (State-hood Day, Army Day). They also blended time foci. For example, they simulta-neously reported on current celebrations and on historical events. In reports on current celebrations, prominent voices were those of state, church, and military elites. Notably, prime ministers linked their political agendas to past events. They frequently explicitly defined the role of historical memory: it should help Serbia with its present tasks. Media presentations suggest that Đinđić's main concern was to create a modern state, a European country governed by the rule of law. He frequently used historical analogies related to the Candlemas Constitution. In contrast, Koštunica concentrated on the best strategies for "keeping Kosovo in Serbia," and frequently referred to Karađorđe and the Uprising. The two prime ministers' attitudes reflected the two discursive models of Serbian culture, with Đinđić emphasizing the civic-democratic model and Koštunica emphasizing the national-liberation model. Prime Minister Cvetković evoked the models less clearly. He concentrated on current issues in his Statehood Day speeches in 2009 and 2010 (the economic crisis, economic and geostrategic developments, mea-sures against corruption, and Serbia's EU prospects). Liberally oriented media, such as the radio station B92, reported on the whole range of topics in his speech held in Orašac 2009,[35] whereas the conservative-oriented *Večernje novosti* con-centrated on the part of his speech thematizing Kosovo.[36]

---

35. "Dan državnosti Srbije," 15 Feb. 2009. http://www.b92.net/info/vesti/index.php?yyyy=2009 &mm=02&dd=15&nav_id=345054, accessed 3 July 2010.

36. http://wwww.novosti.rs/vesti/naslovna/aktuelno.69.html:232290-Drvo-slobode-niklo-u-Orascu, accessed 3 July 2010.

4. Conclusions

In the period from 2002 to 2010, Serbian media regularly dealt with Statehood Day. Media texts may have contributed to building patriotism and constructing national identity, but they did not seem to make Statehood Day widely popular in the period under scrutiny.[37] Significantly, fewer articles appeared in 2010 than in previous years. Arguably, media refrained from reporting about the celebrations in Orašac because in February 2010 the prime minister did not attend.

The anchor topics of the Statehood Day narrative in the media included liberation of Serbia after centuries of foreign rule. Newspapers repeatedly referred to the period of foreign rule using the nouns *ropstvo/robovanje*, 'slavery,' such as in "viševekovno/petovekovno robovanje pod Turcima," 'centuries-long / five-century-long slavery under the Turks.'[38] The media texts highlighted Serbs' self-sacrifices for higher ideals. Sacrifice is repeatedly thematized in the Statehood Day narrative, and the Serbs' wrongdoings are put into a context of fighting for higher ideals. These topics (slavery, sacrifice, and liberation) evoked the national-liberation discursive model. The second anchor topic was Serbia's constitutional tradition. The media characterized the Candlemas Constitution in superlatives, for example: "najviši pravni akt zemlje […] kakvim se u to vreme moglo pohvaliti malo zemalja u svetu," 'The highest legal document of the country […] that few countries in the world could boast of at that time'[39] and "jedan od najliberalnijih u tadašnjoj Evropi," 'one of the most liberal at that time in Europe.'[40] These characterizations evoked the civic-democratic discursive model.

The texts that narrated different aspects of past events may have served either to shape or to reinforce, or both, collective remembering. In the inception phase

37. An online public opinion poll shows that 15 February is not among the most popular red-letter days in Serbia. The most popular holidays are religious holidays. Source: Internet Krstarica. http://www.krstarica.com/lat/anketa/index.php?anketa=725, accessed 29 Apr. 2010. Media texts analyzed occasionally commented on the public's and the media's ignorance of the holiday (e.g., *Borba,* 16 Feb. 2005, p. 3). They stressed that people were confused because the state holiday coincides with the religious one. In a comment in *Danas online* (15 Feb. 2010, http://www.danas.rs/danasrs/drustvo/terazije/slavlje_samo_za_drzavni_vrh.14.html?news_id=183752, accessed 30 May 2010), Katarina Živanović and Dragoljub Petrović expressed their main idea by quoting a retired Yugoslav Army general: "današnje državne praznike obeležavaju samo oni koji moraju, a to je vojni i državni vrh," 'only those that have to do so mark today's holidays: top-ranking state and military officials.'

38. *Danas,* 16 Feb. 2007, p. 5; *Dnevnik,* 15 Feb. 2007, p. 7.

39. *Dnevnik,* 15 Feb. 2007, p. 7.

40. *Politika,* 15 Feb. 2005, p. 9.

of a holiday and immediately after, it is important to inform the community about what happened on the day remembered, who the participants in the historical events were, and why these events and participants are significant. In concentrating on past events, the texts may have influenced acceptance of Statehood Day by explaining, in detail, why the day is celebrated.

Through references to the past, the media informed their audience about the details and importance of historical events underlying Statehood Day. Media texts presented positive aspects of the events: the victorious moments of the First Serbian Uprising, and the modernity of the Candlemas Constitution and its securing of human rights. The media mainly selected words with positive connotations in referring to historical events. The selected words mediated ideologies and attitudes, and possibly contributed to improving collective memory. For example, readers are expected to remember events described as *najvažniji*, 'most significant,' *odlučujući*, 'decisive,' and *istorijski*, 'historical.'

Serbian Statehood Day is an occasion when people have an opportunity, as a collective, to experience and "feel" their nation. The population is reminded of their membership in a nation. Relatively few people participated directly in central celebrations (the media mentioned around a thousand participants in Orašac in 2006 and 2009, for example). Yet, many were informed about celebrations via the media. Thus, the media's role was important. All lengthy media texts narrated relevant historical events. As a rule, they provided very general information, suggesting that the events were not well known.

Daily newspapers and TV are probably not the most influential means for shaping collective memory. They present the information about Statehood Day in holiday-related issues or programs, and information is consumed on one day or for a couple of days, and then forgotten. Other means (e.g., schoolbooks) are more influential because their authors are more authoritative. However, media may repeat the information about underlying events of Statehood Day each year. As this analysis has shown, the media operated with a number of text types to reinforce collective memory and to "popularize" the underlying events.

Explicit references to the link between the two underlying events of the Statehood Day could be found in the material, for example, "Sretenje ustanka i ustava," 'Meeting of the Uprising and the Constitution' (headline in *Večernje novosti*, 14 Feb. 2004, p. 20). This link reflects the duality of Serbia's political and cultural orientation, seeking to unite the two aforementioned opposed models of identity that Ejdus (2007) cites in his discussion of Serbian strategic culture: the civic-democratic and the national-liberation models. Statehood Day unifies both corresponding discursive models into one narrative: the First Serbian Uprising is a key event of the national-liberation model, and the Candlemas Constitution is a key event of the civic-democratic model. Statehood Day thus unifies two distinct value sets, or "meta-narratives" (David 2009: 158). One refers to Serbia as a country with liberation-war traditions, and the other refers to Serbia as a country of constitutional rights and rule of law. This analysis of media genres has showed that neither model is predominant, that participants in the media discourse base their discourse on *both* models. The political orientation of the participants and their concrete aims influenced which model was given more weight, and so did time and context.

Primary sources

Newspapers

Politika, Večernje novosti, Danas, Dnevnik, and *Borba* (34 front pages and 111 inside pages from the period 2002–2010).

Online sources

Glas javnosti, Večernje novosti, Kurir, Politika, Press online, B92, Mondo, RTS, Danas, Dnevnik, Pink, 24 sata, and *Blic* (61 texts).

Law

Zakon o državnim i drugim praznicima u Republici Srbiji (The Law on State and Other Holidays in the Republic of Serbia). *Službeni glasnik RS* 43 (2001), 101 (2007). Available online at *propisi.com*. http://www.propisi.com/zakon-o-drzavnim-i-drugim-praznicima-u-republici-srbiji.html. Accessed 30 June 2010.

CHAPTER 2

The quest for a proper Bulgarian national holiday

Kjetil Rå Hauge
University of Oslo
k.r.hauge@ilos.uio.no

When the former Bulgarian national holiday of 3 March was reinstated in 1990, opinion was divided as to whether 3 March was a good choice. This chapter examines the discussion that followed in Bulgarian media. The argumentation for the other candidates for national holiday status is shown to mostly concern the degree of active Bulgarian participation in the historical events that the days commemorate, and to a somewhat lesser degree also to concern how the days are celebrated.

Keywords: Bulgaria, semantic roles, Bulgarian liberation, Bulgarian unification, Bulgarian independence, St. Cyril, St. Methodius, argumentation, logical fallacy, reductio ad absurdum

1. Introduction

When Bulgaria in 1990 discarded her former official national holiday from the Communist period, 9 September, and reinstated the old national holiday of 3 March, discussion ensued in the media about whether this was the best choice. In the following years, several more days commemorating major events in Bulgaria's history were introduced as official holidays, with 3 March remaining the official *national* holiday, and discussion continued. Other candidates for the status were put forward and myths constructed to support their candidacy.

The set of Bulgarian official holidays is specified in article 154 of the country's Labor Code (*Кодекс на труда*).[1] In addition to New Year's Day, the religious holidays of Christmas and Easter, and May Day (the latter international by definition),

---

1.   Available at the website of *Министерство на труда и социалната политика на Репу-блика България*, http://www.mlsp.government.bg/bg/law/law/, accessed 27 May 2011.

it specifies the following holidays that celebrate events or institutions relating to Bulgaria's history: 3 March, *Ден на Освобождението на България от османско иго* (Day of Bulgaria's Liberation from the Ottoman Yoke); 6 May, *Гергьовден, Ден на храбростта и Българската армия* (St. George's Day, Day of Bravery and of the Bulgarian Army); 24 May, *Ден на българската просвета и култура и на славянската писменост* (Day of Bulgarian Enlightenment and Slavic Literacy); 6 September, *Ден на Съединението* (Day of Unification); 22 September, *Ден на Независимостта на България* (Day of Bulgaria's Independence); and 1 November, *Ден на народните будители* (Enlightenment Leaders' Day) (literally, 'day of popular awakeners'). Only 3 March is given the additional designation of "национален празник," 'national holiday.'

This chapter will examine what Thorsen (2000: 332–333) calls the mythical dimension of these celebrations, that is, the narratives upon which they are based. As indicated by Roudometof (2002: 10), Bulgaria's neighboring states in the Balkan Peninsula all celebrate national holidays that commemorate "an uprising, revolution, battle, or other military victory (or defeat)" (with Serbia's St. Vitus Day, commemorating the Battle of Kosovo, providing the latter exception, KRH), and are connected with "the tales of the peoples' struggles for independence, self-assertion, and national liberation." In other words, these national holidays do not commemorate events relating to formal legitimization, such as ascension to the throne, signing of constitutions, or ratification of treaties. I propose here that the discourse concerning the potential candidates for the official Bulgarian national holiday can be analyzed as an argument over commemoration of *insurgency* versus commemoration of *legitimization*, and I shall use the relatively simple concept of *semantic roles* to show how these manifest themselves in the discourse. I shall also in some cases discuss the argumentation strategies involved.

Semantic roles, also called "thematic roles," describe the underlying semantic (as opposed to syntactic) roles of the entities associated with the verb of a sentence. Thus, in both "Russia liberated Bulgaria" and "Bulgaria was liberated by Russia," "Russia" is the AGENT, acting with volition and carrying out a change in the state of things, while "Bulgaria" is the PATIENT, affected by the action expressed in the verb. The concept of semantic roles has been a current theme in linguistics for several decades, stemming from seminal works like Fillmore (1968). The proposed inventory of roles varies greatly, but this variation need not concern us here in this very basic analysis. We need only a subset of the roles assumed by Aarts ([1997] 2001: 94–95): AGENT: the "doer," or instigator of the action denoted by the verb; PATIENT: the "undergoer" of the action or event denoted by the verb; GOAL: the location or entity in the direction of which something moves; SOURCE, the location or entity from which something moves; BENEFACTIVE: the entity that benefits from the action or event denoted by the verb. A reason why insurgency is preferred over legitimacy could be that descriptions relating to insurgency usually will place the representatives of the (future) nation in the semantic role of AGENT, while legitimacy, especially in the sense of international recognition, is dispensed to the nation by AGENTs outside it, and the nation is represented as a BENEFACTIVE.

In this chapter, I will show how Bulgarian historians, writers, and public figures try to change the Bulgarian "collective memory," defined as "a set of images of the […] past as well as all past figures and events which are commemorated in one way or another and all forms of that commemoration" (Szacka 1997: 120). They do so by presenting their own narratives concerning the current set of holidays in statements and articles in the national media. The material has been collected from major newspapers published on and around the dates, as well as through Internet searches within the major online newspapers in Bulgaria.[2] It consists of articles authored by the participants in the debate as well as interviews with them conducted by both print and on-line journalists. (The latter type naturally carries with it a certain risk of misrepresenting the interviewee's statements. In the references in the text, the cases involving such types are those where the names of interlocutor and author do not coincide.) The academic status of the participants in the debate ranges from that of full professor to second-year student. Most come from the top end of that hierarchy, and interviewers very often use the interviewee's academic title as part of the article's title.

Previous research into this subject is not extensive. Petkov (2005) discusses from a professional historian's viewpoint the character of the events commemorated by the existing holidays and finds the choice inconsistent, even to the extent that some holidays are celebrated per the Gregorian calendar, others per the Julian calendar. He discusses several more occasions in eighteenth- and nineteenth-century Bulgarian history that would better merit national holiday status, with respect to both legitimacy and insurgency. Claudia Weber (2003) mentions

---

2. Print editions of dailies that can be considered quality newspapers were consulted, and relevant pages were photographed in the SS. Cyril and Methodius National Library of Bulgaria in Sofia: *Rabotničesko delo*, the main organ of the Communist Party, 1950, 1955, 1959, 1968, 1972–1973, 1982; *Demokracija*, the main organ of the Union of Democratic Forces, 1990–2000; *Trud*, in the 90s an organ for the Confederation of Independent Trade Unions in Bulgaria, 1990–1991; and three papers published by European media houses: *Standart*, 1990–1999; *Dnevnik*, 2001; *24časa*, 2003; a total of 260 pages with approximately the same number of articles. I express my gratitude to the National Library for providing me with these resources. Internet searches were made for keywords pointing to articles about the relevant dates ("3 mart," "treti mart," "3-ti mart," etc.) and restricted to main media sites ("site:.trud.bg," "site:.standart-news.com," etc.) in order to filter out irrelevant sites. As a result, 140 articles relevant to the subject were downloaded.

national holidays among other aspects of remembrance discourse, from the liberation from Ottoman rule up to the Communist takeover. The first years of the Communist period are covered by Sygkelos (2009); Roth and Roth (1990) discuss Socialist holidays and rituals from an anthropological viewpoint; and Koleva's study (2007) gives an account, based on interviews, of how the man and woman in the street experienced the celebrations.

2.   Day of Bulgaria's Liberation from the Ottoman Yoke, 3 March

During the Russo-Turkish War (in Bulgaria called *Russko-turskata osvoboditelna vojna*, 'the Russo-Turkish War of Liberation') the Russian army conquered large parts of the Ottoman Balkans. Hostilities ended with a truce at Adrianople (Edirne) on 19 January (Julian calendar, "old style")/31 January (Gregorian calendar, "new style") 1878, and on 19 February/3 March,[3] a preliminary peace treaty was signed by Russia and the Ottoman Empire at San Stefano (present-day Yeşilköy, Turkey). The treaty called for the establishment of a Bulgarian tributary principality with home rule and with a prince elected by the Bulgarian people, subject to the approval of the Ottoman Empire and the Great Powers. A Russian commissioner, supported by a Russian occupation force of fifty thousand, would oversee the transition for an approximate period of two years.

Due to pressure from the European Great Powers, this treaty was superseded on 1/13 July of the same year by the Berlin Treaty. This treaty established two Bulgarian political entities: a vassal principality of Bulgaria between the Balkan range and the Danube, and an autonomous province of the Ottoman Empire south of the Balkan range, under the name of Eastern Rumelia. A governor-general appointed by the Sublime Porte and approved by the Great Powers headed this autonomous province, with its capital at Plovdiv. Its three official languages were Bulgarian, Greek, and Turkish. No Bulgarian officials were involved in concluding either treaty.

The non-agentiveness of the Bulgarian side is implicit even in this holiday's name: a verbal noun, *освобождение*, 'liberation,' followed by a *na*-phrase, *на България*, 'of Bulgaria,' which here indicates the semantic role of PATIENT for the transitive verb from which the verbal noun is derived. As for what Bulgaria was liberated from, the present name contains a word that can only be understood metaphorically, never literally, in this context: *иго*, 'yoke,' and this noun is determined by an adjective that refers to a political relation: *османско*, 'Ottoman.'

---

3. All dates hereafter written with the diagonal (/) refer to the old-/new-style calendars, respectively.

This adjective has not always been used – the main party organ *Rabotničesko delo* (Workers' cause), on 3 March 1950, celebrated the seventy-second anniversary (3 March was not a holiday during Communist rule) of liberation from *турско робство,* 'Turkish slavery,' that is, with an epithet that refers to ethnicity and a noun that may be understood not only in a metaphorical sense, but also in a literal sense. In *Rabotničesko delo* of 3 March 1968, the wording is "Ottoman yoke," and on the same date in 1973, "Ottoman slavery."

This holiday was first celebrated in 1880, as *Възшествието на престола на император Александър II и заключение на Сан-Стефански мир* (Enthronement of Emperor Alexander II [of Russia] and the concluding of the San Stefano peace).[4] In 1888, it was renamed *Ден на освобождението на България* (Day of Bulgaria's liberation) (Todorov 1992).

As some participants readily admit, the debate on the status of 3 March tends to be a debate between Russophiles and Russophobes, between left and right. Both sides construct their own narratives about the events the holiday commemorates, emphasising or deemphasising historical facts per their respective purposes. In many ways, the situation echoes that of the first years after the liberation from Ottoman rule: "The very Russophilic version of national holidays was replaced by a Bulgarian one" (Detchev 2003: 142).

Those who argue against national holiday status for 3 March frequently stress aspects of Bulgaria's non-agentiveness, for instance, that there was no Bulgarian representation at San Stefano. For example, as expressed by Associate Professor Petko Petkov of Veliko Tărnovo University, in an interview in the national newspaper *Monitor* (Monitor) on 13 April 2009: "две империи – руската и турската, просто са седнали и са се разбрали как да си оправят отношенията след една война," 'Two empires, the Russian and the Turkish, have just sat down and reached an agreement about how their matters should be settled after a war.' Even clearer is the statement by Kalin Dimitrov, associate professor of history at Sofia University, writing as a staff writer of the daily *Dnevnik* (Journal):

> Победител и победен са две несъществуващи днес империи, а не нещо, с което ние бихме могли да се идентифицираме. Парадоксално се оказа, че честваме като национален празник историческо събитие, в което българите не са субекти и което в най-добрия случай ги свежда до обект.
>
> (Dimitrov 2001)

---

4. That the signing happened on the day of the enthronement was a coincidence, slightly helped along by the Russian delegation leader, Count Ignatiev's hurrying of the signing. However, that the enthronement made its way into the official name might not be a coincidence, given the Russian occupying forces' policy of "nation-building as a byproduct" (Weber 2006: 52–63).

The victor and the defeated are two no longer existing empires, not something that we would be able to identify with. It turned out, paradoxically, that we celebrate as a national holiday a historical event in which the Bulgarians are not subjects and which, in the best case, reduces them to object [status].

This line of thought was also developed by the chancellor of Sofia University, literary scholar and author Bojan Biolčev, in his speech on the occasion of 24 May in 2002. He alludes to and hyperbolizes the switch from celebrating the Ottoman liberation by the Russian army on 3 March to celebrating the alleged liberation by the Soviet army (9 September), and back again:

не познавам друг народ, който толкова да се е колебал, кой е всъщност националният му празник. При хиляда и триста години история ние винаги избираме дата, когато някой е направил нещо вместо нас, когато някой ни е освободил. От едно освобождение скачаме към друго, подлагайки на съмнение или преоценка предишното. И в крайна сметка винаги сме не субект, а обект на националния си празник.   (Biolčev 2002)

I do not know of any other people that has been so indecisive about what is actually its national holiday. With one thousand three hundred years of history on record, we always choose a date when somebody has done something on our behalf, when someone has liberated us. From one liberation, we jump to another, putting the previous into doubt or reconsideration. And when all is said and done, we are never subjects, always objects of our national holiday.

Notice that in the two last quoted statements, by Dimitrov and Biolčev, the authors are very close to employing the same analytical tools that I use here – the difference is that they use the terms "subject" and "object" of surface syntax.

Others claim that the use of "liberation" is unwarranted, or as London-based writer Julian Popov expresses it in an article at the news site mediapool.bg:

Руската пропаганда и вазовото митотворчество са наложили широко-прието схващане, че става дума за освобождение от робство. В действителност нито става дума за освобождение, нито за робство, но инерцията на този мит е много силна.   (Popov 2003)

Russian propaganda and [national literary figure Ivan] Vazov's myth-making has imposed the prevalent view that we had to do with liberation from slavery. In actual fact, there was neither liberation nor slavery, but this myth has strong inertia.

Popov's statement is an allusion to some of the provisos of the San Stefano Treaty. In an interview in the online newspaper *FrogNews*, Plamen Cvetkov, professor of history at New Bulgarian University, Sofia, goes into detail about these provisos (Stojanova 2009). He stresses that the treaty specifies no time limit for the extraction of the Russian armed forces after the stipulated two years of occupation, whereas it explicitly states that the Russian army should evacuate all former Ottoman territories except Bulgaria.[5] It provides for no international control over the Russian administration,[6] and the expenses for the occupation are to be met by the occupied country. The real treaty, says Cvetkov, is the Berlin Treaty, which reduces the period of occupation to nine months, and provides for the withdrawal of the Russian forces as well as for international control of the occupation from its start, something which forced the occupation administration to initiate the setup of Bulgarian state organs. Furthermore, the San Stefano Treaty did not guarantee rights for religious and ethnic minorities, whereas the Berlin Treaty required not only Bulgaria, but also Romania, Serbia, and Montenegro to observe such rights, thereby requiring them to meet European standards.[7]

Cvetkov blends his historical facts with flaming rhetoric against his opponents: "Това се знае само от специалисти, а добре платени фалшификатори на историята […] продължават да бълват тази зловредна легенда за Санстефанския договор." 'This [the facts about the occupation, KRH] is known only by specialists, while well-paid falsifiers of history […] continue to spew out this harmful legend about the San Stefano Treaty' (Stojanova 2009).

Another claim is that 3 March cannot be celebrated wholeheartedly by all members of Bulgaria's multiethnic population,[8] thus again Julian Popov:

---

5.   At the risk of sounding pedantic, I must interject that the treaty did indeed set a time limit of two years, but only "approximately": "Военное занятие Болгарии будет одинаково ограничено приблизительным сроком в два года," 'The military occupation of Bulgaria will in a similar way be limited to an approximate period of two years.' San Stefano Treaty, Article 8 (Koz'menko 1952: 165).

6.   The treaty does provide a very hedged possibility for control: European governments may send emissaries to the Russian commissioner one year after the establishment of a prince and a constitution if this is accepted (the treaty does not say by whom) as necessary and the involved governments, Russia and the Sublime Porte agree: "По прошествии первого года со времени введения нового порядка европейские кабинеты – в случае, если это будет признано нужным и если по сему предмету последует соглашение между ними, Россией и Блистательной Портой – могут присоединить особых уполномоченных к российскому императорскому комиссару." San Stefano Treaty, Article 7 (Koz'menko 1952: 165), disclaimer as in Footnote 2.

7.   Article 7 of the San Stefano Treaty demands "должное внимание на права и потребности," 'due observance of the rights and needs' of the Turkish, Greek, and Vlach populations in mixed areas at elections and in the drafting of the constitution. This passage is repeated in its entirety in the Berlin Treaty, while a separate article of that treaty goes into considerably greater detail.

8.   In the 2001 census, 83.9% declared themselves as being of Bulgarian ethnicity, 9.4% of Turkish ethnicity, and 4.7% of Roma ethnicity (figures computed from numbers available at http://www.nsi.bg/Census/Ethnos.htm).

> Като се изключи Баба Марта и Съединението, май няма много празници,
> които са си съвсем наши и които да не предизвикват остри спорове сред
> хората, които живеят на територията на България. И 3-ти март е такъв ден.
> Турците надали го смятат за свой.
>
> (Popov 2007)

> Not counting Baba Marta [the folkloristic, non-holiday celebration of 1 March]
> and the [Day of] Unification, there seem not to be many holidays that are com-
> pletely ours and that do not cause heavy disputes among those who live on Bul-
> garia's territory. And 3 March is one of the latter kind. The Turks [of Bulgaria]
> hardly consider it as their own.

Assistant Professor Valeri Kolev of Sofia University, interviewed by *FrogNews*, assigns to Bulgarian liberation the role of GOAL of the activity of warfare:

> българите са причина да има 3 март. Националноосвободителното ни
> движение е един от основните елементи в голямата Източна криза – 1875–
> 1878 година, чийто апогей е Руско-Турската война. В корена на войната
> стои българският въпрос. Заради него Русия води войната, тъй като точно
> българите изострят тази криза.
>
> (Stojanova 2010a)

> the Bulgarians are the reason why 3 March exists. Our national liberation move-
> ment is one of the fundamental elements of the great Eastern crisis of 1875–1878,
> whose culmination is the Russian-Turkish War. At the root of the war stands the
> Bulgarian question. Because of it, Russia wages war, as the Bulgarians are those
> who aggravate this crisis.

One of the staunchest defenders of national holiday status for 3 March, and
someone frequently interviewed on the subject of national holidays, is Professor
Andrej Pantev of Sofia University. In an interview in the newspaper *Trud* (Labor)
on 1 March 1991, he stresses that Bulgaria was not in the passive role of BENEFAC-
TIVE, under a headline that clearly accentuates this role – "Трети март не ни е
подарък," '3 March is not a gift to us' (Gančovski 1991) – because Bulgaria provided the necessary conditions for Russia's action:

> задайте си въпроса, защо тъкмо през 1878 г. руската въоръжена акция
> довежда до възстановяване на държавата ни след като това не е първия
> път, когато руски войски преминават Дунава и Балкана? Защото нашите
> революционни натрупвания и националните акции създават обективните
> условия за успешния и завършек. Ако не беше например Април 1876 г.,
> нямаше да има и Трети март 1878 г., да не споменаваме за другите начинания
> преди!
>
> (Gančovski 1991)

> ask yourself: Why does the Russian armed intervention lead to the re-establish-
> ment of our state precisely in 1878, while this is not the first time that Russian
> troops have crossed the Danube and the Balkan Range? Because our accumu-
> lated revolutionary and national actions create the existent conditions for its

successful completion. If there were no April 1876, there would be no Third March 1878 either, not to speak of the other initiatives before that!

Pantev, some years later, in an article in the newspaper *Monitor*, counters the argument concerning the lack of Bulgarian participation in the events of 3 March 1878 (and those leading up to it) with the claim that almost no nation has liberated itself, not even the Americans, and "в началото на миналия век само Норвегия се е появила на европейската карта без война," 'at the beginning of the former century, only Norway appeared on the map of Europe without a war' (Pantev 2005). A similar claim had been made some years earlier by Professor Ilčo Dimitrov, a historian, in a piece entitled "А тръгнахме от пет процента грамотност: Разговор с Илчо Димитров и Иван Илчев," 'And we started with five percent literacy: A conversation with Ilčo Dimitrov and Ivan Ilčev,' in the weekly *Kultura* (Culture) of 3 March 1998.[9] The interviewer suggested that the Greeks had indeed freed themselves, but Dimitrov pointed to the help that Greece received from Great Britain, and went on to assert that the Czechs and Slovaks had to wait for the downfall of the Austro-Hungarian Empire, and the Poles for the Russian Revolution. These statements seem to imply that in the minds of these discussants, in actual practice, or at least in the practice of the nineteenth century, the action of "liberation" could never be reflexive, that is, the role of AGENT for that action would never belong to the same entity as that having the role of PATIENT.

On a more symbolic note, Pantev, in the same issue of *Kultura* (Pantev 1998), called 3 March the day when the fezes were knocked off the heads, symbolically and in actual fact, of a considerable part of the Bulgarian population. Later on, in 2006, interviewed on a news show on the private channel Nova TV, he uses argumentation obviously colored by Bulgaria's imminent membership in the European Union. He makes an allusion to the reports of "Bulgarian atrocities" that caused an uproar in Great Britain from 1876 onwards, and holds that Bulgaria managed to attain statehood "и под натиска на това, което днес наричаме гражданско общество в Европа," 'also by the pressure of what we nowadays call civic society in Europe,' and he considers that this European interest and attention are what should be celebrated (Pantev 2006), thus adding non-government European AGENTS to the event of Bulgarian liberation.

Professor Georgi Markov, director of the Institute of History at the Bulgarian Academy of Sciences, in an interview by the daily *Monitor*, accentuates the anterior position of the San Stefano Treaty in the chain of events: "ако го нямаше Трети март, какво щяхме да съединяваме на 6 септември? Чия независимост

---

9. http://www.kultura.bg/media/my_html/2018/passage.htm. 3 Mar. 1998.

щяхме да отбелязваме на 22 септември?" 'if there were no 3 March, what would we unite on 6 September? Whose independence would we observe on 22 September?' (Michajlova 2006). He thus implicitly assigns to it the role of SOURCE in relation to the events celebrated on 6 and 22 September. This viewpoint is also subscribed to by the president of the republic, Georgi Părvanov, a historian by education, and he has voiced it on more than one occasion.[10]

In a 2009 interview in *Monitor*, Pantev stresses the active role and agency of the Bulgarian volunteers in the war, and simultaneously lapses into dubious logic:

> Ако погледнем по значение, 3 март си остава най-българският – не само защото руската армия побеждава, но и защото в руската армия се сражават опълченците. Ние не можем да кажем, че тази армия, която идва тук, е била окупаторска, защото тогава излиза, че опълченците са помагали на окупаторите.
> (Draganov 2009)

> If we go by importance, 3 March remains the most Bulgarian [holiday] – not only because the Russian army is victorious, but also because the [Bulgarian] volunteers fight in the Russian army. We cannot say that this army, which comes to us, is an occupying army, because then it turns out that the volunteers helped the occupiers.

He repeats this argument the next year in an interview on the news site *vsekiden.com*: "Ако 3-ти март е черна дата, тогава какви са опълченците, питам аз? Излиза, че те са участвали в една завоевателна война," 'If 3 March is a dark day, what are then the volunteers, I ask? It turns out they have participated in a war of aggression' (Červenakova 2010). This might be an attempt at irony on Pantev's behalf, but it rests on the assumption that the public automatically will commit the logical fallacy of division (assuming that what is true of a whole is also true of its parts), and will assume that if the Russian army had intentions of occupation, then the Bulgarian volunteers in the war had the same intentions. He follows up with an attempt at reductio ad absurdum: "Ако е така, би трябвало да си зададем въпроса защо е нямало дружески българо-турски отпор, когато руснаците идват тук," 'If that is the case, we should ask ourselves why there was no joint Bulgarian-Turkish resistance when the Russians came' (Červenakova 2010).

Some historians argue for 3 March, relying not on the historical event itself, but rather on its discursive impact at the time of the event. Among them is Professor Ivan Ilčev of Sofia University, in a newspaper article entitled "The ridiculous tears about 3 March":

---

10. "Dăržavnoto răkovodstvo: Ne biva da smenjame nacionalnija praznik," *Mediapool,* 3 March 2006, http://www.mediapool.bg/show/?storyid=114975&srcpos=1; "Vlast i elit v 'Bojana'," *Standart* (Standard), 5 Mar. 2009.

Трети март е и ден на узаконяване на връзката ни с Европа. Самото поставяне на въпроса е странно. Щото в народното съзнание той е решен. На Трети март е теглена междата между «робското» минало и свободното днес. Не при свикването на Учредителното събрание в Търново, не при идването на първия български княз, не при съставянето на първото правителство, а в Сан Стефано на 3 март 1878 г.   (Ilčev 2006)

Three March is the day of legalization of our connection with Europe. Even questioning this is odd. Because, in the understanding of the people, this is a settled matter. On 3 March, the borderline between the "slavery" of the past and the freedom of the day was drawn. Not at the convening of the Constitutive Assembly at Tărnovo, not on the arrival of the first Bulgarian prince, not at the formation of the first cabinet, but at San Stefano on 3 March 1878.

In a similar vein and using religious metaphors, staff writer Borislav Evlogiev at the large Internet-only news site *Dnes.bg* calls 3 March "денят на българското възкресение след 500-годишното османско иго," 'the day of Bulgarian resurrection after the 500-year Ottoman yoke' and claims that it contained moments of "национален възторг и духовно извисяване," 'national rapture and spiritual upsurge' (Evlogiev 2008). He counters the arguments about the Russo-Turkish War's being about the political goals of only the ruling elite by quoting enthusiastic comments about the war made by Russian writers of the period: Dostoevskij, Garšin (himself a volunteer in the war), Tolstoj, and Turgenev.

Thus, Bulgaria's non-agentiveness is the main argument against the status of 3 March as the national holiday, with the celebration's non-inclusiveness playing a secondary role. Arguments pro stress that the historical event had Bulgarian liberation as a GOAL; that prior events in the Bulgarian lands had created the necessary conditions for it; that no nation has been the single-handed AGENT of its liberation; that the moral support of European AGENTS should be celebrated; that the event was the SOURCE for the further steps toward full independence; and also stress the discursive impact of the 3 March event.

3.   Day of Bulgarian Enlightenment and Slavic Literacy, 24 May

In 864, the Bulgarian ruler, Boris I, converted to Orthodox Christianity and initiated the Christianization of Bulgaria. Some twenty years later, the disciples of Cyril and Methodius, Byzantine missionaries who had introduced Slavic translations of the Bible in Greater Moravia, were expelled from that kingdom. They were invited to Bulgaria and continued their theological work in Slavic, using the alphabet that is now known as Cyrillic and used by many nations outside Bulgaria.

The present name of the holiday camouflages the fact that it originated as the feast of Saints Cyril and Methodius. As such, it has roots dating to before the liberation from Ottoman rule. Its first celebration, in Plovdiv on 11/24 May 1851, on the initiative of scholar and lexicographer Najden Gerov, was followed by regular celebrations in many towns in the Bulgarian lands from 1857 (Aleksova n.d.). These celebrations centered on Bulgarian culture and language (Petrov 2003), despite church rituals being in Greek up to the establishment of a Bulgarian exarchate in 1870. Even a celebration as early as 1813 was noted by an Armenian traveller (Ormandžijan 1984:216). This and May Day are the only official holidays from the Communist repertoire that have been kept after 1989. Just one word has been dropped from the original title: *bălgarskata narodna prosveta*, 'Bulgarian popular Enlightenment' is now just *bălgarskata prosveta*, 'Bulgarian Enlightenment.' The church and some schools arrange celebrations on 11 May (old style), while the state and institutions of higher learning celebrate on 24 May (new style).[11]

The holiday of 24 May is often called "най-българският ден," 'the most Bulgarian day,' and it represents a pattern of national identity in which the nation is understood as a cultural community rather than as a political community (see Szacka 1997:126 for Polish analogues). The myth associated with it is epitomized in a line from Ivan Vazov's poem "Paisij" (1882), "и ний сме дали нещо на светът / и на вси Словене книга да четат," 'we have also given something to the world / and to all Slavs book[s] to read.' However, this day also has inconvenient features with respect to agency. The following sentences by Bistra Veličkova, a student of journalism, from an article provocatively entitled "Как Византия създаде славянската писменост," 'How Byzantium created Slavic literacy,' sum up the prevailing national myth:

> Повечето българи погрешно смятат, че братята Кирил и Методий са българи. Няма никакви исторически доказателства за това. Погрешно се смята също така, че създаването на "българската" писменост (по-точно славянска) е някакво родолюбиво дело на "Солунските двама братя". Всъщност това е поръчка на византийския император.   (Veličkova 2007)

---

11. Other countries in the region have similar holidays commemorating events relating to writing, language or literature: Macedonia also celebrates 24 May and in addition the Day of the Albanian Alphabet on 22 November; Slovenia has Reformation Day, commemorating Primož Trubar (1508–1586), a Protestant priest who endeavored to write books in a language that could easily be understood by all Slovenians, on 31 October, and has the Day of Slovenian Culture, also called Prešeren's Day, after the Romantic poet, on 8 February; and both the Czech Republic and Slovakia observe SS. Cyril and Methodius' Day on 5 July. In Russia, 24 May is observed with church services.

> Most Bulgarians erroneously consider the brothers Cyril and Methodius to have been Bulgarians. There is no historical proof of that. Erroneous is also the notion that the creation of the "Bulgarian" literacy (Slavic, rather) is some kind of patriotic act by the "two brothers from Thessalonica." It was in fact a commission from the Byzantine emperor.

Veličkova's statements may be deliberately overly provocative,[12] but they touch the main point where Bulgarian agency is lacking: the Moravian mission had no relation to Bulgaria. However, there is no lack of Bulgarian agency in the brothers' disciples' literary and missionary activities after this mission, and that seems to be reason enough for celebration. "Когато този духовен празник и ден на национална гордост и величие стане първият ден на българите," 'When this spiritual celebration and day for national pride and grandeur becomes the Bulgarian's first day,' claims historian Petko Petkov, vice-chancellor of Veliko Tărnovo University, in an interview in *Monitor*, "значи сме се оправили 100%," 'it will mean that we are fully restored' (Părvanov 2009). A more detailed explanation was given in Petkov's article on national holidays mentioned at the beginning of this chapter:

> 11/24 май не може да се сравнява с останалите т.нар. национални празници. Неговото историческо значение е толкова голямо, проекциите му към минало, настояще и бъдеще са толкова осезаеми, че националнополитическите страсти, от които е провокирано величието на дни като 3 март, 6 и 22 септември, изглеждат незначителни на фона на многовековното духовно излъчване на делото, което отбелязваме в този ден. Затова съм убеден, че ако Националният празник на българите трябва да е един, то това несъмнено е 11/24 май. Защото националният празник трябва да е ден, обединяващ всички българи или поне всички българи, живеещи днес в България.   (Petkov 2005)

> Eleven/twenty-four May cannot be compared with the remaining so-called national holidays. Its historical importance is so great, its projections to the past, present, and future so tangible, that the national-political passions that provoked the greatness of days like 3 March, 6 and 22 September, appear insignificant on the background of the centuries-long spiritual emanation of the achievement that we commemorate on that day. Therefore, I am convinced that should there be one National holiday of the Bulgarians, that should without doubt be 11/24 May.

---

12. She is also the author of a definitely ironic piece called "Pismo do Svetite bratia Kiril I Metodi ot edin suvremenen bulgarin," 'Letter to the saintly brothers Cyril and Methodius from a modern Bulgarian,' that is, with the Bulgarian typed out in Latin pseudo-transliteration, complete with a certain word processing program's annoying habit of capitalizing the single word "i" in languages that have such a word.

Biolčev, in his speech as chancellor of Sofia University on 24 May 2002, suggested that the very peacefulness of this occasion and its lack of pomp and circumstance could explain why it was not elevated to national holiday status:

> Няма друг ден, в който българинът да е толкова топло усмихнат в съдружие, няма друг миг, който да обдарява българското съзнание с толкова удовлетворение и уют. От друга страна, наблюдателното око не може да не забележи, че онова, което стопля душите ни, примирява ни и ни въздига със и в самите нас, сякаш ни се струва недостатъчно представително, за да се означим национално с него, да го обявим за национален празник.
>
> (Biolčev 2002)

> There is no other day on which the Bulgarian is so smiling in harmony; there is no other moment that bestows the Bulgarian identity with so much satisfaction and comfort. On the other hand, the observer cannot help notice that what warms our souls, conciliates us and lifts us up with and within ourselves, does not seem to appear sufficiently stately for us to let it take on national meaning, to declare it a national holiday.

This argument, based on the day's discursive impact, is somewhat similar to Borislav Evlogiev's for 3 March at the end of Section 3, only that in Biolčev's case, it is the present-day celebration that is deemed important, as opposed to the original event. And Biolčev lets his argument pull in the opposite direction – contra instead of pro – but see Prodanov's argumentation below for how the pro alternative is also possible.

Concrete action for promoting this holiday to official national holiday was taken in May 2010 by Associate Professor Jurij Prodanov, dean of the Department for Journalism and Media at Šumen University, with an aim to present a petition with more than half a million signatures for this cause to the Bulgarian parliament in May 2011. He counters the SOURCE or "causal chain" argument of those who advocate 3 March and liberation over 6 September (unification) and 22 September (independence) by saying that 24 May, keeping in mind the culture-building and nation-building it symbolizes, was a prerequisite for the steps to complete nationhood that followed some thousand years later. He also stresses its antiquity – it has been celebrated for almost 160 years, and it memorializes events that happened eleven centuries ago. Forestalling counterarguments about too frequent changes of the official national holiday, he suggests that this change will mark, borrowing a metaphor from the domain of computing, coined by Simeon Sakskoburggotski, former king (1943–1946) and prime minister (2001–2005), "smjana na čipa," 'a processor upgrade' for the state:

От управление, залагащо на силови органи за налагане на правила, към управление, подкрепящо институции за възпитаване в правила. И приемащо образованието, науката и културата като основен приоритет.

(Venkov 2010)

From a government depending on organs of power to enforce rules, to a government that supports institutions that educate about rules. And [one that] accepts education, science, and culture as its basic priority.

Prodanov's argumentation for 24 May, as Evlogiev's against it, also involves the rituals and practices that are performed on that day. He asks the interviewer:

Гледахте ли репортажите по националните телевизии на 24 май с колко позитивизъм и настроение бяха заредени? Спомнете си как премина честването на 3 март. Казионни митинги, площади с по 100–200 души, и ако не бяха почетните караули и роти, просто нямаше да има празник. Един обикновен неработен ден за българите. Тогава на улиците излязоха само политиците и институциите. На 24 май излязоха всички.

(Venkov 2010)

Did you see how loaded with positivism and enthusiasm the reports on the national TV channels were on 24 May? Recollect how the celebration progressed on 3 March. Formal rituals, squares with one hundred–two hundred people, and if it were not for the honorary guards and army units, there would not be a holiday. Just another non-working day for the Bulgarians. Only politicians and institutions went out on the streets then. On 24 May everybody went out.

The consequence of this type of argument is that a given holiday's status can be elevated through the quantity and quality of the participation (or rather, so as not to camouflage the semantic roles in this action, the participants in the rituals can achieve such elevation). It is reminiscent of the way observers of Swedish culture call Midsummer the *real* Swedish national holiday. The official holiday, which commemorates a relatively insignificant event of legitimacy, as Sweden never needed to be liberated or to liberate itself, garners very little enthusiasm, whereas Midsummer is an all-out display of cultural and culinary Swedishness.

Ljudmil Georgiev is professor of psychology at Sofia University and national board member of the Movement for Rights and Freedoms, a political party drawing most of its supporters from Bulgarian Turks. On 3 March 2006, he was interviewed on a morning news program aired by the private TV channel bTV. In the interview, he contended that Bulgarians of Turkish origin do not feel 3 March as a unifying date. Bringing back memories of the Ottoman slavery produces discomfort, he said, and next posed the rhetorical question of how present-day Bulgarian Turks could be blamed for their ancestors' being enslavers. The alternative to 3 March, he said, should be 24 May, the holiday for the culture, literacy, and language that all citizens of Bulgaria use to express themselves.[13]

Three days later, in an interview on a different channel, Pantev tried to discredit Georgiev's arguments against 3 March through reductio ad absurdum:

> англичаните не се чувстват наранени, когато американците честват своя Ден на независимостта, нито пък белгийците са оскърбени от това, че французите нарушават неутралитета на Белгия и пеят "Марсилезата", която е напоена с кръв.   (Pantev 2006)

> the English do not feel hurt when the Americans celebrate their Independence Day, neither are the Belgians humiliated by the French violating the neutrality of Belgium and singing "La Marseillaise," which is dripping with blood.

In an interview by *FrogNews*, Cvetkov, who is an advocate for 22 September, finds that the word "Slavic" in the name of the 24 May holiday is misleading:

> 24 май се чества като Деня на славянската писменост и българската култура, макар че писмеността си е българска и е възприета от редица народи, между които само някои са славянски. Между другото славянските народи, които пишат на латиница, са повече от славянските народи, които си служат с кирилицата.   (Stojanova 2009)

> Twenty-four May is celebrated as Day of Slavic Literacy and Bulgarian Culture, although the writing system is Bulgarian and adopted by a number of peoples, among whom some are Slavic. Incidentally, the Slavic peoples who use Latin script are more in number than those who use Cyrillic.[14]

No matter how different 24 May is from 3 March with respect to rituals and commemorated events, we find faint echoes of the argumentation about 3 March in the argumentation about 24 May: On the contra side, 24 May lacks the feature of agentiveness, but on the pro side it can rely on discursive impact, not only of the commemorated event, but also to a large extent of present-day celebrations, and the commemorated event was a necessary condition for the nation-building in later times. In addition to that, there is the added positive feature of antiquity, of both the event and its commemoration, but on the con side, the day's name

---

13. Georgiev's words are quoted from a review of the TV broadcast published in *Business Post*, http://news.bpost.bg/story-read-1962.php. I have not had access to the program itself or to a transcript of it. Therefore, since my source's wording does not reflect Georgiev's words directly, I have chosen not to quote the actual wording of my source.

14. The name that he cites deviates from the official one – see the introduction to this chapter; and the rate of Latin to Cyrillic is actually close to a draw.

implies an exaggerated claim about being a valid reason for celebration for all Slavic peoples.

4. Day of Unification, 6 September

In September 1885, Bulgarian revolutionary fighters in Eastern Rumelia took to arms, ousting the governor-general from his Plovdiv residence on the evening of 6/19 September. On the next day, the provisional government of Eastern Rumelia cabled the Bulgarian Prince Alexander and asked him to declare his support for the annexation of Eastern Rumelia by the Principality of Bulgaria. This he did, issuing a manifesto in Tărnovo on 8/21 September, declaring himself ruler of "North and South Bulgaria."

This date, despite all its qualities as an event wherein Bulgarians were the real AGENTS, performing an action that united two formerly separate parts of the assumed Bulgarian national community, does not seem to have many proponents for elevating it to the status of the official national holiday. It does not even help that the date chosen as significant is not the date of the princely manifesto, but instead 6/19 September, the date on which action was taken by a bona fide insurgent, Zacharij Stojanov, leader of *Български таен централен революционен комитет* (the Bulgarian Secret Central Revolutionary Committee).

In an interview with *FrogNews*, Georgi Markov mentions the formal nature of the 6 September celebrations, that is, the lack of participation by the public. The reason for their formality, he says, is that 6 September, as well as 22 September, have been overshadowed by the celebrations of 9 September during Communism (this coincides with the opinion voiced in Koleva 2007: 190). Although unwilling to reduce the status of 3 March, the anniversary of the event that "поставя началото на новата българска държавност," 'laid the foundation of the new Bulgarian statehood,' he nevertheless considers the present celebration of the September anniversaries lacking in splendour. However, he stresses the active role played by Bulgarian politicians in the events that these two dates commemorate:

> според мен точно тези две дати трябва да бъдат тържествено чествани. Те трябва да ни карат да се чувстваме горди като народ. Защото само 7 години след Берлинския конгрес, според който България бе разпокъсана на пет части, нашият народ наруши волята на Великите сили и обяви Съединението на Княжество България и Източна Румелия против Берлинския договор. В това е силата на това събитие, защото тогава всички се обединяваме – както народа, така и управляващите. В името на една обща кауза съществуващите тогава две партии – либералната и консервативна, загърбват различията.
>
> (Stojanova 2010b)

in my mind, exactly these two days should be celebrated in a solemn fashion. They should make us feel proud as a people. Because only seven years after the Berlin Congress, which split Bulgaria into five parts, our people went against the will of the Great Powers and declared the Unification of the Principality of Bulgaria and East Rumelia in spite of the Berlin Treaty. There lies the might of this event, because we all united then – the people as well as the rulers. In the name of a common cause, the two parties of the time, the Liberals and the Conservatives, put their differences behind them.

Professor Cvetkov finds that both 6 September and 22 September meet the goals of "да обединява нацията," 'uniting the nation' and "да ни приобщава към европейските ценности," 'associating us with European values,' and they are both "чисто българско дело," 'a purely Bulgarian matter,' that is, without a foreign AGENT. His heart, however, lies with 22 September – see next section (Stojanova 2009). That opinion also sums up the score for 6 September in the contest – although with a high score for agentiveness, it loses out to the stronger contender of 22 September, due partly to the embarassing calendric neighborhood, and partly to the commemorated event's being only another step on the path to full independence.

5.   Day of Bulgaria's Independence, 22 September

In 1908, exploiting the chaos after the Young Turk Revolution, Prince Ferdinand proclaimed Bulgaria's full independence at Tărnovo on 22 September/5 October and took the title of *car*, 'king' (*car*, as opposed to *knjaz*, 'prince') of the Bulgarians.

Plamen Cvetkov, in the interview mentioned in sections 2 and 4 of this chapter, categorically states: "България има нужда от нов национален празник и това е 22 септември," 'Bulgaria needs a new national holiday, and that is 22 September.' He sees 22 September 1908 as the last in a series of steps leading to independence, the first of which was the establishment of the Exarchate in 1870.[15]

Journalist Petko Bočarov, born eleven years after the event, claims in the daily *Novinar* (Journalist) that 3 March does not have the quality to be a "символ на възкръсналата българска държавност," 'symbol of the resurrected Bulgarian statehood' – a day answering to that description came only thirty years later.

---

15.   On 28 February/13 March 1870, the Ottoman sultan issued a *ferman* (sultan's edict) for the creation of a Bulgarian Exarchate, thus removing large Slavic-speaking areas from the jurisdiction of the Greek-dominated Orthodox religious community, the *millet*, and for the first time recognizing language as a criterion for political divisions.

Bočarov credits Ferdinand with being the sole architect, the only AGENT, of the achievement of independence, seeing it as a result of crafty diplomatic moves played out by "Ferdinand the Fox." He challenges those who partially credit other actors:

> Покрай сегашния празник чух изказвания на граждани, които непрекъснато говореха за "нашата дипломация" (за ролята на Фердинанд нито дума, разбира се), имаше и такива, които твърдяха, че в постигането на независимостта "народът" не бил участвал, а това било дело само на тогавашните "управляващи". Боже, какви деформации в мисленето е причинил изминалия половин век! (Бočarov 2009)

> At the time of the present holiday I heard statements by citizens who were constantly talking about "our diplomacy" (not a word about Ferdinand's role, of course); there were also those who claimed that "the people" did not take part in the achievement of independence, that being the exclusive feat of the "rulers" of the time. My God, what deformations of thinking have not come out of the past half-century!

In Bočarov's understanding, there is nothing demeaning in giving credit to Ferdinand for the feat of the declaration of independence, and the acquiescence of the people was something on the lines of a prerequisite: "Фердинанд е архитект на независимостта, но нямаше да я изработи, ако 'народът' му не е бил готов да я приеме," 'Ferdinand is the architect of independence, but he would not have effected it had not his "people" been ready to accept it' (Bočarov 2009).

Associate Professor Iskra Baeva of Sofia University seems to hold the view that Bočarov criticizes. In an interview at *vsekiden.com*, she terms the declaration of independence a "формално събитие," 'a formal event' and a "въпрос на процедура," 'procedural question,' and emphasizes that the Bulgarian people took no part in these behind-the-scenes diplomatic negotiations. The 1877–1878 war, on the other hand, involved the population in a very direct way, as did the Unification of 1885 and the war with Serbia that followed. She also reminds readers that despite the apparently self-determined approach of Bulgarian diplomacy, Bulgaria needed Russia's support to settle reparations it owed the Ottoman Empire for taking over the Ottoman Railway Company in 1885, as Russia agreed to waive Ottoman reparations to Russia in exchange (Fileva 2010).

The constitutive text of that event, Ferdinand's manifesto, with its predominant use of the first person, bears eloquent witness to the negligible role played by the Bulgarian people (in Ferdinand's mind, at least):

> Българският Народ […] създаде […] под Мое ръководство […] държава, достойна да бъде равноправен член в семейството на цивилизованите народи. […] Моят Народ днес копнее за своя културен и икономически

напредък […] Такова е желанието на Народа Ми […] държавата Ми се спъва в своя нормален и спокоен развой […] Аз и Народът Ми искрено се радваме.[16]

The Bulgarian People […] created […] under My leadership […] a state that is worthy of being a member on equal footing in the family of civilized peoples […] My People is longing for its cultural and economic development […] Such is the wish of My People […] My state is hindered in its normal and peaceful development […] I and My People are sincerely happy.

It seems that for this commemoration, it is hard to pin the role of AGENT to any other than the crowned head of the state – a monarch who ten years later was blamed for his country's misfortune in WW1 and forced to abdicate. The strongest pro argument seems to be that concerning the event's place as the final achievement on the path to full international legitimacy.

6.   Other dates

Other suggestions arise periodically without having any serious impact on the discussion. Archeologist Ivan Petrinski (2008) recollects discussions about the celebrations of Bulgaria's 1300th anniversary – whether to celebrate the Proto-Bulgarian victory over the Byzantines at Ongal in 680 or the treaty with Byzantium in 681. The decision was to favor legitimacy and the latter over insurgency and the former, because, as he puts it, "битки много, но с международното признаване начева летоброенето на една държава," 'there are many battles, but a state's chronology starts with international recognition' (Petrinski 2008). An obvious problem in elevating this event to national holiday status is that the date cannot be fixed more exactly than sometime between 18 March and 9 August 681. Therefore, he suggests to start celebrations of *Ден на България* (Bulgaria Day) on the evening of 23 May, joining it up with "the most Bulgarian day" on 24 May. No need for it to be non-working, he says, and no need for ministers, parliamentarians and businessmen to participate, but it should be "осмислен," 'filled with meaning' in a wise manner.

A parliamentary motion from Lăčezar Tošev, of *Sinjata koalicija* (The Blue Coalition) for making the former Communist national holiday of 9 September into *Ден за почит към жертвите на комунистическия терор в България след 9 IX 1944 г.*, (Day of remembrance of the victims of Communist terror in Bulgaria after 9 September 1944) in order to get rid of "двусмисленото отношение в

---

16. Manifesto cited from http://www.kingsimeon.bg/archive/viewvideo/id/102. 25 June 2012.

България към датата 9 IX," 'the ambiguous attitude in Bulgaria towards the date of 9 September'[17] never made it past the relevant parliamentary committee.[18]

According to Petkov, several good occasions exist for a national holiday that have been ignored: 27 February, the founding of the Bulgarian exarchate, "първата законнопризната общобългарска институция," 'the first legitimate pan-Bulgarian institution'; 16 April, the signing of the first Bulgarian constitution, in Tărnovo in 1879; 17 April, the election of the first Bulgarian prince in modern times in 1879; 20 April, the start of the largest and most successful uprising against the Ottoman yoke in 1876; and many others (Petkov 2005).

The two official holidays not discussed so far, St. George's Day and Enlightenment Leaders' Day, hardly ever get mentioned as candidates for the official national holiday – only Petkov (2005) makes a convincing case for the historical importance of the Bulgarian Enlightenment period and its leaders. One might surmise that St. George's Day lacks any connection to events in Bulgarian history, while Enlightenment Leaders' Day is too vague, with its celebration of a long period of history and an indefinite number of personalities from that period.

And finally, as an out-and-out appeal to legitimacy, on 6 April 2009, the daily *24 časa* came in a glossy wrapper where it was suggested that 6 April was the *real* day of Bulgarian independence, because on that date (6/19 September) in 1909, the protocol was signed whereby the Ottoman Empire renounced all financial and territorial claims on Bulgaria, thereby essentially recognizing its independence.

7.   Conclusion

It seems that 3 March lacks some of the qualities that are expected of an official national holiday. It represents a kind of legitimacy, but one that was short-lived and that implied a territorial claim that has never been enforced, and that would create international political turmoil if voiced again. It also scores low on insurgency. Because non-Bulgarian AGENTs made most of the achievements and only a few were made by Bulgarians (the Bulgarian volunteer fighters), descriptions of the general event that 3 March commemorates must necessarily put Bulgaria into the semantic role of BENEFACTIVE, and therefore only accounts of sub-events can present Bulgaria or Bulgarians as AGENTs.

---

17. http://parliament.bg/bills/41/954-01-8.pdf. 9 Sept. 2009.

18. "Sin deputat iska 9 septemvri da băde praznik," *Trud*, 23 Sept. 2009, http://www.trud.bg/Article.asp?ArticleId=234839.

The runners-up for the status of the official national holiday have the advantage of already being non-working days with certain rituals and celebrations. Some commentators, as we have seen, attach importance not only to the degree of Bulgarian participation in the historical events that these days commemorate, but also to the mood and degree of participation in the commemorative rituals and celebrations. Their doing so may represent the beginning of a change, from understanding the nation as a political community towards understanding it as a cultural community. Here there might be possibilities for further research.

And maybe writer Georgi Gospodinov is right, when (in the daily *Dnevnik* of 5 March 2001) in a column entitled "Kak (ne) praznuvame," 'How we (do not) celebrate,' and referring to the colors of the Bulgarian flag, he muses about how perhaps the average Bulgarian is at his happiest when his salad

> грее в средата на масата с бялото на сиренето, зеленото на марулите и червеното (малко бледо) на доматите. И в това нерефлектирано трибагрено всекидневие този човек може би е по-искрен от снабдените с празничен език мъже на държавата.

> is glistening in the middle of the table with the white color of the feta cheese, the green color of the lettuce, and the red color (somewhat washed-out) of the tomatoes. And in this unreflective tricolored round of everyday life, this person is perhaps more sincere than the state officials with their holiday phrases.

Primary sources

Aleksova, Krasimira. n.d. "24 Maj - Praznik na slavjanskata pismenost, na bălgarskata prosveta i kultura." http://www.balkanfolk.com/bg/news.php?id=23.

Anonymous. 1998. "A trăgnachme ot pet procenta gramotnost. Razgovor c Ilčo Dimitrov i Ivan Ilčev." *Kultura*, 21 Feb. http://www.kultura.bg/media/my_html/2018/passage.htm.

Biolčev, Bojan. 2002. "Akademično slovo." *Kultura* 22, 31 May. http://www.kultura.bg/media/my_html/2230/slovo.htm.

Bočarov, Petko. 2009. "Nacionalen, ama ne săvsem: Na koja data čuždite diplomati pozdravjavat Bălgarija s praznika ì." *Novinar*, 24 Sept.

Červenakova, Genoveva. 2010. "Istorikăt prof. Andrej Pantev: Revizijata na 3 mart e provokirana ot kompleks za malocennost." *vsekiden.com*, 16 Jan. http://www.vsekiden.com/46347.

Dimitrov, Kalin. 2001. "Obratnata strana na 3 mart." *Dnevnik*, 4 Mar.

Draganov, Marijan. 2009. "Prof. Andrej Pantev, istorik i politik: S Osvoboždenieto ni Rusija izvărši velika evropejska misija." *Monitor*, 1 Mar.

Evlogiev, Borislav. 2008. "Treti mart - vreme za obedinenie." *dnes.bg*, 3 Mar. http://www.dnes.bg/redakcia/2008/03/03/treti-mart-vreme-za-obedinenie.48292.

Fileva, Marija. 2010. "Istorikăt Iskra Baeva: Nezavisimostta e čast ot uspechite, koito davat izlišno samočuvstvie." *vsekiden.com*, 6 July. http://www.vsekiden.com/58228.

Gančovski, Živko. 1991. "Treti mart ne ni e podarăk, a Bălgarija ne e izkustveno săzdadena dăržava." *Trud*, 1 Mar.

Ilčev, Ivan. 2006. "Smešnijat plač za Treti mart: Otričaneto na praznika obižda nacijata." *Standart*, 4 Mar.

Michajlova, Katja. 2006. "Istorikăt prof. Georgi Markov: Neka pone dnes da ne se chvaštame za gušite." *Monitor*, 3 Mar.

Pantev, Andrej. 1998. "Četvărtoto izmerenie na edna vojna." *Kultura* 9 (2018), 6 Mar. http://www.kultura.bg/media/my_html/2018/pantev.htm.

———. 2005. "Treti mart i ravnovesieto." *Monitor*, 2 Mar.

———. 2006. "'Ataka' e estestven produkt na 10–12-godišnata politika v Bălgarija: Profesor Andrej Pantev, istorik, gost v predavaneto na Nova televizija 'Na četiri oči.'" [transcript of] *Nova televizija, "Na četiri oči*," 6 Mar. http://www.focus-news.net/?id=f4205.

Părvanov, Ivan. 2009. "Doc. Petko Petkov, zam.-rektor na VTU 'Sv. Kiril i Metodij': Bălgarinăt običa da se krie zad kolektiva." *Monitor*, 13 Apr.

Petkov, Petko St. 2005. "Bălgarskite nacionalni praznici i bălgarskijat nacionalen ideal." *LiterNet* 11 (72), 17 Nov. http://liternet.bg/publish11/petko_petkov/bylgarskite.htm.

Petrinski, Ivan. 2008. "V părvite si 100 g. Bălgarija e bila federativna." *Sega*, 15 May. http://www.segabg.com/online/article.asp?issueid=2973&sectionid=5&id=0001201.

Petrov, Vasil. 2003. "Denjat na Sv.sv. Kiril i Metodij prez Văzraždaneto." *Kultura* 21, 23 May. http://www.kultura.bg/media/my_html/2276/kim.htm.

Popov, Julian. 2003. "1vi, 3ti, 5ti mart!" *Mediapool.bg*, 28 Feb. http://www.mediapool.bg/show/?storyid=20262.

———. 2007. "Părvijat svobodno praznuvan Den na svobodata." *Mediapool.bg*, 2 Mar. http://www.mediapool.bg/show/?storyid=126620&p=31.

Stojanova, Maja. 2009. "Prof. Plamen Cvetkov: Izučavame istorijata si s rusofilski, a tova označava protivobălgarski pogled." *FrogNews*, 4 Mar. http://frognews.bg/news_10525/Prof_Plamen_TSvetkov_Izuchavame_istoriiata_si_s_rusofilski_a_tova_oznachava_protivobalgarski_pogled/.

———. 2010a. "Doc. Kolev: Sanstefanskijat dogovor e podpisan v denja na obesvaneto na Levski." *FrogNews*, 2 Mar. http://frognews.bg/news_20760/Dots_Kolev_Sanstefanskiiat_dogovor_e_podpisan_v_denia_na_obesvaneto_na_Levski/.

———. 2010b. "Prof. G. Markov: Zachari Stojanov sătvori Săedinenieto." *FrogNews*, 5 Sept. http://frognews.bg/news_26695Prof_G_Markov_Zahari_Stoianov_satvori_Saedinenieto/.

Todorov, Manol. 1992. "Kakvo vsăštnost stoi zad datata 3 mart: Trjabva da si izberem bălgarski nacionalen praznik." *Demokracija*, 3 Mar.

Veličkova, Bistra. 2007. "Kak Vizantija săzdade slavjanskata pismenost." *e-vestnik.bg*, 24 May. http://e-vestnik.bg/?p=1151&cp=1.

Venkov, Venci. 2010. "Proektăt 2405." *24 časa*, 25 May.

CHAPTER 3

The multiple symbolism of 3 May in Poland after the fall of communism

Elżbieta Hałas

University of Warsaw

ehalas@uw.edu.pl

The chapter shows the complex symbolism associated with 3 May, wherein secular and religious elements interact. In 3 May, two holidays coincide: the state National Holiday of May Third and the church Feast of Our Lady, Queen of Poland. The National Holiday of May Third commemorates the anniversary of proclaiming the 3 May Constitution in 1791. This event is considered a cornerstone of Polish political symbolism, on which the entire construction of modern Polish national and state identity is founded.

The analysis, done from a symbolic constructionist perspective, focuses on discursive symbolism and its use in symbolic politics after the fall of communism in Poland. Rhetorical categories such as genres and topoi, as well as Kenneth Burke's dramatistic pentad are employed. In terms of Burke's dramatistic pentad, it is pointed out that President Lech Wałęsa focused on the acting "agent," with the nation as a collective subject; in President Aleksander Kwaśniewski's rhetoric, the "act" became central, whereas in President Kaczyński's rhetoric, the "purpose" moved to the foreground. The chapter presents how Polish presidents and church dignitaries used discursive symbolism to shape state and national identity. It shows the complex interaction of civic, national, and religious identities in the context of Poland's most important holiday.

Keywords: dramatistic pentad, Kenneth Burke, metaphor, national holiday, Poland, presidential discourse, symbolic politics, religious symbolism, topoi

1.   Introduction

The analysis in this chapter is based on the assumption that a collectivity needs images and symbols to represent its continuity and its transformation (Hałas 2008; Stråth 2000: 19–46). Such a symbolic constructionist perspective on questions of nation-states and national identities comes close to the perspective of symbol-ization politics (Hedetoft 1998). Symbols, especially when used by leaders, gain political relevance via giving meaning to reality through struggles over a symbolic definition of situation (Hinckley 1990: 1–15). This chapter focuses on how Polish presidents and church dignitaries used discursive symbolism to shape both state and national identities after the downfall of communism. I present the complex symbolism associated with 3 May, wherein secular and religious elements inter-act. In 3 May, two holidays coincide: *Święto Narodowe Trzeciego Maja* (National Holiday of May Third, henceforth 3 May Holiday) and *Uroczystość Najświętszej Marii Panny Królowej Polski* (Feast of Our Lady, Queen of Poland). The 3 May Holiday commemorates the anniversary of proclaiming the Constitution of 3 May in 1791. In the frames of this holiday, two autonomous fields of discursive construction of national identity affect each other: the civic field of the state and the religious field of the Church.

The entire construction of modern Polish national and state identity is found-ed upon the Enlightenment Constitution of 3 May 1791 – a cornerstone of Pol-ish political symbolism (Hałas 2005: 52). The 3 May Holiday was established as a state holiday in 1919, after Poland regained independence following World War I. The communist regime abolished it in 1951. It was reestablished in 1990 after that regime's downfall, during systemic transformation in Poland (Hałas 2002a, 2002b). The church holiday – Feast of Our Lady, Queen of Poland – on the same date was established in 1924. It is rooted deeper still, in a tradition that reaches back to 1656 and oaths taken by King Jan II Kazimierz during the Swedish inva-sion (the so-called Swedish Deluge). Continued celebration of this holiday signifi-cantly contributed to tension between the Church and the state apparatus under communist rule (1944–1989).

My analysis of two types of public discourse, state and ecclesial, shows the complex interaction of civic, national and religious identities in the frames of 3 May. For discourse analysis, I employ basic concepts of rhetoric such as genres, topoi, and metaphors, as well as the categories of Kenneth Burke's dramatistic pentad (Burke 1989: 135): "act," "scene," "agent," "agency," and "purpose." The dra-matistic pentad is the core concept of Burke's new rhetoric; he relates five rhe-torical elements to questions: "what is the action?" (act); "when?" and "where?" (scene); "who?" (agent); "how?" (agency); "why?" (purpose). These five elements serve as criteria for discourse typology. In my analysis of parliamentary and presi-dential speeches, I determine which of Burke's categories dominate a speaker's discourse. On the other hand, my analysis of sermons given on the church holiday is inspired by Burke's concept of the social reality of drama. The results of this analysis show the symbolic recreating of collective identity, as well as the meaning of the "redemption" metaphor.

1.1   The "scene" and the reinstatement of the holiday

On 6 April 1990, the lower house of the Polish parliament, the *Sejm*, issued a law[1] reinstating the 3 May Holiday. Two parliamentarians spoke on that occasion: *Sejm* Deputy Jan Świtka, who presented the bill, and Senator Jerzy Pietrzak, who spoke on behalf of the organ proposing the bill, the Senate.[2] An analysis of their speeches shows that both employ the same rhetorical strategy.[3] They focused on the "scene," in other words, on the circumstances that led to formulating the proposal to reinstate the 3 May Holiday. Emphasizing the circumstances, both parliamentarians diminished the significance of the agent, and thus also of the act and its supposed purpose: the symbolic act of reinstating the 3 May Holiday.

In his short narrative, Deputy Jan Świtka described the history of celebrations associated with the anniversary of the Constitution of 3 May. He also presented arguments referring to the authority of tradition and to fixed national patterns of commemoration. Indeed, at the beginning of his speech, the Deputy ascribed mainly emotional significance to the Senate's initiative of reinstating the 3 May Holiday: "tak mocno poruszyła polskie serca," 'it has moved Polish hearts so strongly.' Thus, he considered 3 May primarily as a vehicle for patriotic feelings. He focused on the 3 May Holiday as a cultural construct, an objectivized symbol representing a lost property of the Polish nation, a property which should be returned. The final justification, in fact, gives no "in-order-to motives" for this legislative act. Deputy Świtka's entire argumentation rests on "because motives,"[4] referring only to the need to respect tradition under conditions which make acting otherwise impossible: "przemiany ustrojowo-polityczne w Ojczyźnie wymagają tego, aby Święto Narodowe Trzeciego Maja [...] zostało przywrócone," 'the systemic and political changes in our Homeland require that the National Holiday of May Third [...] be reinstated.'

---

1.   *Ustawa z dnia 6 kwietnia 1990 r. o przywróceniu Święta Narodowego Trzeciego Maja* (Law of 6 April 1990 on Reinstating the National Holiday of May Third), *Dziennik Ustaw Rzeczypospolitej Polskiej* 28 (160) (1990). Available at http://isap.sejm.gov.pl/DetailsServlet?id=WDU19900280160, accessed 24. Mar. 2011.

2.   Deputy Jan Świtka represented *Stronnictwo Demokratyczne* (Democratic Party), a satellite of the communist party – *Polska Zjednoczona Partia Robotnicza* (Polish United Workers' Party). Senator Jerzy Pietrzak, a historian, represented *Komitet Obywatelski* (Civic Committee), a formation advocating systemic transformation.

3.   The speeches are quoted from the stenographic reports of the *Sejm* (*Sprawozdania stenograficzne 1990*).

4.   Regarding in-order-to motives referring to the future and because motives referring to the past, see Schutz (1982:69–72).

Senator Jerzy Pietrzak used similar arguments. He emphasized the "scene," the situation that determines reinstatement of the 3 May Holiday. Like Deputy Świtka, he justified the reinstatement by invoking tradition and authority. Primarily, the Senator's speech focused on the holiday's emotional significance: "Naród jednak trwał w sentymentach trzeciomajowej tradycji," 'The nation, however, retained the sentiments of the tradition of 3 May' and "Senat [...] nie rozminął się z odczuciami narodu," 'The Senate [...] did not fail to recognize the feelings of the nation.' In the section containing arguments, the speaker concentrated on how the 3 May Holiday functions to maintain continuity of tradition, memory, and identity. The holiday is presented as a sentimental keepsake. Both parliamentarians focused on habitual and sentimental aspects of the 3 May Holiday, without explaining its symbolic meanings that might have been used to interpret postcommunist changes, for which a course had to be set by giving reality a meaning.

2.   **Using the symbolism of the Constitution of 3 May: Three presidential discourses**

Presidential discourse associated with 3 May was initiated in the Third Republic of Poland when President Lech Wałęsa, the first president elected in a free, general election, gave a speech on this occasion in 1991.[5] An analysis of the presidential speeches of Wałęsa and his successors, Aleksander Kwaśniewski and Lech Kaczyński,[6] clearly shows that the speeches represent three different types of discourse.[7] The differences lie both in their rhetorical definitions of the state of things (in other words, differences stem from how the presidents ascribed meaning to the symbol of the Constitution of 3 May) and in their ways of reinterpreting this meaning in the contemporary contexts of the state and of the nation. In terms of discourse structure, the speeches clearly differ regarding their choice of the

---

5.   "The Third Republic" is a designation of the Polish state. It emphasizes the split with the Polish People's Republic and the symbolic and moral junction with the Second Republic (1918–1939), as well as with the First Republic – the Polish-Lithuanian Commonwealth, which came under the rule of the partitioning states (Prussia, Russia and Austria) in 1795.

6.   Lech Wałęsa – president of the Republic of Poland in 1990–1995; Aleksander Kwaśniewski – president of the Republic of Poland in 1995–2005; Lech Kaczyński – president of the Republic of Poland in 2005 – April 10, 2010 (died before the end of his term in the plane crash near Smoleńsk, Russia).

7.   The speeches of all three presidents are quoted from unpublished archive documents containing the authorized texts, provided to the author by the Chancellery of the President of the Republic of Poland. See the list of primary sources at the end of this chapter.

dominant category of Burke's dramatistic pentad. President Wałęsa focused on the acting "agent," with the nation as a collective subject. In President Kwaśniewski's rhetoric, the "act" became central, whereas in President Kaczyński's rhetoric, the "purpose" moved to the foreground.

2.1   The "agent": The nation and its fragile potency

The bicentenary of the Constitution of 3 May occurred in 1991, during the early period of postcommunist transformation, a period particularly susceptible to politicization of symbols (Hałas 2000). This occasion created an opportunity for, and simultaneously required, rhetorical articulation of the nation-state's identity and its regained collective memory. The heritage of the 3 May Constitution's symbolism and that event's historical narration provided many potential topoi for defining the transformational situation and for projecting the significance of historical events. In his first 3 May presidential speech, Lech Wałęsa, the legendary leader of the Solidarity movement, openly employs the current frame for interpreting the 3 May Constitution's historical significance: "Rodacy! To przesłanie jest nadal aktualne!" 'Fellow countrymen! This message is still valid!' The statement's style is shaped by placing emphasis on the collective agent, in whose name President Wałęsa is speaking. In his first 3 May speech, he highlights citizenship rather than nationality in the ethnic sense. For instance, he speaks about *ogół obywateli III Rzeczypospolitej*, 'all the citizens of the Third Republic.'

In President Wałęsa's speech, the acting collective subject's most significant attribute is liberty, as indicated by the proclamation: "O naszym losie decydujemy sami," 'We alone decide our destiny,' which exaggerates unrestricted collective sovereignty and agency. The fundamental significance of the 3 May Holiday lies in the moral message of the idea of liberty, a message which transcends historical time: "Wolność nigdy nie jest dana raz na zawsze. Jest zadaniem, które musi podejmować każde nowe pokolenie," 'Liberty is never given forever. It is a challenge which every new generation must undertake.'

President Wałęsa depicts the main participants in the current political drama by using an analogy to the 1791 event: "zwycięstwo Solidarności podobne jest do zwycięstwa obozu patriotycznego przed dwustu laty," 'the victory of Solidarity resembles the victory of the patriotic camp two centuries ago.' The two victories are depicted as analogous: the victory of Solidarity and the victory of the patriotic camp during the Four-Year Sejm, 1788–1791. Throughout the speech, drawing comparisons to historical events and situations helps ascribe a symbolic sense to contemporary events.

The rhetorical state of things is depicted by defining the event which occurred two hundred years ago as the "repair of the Polish Republic." The current reinterpretation consists in rhetorically identifying historic moments – past and present: "i my żyjemy w czasach wielkiej naprawy Rzeczypospolitej," 'we, too, live in times when a great repair of the Republic is underway.'

"Repair," in the word's literal sense, assumes that something has previously functioned properly. In the discourse of transition, the term "repair" characterizes the process as a reform rather than as a revolution. President Wałęsa's first 3 May speech uses the convention of moralizing discourse, reminiscent of the judicial genre of speech. The moral message of his first speech reaches a lofty culmination in the following statements: "Po dwóch stuleciach przejmujemy wielkie dziedzictwo. Nie możemy go zmarnować," 'After two hundred years we are taking over a great legacy. We cannot waste it'; "tym bardziej jesteśmy odpowiedzialni przed Bogiem, historią i przyszłymi pokoleniami," 'our responsibility before God, history and the future generations is all the greater.'

In his 1994 speech, President Wałęsa presupposed a politically unrealistic unanimous consensus and thus moralized in his presidential discourse: "Warunkiem powodzenia takich przemian jest jednak społeczne przyzwolenie. Powszechna zgoda," 'However, such changes can only take place under the condition of social agreement. General consent.' President Wałęsa also portrayed the moral state of society in 1993, using the metaphors "building" and "connecting" – creating ties:

> Gdy kończy się walka, nastaje czas budowania. Żyjemy właśnie w takim czasie, przed nami ogrom zadań. Łatwiej im podołamy, kiedy skupimy się na tym, co nas łączy, nie na tym, co dzieli.
>
> When the fighting ends, a time for building comes. We live in precisely such a time, before us lies a multitude of tasks. It will be easier to tackle them when we focus on that which connects us, not on that which divides us.

President Wałęsa's moral discourse during his last two years in office (1994–1995) assumes a tone of admonishment. The main political problem of that period was the parliamentarians' inability to adopt a new constitution. His last speech, in 1995, is constructed around a vocabulary of negative emotions. Here, the way of depicting the state of things evokes unease and pessimism, because the historical events which occurred two centuries ago are shown from their tragic side: treason, foreign intervention and, ultimately, the country's disintegration.

> O losie Rzeczypospolitej decydowano już na obcych dworach. W Warszawie karty i pieniądze rozdawał poseł rosyjski. Werbował ludzi przekupnych do posłusznego imperatorowej legionu. Legionu rodzimych zdrajców, który miał uwiarygodnić obcą agresję.

> The fate of the Republic was already being decided at foreign courts. In Warsaw, cards were dealt and money was counted out by the Russian envoy. He recruited corruptible people to a legion that was loyal to the empress [Catherine the Great]. A legion of native traitors that was to justify the foreign aggression.

In contrast to President Wałęsa's earlier speeches, especially his 1991 speech, which underscored the epochal significance of the Constitution of 3 May, in 1995 rhetorical amplification gives way to reduction: the speaker states that the Constitution was "w tych dziejach epizodem. Wydarzeniem, które nie zmieniło biegu historii, nie zatrzymało procesu upadku Rzeczpospolitej," 'merely an episode in history. An occurrence which did not change the course of events, did not halt the process of the Republic's decay.'

In 1991, President Wałęsa also initiated the discourse associated with the constitution, paralleling such connotations of the 3 May Holiday as "liberty" and "repair of the Republic." This speech was given before the first free general parliamentary election in postcommunist Poland: "Nie wyłoniliśmy Sejmu, który miałby prawo opracować i uchwalić nową konstytucję. Konstytucję na miarę czasów, w których żyjemy," 'We have not chosen a *Sejm* which would have the right to draw up and adopt a new constitution. A constitution to match the times we are living in.'

President Wałęsa's first and last speeches delivered on the occasion of 3 May during his presidency contain opposing characterizations of the collective subject, the nation, as the agent. In his first speech, the nation achieves great things and participates in important historic events. The last speech focuses on the failure to act and to cooperate.

2.2   The "act" or what is to be done

President Kwaśniewski assumed office in December 1995. During communist rule in Poland, he had belonged to the *nomenclature* of the Party. President Kwaśniewski's 3 May discourse differs significantly from that of his predecessor. Unlike the epideictic (demonstrative) rhetoric of President Wałęsa, who passed judgment on the contemporary state of affairs, the rhetoric of President Kwaśniewski's discourse is deliberative and didactic: he deliberates on what has been done and focuses on what needs to be done. The key difference as compared to President Wałęsa's speeches lies in making the "act" the leading category. The act-oriented rhetoric of Kwaśniewski's presidential speeches creates a perspective of realism, founded on the principle of pragmatism. Pragmatism is explicitly declared as a priority.

Despite differences between his speeches and those of President Wałęsa, President Kwaśniewski elaborates on some of his predecessor's topoi. Certain elements defining the 3 May Holiday reappear – specifically, rhetorical depictions of the state of things and reinterpretations to give the 3 May Holiday a meaning of contemporary relevance. Significantly, his reinterpretation involves an orientation towards the future, already discernible in the speeches of President Wałęsa, who demanded proper management of the past's significance. This orientation becomes consistently elaborated in the speeches of President Kwaśniewski, whose electoral campaign slogan was *Wybierzmy przyszłość*, 'Let's choose the future.' The topos of "compromise" is also continued and expanded.

President Kwaśniewski adopted the term "repair of the Republic" to define the symbolic meaning of the Constitution of 3 May in his first presidential speech on that occasion. In subsequent years, "repair of the Republic" no longer served as a key term, and it disappeared almost entirely from his vocabulary. The 1791 event gains a new, moral frame of significance. In 1998, President Kwaśniewski defines the 3 May Holiday, above all, as the commemoration of an "act of civic maturity": "Święto Trzeciego Maja to upamiętnienie dojrzałości obywatelskiej najświatlejszych Polaków," 'The Holiday of May Third commemorates the civic maturity of the most illustrious Poles.' Maturity of the elites is emphasized. The symbolic equation consists in identifying the elites of the patriotic camp in the Four-Year Sejm of the 18th century with the elites responsible for the modern project and for progress of the transformation that started in 1989. The nation's lack of civic maturity is presented as a problem. In President Kwaśniewski's view, the civic society turns out to be immature, which appears to be all too natural, since the maturation process requires time.

In 1999, the Constitution of 3 May is referred to as a "part of history," "deserving the highest respect": "Polskie dzieje pełne są lekcji wartych namysłu i zapamiętania. Konstytucja Trzeciego Maja jest godną najwyższego szacunku częścią naszej historii," 'Polish history is full of lessons worth consideration and remembering. The Constitution of May Third is a part of our national heritage that deserves the utmost respect.' In subsequent years a number of expressions describing the 3 May Holiday appear in the discourse; together, they form a semantic field of civic virtues. In addition to civic maturity, we encounter: "a holiday of wisdom," "a holiday of civic sagacity." In 2000, the metaphor "gift of agreement" appears, whereas in 2002 the 3 May Holiday is referred to as "a holiday of national concord and reconciliation": "Jest więc dzień Trzeciego Maja świętem odwagi myśli, siły wartości państwowych, narodowej zgody i pojednania," 'Thus, the day of May Third is a holiday that lauds courage in thought, the strength of state values, national concord, and reconciliation.' This discourse builds an image of positive national habitus or national character.

However, during President Kwaśniewski's first term, the "repair of the Republic" still accompanies the topos of "civic virtues" in his rhetoric: it is a symbolic link between contemporaneity and the events of two centuries ago, as well as a basis for analogy. In contrast, during his second term, the topos of "constitutionalism" replaces the topos of "repair" in the 3 May discourse. In 2001, President Kwaśniewski called 3 May a "holiday of constitutionalism" when interpreting its meaning. In his presidential speeches, much space is devoted to praising the new constitution, adopted in 1997.[8]

The first speech in 1996 contained an opposition of the symbolic sphere and the sphere of practical actions. In other words, the speech questioned the significance of the 3 May Holiday as a symbol of aspirations to liberty and independence, as well as its identity-creating function:

> Przywołujemy dziś pamięć najświatlejszych Polaków XVIII wieku. Pamiętajmy więc, że chcieli oni zasłużyć „na błogosławieństwo i wdzięczność przyszłych pokoleń" nie za stworzenie symbolu, ale za praktyczne uregulowanie spraw Ojczyzny.

> Today we recall the memory of the most illustrious Poles of the eighteenth century, so let us remember that they wanted to earn "the blessing and gratitude of future generations" not for creating a symbol, but for setting the affairs of the Homeland in order in a practical sense.

This interpretation not only contradicted the actual intentions of the 3 May Constitution's authors, who had simultaneously established "a national keepsake" in the form of the anniversary-commemorating feast, but it also missed the mark in terms of understanding the function of symbolism. The speeches given in subsequent years corrected the latter: they firmly emphasized the symbolic significance of the constitution.

President Kwaśniewski presented another opposition in his first speech – a transposition of the Marxist opposition between theory and practice:

> Dzisiaj pomni polskich doświadczeń wiemy, że patriotyzm nie wyraża się w górnolotnych hasłach i teoretycznych rozważaniach, ale w konkretnej pracy dla dobra i pożytku ludzi – obywateli Rzeczypospolitej Polskiej, dla Polski!

> Today, remembering Polish experiences, we know that patriotism is not expressed in lofty slogans and theoretical reflections, but in actual work for the good and benefit of people – the citizens of the Republic of Poland, for Poland!

---

8. *Konstytucja Rzeczypospolitej Polskiej* (Constitution of the Republic of Poland), *Dziennik Ustaw Rzeczypospolitej Polskiej* 78 (483) (1997). Available at http://www.sejm.gov.pl/prawo/konst/konst.htm, accessed 19 May 2011.

In this way, the metaphor "repair of the Republic" has been translated into categories of practical action and into instructions about how to act. This translation is associated with a special feature of this discourse – valorization of everyday life. As a result, the rhetorical style of these speeches differs markedly from the lofty rhetoric of historical responsibility in President Wałęsa's discourse.

Unlike the 3 May rhetoric towards the end of President Wałęsa's term, loaded with moralizing and criticism of society, President Kwaśniewski's discourse over a period of ten years never ceases to be a voice of the high collective self-esteem of Poles, expressed in a vocabulary of positive emotions, of pride and of satisfaction. The discourse represents a certain rhetorical logotherapy – it dispels doubt, awakens trust and hope, and banishes negative emotions. President Kwaśniewski's proclamation in 1999: "Historia dała nam, Polakom, niejeden powód do dumy," 'History has given us Poles more than one reason to be proud of ourselves,' refers in particular to the most recent history – to the systemic transformation. President Kwaśniewski's speeches draw an analogy between the reforms carried out during the Enlightenment, the Round Table agreements between communist party leaders and the opposition in 1989 and the adoption of the Constitution in 1997. The vocabulary of positive emotions functions as material for a narrative which assumes the form of a success story. Furthermore, it recommends an appropriate collective effort to master emotions. The proposed temporal strategy, as exemplified by the expression from 2001, is closely linked with an effort at emotion control – if the past is not a source of pride and satisfaction, it must be marginalized: "Ludzie wierzący w siebie, wierzący we własny indywidualny i zbiorowy sukces – wracają do przeszłości po to, by umacniać dumę i narodową tożsamość," 'People who believe in themselves, who believe in their own individual and collective success, return to the past in order to strengthen their pride and national identity.'

In President Kwaśniewski's discourse, the politics of positive emotions in defining a collective "here and now" goes hand in hand with anti-historical politics. He stated this explicitly in 2001, using a maxim taken from the thoughts of Montesquieu: "Warto pamiętać starą prawdę, że narody szczęśliwe nie muszą ciągle odwoływać się do historii," 'An old truth is worth remembering – happy nations don't need to constantly refer to history.'

Such a politics of memory and emotions is directly utilized in the discourse to manage the significance of the recent past – the period of transformation. Here, worth noting is a characteristic technique of neutralizing guilt by accusing the accusers and by referring to the highest moral arguments. In a postmodernist style of pastiche, the secular speaker unhesitatingly paraphrases the Gospel:

Ale warto i trzeba także samokrytycznie spojrzeć na zaniechania i popełnione błędy i przypomnieć słowa: "Kto bez winy, niech rzuci kamieniem". Nie ma cudownych sposobów, pozwalających błyskawicznie uzdrowić system.

But it is worthwhile and necessary to also take a self-critical look at omissions and errors, and to recall the words: "He who is without fault should cast the first stone." There are no miraculous ways to instantly cure the system.

President Kwaśniewski's pragmatic discourse is oriented towards efficient action. Therefore, the vocabulary of positive emotions and the anti-historical politics of memory fit well into it. The speeches present an image of achieved successes. The topos of "success," introduced in his first presidential speech in 1996, contrasts with the pessimistic last speech of President Wałęsa.

The vocabulary of positive emotions, civic virtues, and success represents material for a discourse which may be termed "postpolitical" because it creates a critical distance towards politics, which becomes contrasted with everyday life. Postpoliticality implies introducing alternatives to politics and criticizing its negative aspects. It is a rhetoric that discourages interest in politics. In his first speech in 1996, President Kwaśniewski already strongly demarcated the world of politics from the world of everyday life.

"Nie ma żadnego powodu, by Polacy musieli przez cały czas żyć wdzierającą się do ich domów agresywną polityką," 'There is no reason for Poles to have to constantly live with aggressive politics that forces its way into their homes.'

President Kwaśniewski gives his discourse a postpolitical character by taking a relativistic view of political opposites and by emphasizing consensus – an agreement. Ultimately, the most significant component of President Kwaśniewski's postpolitical discourse is community. The semantic core *współ*, meaning 'common,' appears in his leading slogans, such as: *wspólna Polska*, 'a common Poland,' *współdziałanie ponad podziałami*, 'cooperation above divisions.' This "community parlance" frequently simulates religious language. This simulation is particularly apparent in the speech delivered in 2005, the year Pope John Paul II died. President Kwaśniewski's discourse sets a double contrast between politics and shared everyday life on the one hand. On the other hand, politics is contrasted with a community of faith and future prospects that transcend this everyday reality.

2.3   The "purpose" and the significance of political action

President Lech Kaczyński's 3 May discourse reflects the store of meanings and symbols carried by historical narratives regarding the Constitution of 3 May, as well as creative rhetorical possibilities of their interpretation. It differs significantly from his predecessor's discourse and, although some elements of the vocabulary used are common to both, Kaczyński's rhetoric is de facto based on different topoi. Furthermore, it deconstructs most of the leading topoi from President Kwaśniewski's discourse. First, it restores the perspective of political action. President Kaczyński's discourse has an openly political rhetoric, presenting an agonistic vision of reality: allies and foes. The acting subjects participate in political strife, which is not limited to a discrepancy of individual interests, but rather consists of a struggle to realize social values by properly shaping democratic institutions. In contrast to the previously analyzed discourses, organized around a "scene" (or situation), the "agent" or "act," in this discourse the "purpose" of the act plays a central role.

Following Kenneth Burke (1989), one may identify different types of discourse: deterministically oriented (when emphasis is placed on the act's circumstances – the scene), idealistically oriented (emphasis placed on the agent), realistically oriented (emphasis placed on the act), or pragmatically oriented (emphasis placed on the agency). Unlike these discourses, President Kaczyński's discourse is oriented towards a need to give political action a higher sense, an ultimate meaning (emphasis placed on the purpose of the dramatistic pentad). In 2007, President Kaczyński introduced a new topos – "honest authority":

> Będziemy walczyć aż do chwili, gdy w Polsce prawo będzie rzeczywiście równe dla wszystkich, a obywatel będzie mógł podejmować demokratyczne decyzje w oparciu o gruntowną wiedzę, zarówno o naszej dzisiejszej rzeczywistości, jak i o niedalekiej przeszłości. To bardzo istotne, to podstawowe przesłanie dla każdej uczciwej władzy – każdej uczciwej władzy w naszym kraju. Z tej drogi nie zejdziemy ani dziś, ani jutro. Rocznica 3 Maja jest znakomitą okazją, żeby to właśnie podkreślić.

> We shall fight until a time comes when the law in Poland is truly the same for everyone and every citizen is able to make democratic decisions based on thorough knowledge, both about the present reality and about the recent past. This is extremely important, this is the basic message for every honest authority – every honest authority in our country. We will not stray from this path, neither today nor tomorrow. The anniversary of 3 May is an excellent occasion to emphasize this.

In contrast to President Kwaśniewski's 3 May discourse during his second term, in the discourse of President Kaczyński the metaphor of "repair" is brought back, but "renewal" and "cure" appear as well, livening the metaphor of "repair" and giving it new overtones. This discourse emphasizes the significance of civic ties, and thus also the significance of a political society, the existence of which cannot be reduced to the level of everyday life. All this is stressed in the 2006 speech:

Jestem przekonany, że również i dziś [...] Rzeczpospolita Polska, nasze niepod-
ległe państwo, nasz sukces sprzed szesnastu, siedemnastu lat, najwyższa wartość,
która łączy wszystkich Polaków zostanie odnowiona, że zwyciężą ci, którzy tej
odnowy chcą, bo ona jest dziś potrzebna.

I am certain that today, also, [...] the Republic of Poland, our independent state,
our success achieved sixteen, seventeen years ago, the highest value that connects
all Poles will be renewed, that those who want this renewal will prevail, because
it is needed today.

The speech, however, assigns a leading role to the topos of "constitutionalism,"
obviously associated with commemorating the events of 1791. This discourse is
plain, uses metaphors sparingly and is careful in employing metonymy, although
it also obliges the speaker to use the symbol of the Constitution of 3 May to give
meaning to contemporary phenomena. When defining the state of things – explaining what the 3 May Holiday stands for symbolically – President Kaczyński
concentrates his attention on denotation. He focuses on the current anniversary
(216th and subsequent ones) of the historical fact and act which are commemorated. Here, in turn, rhetorical inventiveness lies in the difference in presentation.
Unlike his predecessors, President Kaczyński in his discourse refers neither to
an episode nor to an event, but rather to a stage in the long historical process of
reformative efforts to strengthen the state. Thus, emphasis is placed on the significance of purposeful action over a long time, not just on an isolated moment
in history.

President Kaczyński's first speech in 2006 and his subsequent ones adopt a
definition of 3 May as a holiday of the constitution that aimed at a repair of the
state and at Poland's return to its proper place in Europe. Emphasis is placed on
the fact that this is an anniversary of the first constitution in Europe. Once again,
President Kaczyński proves inventive in modifying this topos, which was also
present in his predecessors' speeches. Here, the discourse underscores the significant role played by the tradition of Polish juridical and reformative thought in
drawing up the Constitution of 3 May. The discourse is pro-European, but simultaneously it clearly highlights the distinct Polish identity.

The symbolic equation consists in identifying the entire Polish nation with
the creators of the Constitution of 3 May: the Constitution becomes linked with a
nation existing through generations, and not merely its elites, some political camp
or trend of political thought. Compare the speech of 2009: "218 lat temu uchwalo-
no pierwszą w Europie Konstytucję. Kto to zrobił? My Polacy," 'The first Constitution in Europe was announced 218 years ago. Who achieved this? We Poles.'

As it reconstructs the cognitive layer of the symbol of the 3 May Constitution – in other words, selected and relevant elements of knowledge about this

event – this discourse simultaneously introduces a language of positive emotions: joy, satisfaction, and national pride. This rhetoric retains a feeling of security, which is also depicted as the *differentia specifica* in defining the situation more than two centuries earlier as opposed to the present-day situation. Thus, it builds a distance between these two historical situations. It also creates a need to seek a suitable ground for analogy to interpretatively use the symbolism associated with the Constitution of 3 May, facilitating the comprehension of present conditions in Poland.

To highlight the contemporary situation, President Kaczyński concentrates on one thread of events from the historical tale about the events of the 3 May Constitution: the actions of its opponents, the drama of national treason. His goal is to focus attention no longer on the sagacious elites, but rather on the treacherous oligarchy. The topos of "endangered democracy" extracted from the story of the 3 May Constitution in the 2009 speech serves, primarily, to help interpret the contemporary state of events: "Jak twierdzili: w imię demokracji […] została obalona konstytucja, która […] była uwieńczeniem dzieła naprawy naszego państwa," 'According to their claims: in the name of democracy […] the constitution was overturned, that constitution which […] was the crowning achievement of the efforts undertaken to repair our state.'

In this discourse, attention is focused on the process of communicating and on the possible divergence of actual intentions in communication, on the content of the message and on the perceived meanings. The topos of "oligarchy" and the struggle against it give the discourse associated with 3 May a political character: it relates to a fight for true democracy, an essential requirement of which is adequate knowledge about the present and the past. This discourse never openly discusses the topic of the communist past. It only occasionally alludes to that period as "the bad times." In contrast, frequent references are made to social solidarity. Describing privileges (and their defense by oligarchy two centuries ago) with the help of these images of past social relations, President Kaczyński characterizes the contemporary situation of the Polish society, deconstructing the topos of "success" which dominated in the rhetoric of his predecessor.

Repair, renewal or curing the Polish state is in this discourse not merely an autotelic aim of home politics, but also has a European dimension. The European angle of the narrative referring to the Constitution of 3 May, the fact that it was the beginning of European constitutionalism and the then-valid political model of the Polish-Lithuanian Commonwealth, serves to help interpret the contemporary situation. It permits formulating the modern international mission of the Polish state, especially in Central and Eastern Europe. The 2008 speech presents the Constitution of 3 May as a work of two nations – Polish and Lithuanian, and in truth others as well – which together constituted the Polish-Lithuanian Commonwealth:

> Znów mamy do czynienia z sytuacją, w której solidarność Polski i Litwy, solidarność Polski i innych narodów bałtyckich i solidarność Polski z narodami, które leżą na południowy wschód od Polski jest wielką wartością.

> Once again we must deal with a situation in which the solidarity of Poland and Lithuania, the solidarity of Poland with other Baltic countries, as well as the solidarity of Poland with nations situated to the southeast of Poland is of great value.

Thus, events which took place in the eighteenth century – even bearing in mind that the analogy concerns a quite distant time – supply a script for interpreting contemporary international relations in Central, Eastern, and Southern Europe. The speech uses a foreign intervention in 1792, which supported opponents of the Constitution of 3 May (under the pretext of defending democracy in the form of the Polish *demokracja szlachecka*, 'democracy of the nobility'), to allude to the contemporary situation in Georgia.

The topos of "constitutionalism" appears in all three presidential discourses. If the first discourse portrayed a need for a new constitution, and the second one did likewise, only to subsequently praise the Constitution of the Republic of Poland adopted in 1997, President Kaczyński's speeches mention the need for changes and improvement. Simultaneously, they emphasize – as in 2009 – respect for the existing constitution. "Konstytucje można naprawiać, zmieniać, ulepszać, ale dzisiaj stoi ona ponad wszystkimi różnymi źródłami prawa, powtarzam, tak jak została zapisana," 'Constitutions may be amended, changed, improved, but today it [the existing constitution] stands above all the various sources of law, I repeat – just as it has been drawn up.'

The presidential discourses analyzed here are almost exclusively limited to secular meanings and values. They lack religious content, even though 3 May has a long tradition as a church holiday. The ecclesial discourse associated with 3 May is different in this aspect – here religious, national and civic topics intermingle.

3.   The spirituality of the nation: Ecclesial 3 May discourse

The ecclesial discourse, structured in a completely different sphere of symbolic imagination, is marked by the discernment of inner-worldliness and other-worldliness. Thus, the structure of this discourse focuses on the visible and the invisible worlds, the sacred sphere that exists beyond the profane reality (Weber 2004: 81–100; Schluchter 1990: 249). The religious symbolic system constitutes a spiritual dimension in the experience of a suprareality (Wuthnow 2001). Consequently, the rhetorical categories of the dramatistic pentad are shaped in a unique fashion, since here we are dealing with the action of a divine factor and the dramaturgy of redemption which transcends historical time.

The homiletic rhetoric largely employs a language of metaphors, not just metonymies and analogies. Sermons delivered on the occasion of the church holiday of 3 May, both before and after the transformation, are characterized by a marked persistence of symbolic forms of expression, created by the late Primate Stefan Wyszyński (1901–1981) and condensed within the "Millennium Act," announced in 1966 on the thousandth anniversary of the Christianization of Poland. A few months before becoming pope, Cardinal Karol Wojtyła summed up and repeated this paradigm of symbolic actions in his sermon in the sanctuary at Jasna Góra on 3 May 1978 (Wojtyła 1979: 327–335). He distinctly explicated the meaning of this symbolism and simultaneously consolidated it as the "Akt oddania Polski w macierzyńską niewolę Maryi za wolność Kościoła w świecie i w Polsce," 'Act of surrendering Poland into the motherly servitude of Mary in return for the freedom of the Church in the world and in Poland.' Explaining the paradoxical connection between freedom and servitude, Cardinal Wojtyła said: "Najpełniejszą wolnością jest ta, która płynie z najpełniejszego oddania się Bogu. Człowiek wolny to jest człowiek bez reszty oddany Bogu [...] Tak jak Maryja Służebnica Pańska," 'The fullest freedom is that which comes from the fullest devotion to God. A free man is a man completely devoted to God [...] Just like Mary, Servant of God.'

This teaching simultaneously shows the universal and the national meaning of the holiday's symbolism. The message is directed concurrently at the person and at the community, both in the universal and in the local sense, because the addressee is both humanity and the nation: "Przez serce każdego człowieka idą niejako wszyscy ludzie, nikt nie jest sam [...]. Możemy też powiedzieć, że przez serce jednego Polaka przechodzi cały naród," 'In a way, all people walk through the heart of every man, nobody is alone [...]. We can also say that the entire nation walks through the heart of a single Pole.'

The discourse of the sermons from Jasna Góra binds together the identity of the person with the identity of the community, and religious identity with national identity. The latter two identities intermingle:

> Żyjemy całym dziedzictwem, któremu na imię Ojczyzna, któremu na imię naród. I żyjemy jako chrześcijanie, tym naszym, polskim dziedzictwem, tym naszym polskim Millenium, tym naszym polskim chrześcijaństwem. Takie jest prawo rzeczywistości.

> We live with our entire heritage, the name of which is Homeland, the name of which is nation. And we live as Christians, with our Polish heritage, with our Polish Millennium, with our Polish Christianity. This is the law of reality.

Noteworthy here is that Cardinal Wojtyła represented religious identity by a more general category than Catholicism – Christianity. This representation differs from the widespread stereotype of the "Catholic Pole." Religious symbolism, with its coincidence of oppositions that overcomes antinomies, especially the antinomy of death and life, lends a spiritual dimension to identity, both individual and collective. The theological foundations of this holiday, belonging to the cult of the Virgin Mary, can be traced to the Gospel (John 19:26–27), in other words, to a belief in redemption, which is simultaneously a rebirth (hence the expression "confiding ourselves to the motherly care of Mary"). This holiday, which commemorates an occurrence on Calvary (Jesus's words to Mary and to the disciple John standing by the cross) and thus an occurrence in the history of redemption, is simultaneously a holiday of the Polish nation's memory as a Christian nation's memory. Cardinal Tarcisio Bertone, the Vatican secretary of state, succinctly and accurately characterized this holiday in a 2009 sermon, recalling Cardinal Wojtyła's speech delivered in 1978: "Ta ewangeliczna scena została wybrana na Uroczystość Królowej Polski, święto Matki, która w doświadczeniach, przez jakie przeszedł Wasz naród, nigdy Was nie opuściła," 'This gospel scene has been chosen for the Feast of the Queen of Poland, a holiday of the Mother who, during all the hardships your nation has gone through, has never deserted you' (Bertone 2009). Thus, this holiday, with its specific spirituality centered around the Virgin Mary, represents the Polish national identity, reinforced by religious culture. As we can see from the analyzed sermons, this discourse takes place both on the level of the symbolic language and on the level of metalanguage when it refers to symbols: "Królowa i Matka z Jasnej Góry stała się symbolem narodowej wolności i uczuć religijnych Polaków," 'The Queen and Mother from Jasna Góra has become a symbol of national freedom and of the religious feelings of Poles' (Bertone 2009). Cardinal Bertone uses metaphors when speaking about the sanctuary: "the Polish Nazareth," "the Polish Cana," "the Polish Calvary." These metaphors can easily be translated into narratives interpreting collective past experiences. The mystical meaning of the cross is conferred on the national experience: "To sanktuarium jest też 'polską Kalwarią', gdzie pod krzyżem Chrystusa i pod krzyżem historii Polaków jest zawsze obecna Maryja," 'This sanctuary is also the "Polish Calvary," where by the cross of Christ, as well as by the cross of the history of Poles, the Virgin Mary is forever present' (Bertone 2009). He also paid tribute to the work of Cardinal Wyszyński and Cardinal Wojtyła which, thanks to the pontificate of the latter as John Paul II, became "dziedzictwem Kościoła powszechnego", 'a heritage of the universal Church.' The speech constructs a perspective of the continuing existence of Christianity and a millennial perspective of Polish history, as well as of the Polish nation's future.

This church holiday, established in 1924 by Pope Pius XI on the day com-memorating the Constitution of 3 May, transcends historical time as a religious holiday, but simultaneously lends a spiritual dimension to the Polish nation's past, bringing this past into the dimension of the history of redemption. Therefore, sermons constantly carry memories of the Constitution of 3 May, an achievement which was, as Cardinal Wojtyła repeated in 1978: "początkiem nowego dążenia do niepodległości, z której naród polski nigdy nie zrezygnował," 'the beginning of a new drive towards independence, which the Polish nation never forsook' (Wojtyła 1979: 327).

The duality of this holiday is clearly articulated and emphasized. In the words of Cardinal Wojtyła in 1978: "przybywamy więc tutaj prowadzeni podwójną mo-tywacją. Zresztą ta dwoistość motywacji zawiera się w samym tytule Bogarodzicy, który nas tutaj dzisiaj sprowadza – Maryi, Królowej Polski," 'we thus arrive here led by a dual motivation. Moreover, that duality of motivation is contained in the very title of the Mother of God which brings us here today – Mary, Queen of Poland' (Wojtyła 1979: 327).

In 1991, this duality was suggestively depicted by Primate Józef Glemp:

> 3 maja w kalendarzu naszych świąt to święto wyjątkowe. Przepojone jest ono wartościami religijnymi i narodowymi. Nie potrafimy ich dobrze rozgraniczyć. Z jednej strony kierujemy nasze uczucia ku Matce Najświętszej, wyznając wiarę i zaufanie w Jej opiekę, a jednocześnie kierujemy wzrok na Orła Białego, widząc w nim wartość naszej narodowej egzystencji, naszych zmagań, walki, cierpień i zwycięstwa. I te wartości – religijne i narodowe, nadprzyrodzone i ziemskie, nie tylko są obecne, ale scalają się w polskiej duszy.

> In our calendar of holidays, 3 May is unique. This holiday is saturated with re-ligious and national values. We cannot clearly differentiate them. On one hand, we direct our feelings towards Our Lady, having faith and trust in Her care, but simultaneously we gaze at the White Eagle [emblem of Poland], which to us em-bodies the value of our national existence, our struggles, our fighting, sufferings, and victory. (Glemp 2004: 229)

The Feast of Our Lady, Queen of Poland, unlike the National Holiday of May Third, continued to be celebrated under communist rule. Hence the civic sig-nificance of this holiday's symbolism was also transmitted unceasingly, closely connected with its religious content, creating an image of the national commu-nity where, as expressed by Cardinal Glemp in 1985, "identyczność narodowa i identyczność wiary," 'national sameness and sameness of faith' remain tightly intertwined (Glemp 2004: 88).

4. Conclusion

The power of the 3 May Holiday's symbolism stems from its long tradition. It is the oldest of Polish public holidays, representing the sovereignty of the state, constitutionalism, and national identity. In the symbolic politics of systemic transformation, the holiday was reinstated after the foundational symbol of the Second Republic, *Narodowe Święto Niepodległości* (National Holiday of Independence) celebrated on 11 November , was reintroduced by the communists on 15 February 1989. The symbolism of 3 May fuses the secular and the sacred. This is reflected in the state and ecclesial discourses associated with this double holiday. The discourses, secular (in Warsaw) and religious (at Jasna Góra sanctuary), are differentiated from one another in terms of spatial location and belong to separate institutional areas of the public sphere, in accordance with the principle that the state and the Church should remain autonomous. However, in the temporal dimension they coexist, underscoring the dual character of 3 May, which is simultaneously a national holiday and a church holiday. The state discourse is free of religious content, whereas in the ecclesial discourse, a central role is played by the sacral symbolic universum, into which the symbolism of the national community fits by means of its identification with the community of faith. In this way, the spiritual dimension of the double holiday of 3 May becomes its distinctive feature and a significant trait of Polish national culture. The 3 May holiday is a symbol of the national identity in the civic sense, and the church holiday symbolizes the nation's cultural identity, wherein Christianity has always been a constitutive factor.[9] The conceptual opposition between the nation in a cultural sense and the nation in a civic sense turns out to be non-applicable in the case of Poland, where collective identity is articulated in both ways. These discourses show the complex symbolic construction of the Polish national identity, which lacks primordial ethno-symbolic depictions of kinship, race, and territory.

The strength of the symbolism associated with the 3 May Holiday has undergone trials, including the rule of the communist regime, and has emerged unshaken. The symbolism of the 3 May Constitution has been a source of flexible interpretations on the threshold of the systemic transformation and in rhetorical strategies of successive presidents. The ecclesiastical discourse from that period reproduces the fundamental rhetorical pattern of national drama. So far, the persistent use of this symbolism signals its lasting presence in the Polish public sphere, with continuing autonomy of the civic and religious spheres, but with no immediate possibility of breaking their subtle connection.

---

9. For a comparative perspective, see Thorsen (2000).

Primary sources

Bertone, Cardinal Tarcisio. 2009. "Widzieć świat oczyma Boga" [To see the World with the Eyes of God]. *Jasna Góra* 4 (2009), 4–5.

Glemp, Cardinal Józef. 2004. "Uczyń nas świątynią Jezusa, Bogurodzico!, Z jasnogórskiego szczytu" [Make Us the Temple of Jesus, Mother of God! From the Peak of Jasna Góra], 229–234. Częstochowa: Paulinianum.

Kaczyński, Lech. *Przemówienia Prezydenta z okazji rocznicy uchwalenia Konstytucji 3 maja 2006–2009* (Speeches of the President on the Anniversary of Proclaiming the Constitution of 3 May 2006–2009). Warszawa: Kancelaria Prezydenta RP.

Kwaśniewski, Aleksander. 2005. *Przemówienia, listy, wywiady: wybór / Prezydent Rzeczypospolitej Polskiej Aleksander Kwaśniewski* [Speeches. Letters. Interviews]. Warszawa: Kancelaria Prezydenta RP.

Sprawozdanie stenograficzne z 25 posiedzenia Sejmu Rzeczypospolitej Polskiej w dniach 5 i 6 kwietnia 1990 r. [Stenographic Report from the 25th Session of the *Sejm* of the Republic of Poland on 5 and 6 April 1990]. Kancelaria Sejmu RP.

Wałęsa, Lech. 1995. *Wszystko co robię, robię dla Polski: przemówienia, posłania 1990–1995* [Everything I Do, I Do for Poland: Speeches, Messages 1990–1995]. Warszawa: Kancelaria Prezydenta RP.

Wojtyła, Cardinal Karol. 1979. *Oto Matka Twoja* [Here is Your Mother], 327–335. Jasna Góra – Rzym: Paulini.

CHAPTER 4

"Dan skuplji vijeka," 'A day more precious than a century'

Constructing Montenegrin identity
by commemorating Independence Day

Tatjana Radanović Felberg
Oslo and Akershus University College of Applied Sciences
tatjana@felberg.com

This chapter describes how one version of Montenegrin identity was constructed in the Montenegrin newspaper *Pobjeda online* (Victory online). This construction was analyzed in connection with commemorations of the Montenegrin *Dan nezavisnosti* (Independence Day), 21 May, from 2006 to 2009. The elements analyzed within a social semiotic approach are layout, photographs, verbal text, and discourse models. The results of the analysis suggest that Montenegrin identity was constructed as a continuation of independence achieved in the past, and then unwillingly interrupted. The results indicate, moreover, that identity was also constructed as having been achieved through conflict with both internal and external enemies, and through concepts like independence, democracy, modernity, and European values.

Keywords: Montenegro, *Pobjeda online*, Montenegrin identity, Milo Đukanović, front pages, discourse models, social semiotics

1. Introduction

This chapter shows how one version of Montenegrin identity was discursively constructed in the newspaper *Pobjeda online* (Victory online). This construction was analyzed in connection with the commemoration of the Montenegrin *Dan nezavisnosti* (Independence Day), 21 May, from 2006 to 2009. Two important areas of social life are therefore covered, politics and the media, as is their connection with language. Both political and media discourses contribute to building identities and relations through the construction of, for example, closeness vs. distance, space vs. time, and the division us vs. them, and thus contribute to building the knowledge and belief systems within a particular society. The way identities and relations are built affects the construction of national ideologies as well. Because "national holiday commemorations are key sites for the affirmation and reaffirmation of national bonds" (Fox and Miller-Idriss 2008: 546), this chapter focuses particularly on Montenegrin Independence Day.

National holidays are celebrated every year; they consist of ritualized actions and abound in symbols. Because online newspapers are multi-modal, they are perfect places for reenacting national holidays. *Pobjeda online* was chosen not only for this reason, but also because it represents an official voice. Voice is always connected with identity (signaling who is speaking) and power (showing who is allowed to speak). My research question is therefore: How is Montenegrin identity constructed in the Montenegrin government-friendly newspaper *Pobjeda online* through the Independence Day commemoration?

Following a brief historical and political overview focused on relations between Montenegro and Serbia, and on the role of *Pobjeda*, I describe the data analyzed and explain the study's theoretical and methodological frameworks. This chapter continues with an analysis of homepages and selected articles from *Pobjeda online*, and concludes by giving a possible answer to the research question regarding this newspaper's construction of Independence Day and Montenegrin identity.

2. Background

After the Socialist Federal Republic of Yugoslavia collapsed in 1992, national holidays were redefined and new holidays were introduced in the successor states. According to the Law on State and Other Holidays adopted in May 2007, Montenegro has four official, secular holidays: *Dan nezavisnosti* (Independence Day), 21 May; *Dan državnosti* (Statehood Day), 13 July; *Nova godina* (New Year's Day), 1 January; and *Praznik rada* (Labor Day), 1 May.[1]

The explanatory text following paragraph IV in the law connects Statehood Day with freedom and independence:

> Trinaesti jul kao Dan državnosti Crne Gore simbolizuje kontinuiranu težnju Crne Gore i njenog naroda za slobodom i nezavisnošću i predstavlja istorijsku

---

1.   *Zakon o državnim i drugim praznicima,* available at the website of *Sindikat trgovine Crne Gore,* http://www.stcg.me/files/zakon_o_dravnim_i_drugim_praznicima.pdf, accessed 20 Feb. 2010.

vertikalu njenog državnog identiteta od 13. jula 1878. godine i Berlinskog kongresa kada je prvi put međunarodno priznata, 13. jul 1941. godine kada je ustala protiv fašizma do savremenog značaja ovog datuma.

> Thirteenth of July as Statehood Day symbolizes the continuous yearning of Montenegro and its people for freedom and independence and represents the historical connection of its state identity – from 13 July 1878 and the Congress of Berlin, when it was internationally recognized for the first time, to 13 July 1941, when it rose up against fascism – to the contemporary importance of this date.[2]

This explanatory remark constructs independence as a continuum starting at the time of Montenegrin independence in 1878, connecting it with the uprising against fascism in 1941 and further with the present time. Contrary to this construction, there exists another construction of the same historical events in which Montenegro is constructed as part of Serbia and in which Montenegrin and Serbian similarities are foregrounded (Morrison 2009: 210). This version is based on Montenegro's joining the Kingdom of Serbs, Croats, and Slovenes in 1918 and sharing a common state with Serbia from 1918 to 2006. These competing constructions of history are connected with political differences within Montenegro today (Morrison 2009). Montenegrins are thus divided into two groups: those in favor and those against an independent Montenegro. Those in favor of the union with Serbia build upon the storyline that the Kingdom of Montenegro voluntarily joined the Kingdom of Serbs, Croats, and Slovenes in 1918. In a referendum in 1992, the majority opted to continue the union with Serbia. Those in favor of an independent Montenegro build upon the independence and statehood that Montenegro had prior to 1918 and consider the union in 1918 to have been forced (Gallagher 2003; Andrijašević and Rastoder 2006). In the 2006 referendum, 55.53% of voters opted for an independent Montenegro, which was 0.53% more than the EU's proposed margin (Morrison 2009: 219).

Montenegrin independence is publicly connected with one dominant political figure: Milo Đukanović. Đukanović has been active in Yugoslav and Montenegrin politics since 1991, when he was elected prime minister at the age of twenty-nine. Since then, he has held various important positions as prime minister, president, or chairman of the leading party, the Democratic Party of Socialists of Montenegro (DPS). Đukanović has lived through difficult political times. He had a common political platform with Slobodan Milošević from 1989 to 1997 (Huszka 2003; Andrijašević and Rastoder 2006). This union ended when Đukanović decided to distance himself from Milošević, a process that was particularly obvious during the NATO bombing of Yugoslavia in 1999 (Felberg 2008) and continued

---

2.   All translations by the author.

until Milošević's fall from power in 2000. Distancing himself from Milošević also meant stepping up discourse about Montenegrin independence.

A possible referendum on Montenegrin independence was discussed several times in international fora, resulting in the referendum's postponement until 2006. The international community, represented by the EU, was involved in this process. National and international observers, and the media monitored the referendum. In contrast to the violent events during Yugoslavia's collapse, the Montenegrin referendum was peaceful.

Montenegro's media landscape for newspapers consists of three main dailies: *Dan* (Day), *Pobjeda*, and *Vijesti* (News). *Pobjeda* is the longest-running newspaper in Montenegro; it had a strong influence on public opinion during Yugoslav times, albeit primarily in Montenegro.[3] *Pobjeda* was state owned, under the influence of the ruling Communist Party until the multiparty system was reintroduced in Yugoslavia. The process of transforming *Pobjeda* into a shareholder-owned company began in 2003 and ended in December 2005, with the majority of shares belonging to the state (*Pobjeda*, 2 Jan. 2006). After the reintroduction of a multiparty system, *Pobjeda* continued to support the government (Felberg 2008). In 2003, *Pobjeda* started publishing its online version. *Pobjeda* did not have any competition in Montenegro until 1997, when *Vijesti* appeared, and then *Dan* a year later. *Vijesti* is considered an independent newspaper, whereas *Dan* is considered pro-Serbian (Lakić 2005; Pavićević and Đurović 2009).

This chapter concentrates on *Pobjeda online* as an official voice supporting independence and a separate Montenegrin identity.

3. Theoretical and methodological frameworks

When reading online newspapers, readers construct meaning from the reality represented and mediated through that particular online newspaper. This mediated version of reality is the object of this study, and it is constructed and represented by means of linguistic and other semiotic resources. The relation between language and society is here understood through the metaphor of a construction site (Potter 2003: 97), which foregrounds the idea that people construct different versions of the world through different use of language. People can choose from a number of language resources. The language resources they choose reveal something about the construction of a particular event. This idea is also found in social semiotics (van Leeuwen 2005), a field of research that has adapted systemic

---

3. The first issue of *Pobjeda* was published on 24 October 1944.

functional linguistics (Halliday and Hasan 1989) to analyzing semiotic resources beyond verbal language. Verbal and visual elements that form different semiotic systems are referred to as modes or modalities, and require a specific analytical approach. Because the *Pobjeda online* website contains not only verbal elements, but also visual elements such as photographs, graphs, charts, and political cartoons, social semiotics proves useful for this analysis. The main principle of this theory is that multimodal texts combine effects of various semiotic systems, thereby constructing meaning. The two important questions are how these different systems combine and how that combination contributes to meaning making.

Both verbal and visual texts use their respective systems of possible forms and combinations, and create meaning that is interpreted according to a particular culture's practices. Accordingly, in this analysis, the theory and methodology of the texts and images from Montenegro are applied within the Montenegrin context. While moving reflexively from context to texts, and back, to understand how these constitute one another, certain structures come to light. Following Gee (2005), these are called discourse models (DMs). DMs are often subconscious simplifications that help people make sense of their surroundings. If, for example, a DM of a wedding is evoked, the majority of people in Montenegro would have "a theory" about what a wedding is supposed to be like. That theory would have many common elements such as a bride, a groom, a best man, possibly a priest, and so on. The DM of a wedding would be somewhat different in different cultures. Common among DMs is that all of them consist of participants, relations, actions, aims, and inferences. Speakers can use several, sometimes contradictory, models; DMs can also be partial. Usually one model is the main model onto which other models can connect. New DMs can be based on old ones, ensuring better understanding. Each DM, like each text, is an engagement in some preexisting debate (following a Bakhtinian understanding of dialogism). Recapturing that preexisting debate requires knowledge of various elements of text and context.

3.1   Data and methodology

The data analyzed in this chapter consist of homepages of *Pobjeda online* and a selection of articles:

1. Four homepages of *Pobjeda online* – 22 May 2006 (the day after the referendum), 20 May 2007,[4] 21 May 2008, and 21 May 2009 – were selected

---

4. *Pobjeda* was not published on 21 May 2007.

because they were published on the expected dates for commemorating Independence Day.[5]

2.   Three articles, one from each of three issues after independence, were chosen because they give a summary of Independence Day and because they represent newspapers' construction of Independence Day and thus of Montenegrin identity:

   a.   "Dan skuplji vijeka," 'A day more precious than a century' (20 May 2007) by Radomir Tomić

   b.   "Čekali smo dugo – isplatilo se!" 'We've been waiting for a long time – it was worth it!' (21 May 2008) by Radomir Tomić

   c.   "Svečanost povodom obilježavanja 21. maja – Dana nezavisnosti Crne Gore, Spomenik u čast 90. godišnjice Božićnog ustanka," 'Celebration commemorating 21 May, Montenegrin Independence Day, monument in honor of ninetieth anniversary of Christmas Uprising' (21 May 2009) by I. K. (only initials are given).[6]

3.   Two interviews given by Milo Đukanović for Independence Day were chosen because Milo Đukanović is considered "the foremost fighter for Montenegrin independence" and as such is expected to give an official construction of the independence and of Montenegrin identity. The popularity of his interviews is also shown through the column "most read news today," showing that both interviews by Đukanović were among the five most read news items on the days they were published.

   a.   "Crna Gora je danas stabilna država," 'Montenegro stable country today' (20 May 2007)

   b.   "Crna Gora pouzdano drži kormilo evropske budućnosti u svojim rukama," 'Montenegro confidently holds rudder of European future in its hands' (21 May 2009)

The data were analyzed using the following methodological steps:

1.   Analyzing *Pobjeda*'s construction of Independence Day by

   a.   Analyzing choices of layout, photographs, and main news of four front pages,

---

5.   *Pobjeda online* changed its web presentation in 2011. As a result of that change, the homepages analyzed were removed from the archive and replaced with different, text-only versions of the homepages.

6.   The Christmas Uprising was a protest against Montenegro's decision to join the Kingdom of Serbs, Croats, and Slovenes in 1918.

b. Analyzing views expressed through qualitative content analysis and analysis of discourse models[7] in three articles summarizing the Independence Day commemoration,

2. Analyzing Đukanović's construction of Independence Day and of Montenegrin identity in his two interviews by analyzing views expressed through the choices of topics and discourse models used, and

3. Comparing *Pobjeda's* and Đukanović's constructions of Independence Day.

4. Analyzing *Pobjeda's* construction of Independence Day

4.1   Layout

Web pages are generally dynamic and they have an action potential (Baldry and Thibault 2006: 104). These features mean that people can click their way around a website, choose their own path while browsing, and interact with online newspapers. The homepage has a special function because it provides links to other pages on the website; it is a portal into the newspapers and serves a front-page function. It has both an aesthetic aspect, which is designed to attract readers, and a functional one as a recognizable point of entry that structures the news. The homepages of *Pobjeda online* resemble the front pages of its paper editions regarding the photographs chosen and the news presented. This resemblance is obvious from comparing the homepages with images of front pages shown in the lower right corner of all issues. As mentioned earlier, all homepages are multimodal because they can include various semiotic resources such as verbal text, photographs, colors, videos, music, layout, various font types, and various font sizes. The dynamic nature of web pages is also apparent in the fact that they can be constantly updated. However, *Pobjeda's* homepages from the period analyzed are published once daily, are not updated during the day, and offered no possibility for immediate interactivity as is the case with some other European online newspapers (Redden and Witschge 2010: 171–186). There is one exception, however: One part of the page, in the upper corner of the middle panel, is updated. This panel features a ticker bar with breaking news similar to ticker bars on television news.

Given the four screenshots (here shown in black and white, see Figures 1–4) and comparing other homepages not shown here, one can see some general characteristics of *Pobjeda's* web layout:

---

7. An analysis of discourse models in three articles is not presented in this chapter due to lack of space.

1. The site name *Pobjeda online* is in the homepage's upper left corner. *Pobjeda* is written in Cyrillic in red, and *online* is written in the Latin alphabet, perhaps reflecting the impact of globalization. The rest of the text in the online version is written in the Latin alphabet, whereas the paper version of *Pobjeda* uses Cyrillic. This changed on 21 May 2010 (on Independence Day), when *Pobjeda* switched from Cyrillic to the Latin alphabet.[8]

2. The top banner is reserved for information to readers and it changes from time to time (e.g., information about change of e-mail address, information that the online version from that day is uploaded after 3 pm, etc.).

3. The rest of the page is divided into three panels:

   a. The left panel consists of hyperlinks to main sections in the newspaper (politics, business, society, etc.).

   b. The middle panel consists of the foregrounded most important news chosen by *Pobjeda online*.

   c. The right panel consists of a list of the most read news that day, space for ads, a search engine, an image of *Pobjeda*'s front page, links to *Pobjeda*'s sports section, and the weather report.

4. The bottom bar consists of copyright information as well as links to the main sections of the newspaper.

Generally, *Pobjeda online*'s layout seems designed to resemble that of other modern online newspapers and simultaneously to preserve features that make it recognizable to its readers, as, for example, its name written in Cyrillic. The main difference is the lack of news dynamics and interactivity. *Pobjeda* structures global events for its readers by choosing and foregrounding a few news items daily. The number of photographs is very low, and only the very important news stories feature photographs.

4.2   Photographs

Pobjeda online uses few photographs on its homepage, so that the photographs and the news connected to them become even more salient. All photographs appear in the middle panel's upper left corner, the most prominent space on a page

---

8. The editor-in-chief of *Pobjeda*, Srđan Kusovac, explained the reasons for changing the font from Cyrillic to Latin in the article "Pobjeda latinicom! Pragmatizam ili jeres?" 'Pobjeda in Latin alphabet! Pragmatism or heresy?' published on 21 May 2010, as threefold: (1) young readers prefer the Latin alphabet, (2) it makes *Pobjeda* more easily accessible to the minorities in Montenegro who do not have Montenegrin as their mother tongue, and (3) it is cheaper and technically easier to use the Latin alphabet.

Figure 1. *Pobjeda online*, 22 May 2006

according to Kress and van Leeuwen (1996), and to a *Pobjeda* journalist I interviewed (Felberg 2008). The photograph published on the day after the referendum, 22 May 2006 (see Figure 1), shows people on the street with Montenegrin flags celebrating Montenegro's independence. One of the flags visible in the center

Figure 2. *Pobjeda online*, 20 May 2007

of the photograph is an older version of the Montenegrin flag. It is red with a big, yellow cross in the middle. The main space was thus given to the national symbols and the people – a collective representing the 55.53% of the Montenegrin population that voted for independence.

On the first anniversary of independence, 20 May 2007, a photo of Milo Đukanović, taken from a close-up shot, was placed next to the interview that he gave to the newspaper (see Figure 2). At that time, he was his party's leader but not Montenegro's leader. Giving him front-page and homepage space in the newspaper was a strong statement connecting him to Montenegrin independence. The

Figure 3. *Pobjeda online*, 21 May 2008

photograph's background is neutral but the mood is official. Đukanović is wearing a suit with a red tie and his hands are in midair, suggesting gesticulation as though he is talking. State symbols, such as the flag or coat-of-arms, are not present here. The photo is connected to the text of the interview he gave to the newspaper: "Crna Gora je danas stabilna država," 'Montenegro stable country today.'

On the second anniversary, 21 May 2008, a photo shows the new president, Filip Vujanović, starting his second term with a celebration in Cetinje, Montenegro's secondary capital and the president's official residence (see Figure 3).[9] The photograph depicts soldiers in green, blue and white uniforms, representing the army, air force, and navy respectively. Montenegrin flags are prominent on the building behind the soldiers. The red carpet symbolizes the importance of the people walking on it: Montenegrin President Filip Vujanović and Speaker of Parliament Ranko Krivokapić. It is important to note that these two are shown from an impersonal distance and are not easily recognizable. The second photograph in this issue shows Đukanović together with the Hungarian president; so, he is shown in this issue as well.

The homepage on the third anniversary, 21 May 2009, shows Milo Đukanović, who was in office again (see Figure 4). Now he is in a relaxed position, giving an interview. The Montenegrin flag is visible to his left, as is the painting *Crni panter* (Black Panther) by the Montenegrin painter Petar Lubarda. That painting connotes important official meetings. The other photograph on this day shows the unveiling of a monument in Cetinje, commemorating the ninetieth anniversary of the Christmas Uprising.

The comparison of the layouts and the photographs of front pages in *Pobjeda* from 2006 to 2009 does not show any significant change. The layout follows general conventions of online newspapers framed by the technology at *Pobjeda*'s disposal. The conventional representation of the people waving flags and celebrating independence is followed by a conventional representation of the "strongman" Milo Đukanović, who is by far the most prominent political personality presented because he is shown on all three anniversaries. Other leaders of the ruling party – Filip Vujanović and Ranko Krivokapić – are both shown in one edition, but are not presented as central. *Pobjeda online* constructs the commemoration of Independence Day in all four issues as a solemn occasion in which state symbols such as flags and military uniforms, as well as business suits, are part of *Pobjeda*'s aesthetics. It is important to note that no explicit religious symbols are present, other than crosses, as an integral part of the Montenegrin flag. The lack of religious symbols possibly supports a proclaimed view by the ruling party that Montenegro is a state for all citizens and not only for the followers of one particular religion.

---

9. Cetinje was historically the royal capital, and today it is the secondary capital of Montenegro; the primary capital is Podgorica.

Figure 4. *Pobjeda online*, 21 May 2009

4.3   Main news

Pobjeda online structured the news for its readers by graphically marking its homepages; the titles of articles are written in red, and there is a short lead introducing news items. These are clickable so that the readers can decide whether they want to go on reading the particular story. The main news items chosen by Pobjeda online on the first, second and third anniversaries are shown in Table 1.

Table 1 shows that the homepages were, as expected, structured around the main news of the day: commemorating Independence Day.

How did *Pobjeda*'s journalists construct Independence Day verbally?

Table 1. *Pobjeda online*'s choice of news

20 May 2007	21 May 2008	21 May 2009
1. "Crna Gora je danas stabilna država," 'Montenegro stable country today'	1. "Vujanović počeo drugi mandate," 'Vujanović starts second term'	1. "Intervju: Crna Gora pouzdano drži kormilo evropske budućnosti u svojim rukama," 'Interview: Montenegro confidently holds rudder of European future in its hands'
2. "Svim građanima Crne Gore čestitamo Dan nezavisnosti," 'We congratulate all Montenegrin citizens on Independence Day'	2. "Crnogorski premijer Milo Đukanović juče boravio u zvaničnoj posjeti Mađarskoj," 'Montenegrin prime minister Milo Đukanović on official visit to Hungary yesterday'	2. "Svečanost povodom 21. maja: Spomenik u čast 90 godina Božićnog ustanka," 'Celebration commemorating 21 May, monument in honor of ninetieth anniversary of Christmas Uprising'
3. "U prazničnom broju govori," 'Speeches in holiday issue'	3. "Datumi – dvije godine od nezavisnosti," 'Dates: two years of independence'	3. "Svim građanima čestitamo Dan nezavisnosti," 'We congratulate all citizens on Independence Day'
4. "Poklon čitaocima," 'Gift to our readers'	4. "Svim građanima Crne Gore sretan Dan nezavisnosti," 'Happy Independence Day to all Montenegrin citizens'	4. "Sljedeći broj Pobjede izlazi u subotu 23 maja," 'Next issue of *Pobjeda* to appear on Saturday 23 May'

4.4   Journalists' construction of Independence Day

The first anniversary of independence is summarized in an article called "Dan skuplji vijeka," 'A day more precious than a century.' The title is a play on the love poem *Noć skuplja vijeka* (A night more precious than a century) written by Petar Petrović II Njegoš, Montenegro's bishop-ruler in 1845. Interesting to note is that Njegoš is used by some as proof of a unique Montenegrin identity and by others as proof of the Serbian origin of the Montenegrin people. This chapter uses the connotation to symbolically represent the importance of independence, comparing it to the importance of love. Njegoš is thus indirectly connected with independent Montenegro. The gender perspective is indirectly present because the feminine noun *država,* 'state' is conceptualized as a woman to be loved. Because Orthodox bishops were not supposed to marry and thus not supposed to have amorous

Table 2. The journalist's choice of topics, summarized

"A day more precious than a century" (20 May 2007)	"We've been waiting for a long time – it was worth it!" (21 May 2008)

1. Remembering 21 May 2006:
   a. Restoring Montenegro's independence
   b. Retelling the story of the referendum, concentrating on difficulties with the opposition, Serbia, and the EU
2. Sixteen babies born
3. Connecting with the past
4. Honoring Iceland as the first country to recognize Montenegrin independence
5. The importance of the Montenegrin flag on the East River (UN)
	1. Historical background:
	   a. Negative attitude towards Slobodan Milošević
	   b. Negative towards the EU in 2000 because it did not support Montenegro in its bid for independence
	   c. Mentioning the special conditions given by the EU in order for the referendum to be valid: 55% of the votes required
	2. Political events after independence: parliamentary elections; DPS/SDP wins; Đukanović withdraws from politics in October 2007; Željko Šturanović, elected president, signs the agreement on stabilization.
	3. Sixteen children born on Independence Day are celebrating their second birthday.
	4. Montenegro's membership in sports organizations

relations, there is an element of forbidden love connected to the long-denied desire by some Montenegrins for independence. The title is powerful because it evokes emotions and connects readers with history.

The second anniversary is summarized in the article "Čekali smo dugo – isplatilo se!" 'We've been waiting for a long time – it was worth it!' The article was written by the same journalist, Radomir Tomić, who wrote the above-mentioned article "Dan skuplji vijeka." The title refers to historical time: "Waiting for a long time" here refers to the last time Montenegro was independent, in 1878.

Pobjeda's journalist is the narrator in both articles and his voice is dominant. The journalist's voice is seen through the choice of topics and the type of language used, summarized and shown in Table 2.

The main topics in both issues contextualize "waiting for" Montenegrin independence in time and space. Particular historical events are evoked, other countries are mentioned as political players, and some other historical events are backgrounded. For example, by using the phrase "restoring independence eighty-eight years on," the journalist evokes the Christmas Uprising, and clearly articulates his position of constructing Montenegro's independence as a continuum and Montenegro as a separate, independent state:

> Kada je uoči ponoći, 21. maja 2006. postalo jasno da je većina građana Crne Gore odlučila da nakon 88 godina povrati samostalnost jednoj og najmanjih država na svijetu, dilema nije bilo: Ta nedjelja je definitivno – DAN SKUPLJI VIJEKA!!!
>
> (*Pobjeda online*, 20 May 2007)

> When it became clear just before midnight on 21 May 2006 that the majority of citizens of Montenegro had decided after eighty-eight years to restore independence to one of the smallest countries in the world, there was no question: that Sunday was definitely: A DAY MORE PRECIOUS THAN A CENTURY!!!

This citation also exemplifies how typography and exclamation marks can be used to emphasize the importance of particular elements in the verbal text. "A day more precious than a century" is highlighted through use of both capital letters and triple exclamation marks.

The time of sharing a common state with Serbia is downplayed and represented as negative, as shown in the following example. Moreover, the example shows how Montenegro is constructed as a victim that succeeded in changing its role into that of a victor.

> Od konačnog državnog i sloma dinastije Petrović Crna Gora je do drugog svjetskog rata sistematski potirana u svakom pogledu da bi tek nakon NOR-a vratila elementarno dostojanstvo kao najmanja ali, koliko je to bilo moguće – ravnopravna članica ondašnje zajednice "bratskih republika naroda i narodnosti". Nakon surovog raspada SFRJ, krajem aprila 1992. godine ušla je u zajednicu sa Srbijom, konstituišući Saveznu Republiku Jugoslaviju, državu kojom je, naročito do početka 1997. godine, gospodario neprikosnoveni Slobodan Milošević.
>
> (*Pobjeda online*, 21 May 2008)

> From the final collapse of the state and the Petrović dynasty, Montenegro was systematically trampled in every way and only after the People's liberation war did it gain back its elementary dignity as the smallest but (as much as was possible) an equal member of the community of "brotherly republics of nations and nationalities." After the harsh collapse of the Socialist Federal Republic of Yugoslavia, by the end of April 1992, it entered into a federation with Serbia, thus constituting the Federal Republic of Yugoslavia, a country that, especially until the beginning of 1997, was ruled by the untouchable Slobodan Milošević.

A clear us/them distinction exists in both articles, "us" being pro-independence, and "them" being anti-independence and thus unionists with Serbia. "Us" is addressed in positive terms, supported by emotional elements such as naming babies born on Independence Day and calling them "the most beautiful gifts." The names of the newborn babies are given together with the cities they were born in. Emphasis is placed on the birth of twins and the fact that eight boys and eight girls were born. Babies represent a symbol of rejuvenation of the nation, a new start.

The journalist used various language resources to support his own construction of the event. He also established the truthfulness of his newspaper by doing the following:

1. Giving facts in the form of numbers:

    "U nedjelju, 21. maja 2006 godine od upisanih 484.718 birača, glasalo 419.236. Za samostalnu Crnu Goru opredijelilo se 230.661 ili 55,5 odsto," 'On Sunday, 21 May 2006, out of 484,718 voters, 419,236 voted. Of these, 230,661, or 55.5%, voted for an independent Montenegro' (*Pobjeda online*, 21 May 2008).

2. Using superlatives for his own newspaper:

    "ali podatke je najtačnije objavila Pobjeda," 'but the most correct information was published by *Pobjeda*' (*Pobjeda online*, 21 May 2008).

3. Criticizing Serbian media and implicitly saying that *Pobjeda* is not like that:

    > Većina najtiražnijih dnevnika i najgledanijih televizija u Srbiji (Novosti i RTS, na primjer) izdašno su medijski sokolili unioniste na čelu sa Socijalističkom narodnom partijom i njenim tadašnjim predsjednikom Predragom Bulatovićem. No, i pored toga, najmanje mjesec i po prije referenduma svim dobrim poznavaocima prilika u Crnoj Gori bilo je jasno da je novinarska kampanja iz Beograda – apsolutno kontraproduktivna.   (*Pobjeda online*, 21 May 2008)

    > The majority of the most read news and the most watched TV channels in Serbia (*Novosti* and Serbian Broadcasting Corporation, for example) fully supported the unionists led by the Socialist People's Party and their leader Predrag Bulatović. Nevertheless, at least a month and a half before the referendum, everyone that knew the conditions in Montenegro was well aware of the fact that the journalistic campaign from Belgrade was absolutely counterproductive.

On the third anniversary, *Pobjeda online* did not run a summary article as it had the two previous years. Instead, it ran an article about a new monument honoring the ninetieth anniversary of the Christmas Uprising. The article is signed with initials (I. K.) and consists mainly of quotes from the speech given on the occasion by Milo Đukanović. The two main topics concern the unveiling of the monument honoring the ninetieth anniversary of the Christmas Uprising and Đukanović's retelling of the history of 6 January 1919. He glorified the people that tried to keep Montenegro independent and his speech abounds in traditionalisms such as *čast*, 'honor'; *obraz*, 'face'; *sloboda*, 'freedom'; and *dostojanstvo*, 'dignity.'

The photograph of the occasion shows the monument, an obelisk surrounded by a group of people with two banners waving in the wind: the Montenegrin and American flags (see Figure 5). The Montenegrin flag is being aligned with power symbols: an obelisk and the flag of the world's most powerful country, the United States.

Figure 5. The monument honoring the Christmas Uprising, photo published in *Pobjeda online*, 21 May 2009

In summary, these three articles construct Montenegrin independence and thus Montenegrin identity on the basis of a historical continuum of Montenegrin independence and national identity. The fact that Montenegro was an independent state in 1878 is foregrounded in all mentioned articles. Montenegrin identity is also constructed in opposition to Serbian identity by portraying the union between Montenegro and Serbia as unnatural and forced. The articles clearly support an "us vs. them" division in which "us" is all Montenegrins in favor of independence and "them" is all those against an independent Montenegro. Milo Đukanović is given ample space both in photographs and through interviews.

Seemingly, during these three years, journalists tended to increase the amount of historical details in their articles, but more research must be done to support or refute this impression.

5.   Đukanović's construction of Montenegrin identity in two interviews

Pobjeda online shows its attitude toward Đukanović by explicitly writing that he is "u javnosti prepoznat kao glavni nosilac obnove države Crne Gore," 'recognized by the public as the main force in regaining the independence of Montenegro' (*Pobjeda online*, 20 May 2007). *Pobjeda online* gives him the most prominent place on two Independence Day homepages in 2007 and 2009. Đukanović is also present on the homepage in 2008, but then in connection with a state visit, not with Independence Day. Both interviews are quite long, consisting of almost four thousand words each, and are written by the same journalist, Andrija Racković.

In both interviews, Đukanović constructs the history of the referendum and the achievement of independence, justifying independence, glorifying his own and his party's role, justifying the international community's moves, and attacking the opposition. Both interviews address history, but also the future of Montenegro.

As mentioned earlier, the title of the interview given in 2007 is "Crna Gora je danas stabilna država," 'Montenegro stable country today.' Đukanović, who was then the leader of the Democratic Socialist Party, constructs independence as a historical continuation, or *obnova državnosti*, 'restoration of statehood,' and gives an overview of various social, economic, and political events and tendencies in Montenegro.

Two years later, Đukanović was back as prime minister of Montenegro. The title of the interview from 2009 is "Crna Gora pouzdano drži kormilo evropske budućnosti u svojim rukama," 'Montenegro confidently holds rudder of European future in its hands.' The most important points from the interview of 2009 are summarized in the lead by the journalist: the affirmation of Montenegro on the international scene, the global financial crisis and measures taken by Montenegro's government, Montenegro fighting corruption, and future investments in Montenegro.

In both interviews, Đukanović constructs "us" and "them" groups. "Us" is the citizens of Montenegro that voted for independence, whereas "them" includes Serbia (in the first interview) and the opposition/unionists (in both interviews). This construction overlaps with the "us vs. them" dichotomy of the *Pobjeda online* journalist.

The use of the term *građani*, 'citizens' rather than *narod*, 'people' signals Đukanović's desire to imply the equal status of all members of society and thus to claim democratic discourse. An analysis (Felberg 2008: 169) of *Pobjeda online*'s articles during the NATO bombing of Yugoslavia in 1999 showed that the term "citizens" was used by Đukanović and that it connoted a democratic government, whereas the term "people," which was used by Milošević, connoted a national-istic, undemocratic government. However, the situated meaning of "citizens" in both interviews is citizens in favor of independence. They are also constructed as a majority, whereas other citizens are still "unaware of the advantages of in-dependence": "Ponekad mi se čini da dio naših građana nije još uvijek u punoj mjeri spoznao prednosti i šanse koje nam je svima donijela odluka od 21. maja 2006. godine," 'Sometimes it seems to me that some of our citizens still have not fully realized the advantages and opportunities that the decision of 21 May 2006 brought us all' (*Pobjeda online*, 20 May 2007).

The citizens of Montenegro are constructed as brave, modern, self-controlled, understanding, and democratic: "građani Crne Gore na demokratskom referen-dumu donijeli odluku o obnovi crnogorske nezavisnosti," 'Montenegrin citizens made a decision about restoring Montenegrin independence in a democratic referendum' (*Pobjeda online*, 20 May 2007); "crnogorsko društvo je pokazalo političku zrelost," 'Montenegrin society showed political maturity' (*Pobjeda online*, 20 May 2007).

> Pokazali smo neke nove odlike savremenog građanina Crne Gore: mudrost uz hrabrost, tolerantnost uz odlučnost, realnost da prihvatimo lošiju startnu poziciju u razgovorima i da zbog toga i po milion puta ponovimo argumente u koje vjerujemo, samokontrolu da na žaoke iz susjednog dvorišta ne uzvratimo, poštujući istorijsku bliskost i projekcije zajedničke evropske budućnosti. Poslali smo time jasnu poruku da su nove generacije u Crnoj Gori spremne da žive po pravilima demokratskog evropskog okruženja.   (*Pobjeda online*, 20 May 2007)

> We showed some new characteristics of the modern citizen of Montenegro: wisdom with bravery; tolerance with decisiveness; in touch with reality to accept a worse starting position in talks and because of that and for a millionth time to repeat the arguments we believe in; self control not to respond to barbs from the neighboring garden, respecting historical nearness, and projections of our common European future. We have sent a clear message that the new generation in Montenegro is ready to live according to the rules of its democratic European surroundings.

The opposition is constructed as unionists – in other words, as pro-Serbian and in favor of reunification with Serbia. Furthermore, they are characterized as being unable to bury dead politics.

Zar ne vidite da su, ne samo opozicioni lideri, nego i njihovi intelektualni i medijski oslonci, samoproklamovani mislioci, analitičari, neshvaćeni kritičari globalnog poretka, inače u mojoj komunikaciji sa njima poznati kao neostvareni, danas mrtvi ljuti i na međunarodnu zajednicu što ne obavi posao umjesto njih nesposobnih i ne promijeni vlast u Crnoj Gori. […] ko god ih čuje, svejedno da li je iz Brisela ili Gornje Morače, jasno mu je da ne može vjerovati ljudima koji tako pljuju po svojoj državi, jasno mu je da je riječ o politički ambicioznim i neuspješnim, isfrustriranim ljudima, od kojih će nekima, kako vrijeme odmiče, sve manje trebati vlast, a sve više pojačana porodična pažnja ne bi li bar ostali podnošljivo agresivni u svom radnom i životnom okruženju.

(Pobjeda online, 21 May 2009)

Don't you see that, not only the opposition leaders, but also their intellectual and media supporters, self-proclaimed thinkers, analysts, not understood critics of the global establishment, in my communication with them recognized as unful-filled persons, are now furiously angry even with the international community for not doing the job instead of these incompetents and for not changing the government in Montenegro. […] it is clear to everyone that hears them, whether he comes from Brussels or from Gornja Moraca, that you cannot trust people that spit on their own country, it is clear that this is about politically ambitious and unsuccessful, frustrated people, some of whom, as time goes by, will not need power, but stronger family care, so that they can remain bearably aggressive in their work and life surroundings.

In this interview, Đukanović strongly criticizes the opposition, characterizing them as mentally ill. According to Đukanović, citizens were fighting for independence through a democratic referendum. Because their fight was just and because democracy was constructed as positive, the Montenegrins won the referendum. The opposition, in trying to hamper Montenegro's independence, acted negatively from Đukanović's perspective. Furthermore, Đukanović constructs Montenegro as a democracy. As a democracy, Montenegro wants to be a member of Europe. Thus, the main goals of Montenegro are identified as joining the EU and NATO, and making Montenegrin citizens wealthy. Achieving these goals is constructed as movement along a road.

From the analysis above, it is possible to identify three DMs: Montenegro as a democracy, Montenegro fighting opponents in general, and Montenegro fighting the opposition (see Table 3).

In both interviews, Montenegro is constructed as a democracy. The citizens of Montenegro are described as politically mature and as having a clear objective: regaining independence. The fight for independence was constructed as a long process. Enduring such a long process was crowned by a victory: independence through democratic means. In the first interview, the opponents were identified

Table 3. Montenegrin discourse models

	Discourse models		
	Montenegro as a democracy	Montenegro fighting its opponents	Montenegro fighting the opposition
Participants	Citizens of Montenegro (politically mature)	Montenegrin citizens, the EU, Serbia, the opposition	The leading party, the opposition
Activity	"Regaining" independence (*obnova državnosti*)	EU, Serbia, and the opposition are trying to hamper Montenegro's citizens in achieving independence.	Trying to lead Montenegro into Europe (NATO) / hampering Montenegro's prosperity
Aim(s)	Independence	Montenegrin citizens want independence; the opposition and Serbia want to keep Montenegro in union with Serbia.	Montenegro as a member of the EU and NATO / Montenegro as a part of Serbia
Process	Democratic referendum	Achieving independence	Fulfilling all EU conditions / betraying Montenegro
Position	Morally better than the opponents	Democratic means from Montenegrin citizens / dirty play from the opponents and Serbia	Montenegro is morally better
Inference (expected action)	Democracy is winning	Fighting	Montenegro wins

as Serbia, the opposition, and at one time the EU. This point is where the DM of fighting opponents connects with the DM of a democratic Montenegro. Montenegrin citizens play a fair game in contrast to the others, who play dirty.

In the second interview, the DM of fighting the opponents changes into the DM of fighting the opposition. Đukanović aligns the leading party with Montenegro and launches a heavy attack against the opposition. The inference he makes is again one of an independent Montenegro winning in the metaphorical, eternal fight between good and bad.

The constructions by *Pobjeda* and by Milo Đukanović overlap so much that they can be considered one official voice. This is seen through almost identical constructions of the main participants' activities in the articles analyzed as well as their positioning. It seems that both Đukanović and *Pobjeda* are becoming harsher in expressing negative views of their opponents – again, an impression that requires more analysis.

6. To be continued …

The work of building any country's identity is a parallel, ongoing activity in both the public and private spheres. Montenegro's independence in 2006 intensified the work of building Montenegrin identity. This chapter focused on only one of many voices that participate in building Montenegrin identity: that of the government-friendly newspaper *Pobjeda online*. *Pobjeda online* represents one version of understanding Montenegrin identity, and because that version is the version of the party in power, it has a powerful place in Montenegrin society. The important event of achieving independence was chosen as a case study of identity building. The question posed in this chapter's introduction about the construction of Montenegrin identity through commemorating Montenegrin Independence Day in *Pobjeda online* could be answered as follows: as an online newspaper, *Pobjeda* had different multimodal resources at its disposal to construct its own version of reality. It framed the events through its choice of layout, photographs, and news. Its journalists used a subjective, emotional style in summarizing independence. *Pobjeda online* gave ample space to Milo Đukanović, who constructed his version of Montenegrin identity in two interviews. *Pobjeda online*'s and Đukanović's versions overlap greatly and, from the perspective of this analysis, are considered to be one voice.

Montenegrin identity is constructed through independence, democracy, modernity, and European values. Independence is further constructed as based on history as a continuation of independence achieved in the past, and then unwillingly interrupted. Religion did not play an explicit role in the material analyzed. It was present though as an integral part of the Montenegrin national flag. Independence did not come by itself, but rather was achieved through a fight with internal enemies, the opposition, and external enemies (Serbia). Independence was also constructed as leading to democracy and to Euro-Atlantic integrations, particularly in Đukanović's interviews. Positive values such as improving the economy and fighting corruption were highlighted. These positive values are aligned with the ruling party, whereas negative values are aligned with the opposition.

This construction of Montenegrin identity has shown minor fluctuation over the first three years following independence. History has been evoked in every issue every year, but the details differed somewhat and there has possibly been a tendency to increasingly dwell on historical elements. The theme of fighting the opposition also seems to be stronger in recent years, whereas fighting outside enemies has become weaker. Calling upon democracy is still a prominent feature of political discourse and questions such as corruption, economic development, and globalization have appeared.

The scope of this study is limited and, as such, it is meant to be a catalyst for further research to support or refute these perceptions. Thus, like any work on identity, this one is to be continued.

CHAPTER 5

Croatia in search of a national day

Front-page presentations of national-day celebrations, 1988–2005

Ljiljana Šarić
University of Oslo, ILOS
ljiljana.saric@ilos.uio.no

This chapter analyzes the identity-building force of and controversies associated with national days in Croatia by examining the front pages of three influential Croatian dailies (*Vjesnik, Slobodna Dalmacija*, and *Novi list*) from 1988 to 2005. Following a social semiotics approach (Kress and van Leeuwen 1998; van Leeuwen 2005), I look at several front-page elements (congratulatory items, the relationship of visual and verbal elements, keywords of headlines and leads), and I analyze their function in three periods. The analysis seeks to explain how the changes in featuring Statehood Day on front pages relate to opposing Statehood Day narratives in Croatian public discourse, and to explain what factors contribute to the unstable nature of Statehood Day as a state symbol. Applying discourse-analytic categories of legitimization and othering, I examine how the newspapers and various participants in public discourse have used the holidays to create positive self-images and negative other-images.

Keywords: Croatia, Croatian statehood days, Croatian newspapers, contested national days, newspaper front pages, othering, legitimization, social semiotics, visual-verbal analysis

1.   Introduction and background: Underlying events and controversies of national days as state symbols

The timeframe[1] analyzed in this chapter relates to social transformations affecting Croatian national days.[2] Formal changes, such as the change from a one-party to a multiparty system and gaining independence, normally lead to the introduction of new state symbols[3] (Geisler 2005), including new national days. Creating a new state identity at a general level in Croatia was followed by forming new political identities at the micro-level of political groups. National days also experienced structural changes, expressed in how they were observed and featured on newspapers' front pages.

Coverage of holidays in transition years receives particular focus in this analysis: the last year(s) of observance of Yugoslav Republic Day in Croatia, the first year(s) of the first Croatian Statehood Day, and the first year(s) of the second Croatian Statehood Day. Background information on national days' underlying events in this section is followed by an account of the reasons for introducing and abolishing the days, an explanation of the methodological steps and analysis of front pages in three periods (Section 2), and a conclusion (Section 3).

An overview of the holidays analyzed is provided in Table 1.

Republic Day commemorated an event underlying the federal postwar organization of Yugoslavia, and was the most important Yugoslav public holiday, as well as the most important holiday in the Yugoslav republics, including Croatia.[4] Although Croatia was part of Yugoslavia until 1991,[5] Croatia was already on its way to independence in 1990, when the first multiparty elections were held and when Croatia last observed (Yugoslav) Republic Day.

---

1.   This period from 1988 to 2005 was chosen because it encompasses two significant transitions. The media material after 2005 did not reveal any relevant changes.

2.   "National day" refers to any day "celebrating nationhood" (Fuller 2004: 3). Nationhood may be symbolized by the date of independence, or by another significant date.

3.   Regarding other national symbols in Croatia since 1990 and before, see Brkljačić and Sundhaussen (2003).

4.   Yugoslav Republic Day was celebrated with numerous rituals at the state and local levels (e.g., induction of first graders into the Pioneer movement) and unofficial customs (e.g., shopping trips).

5.   In the last phase of Yugoslavia's existence, the Croatian government formally tried to negotiate with the Serbian government to create a confederated Yugoslavia with decentralized power.

Table 1. Overview of the holidays analyzed

Republic Day (*Dan Republike*, 29 November)	(Old) Statehood Day (*Dan državnosti*, 30 May)	(New) Statehood Day (*Dan državnosti*, 25 June)
1. Former Yugoslav national day 2. Underlying events: second AVNOJ conference in Jajce, Bosnia-Herzegovina (November 1943); proclamation of Yugoslavia as a socialist republic on 29 November 1945 3. Last observed in Croatia in 1990	1. Observed 1991–2001 2. Introduced by the Law on Holidays in 1991[6] 3. Underlying event: first post-communist multiparty parliament constituted on 30 May 1990	1. Observed 2002–present 2. Introduced by the Law on Changes and Supplement to the Law on Holidays in 2001[7] 3. Underlying event: parliamentary proclamation of independence from Yugoslavia on 25 June 1991

States introduce new symbols when creating a new identity. Newly independent nations seek to erase or overwrite symbols from the undesired past (Geisler 2005). Croatia also introduced a new national day after proclaiming independence. Changing holidays as part of changing a state's symbol system accompanies other symbol changes (e.g., flag, coat of arms, anthem). The introduction of a new national day was to be expected after Croatia proclaimed independence. The first Croatian post-Yugoslav Statehood Day (the old SD) was first observed in 1991, when Croatia was still formally part of Yugoslavia. The context of the event this SD commemorated is relevant for understanding its controversial nature and short existence. On 30 May 1990, the nationalist Croatian Democratic Union (HDZ) won almost two-thirds of the seats in the new multiparty parliament. A number of sub-events related to the HDZ's election victory later proved relevant for accepting and rejecting this day (Knežević 2004; Lipovac 2006; HRT). These events included the inaugural session of parliament, at which the HDZ leader, Franjo Tuđman, was elected president of the Croatian presidency,[8] and a pompous public celebration in Zagreb's central square with over one hundred thousand participants (Barišić 1999). Sources record an outburst of patriotic emotions, national symbols, and kitsch on that occasion. Images and texts helped to make

---

6. *Zakon o blagdanima i neradnim danima u Republici Hrvatskoj, Narodne novine* 14 (1991), 25 March. Available online at http://narodne-novine.nn.hr/, accessed 27 May 2011.

7. *Zakon o izmjenama i dopuni Zakona o blagdanima, spomendanu i neradnim danima u Republici Hrvatskoj, Narodne novine* 96 (2001), 7 Nov. Available online at http://narodne-novine.nn.hr/, accessed 27 May 2011.

8. In the Yugoslav federation, all constituent republics had presidencies, and these had presidents.

this event part of collective memory. The parliamentary session and celebration were televised. This day is thus remembered by many, but the meaning ascribed to it varies. Many people link the events of 30 May 1990 with the HDZ, which discredited itself in the next decade (Kusovac 2000; Søberg 2007). The day thus became controversial and was rejected by some groups. A public discussion and two narratives arose regarding the suitability of this date as a national day. After eleven observations, the holiday lost its official national-day status and became a lower-ranking memorial day (*spomendan*):[9] *Dan hrvatskoga sabora* (Croatian Parliament Day).

The current SD, 25 June, was introduced in 2002. It refers to Croatia's declaration of independence in 1991.[10] The official discussion on the suitability of the old SD was initiated by Member of Parliament Ivo Škrabalo, who endorsed the date 25 June 1991 on which Croatia formally and finally proclaimed independence. His proposal became part of a compromise solution: Croatia obtained two new national days, a solution symbolically mirroring the difficulties in acquiring independence. Alongside the new SD, Independence Day (*Dan neovisnosti*, 8 October), which commemorates the date independence was implemented, has been observed in Croatia since 2002.[11]

All three Croatian post-Yugoslav national days commemorate the recent past and remember the same macro event: independence from Yugoslavia. However,

---

9. Croatian laws on holidays define two groups of red-letter days: *blagdani* (official holidays, non-working holidays), and *spomendani*, 'memorial days' (workdays). Curiously, laws include remarks on how to mark *spomendani* but no such details exist for *blagdani* (*Zakon 1996, Zakon 2002, Zakon o dopunama 2005*).

10. In the referendum on independence, which was boycotted by most Croatian Serbs, over 90% of voters supported Croatian independence. Serb-populated areas tried to form an enclave so as to separate from Croatia if Croatia itself separated from Yugoslavia. Serb-controlled areas of Croatia became part of the self-proclaimed Republic of Serbian Krajina (Barić 2008). After Croatia declared independence, armed conflicts began between the Croatian police and militant Serbs backed by the Yugoslav Army (Petričušić 2008).

Constitutional relations with Yugoslavia were severed in October 1991. Croatia was internationally recognized in January 1992 by the European Union and the United Nations, and was admitted to the UN in May that year.

11. In Internet discussions on SDs and Independence Day, the new holidays are labeled *Škrabalovo* (Berković 2002). This word-formation pattern imitates the colloquial derivation of names of saints' days, in which the suffix *-ovo* is added to the name stem: for example, the Feast Day of Saint Peter and Saint Paul is officially termed *Sveti Petar i Pavao* in Croatian, or colloquially *Petrovo*. Church holidays not containing proper names also follow this pattern, for example, *Tijelovo* (< *tijelo*, 'body'), 'Corpus Christi.' Hence, with *Škrabalovo* an ironic effect is achieved because the derivational pattern suggests the meaning 'The Feast Day/Holiday of (Ivo) Škrabalo.'

their reference points are slightly different sub-events that lack a clear profile; two even relate to the same year (1991). The change of the SD's date in Croatia in 2001 reflects neither a radical change in the political system nor the creation of a new state. Thus, acceptance of Independence Day and of the new SD has remained controversial. This is reflected in public confusion regarding the dates and symbolic value of Statehood Day and Independence Day; such confusion is documented in, for example, public opinion polls, newspaper readers' comments (see, e.g., Kustura 2008; Mazzocco 2005), and on-line discussion forums.

2.   Analysis: Categories and premises

2.1   Front pages

To analyze the identity-building force and controversies of national days in Croatia, I look at the front pages of three important Croatian newspapers – *Vjesnik* (Gazette), *Slobodna Dalmacija* (Free Dalmatia), and *Novi list* (New Paper)[12] – from 1988 to 2005.[13] Secondary material includes inside pages related to the front

---

12. Relevant texts from *Večernji list* (Evening News, highest circulation in the 1990s) and *Jutarnji list* (Morning News, a tabloid) were preliminarily evaluated, but were left out from this analysis. The reason is that *Večernji list* follows the patterns identified for *Vjesnik* and *Slobodna Dalmacija* (they all were controlled by the HDZ; see Malović and Selnow 2001: 4, 122). *Jutarnji list* was not launched until 1998, and therefore is not suitable for a comparison with other newspapers prior to 1998. Reliable 1990s circulation data for Croatian newspapers are difficult to find. In 1993, *Slobodna Dalmacija*'s circulation was supposedly 90,000 to 120,000 (Nizich, Markić, and Laber 1995; Erceg 2000); *Vjesnik*'s circulation in 1997 was about 13,500 (Izvješće 2006). The current circulation (48,000) of *Novi list* is similar to that of the 1990s (CML 2008).

13. *Vjesnik* is published in Zagreb. In 1990, it came under the control of the ruling party, the HDZ, and took a pro-government editorial stance in the next decade. *Slobodna Dalmacija* is published in Split. Between 1983 and 1993, a diverse group of columnists, unburdened by political bias, wrote for it. The daily was privatized and formally taken over in March 1993 by Miroslav Kutle, a HDZ-sponsored (and later imprisoned) business magnate (Vezic 2001: 2; Jurisin 2002). The new owner's editorial policy promoted hardline nationalism, a stance retained even during the first year of Prime Minister Ivica Račan's center-left government (Erceg 2001). *Novi list* is the oldest Croatian daily published in Rijeka. Its core readership is Primorje–Gorski Kotar County. It was the only Croatian daily newspaper to maintain a critical distance towards the Tuđman government during the 1990s (regarding policies towards the media in the 1990s; see Ramet 2008: 47–49). In the late 1990s, *Slobodna Dalmacija* was almost financially ruined, and was again taken over by the government. In May 2005, it was reprivatized and sold to the Europapress Holding company. *Vjesnik* is still state-owned. The owners of *Novi list* are the newspaper's employees (Jurisin 2002).

pages. I consider these newspapers representative of the entire Croatian media landscape in the period analyzed. Although their core readership is in three different regions, they are distributed, sold, and read nationwide.

The material analyzed consisted of 106 front pages and 47 inside pages altogether.[14] The selection of the most relevant material was made on the basis of formal and content criteria: The formal criterion for selection was that front pages contain elements that thematize the holiday (first step). Inside pages with texts thematizing the holiday were also collected in the second step. Only some of these texts were included in the analysis; namely, those closely related to the front pages (e.g., some front pages featured the headline and sub-headline of a holiday-related text, whereas the continuation of the text could be found on inside pages). The texts merely mentioning the holiday and discussing non-related topics were ignored.

I analyzed holiday, pre-holiday, and post-holiday editions of the three dailies. The holiday editions were usually two- or three-day special holiday editions. The pre-holiday and post-holiday editions announced or reported on national day-related events.

Front pages contain core information that first attracts readers' attention, and front pages are often the only pages actually read by busy readers. The social semioticians, Gunther Kress and Theo van Leeuwen (1998), see front pages as "complex signs, which invite and require an initial reading as one sign," and highlight three crucial categories in the semiotics of their composition: information value (position of elements creating a given and new value), salience (realized through a combination of color contrast, placement, and size of elements), and framing (lines used to (dis)connect or differentiate layout elements). For the front pages analyzed here, the left-right distribution in Kress and van Leeuwen's (1998) sense of "given" and "new" is not evident. However, it could be observed that upper-left elements and those in the central section had great salience. Both the visual and the content salience of elements elsewhere were enhanced through typesetting.

---

14. The newspaper material was collected in archives in Croatia. Each relevant newspaper page was photographed and is available in the digital project archive of the Red-Letter Days project group at the University of Oslo. The initial material collected is much more extensive than the selection used in this analysis.

2.2   Elements analyzed

I examine front-page congratulatory items,[15] photos, the relationship of visual and verbal elements,[16] and keywords of headlines and leads. Leads are the "story in microcosm" (Bell 1991:174), and headlines often show newspapers' ideological attitudes. I concentrate particularly on the most salient keywords in longer texts, be they single words or complex phrases. The identification of keywords resulted from a close reading of newspaper texts. It was not based on the analyst's vague impression. Instead, the criterion for the selection of keywords and phrases was that they be prominent through repeated usage in texts: content words and phrases were understood as keywords and phrases if they appeared several times within the same text (e.g., in a text's headline or kicker, and in its introductory and concluding part; or in a text's headline, lead, and/or its sub-heads). These keywords summarize the main message and tone of a text. In my corpus, the keywords are often positively or negatively evaluative (see, e.g., Section 2.5). They contain the core information and are thus most relevant for the denotative and connotative level of the messages, and consequently for intended or unintended effects of the texts.

Significant parameters of congratulatory items are their presence or absence, and their position on the page (i.e., salience and framing). Structural characteristics are also relevant: congratulatory items can be written words, or combinations of written words and images, and personalized or impersonal; senders and addressees can be explicitly coded or left undefined. The number of words is also significant. Congratulatory items overtly remind readers of the holiday. They thus fulfill an educational function in people's "learning national identity" (Kolstø 2006:676), make the holiday visible, and perhaps popularize the holiday (Jedlicki 1999). They also overtly or covertly convey part of the newspaper's content and the newspaper's attitude towards a holiday.

Holiday-edition front pages generally contained congratulatory items. *Novi list* featured them prominently (except for 1990), often to the right of the nameplate. The layout and text structure of these items varied. The practice in *Vjesnik* varied between 1991 and 2001: only some holiday editions featured official congratulations (1991, 1993, 1994, 1995, and 1999). Between 2001 and 2005, *Vjesnik*

---

15. "Congratulatory items" are newspaper genres usually including written words (e.g., "we congratulate on the occasion […]") and images (e.g., an image accompanying the text, characters in specific shapes and sizes, frames, etc.).

16. In this chapter, the terms "visual" and "verbal" sometimes occur in contrasting different elements: in such contexts, "visual" refers to images (e.g., photographs, drawings) and "verbal" to texts or written words.

featured a framed congratulatory item in 2001 only (the last year of the old SD celebration). *Slobodna Dalmacija* regularly featured congratulatory items. Their position varied, as well as their structure: sometimes they included attributions (e.g., *redakcija*, 'the editorial board,' or merely the newspaper's name) or images; for example, in 2000 the congratulatory item contained an image of soldiers in uniforms and an image of the Croatian flag.

From 1988 to 2000, the front pages regularly featured SD-related photos, but there were differences in how different visual elements were linked and in how social actors were presented. The analytical questions in this chapter concerning front-page photos and their meanings are: Which participants were foregrounded, backgrounded, or absent? What does each imply? What relation links textual and visual elements? Did photos merely illustrate textual segments, or did they continue text narratives or stand in opposition to them? (See, e.g., van Leeuwen 2005: 12–13.) Since 2000, SD photos have almost disappeared from front pages.

Important questions regarding the textual elements of front pages are: What textual items were featured? What were worthy topics for textual items: presidential addresses, parliamentary session reports, military parades, reports on openings of important facilities, or local celebrations? Did textual elements establish a hierarchy of SD events (and participants)? What keywords were dominant in kickers,[17] headlines, and leads, and other textual fragments featured? Generally, the keywords of holiday-related items were a selective mirror of reality and provided selected contextual information. All of the SD items fulfilled specific functions such as popularizing and/or forgetting SD; promotion of state officials: backing the current government; reinforcing othering among various social actors; and othering SD itself. "Othering" refers to discursive practices of constructing "oneself" by establishing a strong opposition to a simultaneously constructed "opposite." The items examined either reported a selected number of SD events, or focused on the meaning and appropriateness of these events, or did both. In doing so, front pages informed the public about SD(s), and perhaps contributed to their popularity (e.g., by featuring numerous related items). Naturally, by featuring no related items, front pages also contributed to holidays' being forgotten.

The relation and presence of these strategies differed across periods. I identified three periods, analyzed below. These periods relate partly to three different national days and partly to changes in how newspapers featured them.

The first and last year of observance receive particular focus, as well as years of significant changes in observances or participants – for example, a change of main actors in SD celebrations. The year 1990 had significant changes: the holiday

---

17. This is a headline placed above the main headline (Johnson-Cartee 2005: 173).

existed formally and on dailies' front pages, but was a workday after long having been a day off. The year 1991 was atypical: the first observance of the new SD took place, but Croatia was still formally part of Yugoslavia. The years 1999 and 2000 are interesting, 1999 as the last observance under Tuđman and 2000 as the first observance after his death, as is 2002, the new SD's first observance.

2.3   The first period: The decline of Yugoslavia

The period from 1988 to 1990 comprises the last three observances of the former Yugoslavia's Republic Day. In Croatia, the holiday deteriorated already in 1989 and 1990. This is observable on the front pages that featured fewer holiday-related items. These items were absent from the post-holiday editions of *Vjesnik*. The number of issues devoted to the holiday also had symbolic importance: in 1990, all three dailies published a single-day edition (29 November) instead of a two- or three-day holiday edition. *Novi list* did not feature Republic Day-related items at all on its front pages in 1990, whereas the editorial board of *Slobodna Dalmacija* published a congratulatory item in 1990. The absence of congratulatory items had strong symbolic value in the holiday editions of *Vjesnik* and *Novi list* in 1990 because they had been present before, indicating that the holiday had become less salient in official discourse. This absence and reduced salience may have affected readers' attitude toward the holiday.

I present some interesting examples that break the norms for congratulatory items. The 1988 and 1989 holiday editions of *Slobodna Dalmacija* had a congratulatory item at the bottom of the front page. This position was thus neither central nor most salient. However, another element provided salience in 1988: The text *Dan Republike 1988* was part of the nameplate and placed in a black circle: the text replaced the date, which was usually placed in a similar black circle. In effect, Republic Day overshadowed the calendric measuring of time: compare the 1988 holiday and post-holiday editions in Figure 1.

A symbolic change in *Slobodna Dalmacija* is observable in 1990. The holiday-edition nameplate featured the date, not the holiday label. Hence, the holiday had become much less salient, although the position of the congratulatory item itself was more salient than in 1988 – it was framed and to the right of the nameplate. The congratulation was personal this time, from the editorial board ("Čestitamo Dan Republike. REDAKCIJA," 'We Congratulate on Republic Day. The editorial board') (see Figure 2), whereas the 1988 and 1989 items contained no attribution; the addresser was absent.

The congratulatory item was particularly salient in *Vjesnik*'s 1988 holiday edition: A framed congratulation with capitalized text was part of the nameplate (see

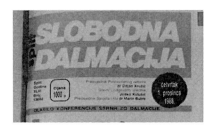

Figure 1. *Slobodna Dalmacija*, 28–30 November 1988 holiday edition and *Slobodna Dalmacija*, 1 December 1988 post-holiday edition

Figure 2. *Slobodna Dalmacija*, 29 November 1990 holiday edition

Figure 3. *Vjesnik*, 28–30 November 1988 holiday edition

Figure 3). The nameplate establishes and communicates the newspaper's identity, and putting elements here establishes the closest possible connection between the newspaper's identity and what the item that visually coincides with it means or symbolizes. No such salience is seen for congratulatory items for subsequent Croatian national days in the newspapers analyzed.

As a rule, photos related to Republic Day appear on front pages as illustrations of the texts, or as their complements. However, photos also appear juxtaposed with texts. *Vjesnik*'s 1990 holiday edition has an interesting example of a contrast between words and images. A large central photo was most salient and contradicted the context and the text. In the year when Yugoslavia was obviously falling apart (Mønnesland 1997: 329–345), this photo showed something else: the president of the Yugoslav presidency, the vice president, and the prime minister celebrating the holiday in good spirits. The celebration was perfect as a ritual performance: its visual representation signaled no change from previous years' representations, although the context of the performance had changed. The accompanying text reads that Yugoslavia is not "as it always has been." A similar photo with the same central participants appeared in the holiday edition of *Slobodna Dalmacija*. It complemented a text that did not problematize the celebration but that instead provided only facts about who attended it.

Keywords from 1989 and 1990 contrasted sharply with those from 1988. In 1988, they still painted an idyllic picture of Yugoslavia: *moć zajedništva*, 'the power of togetherness' and *nacionalna ravnopravnost*, 'national equality,' whereas in 1989 and 1990 they hinted at collapse. The 1989 *Slobodna Dalmacija* post-holiday edition was dominated by the key phrases *vrtlog žestokih sukoba*, 'a whirl of severe conflicts,' and *dani koji potresaju Jugoslaviju*, 'days that shake Yugoslavia.' The 1989 front-page editorial of *Vjesnik* featured the key phrases *dani zatrovani krizom*, 'days poisoned by a crisis,' *slavljenički stjegovi 46. rođendana Jugoslavije su forma*, 'the celebratory flags of Yugoslavia's forty-sixth birthday are only for show,' *AVNOJ – pojam iz politikantskih križaljki*, 'the Antifascist Council for the People's Liberation of Yugoslavia: a concept for political games.'

Ambivalence related to the structure and function of the congratulatory items and photos in this period relates somewhat to key words as well. In 1988, the keywords that reflect the tone and attitude of the entire texts on the front and inside pages were still concerned with maintaining the established discursive reality as in the preceding years, in which an idealized holiday symbolized an idealized state. They largely ignored the ongoing changes in the social context. In 1989 and 1990, the emphasis was placed on the rapidly changing context. The holiday's discourse did not disappear (which could have been a possibility). Instead, this discourse became a platform for critical reflections about the state it symbolized, as well as a discursive platform for reflections on the role and the meaning of the holiday; that is, this discourse became self-reflexive.

2.4   The second period: The Tuđman period

In the period from 1991 to 1999, SD-related items regularly appeared on the front pages of all three dailies.

President Tuđman's photos dominated *Vjesnik*'s holiday-edition front pages. They regularly featured two to four SD-related items, including a photo of Tuđman. *Vjesnik* thus directly related the most important SD events to Tuđman. A representative example is the 1991 front-page photo showing Tuđman sitting at a desk with several national symbols behind him; see Figure 4.

The photo occupied the most salient, middle section and symbolically promoted Tuđman as the chief social actor of SD events. It assigned him a state-symbol function like that of conventional symbols such as the flag and the coat of arms. He retained the position of the main social actor in *Vjesnik* until his death in 1999, backgrounding other social actors. In 1999, a significantly changed post-holiday edition appeared. The front page featured an entirely different photo,

Figure 4. *Vjesnik*, 30 May 1991 holiday edition

Figure 5. *Vjesnik*, 31 May 1999 post-holiday edition

presenting ordinary people cycling and walking. Flags functioned as a SD symbol, not the president. This photo (see Figure 5) marks the end of Tuđman's symbolic reign over the front pages of *Vjesnik*'s holiday editions.

In *Novi list,* Tuđman's photos never dominated the holiday editions so strongly. He is featured on only three front pages of nine of the newspaper's holiday editions. *Novi list* concentrated on other social actors, symbols, and activities: in addition to state and military officials, it regularly featured photos from Rijeka and from the Gorski Kotar region, or of local celebrations. SD was thus not constructed in relation to the political elite and to events in the capital only; compare the 1991 holiday edition showing, in Figure 6, a building in Rijeka decorated with flags on the occasion of SD celebrations.

Slobodna Dalmacija also featured local events, although much less than did *Novi list.* The most dominant actor in the front-page photos was the president, as in *Vjesnik*.

Turning to keywords, there is initially a strong reference to the war in Croatia in this period; after 1995, the keywords focus on social problems. The keywords of *Vjesnik*'s 1992 holiday edition are *tutnjava topova*, 'the cannon's roar' and *tisuće grobova*, 'thousands of graves.' Similar keywords are found in *Novi list: izbjeglice*, 'refugees' and *antiratni protesti*, 'anti-war protests.' Its 1996 holiday edition focused on social circumstances: *put u izolaciju*, 'the path into isolation.'

Figure 6. *Novi list*, 30 May 1991 holiday edition

In *Vjesnik,* quotes and summaries of Tuđman's address to the nation prevailed, as well as reports on Tuđman bestowing medals and awards, and on ceremonial sessions of parliament. The greatest role in the featured events was performed by the political elite. Moderate prominence was given to events such as introducing the new Croatian currency (in 1994), opening new facilities, congratulations by foreign state officials, and the president's SD receptions. No matter what event front-page texts in *Vjesnik* thematized, Tuđman was the main participant. The "Tuđman cult" in *Vjesnik* culminated in 1995 in six front-page items with him as the main social actor.

Novi list featured items announcing official state events (e.g., celebratory sessions of parliament) and local events. Noteworthy is that in 1992, *Slobodna Dalmacija* featured evaluative textual items commenting on the achievements and failures of Tuđman, concluding that part of his program had been realized, and part had gone wrong. As expected, no such criticism can be found after the HDZ tycoon Miroslav Kutle took over the paper in 1993. Subsequent holiday editions primarily feature items related to Tuđman's SD activities. Notably, he is absent from only one holiday edition (1998), and that edition's front page is dominated by the keyword *izolacija,* 'isolation.' Still, one cannot assume a strong intention of the newspaper to criticize Tuđman in 1998: A change in the newspaper's political orientation is observable only since 2000.[18]

---

18. In 2003, in a front-page commentary, the journalist Krešimir Fijačko states that *Vjesnik* was "in the service of politics" throughout the 1990s.

In 1999, at the SD mass attended by Tuđman, Zagreb's archbishop used his homily to strongly challenge the government. His challenge was thematized only in the *Novi list* post-holiday edition: neither *Slobodna Dalmacija* nor *Vjesnik* mentioned it on their front pages. The key phrase of this edition of *Novi list* was "difficult social and economic situation." The headline in *Novi list*, "Bozanić upozorio Tuđmana na teško socijalno i gospodarsko stanje," 'Bozanić cautions Tuđman on difficult social and economic situation' was featured in the upper front-page section (31 May). The same edition featured an article by Dražen Vukov Colić on page 4 commenting on Tuđman's rhetoric, which constantly promotes fear of "internal and external enemies" and new unwished-for Balkan unions, ignoring the reality of thievery in the economic transformation, moral crisis, and the country's economic destruction. Notably, the same page featured another text headlined "Hrvatska nije ni u čekaonici EU," 'Croatia not even in EU waiting room.'

As for the function of featured items, a strategy of promoting state officials, legitimizing their actions, and backing the current government (i.e., continuous endorsement of Tuđman) was clear in *Vjesnik* throughout the period and in *Slobodna Dalmacija* after 1993: photos featuring the president dominated, as well as the number of textual items that referred to SD events with him as the main participant.

Front-page representations reinforced othering strategies among various social actors. Othering strategies are often interwoven with endorsements of state officials. Front-page items endorsed Tuđman by positioning him against various Others. During the Croatian War of Independence 1991–1995, his prominent Others were the Yugoslav People's Army, Croatian Serbs, all other Serbs, and the international community. After 1995, the role of the Other was more frequently occupied by various domestic political opponents. Nevertheless, all Others already defined in the early 1990s, including the international community, retained this role.

SD items also served for questioning the appropriateness of SD and its (mis)use by various social actors, that is, its use as a means of (de)legitimizing SD. By the early 1990s, this attitude was observable in *Novi list*. In 1992, a page-long negative comment occasioned by SD appeared on the inside pages ("Jubilej samoljublja ili svehrvatskog pomirenja?" 'Anniversary of self-admiration, or of pan-Croatian reconciliation?'). The text reflects on 30 May 1990, recalling that the HDZ (mis)used this day to promote itself, arranging "patriotic concerts" and "historic speeches" by the party's leading politicians (see Section 1). Another example of othering strategies was a negative comment headlined "Parada bahatosti i samodovoljnosti," 'Parade of arrogance and self-sufficiency' occasioned by SD in 1994. The text reflects on the HDZ equating itself with the state, and the state administration's plans to celebrate SD "more ceremonially than ever" (e.g.,

Novi list, 29–30 May 1995 holiday edition   *Novi list,* 31 May 1995 post-holiday edition

Figure 7

by introducing the new Croatian currency, opening the reconstructed medieval fortified town of Medvedgrad, and opening the "Altar of the Homeland").[19] The front page of *Novi list*'s 1995 holiday edition (see Figure 7) announced the analytical comment (featured on page 2) by the journalist Neven Šantić: The kicker "U povodu pete godišnjice Dana hrvatske državnosti," 'On the Fifth Anniversary of Croatian Statehood Day,' and headline "Naša Hrvatska," 'Our Croatia' were placed in the upper-left corner, parallel to the photo and comment on Tuđman opening the new university library. The commentary itself on page two recalls Croatia's statehood tradition as part of various states, and warns that the panegyrics in honor of the "father of the nation" (the author questions the metaphor by using quotation marks) are dangerous, along with efforts to transform the state into a fetish. It warns that totalitarian ideas may hide behind the "rhetoric of national interests." Its symbolic color harmony with the *Novi list* logo provided it with the greatest salience and indicated that the comment was in line with *Novi list*'s policy. "Naša Hrvatska," 'Our Croatia' – whoever the implied "we" may be – was definitely a projection of a state opposed to Tuđman's. The post-holiday edition's

---

19. The *Oltar domovine* (Altar of the Homeland) monument at Medvedgrad near Zagreb is dedicated to Croatian war dead. From 1994 until Tuđman's death, it was an important site of SD celebrations. The post-Tuđman government sought a symbolic break with his policy and symbols. The monument was neglected in the following years; it was renovated in 2006.

structure also resembled the holiday edition. The most important framed item was placed in the upper-left corner.

The upper-right section of the post-holiday edition featured a photo of Tuđman with his close allies at the central SD event that year, the military parade at Lake Jarun in Zagreb. The appearance of the participants, especially Tuđman's posture and uniform, resemble Tito's posture and uniforms. The upper-left corner featured the kicker, headline, and lead of a comment by the journalist Dražen Vukov Colić, thematizing the numerous medals awarded without clear criteria. Through its most salient position, the headline "Opći nedostatak sluha," 'General absence of common sense' comments not only on its direct topic (medals awarded) but also indirectly on other issues related to SD events, especially the military parade and Tuđman's "staging" in the front-page photo.

Disapproving reviews continued to be part of *Novi list*'s front pages in the following years. These reviews disapproved not of SD itself, but rather of what the political elite made of it: how they staged it and themselves through its celebrations.

In the second period, featured items (verbal and visual) functioned as a strategy of promoting state officials and legitimizing their actions (in *Vjesnik* throughout the period and in *Slobodna Dalmacija* after 1993). Front pages reflected othering strategies among various social actors. Front-page items endorsed Tuđman by positioning him against various Others (e.g., the Yugoslav People's Army, Croatian Serbs, the international community, and political opponents). However, SD items also served to question the appropriateness of SD and as a means of (de)legitimizing SD (notably in *Novi list*).

2.5   The third period: After Tuđman

Tuđman died in December 1999. In the general elections in January 2000, a coalition of two major and four minor parties won 95 of the 151 seats in the lower house of parliament and gained control from the HDZ. In presidential elections a month later, Stjepan Mesić won as the candidate of the small Croatian People's Party (HNS).

In this period, the front pages featured increasingly fewer holiday-related items. For comparison, all six front-page items in *Slobodna Dalmacija*'s 1991 holiday edition were related to SD, whereas the holiday became almost absent from its front pages after 2002, the first celebration of the new SD. Similarly, *Novi list* featured no holiday-related items on the front page of its 2002 holiday edition. The congratulatory item is the only reminder (e.g., *Slobodna Dalmacija* featured congratulatory items in 2002–2005, but no other SD items).

SD obviously became a much less worthy front-page topic, or hardly worthy at all, and it was simultaneously contested in public discourse: the suitability of SD's date related to its underlying event became disputed. Possible alternative dates were discussed among the public. Front-page photos featured new participants: one reason was the election of a new president and a new parliament, and the naming of a new prime minister. Another reason was newspapers' changed attitude toward SD. The two were closely interrelated. Items directly related to SD, including photos, almost disappeared from the front pages. The photos on the inside pages featured various state officials: they were not focused on one person only. The dominant motif was one of laying wreaths. By featuring this ceremony, the newspapers presented Mesić as but one of several social actors.

Dominant keywords indicate settling accounts with the ruling structures from 1991 to 2000. The dominant key phrase of the *Vjesnik* holiday-edition front page in 2000 was *bivša vlast – zločinačka/pokvarena organizacija*, 'former authorities – a criminal/corrupt organization.' Keywords also mirrored changes in the manner of SD observances: "Službena počast na Mirogoju, vijenci HDZ-a na Medvedgradu." 'Official honors at Mirogoj, HDZ wreaths at Medvedgrad' (headline in *Slobodna Dalmacija*, 2000 post-holiday edition). The prominent keywords of all holiday editions were *polaganje vijenaca*, 'laying wreaths' and *paljenje svijeća*, 'lighting candles.'

Even in the last period of the old SD, its performances and events changed. New locations for observances and transformed modes of celebrations were introduced. Most SD sub-events from 2000 featured on inside pages related to paying tribute to participants in the war in Croatia. Front pages and related inside pages documented a great change: the SD celebration turned into mourning for Croatian war victims.

Along with the structural change in the holiday, a language shift also occurred. Reports on SD events up to 1999 regularly used the verb *(pro)slaviti*, 'to celebrate,' and from 2000 to 2005 they regularly used the verb *obilježiti/obilježavati*, 'to mark.' The change of attitude in holiday performances blended with the change in holiday language. The difference between the meanings of the two verbs, *(pro)slaviti* and *obilježiti/obilježavati*, matches the change in the attitude towards the holiday: the holiday-related activities were changed from festive and celebrative to commemorative. Consequently, the frame of mind related to the holiday was transformed.

The dominant function of SD-related items on holiday-edition front pages in the transition year 2000 was othering. Newly elected President Mesić positioned himself against the previous government, which became the Other, along with the HDZ, and Tuđman. SD was used as an occasion to recapitulate the previous decade. The central section of the holiday-edition front page in *Slobodna Dalmacija* featured a photo of the new president and an interview announcement headlined "Šakali oko Tuđmana opljačkali Hrvatsku," 'Jackals around Tuđman plundered Croatia.' SD served as a platform for settling the accounts of the new government with the old. The holiday edition of *Novi list* also announced the same interview with Mesić, headlined "Tuđmanova administracija bila je pljačkaška organizacija," 'Tuđman's administration was pillaging organization.' The headlines in both *Slobodna Dalmacija* and *Novi list* suggest different attitudes. *Slobodna Dalmacija* separated Tuđman from the agents in the sentence. His responsibility was thus blurred. *Novi list* characterized his administration as *pljačkaška*, 'pillaging.' The possessive phrase *Tuđmanova administracija*, implied Tuđman's responsibility.

Vjesnik featured similar keywords in its 2000 holiday edition. The comment by Davor Gjenero "30. svibnja – Dan hrvatske državnosti ili tek Tuđmanov spomendan?" 'May 30 – Day of Croatian statehood, or merely a Tuđman memorial day?' indicates a substantial change in the policy of *Vjesnik*, which strongly endorsed this holiday and its main participants from 1991 to 1999. With this comment that aims at delegitimizing and othering the holiday, *Vjesnik* contributed to a sudden problematization of the date and meaning of SD: SD is characterized as a problematic date when an undemocratic government and an authoritarian ruler started to rule over Croatia (Gjenero 2000).

Novi list maintained its critical stance toward the new government and SD celebrations after 2000. It featured no holiday-related items (other than the congratulatory item occupying a non-salient position) on the holiday-edition front page in 2002, the first year the new SD was observed. The keywords of SD-related items on its inside pages in 2002 were *praznik bez slavlja*, 'a holiday without celebration,' and *korupcija*, 'corruption.'

After 2000, the holiday became much less visible on the front pages. This is reflected either in the reduced number of SD-related items, or in their absence.[20] A reduction in number of featured items on holiday-edition front pages was observable in the first period as well (e.g., in *Vjesnik* in 1990, the last year that Yugoslav Republic Day was observed). The holiday also abruptly disappeared from the front pages of *Novi list*. SD's disappearance from the front pages is apparent after Tuđman's death (1999); for example, in 2000 in *Vjesnik*, SD was mentioned only randomly in one non-salient front-page item. This fading away has been especially apparent since the first observances of the new SD. Vanishing indicates that a holiday is in a "weak" period of its existence, as in the case of Yugoslav Republic Day in its last years, or may relate to a changed media policy. The media analyst Zrinjka Peruško (2007:233) points towards the state-building value as

---

20. The inside pages of the post-holiday editions continued to feature SD-related items.

one of most prominent values in Croatian political discourse, including journalism, in the early 1990s. The political elite characterized the media connected with the state-building value as "responsible" because journalists followed the government position. Independent media (such as *Novi list*) were labeled "irresponsible" because of their critical stance towards the government. The way that *Vjesnik* and *Slobodna Dalmacija* presented SD in the 1990s can be interpreted as part of newspapers' "state-building" strategy, whereas neglecting it since 2000 may relate to their opening to freedom of expression, impartiality, and pluralism. To paraphrase Polish sociologist Elżbieta Hałas (2002b: 119), objectivization of the state takes place through the use of symbolism. National days are part of the state's symbolic inventory, and in the Croatian case, this objectivization has become less prominent since 2000.

Concerning changes in featuring SD on front pages, other factors were also relevant: the change of the state ruling structures in 2000, the subsequent change of SD's date, and public discussions regarding the appropriateness of both the old and the new date. Newspaper owners' policies may also be relevant, but such policies are not relevant regarding the dailies analyzed. SD not only disappeared from front pages after 2000, but also started to blend with other holidays and to be forgotten in the public sphere. Newspapers leave the impression that local holiday-related events are absent. The transformation of modes of observance is accompanied by less public involvement in the holiday-related events and the aforementioned change in language. Perhaps it is easier to involve the public in official celebrations (indicated by the verb (*pro*)*slaviti*, 'to celebrate', which was regularly used up to 2000) than in official mourning (indicated by the verb *obilježiti/obilježavati*, 'to mark', which was regularly used after 2000).

3. Concluding remarks

The three Croatian newspapers analyzed show slight differences in presenting SD events in all three periods analyzed: their ideological positions differ (a strong or moderate pro-government line vs. an independent position). Numerous critical reflections challenging SD, published since 2000, reflect a new orientation of the media towards pluralism. Until 2000, the newspapers generally concentrated on the elite production of national symbols and on their ritual performances, presenting people as faithful consumers of national meanings (Fox and Miller-Idriss 2008). The holiday-related items featured on front pages were mainly used to legitimize the political elite's actions, and served in creating their positive self-images. Discussions in the newspapers since 2000 illustrate a process in which people are producers of counter symbols, and are opponents of SD as an official symbol. The SD discourse was used in legitimizing strategies again: this time, the new political actors used the occasion to delegitimize their predecessors.

Through an examination of front pages, this analysis has revealed in Croatian public discourse two opposing lines in discursive constructions of SD that are realized as opposing narratives.[21] The existence of these narratives is also confirmed by studying the additional media material. In the narrative in favor of the old SD, its date is construed as symbolizing the inauguration of the multiparty parliament. The parliamentary tradition is also part of the Croatian constitutional narrative: it is constructed as a symbol of continuous Croatian statehood tendencies throughout history.[22] This narrative emphasizes that the choice of a new SD results from an unconsidered political action: the post-Tuđman government wanted to use symbolic actions such as this change to cover up its inability to make substantial changes (Letica 2009).

In the second narrative, the old date is challenged as the day on which the HDZ celebrated its election victory. It is stressed that this holiday became part of Tuđman's legacy. Its opponents label this day *Tuđmanov spomendan*, 'Tuđman's memorial day', and present its abolition as a legitimate strategy in the "de-Tuđmanization process" (Gjenero 2000). This narrative insists on the new date of the SD as most relevant to proclaiming Croatia's independence. The newspapers I analyzed show that the pro-government media in the 1990s structured the old SD as being closely related to political elites and their ritual performances – in fact, as being their "symbolic property." Thus, the political elites and their performances also provoked the emergence of the narrative against the old date. On the other hand, the material related to Yugoslav Republic Day that I considered shows that the attachment to the holiday was stronger than was the attachment to what it symbolized. The issue concerning which group might claim proprietorship of that holiday's symbolism was neither obvious nor widely discussed in the last period of its observances.

Norwegian nationalism scholar Pål Kolstø (2006: 679) observes that in new, insecure nations, national symbols often fail to fulfill their function as promoters of national unity. In the narrative in favor of the old SD, the change of the holiday's date is an apparent symbol of an insecure nation.

It is difficult to predict which underlying events for national days will turn out to be appropriate and accepted (see also Introduction, this volume), but the problem with underlying events for both Croatian SDs is that they are relatively

---

21. "Narrative" is here understood as a story, part of a story, or a set of stories that follow one main idea and argumentation line in public discourse.

22. See Croatian Constitution (I: Historical Foundations), at: http://www.usud.hr/default.aspx?Show=ustav_republike_hrvatske&Lang=en, accessed 3 May 2010.

recent, and thus a subject of critical reflections by various contemporaries. Both SDs relate to events from the early 1990s, and create a scenario that positions Croatia against the same Others: Yugoslavia and the Serbs. These Others were part of Tuđman's narrative of common suffering in Yugoslavia, incorporated into the discourse of national unity in the 1990s. That narrative had its function in the 1990s but became obsolete afterwards.

Moreover, both SDs and their linkage to the 1990s ignore the constitutional narrative. The Croatian constitution emphasizes a continuous statehood tradition within the various forms of states that Croatia was part of, and relates the earliest tradition to the formation of seventh-century Croatian principalities.[23] A few alternative dates have thus been suggested in public discourse as a better choice. One of these dates is a date from 879 that recalls the first Croatian state with international legitimacy, at that time conferred by the pope. This was Duke Branimir's state (Pavličević 1996; Mijović Kočan 2002). Other dates are those of the independence referendum (19 May 1991) and of international recognition (15 January 1992). Even the founding date of the Independent State of Croatia, a World War II Axis puppet state, is discussed as a possible date among Croatian emigrants.

My analysis of the period since 2000 shows a strong relation of SD observances to commemorations of the Croatian War of Independence (see Pavlaković 2007). That relation blurs the identity of different commemorations, and also calls into dispute the acceptability of this day for all citizens. National days ideally should not carry controversial connotations. However, many disputed issues exist concerning the Croatian War of Independence. The relation to the war makes SD not a day to celebrate, but a day to mourn. New observance modes indicate a rather peripheral national-day type, given that the prototypical national day is one of celebration.

Croatian national days will certainly remain a contested issue for quite a while. Their unstable nature, typical for all new symbols, is perhaps less related to their being new and unfamiliar and more related to their having a strong association with certain persons and certain events. Disputed among different socio-ideological groups, they do not fulfill the most important function of national symbols as defined by Kolstø (2006: 679): to promote national unity. What they do is quite the opposite.

---

23. See Note 22.

Primary sources

Newspapers

Novi list, Slobodna Dalmacija, and *Vjesnik* (1988–2005; 106 front pages and 47 inside pages).

Newspaper articles, TV news, Internet publications

Barišić, Marko. 1999. "Što se sve događalo 30. svibnja 1990. na prvi Dan svehrvatske državnosti?" *Vjesnik*, 29/30 May, 17.

Berković, Zvonimir. 2002. "U podsvijest Hrvata je ugrađen strah od revolucije, iako je nikad nisu imali." *Vjesnik*, 13 June, 5.

CML = The Croatian media landscape – print media. 2008. http://www.wieninternational.at/en/node/11834. Accessed 26 Feb. 2010.

Erceg, Ivana. 2000. "Media After Elections." AIM Zagreb. http://www.aimpress.ch/dyn/trae/archive/data/200001/00124-001-trae-zag.htm. Accessed 26 Feb. 2010.

Erceg, Ivana. 2001. "Hate Speech in the *Slobodna Dalmacija* Newspaper." http://archiv.medienhilfe.ch/News/2001/AIM-CRO02-16.htm. Accessed 3 May 2010.

Gjenero, Davor. 2000. "30. svibnja – Dan hrvatske državnosti ili tek Tuđmanov spomendan?" *Vjesnik*, 31 May, 4.

Hrvatska radiotelevizija (HRT). "Dan Hrvatskog Sabora." http://www.hrt.hr/arhiv/ndd/05svibanj/0530%20DanDrzavnosti.html. Accessed 3 May 2010.

Izvješće 2006: *Izvješće o stanju u društvima: Pregled uređivačke politike lista Vjesnik*. Zagreb: Vjesnik d.d. i Vjesnik-Naklada d.o.o. At: http://www.sabor.hr/fgs.axd?id=4195. Accessed 22 Feb. 2010.

Jurisin, Pero. 2002. "Media Ownership Structure in Croatia: Huge Power of the Media." *Mediaonline.ba. Southeast European Media Journal.* http://www.mediaonline.ba/en/?ID=210. Accessed 22 Feb. 2010.

Knežević, Ivana. 2004. "Četrnaest godina samostalnosti." *Vjesnik*, 24/25 June.

Kustura, Irena. 2008. "Hrvati ne znaju svoje blagdane." *Večernji list*, 23 June.

Letica, Slaven. 2009. "Blagdanska revolucija: Tko je Hrvatskoj ukrao rođendan ili velika osveta podrumskih junaka." *Vijenac* 398, 4 June. Available at: http://www.matica.hr/Vijenac/vijenac398.nsf/AllWebDocs/Tko_je_Hrvatskoj_ukrao_rodjendan_ili_velika_osveta_podrumskih_junaka. Accessed 3 May 2010.

Lipovac, Marijan. 2006. "Sabor iz 1990. trasirao je put u hrvatsku državnost." *Vjesnik*, 30 May, 5.

Mazzocco, V. 2005. "Svi se vesele, a ne znaju što slave." *Večernji list*, 21 June.

Mijović Kočan, Stijepo. 2002. "Dan državnosti: hrvatskih je država bilo podosta, a prva je međunarodno priznata Hrvatska kneza Branimira." *Vjesnik*, 24/25 June, 13.

Vezic, Goran. 2001. "The Knights of the Shitty Coastline: On 'Slobodna Dalmacija.'" *Mediaonline.ba. Southeast European Media Journal.* http://www.mediaonline.ba/en/?ID=74. Accessed 27 Febr. 2010.

Laws

Constitution = The Constitution of the Republic of Croatia. Available at: http://www.usud.hr/
default.aspx?Show=ustav_republike_hrvatske&Lang=en. Accessed 3 May 2010.

Zakon 2002 = *Zakon o blagdanima, spomendanima i neradnim danima u Republici Hrvatskoj.*
Narodne novine 136 (2002). http://narodne-novine.nn.hr/clanci/sluzbeni/309949.html.
Accessed 3 May 2010.

Zakon o dopunama 2005 = *Zakon o dopunama zakona o blagdanima, spomendanima i ne-*
radnim danima u Republici Hrvatskoj. *Narodne novine* 112 (2005). http://narodne-novine.
nn.hr/clanci/sluzbeni/289584.html. Accessed 3 May 2010.

Zakon 1996 = *Zakon o blagdanima, spomendanima i neradnim danima u Republici Hrvatskoj.*
Narodne novine 33 (1996). Available at http://narodne-novine.nn.hr/. Accessed 3 May
2010.

CHAPTER 6

Contested pasts, contested red-letter days

Antifascist commemorations and ethnic identities in post-communist Croatia

Vjeran Pavlaković
University of Rijeka
vjeranp@gmail.com

Commemorations (and counter-commemorations) of the World War Two antifascist resistance movement in Croatia continue to be a source of debates over both political and ethnic identities. This chapter examines the transformation of several red-letter days in Croatia during the post-communist transition, in particular focusing on the content of the speeches given at commemorations. The new official Antifascist Struggle Day (22 June) replaced the former Uprising Day (27 July) after 1990, essentially erasing the latter from Croatia's commemorative culture because it was considered to be too "Serbian." The debate over these World War II commemorations, and their significance in contemporary political and ethnic identity construction will be examined by analyzing the discourse of political speeches delivered at the commemorations, the polemics present in a broad spectrum of the Croatian press, and field research (including interviews) conducted at the actual sites of memory.

Keywords: Croatia, commemorations, commemorative speeches, World War II, culture of memory

1. Introduction

Commemorations and other political rituals are key components of a nation's culture of memory, and therefore are crucial in the construction and reinforcement of multiple identities, whether ideological, political, ethnic, economic, sexual, or numerous others. This chapter examines the transformation of several antifascist commemorations in Croatia during the post-communist transition and the impact this transformation has had on both political and ethnic identities. Red-letter days commemorating World War II were a key component in constructing political legitimacy during communist Yugoslavia, and debates about how to remember that past continue to affect societies in all Yugoslav successor states, including Croatia. The new official Antifascist Struggle Day (*Dan antifašističke borbe*), 22 June, replaced the former Uprising Day (*Dan ustanka*), 27 July, after 1990, essentially erasing the latter from Croatia's commemorative culture because it was considered to be too Serbian. However, in recent years, the 27 July commemoration has been revitalized and is a key element of the cultural memory of Croatia's biggest ethnic Serb political party. This revitalization has provoked counter-commemorations and a sharpened nationalist rhetoric from rightists, who have traditionally challenged Croatia's antifascist tradition. The debate over these World War II commemorations and their significance in contemporary identity construction will be examined by analyzing the discourse of the political speeches delivered at the commemorations and the polemics present in a broad spectrum of the Croatian press, and by field research (including interviews) conducted at the actual sites of memory. Between 2006 and 2011 I attended numerous World War II commemorations in Croatia, and the speeches analyzed in this chapter were chosen because they were delivered for the most part by high political functionaries and emphasized both state-building and identity issues. Unlike several of the other chapters in this volume that examine how Yugoslav successor states constructed completely new state holidays (see the chapters by Ljiljana Šarić and Tatjana Felberg), this contribution analyzes parallel and even counter-commemorations in Croatia that reflect the hotly contested narratives of World War II. By examining the commemorative culture in transitional countries such as Croatia, it is possible to see how various layers of identity are expressed in public rituals. These identities subsequently influence behavior and political decisions in other aspects of Croatian society.

2. Reconstructing the past: Independent Croatia and the post-communist transition

The work of scholars in recent decades has clearly shown the relationship between memory and identity, both of which are constructed and reconstructed. According to John Gillis, "just as memory and identity support one another, they also sustain certain subjective positions, serial boundaries, and of course, power" (Gillis 1994:4). In analyzing the "culture of memory" and its relationship with national identity, and how both the culture of memory and national identity changed from the communist era to the post-communist period, it is necessary to define the three levels at which memory functions. The first level is individual memory, or the remembering of events actually experienced by individuals. Since people who experienced World War II are still living, their oral histories contribute to the communicative memory of and discourse about those events, although the death of this generation will probably change the way this past is remembered (Assmann 2005: 59). The second level is *collective memory*, a term coined by sociologist Maurice Halbwachs, who argued that group memory is socially constructed through interaction with others and reflected the dominant discourses of society (Halbwachs 1992). Institutional memory, the way ruling elites as well as their opponents construct historical narratives, represents the third level at which memory functions and is the most relevant framework for analyzing the post-communist transition in Croatia.

Commemorations, along with other political rituals such as rallies, parades, anniversaries, and other mass gatherings, are symbolic public activities that the political establishment attempts to use to convey its values. Additionally, the commemorative speech plays a key role in political rituals, and as Titus Ensink and Christoph Sauer have shown in their discourse analysis of the Warsaw Uprising commemoration, "without a speech, a commemoration cannot come to pass" (Ensink and Sauer 2003: 29). Although methodologically some aspects of discourse analysis will be used to examine the speeches given at the commemorative events discussed in this chapter, my primary goal is to highlight the contested narratives about the past which are inevitably politicized at the annual commemorations related to World War II.

In communist Yugoslavia, the regime's monopoly over historical narratives meant that the holidays which were celebrated were connected to key moments from the "National Liberation Struggle" (*Narodnooslobodilčka borba*, the name given to the Partisan resistance against the Ustaša[1] regime) or international worker holidays (such as May Day), while religious holidays were ignored and had to be celebrated in private (Hoepken 1999: 196; Rihtman-Auguštin 2000: 116).[2] In 1990, Franjo Tuđman's Croatian Democratic Union (HDZ – *Hrvatska demokratska*

---

1.   The plural form of Ustaša, which means 'insurgent' in Croatian, is Ustaše, and in this text I have used Ustaša when an adjective is appropriate (such as "Ustaša regime"), or Ustaše when referring to more than one member of this movement.

2.   Croats, who felt persecuted and exploited by the Serbian regime during the first Yugoslavia (1918–1941), initially welcomed the establishment of the Independent State of Croatia (NDH) in the aftermath of the German invasion in April 1941. Although the Ustaša movement, a radical Croat nationalist organization influenced by Fascist Italy and Nazi Germany, clearly was not going to create a liberal democratic regime when they took power on 10 April, few could imagine the horrors of mass murder, concentration and death camps, systematic persecution of non-Croat civilians, and widespread destruction that ensued in the next four years of spiraling violence and retribution. The multiethnic and communist-led Partisan movement, as well as the nationalist and monarchist Serb Četniks, fought each other as well as the Ustaše and the

zajednica) won the majority in the Croatian parliamentary elections. Tuđman and the HDZ not only oversaw the ideological transformation of Croatia's streets and monuments, but also reshuffled the calendar and the collection of national holidays; commemorations of Partisan and Ustaša victims were held side by side with Catholic holy days and red-letter days celebrating Croatian independence. Although Tuđman had been a Partisan officer, he tolerated the sustained attack on Croatia's antifascist legacy (in the press, revisionist history books, and textbooks), and tacitly allowed the rehabilitation of the Ustaša (including in the political arena where a number of parties celebrating the Ustaša past sought electoral support) as part of his concept of "national reconciliation" that would unite Croats of all political backgrounds against a common enemy, the Serbs. The Catholic Church in Croatia, which had played a controversial role in the Independent State of Croatia (NDH – *Nezavisna Država Hrvatska*) (Biondich 2009), has significantly influenced the commemorative culture during the transition period, emphasizing the victims of communist repression while generally avoiding antifascist memory sites. A kind of schizophrenic commemorative culture ensued, as new memory days and monuments were financed along with antifascist commemorations retained from the communist era.

Thus, not all Partisan commemorations were extinguished, but some, such as the Uprising Day (27 July), were changed (it became Antifascist Struggle Day and is instead celebrated on 22 June) to reflect the newly reasserted Croatian sovereignty while still commemorating the antifascist foundations enshrined in the Croatian constitution enacted in December 1990. The Communist Party of Yugoslavia (KPJ – *Komunistička partija Jugoslavije*) had been planning an armed uprising since the German attack on Yugoslavia in April 1941 dragged the country into World War II, but it was the German invasion of the Soviet Union on 22 June that sparked the formation of the first Partisan unit in Croatia, in a forest near the industrial town of Sisak (Anić 2005: 20–21). Led by Vladimir Janjić-Capo and Marijan Cvetković, this unit of mostly Croats sabotaged the important railway nearby, representing the first act of armed resistance in Croatia (Goldstein 2008: 279). But it was in the predominantly Serb region of Lika, along the Croatian-Bosnian border, where the massive armed uprising took place in the summer of 1941. The NDH had absorbed what is today Bosnia-Herzegovina as compensation for the loss of the Dalmatian coast to Italy, and the Ustaša authorities persecuted the local Serb population as vigorously as in Croatia. The towns of Srb and Donji Lapac, located in isolated valleys along the Una River, served as the staging area for the Serb uprising against Ustaša extremism, in coordination with Bosnian Serbs in

---

occupying Axis forces. However, the Četniks quickly ceased to be an antifascist force and openly collaborated with the Italians and to a lesser extent with German and NDH units.

Drvar. On 27 July, Serb villagers in Srb and in Drvar organized a massive uprising, nominally under the command of a local KPJ cell, attacking all symbols of the NDH regime and ambushing Ustaša and Domobran forces sent to restore order. However, some of the insurgent forces included Četniks who committed atrocities against Croat and Musilim civilians, as well as burning Croat villages such as Boričevac. The postwar communist regime designated 27 July as the official Uprising Day for Croatia, one of the most important memorial days of each of the Yugoslav republics.

The decision to shift the official commemoration of the 1941 uprising to 22 June was motivated as much by politics as by the desire to properly acknowledge the Sisak Partisans. A Zagreb newspaper declared in 1991 that the change of dates was not only paying off the debt to historical truth, but was a significant liberation of Croatia from the spiritual, cultural, and political oppression that it tolerated for more than seventy years.[3] During the communist era, the discourse of the speeches given by political and military officials at the Srb commemoration emphasized Brotherhood and Unity (i.e., the equal contribution of all ethnic groups in the resistance movement) and the revolution that followed the victory over fascism.[4] After the collapse of Yugoslavia, the commemorative speeches given in both Sisak and Srb are stripped of the ideological phrases and more explicitly refer to Croat-Serb relations.

The old date had several disadvantages compared to the new one in light of the political context in the early 1990s: the Srb rebellion was directed against a Croatian state; it was led by Serbs with only a few Croats participating; the insurgents killed many innocent civilians in reprisal attacks; chronologically it was subservient, as it were, to the uprisings in other republics; and the "Log Revolution" (*Balvan revolucija*) of the Croatian Serbs in 1990 was centered in the region near Lika and northern Dalmatia. In fact, nationalist Serbs issued a declaration of "Serbian autonomy" in Srb on 30 September 1990, providing an additional catalyst for armed rebellion against Zagreb and providing another reason why Srb was problematic as an antifascist memory site (Pauković 2005: 71–72).

Reasserting 22 June as Croatia's proper day for commemorating the resistance to Axis occupation was important in that it challenged communist distortion of the past without rejecting the country's antifascist legacy, unlike many of the other revisions that had taken place. Yet it was not until Stjepan Mesić was elected in 2000 that a Croatian president presided over the Antifascist Struggle Day commemoration, a key moment in restoring respect for the antifascist past in

---

3. *Večernji list*, 27 Apr. 1991:12.

4. *Borba*, 28 July 1971:1, 6.

Croatia. The speeches held on this day since 2000 by Mesić and other politicians not only emphasized European values, but also claimed continuity from the Partisan struggle to the establishment of an independent Croatia and, more recently, harbored thinly veiled attacks against right-wing politicians. The discourses of the commemorative speeches reveal how the post-Tuđman elites sought to reassert the Croatian-ness of the Partisan narrative, as well as to convince the European Union that the country was fit for membership.

The promotion of 22 June meant that the memory of 27 July had to be erased, which physically occurred during the Croatian Army's Operation Storm (*Operacija Oluja*) in 1995. Restoration of Zagreb's control over the so-called Krajina,[5] including Srb, was preceded by a full-scale exodus of the Serb population and the devastation of most houses and cultural monuments, including Radauš's statue.[6] Generally, the first decade of Croatian independence was characterized by a systematic assault on the physical memory of the antifascist past (of some six thousand monuments and memorials, about three thousand were destroyed, removed, or severely damaged), by the construction of monuments to members of the NDH regime (such as commander Jure Francetić and Minister of Education and Culture Mile Budak), and by the transformation of the symbolic landscape to reflect the memory of the Homeland War (Hrženjak 2002).

3.   Parallel commemorations, contested pasts

Tuđman insisted on retaining Antifascist Struggle Day as an official holiday and made considerable efforts to display Croatia's antifascist legacy for the international community's consumption. However, domestically he allowed the Partisan memory to be criminalized and instead focused on the glorification of the Homeland War, the event which reinforced the HDZ's as well as his personal political legitimacy. The 22 June commemorations passed practically unnoticed in the 1990s, with only brief wreath laying ceremonies conducted at the Altar of the Homeland

---

5. The Habsburg Military Frontier (*Vojna krajina* or *Militärgrenze*) was created in the sixteenth century in the parts of Croatia bordering the Ottoman Empire, and was settled by an Orthodox population (including Vlachs) that eventually adopted a Serbian identity. In the 1990s, Serbs in Croatia declared the Republic of Serbian Krajina (RSK – *Republika Srpska Krajina*) with support from Slobodan Milošević's Serbia, and rebelled against the newly independent Croatian state.

6.   While some sources have indicated that the monument was blown up by explosive charges, citizens of Srb claimed that a Croatian Army tank had shot the monument to pieces. Interview with Dragan Rodić and Nikola Čanak, both active in local politics, in Srb, Croatia, 25 Nov. 2009.

(a fabricated memory site constructed in Medvedgrad, in the hills above Zagreb), at the monument to People's Heroes in the Mirogoj Cemetery, and at the monument to fallen antifascists in Zagreb's Dotrščina Park. Tuđman never attended the official ceremonies, sending instead members of parliament, while local antifascist veterans organizations arranged additional commemorations at various sites of memory across the country.[7] Even though the monument near Sisak was officially the symbolic center of commemorative events, commemorations at it during the Tuđman era were attended mostly by local politicians and veterans.

Meanwhile, 27 July was almost completely forgotten in the 1990s. During the war years, the dysfunctional nature of the Krajina para-state, as well as the dominance of pro-Četnik (and anti-Partisan) narratives, meant that 27 July commemorations were not held from 1991 until 1995.[8] The exodus of the Serb population after Operation Storm in August 1995 left no one to commemorate Uprising Day, either formally or informally. Only after 2000, with Croatia's second post-Tuđman transition, this one under a center-left coalition government, were the first tentative steps taken to publicly commemorate 27 July. Initially, a few dozen elderly Partisan veterans, locals, and representatives of Croatian Serb organizations commemorated the uprising by laying wreaths at the base of the devastated monument on 27 July. Photographs from the commemoration in 2003 show the participants walking past the burned out husks of Srb's looted houses, a vivid testimony of the tragedy that struck both in the 1940s and in the 1990s.[9] The mainstream press and electronic media completely ignored the commemoration, even though the atmosphere had changed in Croatia regarding attitudes towards antifascism after Tuđman's death in 1999, at least on the national level. While only about fifty individuals attended the 27 July commemoration in 2002, the numbers steadily grew; in 2003, there were about three hundred participants, in 2006, about six hundred, and in 2008, the press reported that over 1,500 people attended the 27 July commemoration.[10] The Croatian government helped the town of Srb slowly rebuild, but the pile of stones that once formed the central monument symbolically illustrated how the controversies of World War II remained a part of contemporary politics, as described in more detail below.

The process of de-Tuđmanization during the presidency of Mesić meant that the Antifascist Struggle Day commemoration on 22 June was suddenly elevated

---

7. *Novi list*, 23 June 1996: 3.

8. Interview with Dragan Rodić and Nikola Čanak in Srb, Croatia, 25 Nov. 2009.

9. *Novosti*, 1 Aug. 2003: 10–11.

10. *Novosti*, 2 Aug. 2002: 10; *Glas antifašista*, 1 Sept. 2003: 16; *Glas antifašista*, 5 Sept. 2006: 22; *Novi list*, 28 July 2008: 4.

to the level of official recognition that it deserved in a country that based its constitutional foundations and historical continuity on the Croatian antifascist movement. The governments in power after 2000 effectively abandoned the Altar of the Homeland as a commemorative site, and the monument in Brezovica was restored as the dominant site of memory for remembering the events of 1941. In 2006, Mesić became the first Croatian president to participate in the Brezovica commemoration, and in subsequent years, he used this political ritual to lash out at his opponents. The connection between the Partisan movement in the 1940s and the independent state, forged in the Homeland War of the 1990s, became a dominant theme in the speeches given at the 22 June commemoration, challenging right-wing interpretations of history emphasizing the NDH as the legitimate Croatian state in World War II. Vladimir Šeks, one of the HDZ's most senior deputies, personally illustrated the shift in Croatia's attitudes towards the Partisan legacy in his speech on 22 June 2005, when he stated:

> ZAVNOH je uspostavio temelje hrvatske državne suverenosti u jugoslovenskoj državi i vratio Hrvatskoj krajeve koje su sluge okupatora predale nacifašistima. I u nacionalnom i u demokratskom smislu hrvatski antifašizam je neprocjenjiv. Temelji se na partizanskoj borbi u Drugom svjetskom ratu i u Domovinskom ratu, a okrenut je budućnosti. Antifašizam je sastavni i neozabilazni element suvremene Europe.[11]

> ZAVNOH [State Antifascist Council of the National Liberation of Croatia, the governing body of the Croatian Partisans] established the foundations of Croatian state sovereignty within the Yugoslav state and reintegrated Croatian regions that the servants of the occupiers had handed over to the Nazi-fascists. In the national and democratic senses, Croatian antifascism is immeasurable. It is founded on the Partisan struggle during World War II and in the Homeland War, and is turned towards the future. Antifascism is an integral and unavoidable element of modern Europe.

The highest officials in the country thus began to publicly express support for the antifascism that had been vilified in the 1990s; this support culminated in the Croatian Parliament's passing of the Declaration of Antifascism in April 2005.[12]

---

11. *Vjesnik*, 23 June 2005: 5.

12. "Deklaracija o antifašizmu," available at the website of *Hrvatski sabor*, www.sabor.hr/Default.aspx?art=7273, accessed 27 Apr. 2010. Croatian antifascist organizations criticized the government in the years since the enactment of the Declaration, alleging that at the local level not enough was done to promote antifascism, to prohibit the use of Ustaša and other fascist symbols, or to provide sufficient benefits to the dwindling numbers of Partisan veterans.

The reaffirmation of Croatia's Partisan past and the recognition of the 22 June holiday as being significant enough to draw the state leadership also enabled the 27 July date to gradually emerge from behind the veil of amnesia imposed by the Tuđman regime. Although initially some of the participants involved in the Srb commemoration and a few columnists writing in the Croatian Serb press expressed bitterness at the fact that 22 June had been designated as Antifascist Struggle Day to portray only Croats as antifascists,[13] the rhetoric at the commemorations has been one that supports both dates as legitimate memory sites observing the beginning of the fight against fascism in 1941. In 2003, representatives of antifascist organizations and of the Croatian Serb community agreed at the Srb commemoration that "mi se nismo skupili da licitiramo oko toga koji dan ustanka pravi, da li 27. jul ili 22. jun 1941. godine, već da obilježimo značajan događaj i da odamo počast svim poginulima i žrtvama rata," "we have not gathered here to bargain about which uprising day is the real one, either 27 July or 22 June 1941, but instead to mark an important event and to honor all of the dead and victims of war."[14] Speakers at the 22 June event likewise began to mention the legitimacy of the parallel commemoration in Srb, and Partisan veterans groups have for years argued that both dates should be equally remembered as part of a unified history.[15] Although official government delegations have yet to attend the Srb commemoration, the presence of leading politicians from the major opposition parties, Zoran Milanović and Vesna Pusić, indicated at least symbolically that 27 July was being rehabilitated as an integral part of Croatia's cultural memory of World War II.

However, at the same time as the parallel antifascist anniversaries were reaffirmed in a Croatia dedicated to European Union membership, a third commemoration, or more explicitly, counter-commemoration, gained strength. Namely, right-wing organizations and pro-Ustaša groups drew greater and greater crowds each 22 June at the site of Jazovka, a karst pit used as a mass grave for several hundred (or possibly several thousand) individuals believed to have been liquidated by Partisan units in 1943 and 1945. The date of 22 June was chosen not because it was associated directly with the Jazovka site, but specifically to challenge the antifascist holiday on that same day. In 1999, some seven hundred people attended the commemoration, while in 2005 the press reported three thousand people, and in 2009 estimated up to 5,500 people.[16] Although the Jazovka commemoration

---

13. *Novosti*, 28 July 2000: 6.

14. *Novosti*, 15 Aug. 2003: 6.

15. *Glas antifašista*, 15 June 2006: 24; and *Glas antifašista*, 5 Sept. 2006: 4.

16. *Vjesnik*, 23 June 1999: 7; *Vjesnik*, 23 June 2005: 5; and *Hrvatsko slovo*, 26 June 2009: 8.

has been ignored by government officials and attended by politicians from marginal parties such as the Croatian Pure Party of Rights, Croatian state television reported on it and the police have never intervened against individuals displaying Ustaša symbols.

Whereas the 22 June and 27 July commemorations form a common narrative of 1941 and the antifascist struggle that eventually laid the foundations of the modern Croatian state, the Jazovka commemoration offers a diametrically opposed narrative that suggests the Partisan movement was inherently anti-Croat in nature and responsible for war crimes far more hideous than those of the Ustaše. Members of the Croatian Party of Rights (HSP), once the strongest far-right party in the parliament, declared that "the bandits' anniversary does not warrant any celebration," in line with their assertion that all antifascists had inherently fought against a Croatian state (Roksandić 1995: 271).[17] Jazovka provides an annual opportunity to challenge the very idea of celebrating an antifascist holiday, where demands are issued for the parliament "da 22. lipnja nije dan antifašističkog, nego četničko-partizanskog ustanka te [su okupljeni] pozvali Sabor, Vladu i pravosuđe na ispravak Ustava i povijesnih nepravdi," 'to no longer call 22 June "Antifascist Struggle Day," but instead to change it to "Četnik-Partisan Uprising Day," alter the holiday in the constitution, and correct a historical injustice.'[18] The organizer of the commemoration in 1999, Zvonimir Trusić, insisted that "Ti zločinci su 22. lipnja 1941. krenuli u strahotno ubijanje hrvatske države i svega hrvatskog," 'on 22 June 1941, those criminals [the Sisak Partisans] began to horrifically kill the Croatian state and everything that was Croatian.'[19] Looking at the discourse of speeches held at the three commemorations in 2009, it is possible to see how the debates over the World War II legacy continue to shape notions of the Croatian state and of the ethnic identity of its citizens.

4.   Nation states and identity in commemorative speeches

The content of the commemorative speeches held every summer at Brezovica, Srb, and Jazovka provides insight into how certain groups (antifascists and national leaders, the Serb minority, and the radical right) in post-communist

---

17. A recent article in a right-wing weekly, *Hrvatski list*, featured the headline "Once and for all: Ustaše were for Croatia, communists and their followers are always for Yugoslavia." *Hrvatski list*, 24 July 2008: 30.

18. *Jutarnji list*, 23 June 2007: 2.

19. *Vjesnik*, 23 June 1999: 7.

Croatia view the state and ethno-national identity through the prism of World War II. The speeches from the year 2009 were chosen not because of any significant anniversary, but because the polemics over the World War II era were particularly lively. Former President Mesić had given a fiery speech at Jasenovac[20] in April, which was followed by an ideological rebuttal from veteran HDZ deputy Andrija Hebrang at Bleiburg in May; so, Mesić's 22 June speech included even sharper attacks against his political opponents. The speech at Jazovka by Bishop Valentin Pozaić was likewise frank in its political interpretations, which the right-wing press claimed was a reason that it was "hushed up." Finally, the presence of leading opposition politicians at Srb gave greater significance to the commemoration and to the speeches delivered in front of Radauš's devastated monument. Beginning in the summer of 2009, the right-wing press subjected the 27 July commemoration to sustained attacks in part because of the presence of leftist politicians and the efforts to restore the statue. Namely, Croatia's largest Serb political party, the Independent Democratic Serbian Party (SDSS – *Samostalna demokratska srpska stranka*), and the Serb National Council (SNV – *Srpsko narodno vijeće*), have made the renovation of the Srb monument one of their key political and cultural goals. The result is a struggle over not only cultural memory, but also actual political power and identity.

The discourse of Croatian World War II commemorative speeches in the last decade has focused largely on the state-building nature of either Axis collaborators or members of the antifascist movement, as well as on their respective relationships to the Homeland War. In the 1990s, Tuđman tolerated the rehabilitation of the NDH as a legitimate Croatian state. After 2000, Croatian officials used commemorations to reassert the narrative that the antifascist struggle, rather than the Ustaša regime, is the source of Croatian statehood in the second half of the twentieth century. As Titus Ensink and Christoph Sauer note in their analysis of the Warsaw Uprising commemorations, "by means of a commemorative speech [...] links are forged between individual recollections of the past, public remembrance and the collective memory" (Ensink and Sauer 2003: 32), links which are explicit in Croatian commemorative speeches directed to veterans of World War II as well as to the broader Croatian public.

Mesić's speech in Brezovica on 22 June 2009 emphasized the antifascist foundations of the democratic Croatian state and explained how true Croatian

---

20. Jasenovac was the NDH's largest and most infamous death camp, and the subject of continuing polemics about the number of victims (most of whom were Serbs). During communist Yugoslavia, the official number was 700,000 victims, but recent research suggests between eighty thousand and one hundred thousand victims.

patriots chose to accept neither the occupation nor the quisling state.[21] Later on, he clearly rejected the state-building continuity with the Ustaše:

> Naša je država mlada. Izrasla je u Domovinskome ratu, u borbi za slobodu i samostalnost. Ova, današnja Hrvatska, nema ama baš nikakve veze s tvorevinom koja je u vrijeme Drugoga svjetskog rata okaljala hrvatsko ime i koja je odgovorna za besprimjerne zločine protiv Srba, Židova, Roma, Hrvata-antifašista i uopće svakoga za kojega je i posumnjala da bi mogao misliti drugačije. Niti je tzv. NDH bila izraz povijesnih težnji hrvatskoga naroda, niti je današnja Republika Hrvatska na bilo koji način njezin nastavak, ili njezino uskrsnuće. NDH nije bila ni nezavisna, ni hrvatska, a niti je bila država![22]

> Our state is young. It emerged from the Homeland War, a struggle for freedom and independence. This, today's Croatia, has absolutely nothing to do with the entity which tarnished the Croatian name during World War II and is responsible for the unparalled crimes against Serbs, Jews, Roma, Croatian antifascists, and anybody else it suspected could think differently. The so-called NDH was not an expression of the historical aspirations of the Croatian people, nor is today's Republic of Croatia in any way its continuation, or its rebirth. The NDH was not independent, not Croatian, and it was not a state!

In many ways, the speech and many others delivered by Mesić at antifascist commemorations are a reaction to the historical revisionism unleashed by the postcommunist transition in Croatia, and an effort to explicitly associate Croats and the Croatian state with the antifascist movement.

Furthermore, at these speeches Mesić emphasized that not only the foundations of the modern Croatian state derive from the Partisan resistance in World War II, but also the Croatian identity more broadly. During the Jasenovac commemoration on 20 April 2008, Mesić declared that the Croatian people, thanks to their antifascists and to the National Liberation Struggle, finished World War II on the side of the victors, which meant on the side of the struggle for freedom, national independence, tolerance, and the equality of nations and individuals.[23] This position was in contrast with the identity politics of the 1990s, which was

---

21. Mesić, Stjepan, "Govor predsjednika Mesića na obilježavanju Dana antifašističke borbe," 22 June 2009, Brezovica, transcript available at the website of *Ured predsjednika Republike Hrvatske*, http://www.predsjednik.hr/Default.aspx?art=16330&sec=712, accessed 15 Mar. 2010.

22. Ibid.

23. Mesić, Stjepan, "Govor predsjednika Mesića na 63. obljetnici proboja iz logora Jasenovac," 20 Apr. 2008, Jasenovac, transcript available at the website of *Ured predsjednika Republike Hrvatske*, http://www.predsjednik.hr/Default.aspx?art=14986&sec=713, accessed 30 June 2010.

a result of Tuđman's policy of national reconciliation that to some degree legitimated the Ustaša movement as an expression of Croatian national sentiment.[24] Through his commemorative speeches at emotionally powerful sites of memory, Mesić firmly negated that association. At the Antifascist Struggle Day commemoration in 2008, he rejected seeking Croatian ethno-national identity within the Ustaša movement:

> Mi i danas plaćamo danak pogreškama i zastranjivanjima iz prvih godina hrvatske samostalnosti, kada se otvoreno koketiralo s ustaštvom i tolerirala ustašonostalgija. Treba jasno reći da je to neprihvatljivo. Između ustaštva i hrvatstva nema, ne može i ne smije biti nikakvog znaka jednakosti. Nema ga, nikada ga nije bilo i nikada ga neće biti. To prije svega trebaju shvatiti pripadnici naše mlade generacije, koji ponekada – prihvaćajući simbole i parole ustaštva – misle da time pokazuju svoje hrvatstvo, ili čak svoju pripadnost hrvatstvu i katoličanstvu. Oni ne shvaćaju da time vrijeđaju svakoga iskrenoga Hrvata i svakoga iskrenoga katolika.[25]

> Even today, we are paying the toll for the mistakes and deviations during the first years of Croatian independence, when there was open flirting with Ustašaism and a toleration of Ustaša nostalgia. We must say it clearly that this is unacceptable. Between Ustašaism and Croatian-ness there is no, cannot be, and must not be any sign of equality. It does not exist, it never existed, and it will never exist. In the first place, this must be understood by our younger generations who sometimes – by accepting the symbols and slogans of the Ustaše – think that this is a way of expressing their Croatian-ness, or their belonging to the Croatian nation and Catholicism. They do not understand that by doing this they are insulting every sincere Croat and every sincere Catholic.

The references to youth, and to the problematic educational system with nationalistic textbooks in the 1990s, were also frequent motifs in Mesić's commemorative speeches, since he was well aware that the revisionism of World War II had permeated the way history was taught in Croatian schools, with the consequence

---

24. While only a small segment of the Croatian population wholeheartedly and openly embraced Ustaša identity, especially in the political arena, the nature of the post-communist transition and war with Serbia meant that a greater percentage of Croats deem the NDH to have been a legitimate, albeit problematic, Croatian state. However, Serbian public discourse, especially in the 1990s, characterized *all* Croats as Ustaše in order to justify armed aggression against the fledging Croatian state (Pauković 2009: 134–135).

25. Mesić, Stjepan, "Govor predsjednika Mesića na obilježavanju Dana antifašističke borbe," 22 June, 2008, Brezovica, transcript available at the website of *Ured predsjednika Republike Hrvatske*, http://www.predsjednik.hr/Default.aspx?art=15234&sec=713, accessed 28 June 2010.

that young Croats were embracing slickly marketed Ustaša fashion without understanding the true nature of the NDH.

In addition to the themes of Croatian statehood and Croatian identity, the rhetoric of his speeches was especially militant, reflecting the intensity of the debate in Croatia over the World War II past. In Brezovica in 2009, Mesić addressed the large crowd gathered in the forest around the imposing stone monument with the following:

> Moramo obraniti povijesnu istinu. Ako to ne učinimo danas, sutra bi moglo biti kasno. Sada još kao predsjednik Republike, a uskoro kao građanin te Republike ja vodim i vodit ću svoju posljednju bitku, svoj posljednji rat. Ako netko misli da ću možda dobiti bitku, a izgubiti rat, mogao bi se grdno prevariti.[26]

> We must defend the historical truth. If we do not do it today, tomorrow could be too late. Now as the president of the Republic [of Croatia], and shortly as a citizen of that Republic, I am waging and will wage my final battle, my final war. If someone thinks that I might win the battle, but lose the war, they are badly mistaken.

This was a follow-up to his speech in Jasenovac on 26 April, where he accused his political opponents of "očajničkog pokušaja povijesnih revizionista da promijene rezultate Drugog svjetskog rata," 'a desperate attempt at historical revisionism in order to change the results of World War II' and firmly declared "ni ova zadnja osma neprijateljska ofenziva neće proći," 'that even this final, eighth enemy offensive will not pass.'[27] Throughout his mandate, Mesić used commemorations to reinforce the antifascist, and by association European, values of Croatia, which was a significant shift from his predecessor's policies.

While the commemorative speeches on 27 July in Srb and those at the Brezovica commemoration share the same antifascist narrative, the emphasis is not so much on the state-building nature of the Partisan struggle, but rather is on the unified struggle of Serbs and Croats against fascism. For post-Tuđman Croatian politicians such as Mesić, it was important to reaffirm the Partisans as a Croat movement, while for Croatian Serb leaders it was important to restore the

---

26. Mesić, Stjepan, "Govor predsjednika Mesića na obilježavanju Dana antifašističke borbe," 22 June, 2009, Brezovica, transcript available at the website of *Ured predsjednika Republike Hrvatske*, http://www.predsjednik.hr/Default.aspx?art=16330&sec=712, accessed 28 June 2010.

27. Mesić, Stjepan, "Govor predsjednika Mesića na komemoraciji povodom 64. obljetnice proboja logoraša," 26 Apr. 2009, Jasenovac, transcript available at the website of *Ured predsjednika Republike Hrvatske*, www.predsjednik.hr/Default.aspx?art=16145&sec=712, accessed 15 Mar. 2010. The reference to *neprijateljska ofenziva*, 'enemy offensive[s]' was from the communist narrative of World War II, which chronicled seven enemy offensives against Tito's forces.

antifascist status of the Serb population collectively labeled as Četniks in the wars of the 1990s. In 2009, the president of the SNV, Milorad Pupovac, insisted:

> Okupljamo se ovdje i zato da bi u Lici postajala i produbljivala se vjera jednih ljudi u druge. Tu vjeru Srba u Hrvata i obrnuto mi moramo širiti [...] Hrvatska treba više pravde i više odgovornosti, a teret treba raspodijeliti na sve. Ili će se mijenjati politika, ili ćemo se mi mijenjati. Srb nije bio samo mjesto ustanka, već je to bilo mjesto gdje se vjerovalo u pravednije društvo.[28]

> We are gathered here so that the trust of people in each other is created and strengthened in Lika. We must spread the trust between Croats and Serbs [...] Croatia needs more justice and more accountability, and the load must be shared by all. Srb was not just a place of the uprising, but a place where there existed a belief in a more just society.

The previous year he had issued a similar message, which included strong undertones of reconciliation between Serbs and Croats in Croatia:

> Nismo se okupili da se dijelimo u Hrvatskoj jer podjela je ionako više nego što ih možemo podnijeti. Okupili smo se da u ovoj klici sloge pošaljemo poruku da u Hrvatskoj antifašizma bez Srba ima, ali tko to govori ne govori punu istinu jer je o antifašizmu bez Srba nemoguće govoriti.[29]

> We did not gather here to create divisions in Croatia because there are already more divisions than we can tolerate. We gathered here in this embryonic unity to send the message that in Croatia it is possible to speak of antifascism and ignore the Serbs, but whoever says that is not speaking the full truth because it is *impossible* to speak of antifascism without them.

In a seperate interview, Pupovac noted that participation in the National Liberation Struggle was a crucial element of Croatian Serb identity and cultural heritage, and that the systematic destruction of antifascist monuments in the 1990s had served to erase that part of Croatia's cultural memory.[30] For this reason, the SNV has included the renovation of antifascist monuments as one of the key goals in its program (Milošević 2007: 20–21).

Vesna Pusić, who used the commemoration as part of her presidential campaign, issued similar statements of interethnic cooperation:

---

28. *Novosti*, 31 July 2009: 2.

29. *Novi list*, 28 July 2008: 4.

30. Interview with Milorad Pupovac (president of the Serbian National Council) in Zagreb, Croatia, 1 Oct. 2009. Pupovac admitted that some participants at the Srb commemoration were not critical enough of communist Yugoslavia and Tito, but rejected any suggestions that Četnik ideology was celebrated there.

> Kada se govori o prošlosti, onda svakom mora biti jasno da antifašizam u Hrvat-skoj nema alternative. [...] Svi imamo pravo na Hrvatsku, ali moramo preuzeti i odgovornosti za njenu budućnost, jer svako od nas ima mnogo toga korisnog učiniti za ovu državu. Ova država mora biti kao dobra majka za sve svoje građa-ne, bez obzira na bilo koju vrstu njihovu pripadnosti.[31]

> When we speak of the past, we all must be clear that there is no alternative to antifascism in Croatia. [...] We all have a right to be part of Croatia, but we must take on the accountability for its future, because each of us has a lot to contribute to this state. This state needs to be like a good mother to all of its citizens, regardless of what group they belong to.

In the months preceding the actual commemoration in 2009, the organizers had expressed a hope that 27 July would be recognized once again as a memorial day, but not necessarily as an official state holiday. The former president of the Croatian antifascist organization, Ivan Fumić, stated that his organization never differentiated between the two dates and equally commemorated them, adding that 27 July was removed because of political reasons.[32] Thus the Srb commemoration and other significant sites of memory related to World War II serve to reinforce Croatian Serb antifascist identity (and to reject Četnik narratives) as well as to restore Serbs to the broader Croatian antifascist narrative emphasized since 2000.

While on one hand the parallel commemorations of 1941 at Brezovica and Srb complement each other in constructing the Croat and Serb narratives of World War II, on the other hand the growth of the Jazovka commemoration reveals the strength of the right-wing counter-narratives of the Partisan movement and of the defeat of the NDH. The commemorative speeches, including Bishop Pozaić's in 2009, emphasize the anti-Croat, anti-Catholic, and inhuman nature of the antifascist resistance to the Ustaša regime, while simultaneously glorifying the NDH at a commemoration intended to honor innocent victims. Suggesting that former communist (and thus criminal) elites continued to control Croatia, on 22 June 2009 at the entrance of the Jazovka pit, Pozaić declared:

> Te zločine nikada ne smijemo zaboraviti, ni prešutjeti; naprotiv, moramo dizati glas istine i o počiniteljima toga zla: a to je zločinački komunistički antihrvatski, antiteistički – protubožji režim, i njegovi brojni sateliti – koji još i danas sablasno kruže i maršíraju Lijepom našom domovinom, uživajući neizrecive privilegije društvene, političke i financijske.[33]

31. *Novosti*, 31 July 2009: 2.

32. *Novosti*, 26 June 2009: 2.

33. Transcript of Bishop Valentin Pozaić's speech, reprinted in *Politički zatvorenik*, 208–209 (July–August 2009), online version at www.hdpz.htnet.hr/broj208/jazovka.htm, accessed

We must never forget these crimes, nor should we keep them a secret. In fact, we must raise our voices for the truth and about the perpetrators of this evil – the criminal communist, anti-Croatian, Godless regime and its numerous satellites – who continue to freely roam and march about our beautiful Homeland, enjoying unimaginable social, political, and economic privileges.

Whereas the state-forming tradition and the multiethnic nature of the World War II resistance in Croatia were the key themes in the commemorative speeches analyzed earlier, the discourse at Jazovka featured "Truth" as the key theme and also featured the alleged lies of not only the communist era but even of the post-communist period which sought to cover up the actual events of World War II. The word "truth" (*istina*) was used fifteen times in the short speech delivered in 2009. This was even more than Mesić used the term at Brezovica, where he had also repeatedly warned that the historical truth needed to be defended. Pozaić stated:

> Ovdje, na jednome od još uvijek ne-izbrojenih stravičnih mjesta stradanja hrvatskoga naroda, i svih onih drugih revolucionarnim hordama nepoželjnih osoba, […] dužni smo obećati, čvrsto i bespogovorno, da ćemo se oduprijeti svim onim besramnim lažovima koji istinu izvrću ili prikrivaju, ma na kojem se trenutačno položaju nalazili.[34]

> Here, at one of the countless horrific sites of death of the Croatian nation and of all those other individuals unwanted by the revolutionary hordes, […] we must promise, strongly and without hesitation, that we will oppose all those shameless liars that twist or hide the truth, regardless of their current positions.

The last comment was likely a reference to Mesić, whose efforts at restoring the legitimacy of the antifascist movement were at times uncritical of the war crimes and of the liquidations of political opponents committed by the Partisans, especially towards the war's end.

It should not be surprising that a member of the Catholic Church delivered such scathing criticism of the communist-led Partisans, considering the communist repression against organized religion after 1945. However, the revisionist narratives at commemorations such as Jazovka ignore the fact that many Catholic priests supported the Croatian antifascist movement. Moreover, such narratives

---

27 Apr. 2010. The transcript is in the possession of the author. Rightists frequently claim that Partisan veterans enjoy excessive privileges, even though the pensions of World War II antifascist veterans were slashed in the 1990s and are still today approximately half of those of similar veterans of the Homeland War. *Novosti*, 23 Apr. 2010: 16.

34. Transcript of Bishop Valentin Pozaić's speech, reprinted in *Politički zatvorenik*, nos. 208–209 (July–August, 2009), online version at www.hdpz.htnet.hr/broj208/jazovka.htm, accessed 27 Apr. 2010.

overlook the terror unleashed by the Ustaše or by their fascist and Nazi allies, in order to depict the Partisans as an exclusively anti-Croat phenomenon rather than through the prism of a resistance movement. For example, the organizers of the Jazovka commemoration issued an appeal to the Croatian parliament and government demanding that antifascism be removed from the Constitution because:

> hrvatski tzv. antifašisti, t.j. komunistički partizani, njihov Avnoj, Zavnoh i nikakvi jugo-partizanski ustroji nisu borili za antifašističku slobodnu Hrvatsku, nego za genocidnu srbokomunističku Jugoslaviju i za smrt svake hrvatske slobode i države! To naposljedku priznajte, jer danas, 22. lipnja, u Brezovici kod Siska politički vrh Republike Hrvatske opet krivotvori poviestnu [sic] istinu slaveći četničko-komunistički ustanak od 22. lipnja 1941., kada tzv. antifašisti započeše množtveno ubijati hrvatsku slobodu, da sve groznije nastave do god. 1945. i nakonratnih genocidnih vrhunaca![35]

> Croatian so-called antifascists, that is, so-called communist Partisans and their AVNOJ, ZAVNOH [the Yugoslav and Croatian Partisan governing bodies established during the war] and Yugo-Partisan organizations never fought for a free antifascist Croatia, but for a genocidal Serbo-communist Yugoslavia and the death of every Croatian freedom and state! You must admit this, because today, 22 June, in Brezovica, near Sisak, the political leadership of the Republic of Croatia is once again falsifying the historical truth by celebrating the Četnik-communist uprising of 22 June 1941, when the so-called antifascists began to massively kill Croatian freedom and continued until 1945 when it climaxed with the postwar genocide.

The extreme positions of this text, and of speeches that can be heard at commemorations such as Bleiburg, suggest that anyone who fought against the NDH or resisted fascism was automatically a communist, an enemy of Croats, and a genocidal criminal, which are no closer to the truth than the one-sided histories produced during the communist era. The commemorative speeches at Jazovka reveal that waging ideological battles rather than solemnly remembering the victims of war remains a dominant characteristic of Croatia's commemorative culture.

5.   Conclusion

The analysis of the three World War II commemorations in Croatia after the transition from communism reveals that the commemorative culture remains

---

35. "Zahtjev hrvatskom Saboru i Vladi," *Politički zatvorenik*, 208–209 (July–August, 2009), online version at www.hdpz.htnet.hr/broj208/jazovka2.htm, accessed 1 July 2010.

incredibly politicized and divided in both the national and the ideological sense. Although the Homeland War and its accompanying memory sites constitute a more relevant issue to current politics, the memory of World War II is also a source of passionate and emotional polemics that extend into the political sphere. Moreover, the debates about the tragedy of the 1940s have moved far beyond academic debates between historians and scholars, and are waged in the press, at commemorations attended by thousands of people, and in public spaces through-out the country.

While a wave of commemorative reconciliation has seemingly swept through Europe – notable was the Katyn massacre, jointly commemorated by Polish and Russian leaders – World War II remains divisive in Croatia. And most problem-atic is that the details of the historical events are not so much at the center of the controversies, but are rather entrenched representations of the past by oppos-ing political factions. Were the uprisings at Brezovica and Srb the beginnings of Croat and Serb resistance to a brutal fascist regime, or the first phase of an attack against an independent Croatian state? Were the massive losses suffered by col-laborationist forces in 1945 the result of desperate battles even after the capitula-tion of the Third Reich and revenge attacks against war criminals, or deliberate attempts at wiping out nationalist Croats and institutions such as the Catholic Church in order to subjugate Croatia once again to rule from Belgrade? Dense history books, devoid of emotionally charged discourse that present the nuances of the complicated World War II past with its multiple layers of the "truth," are of-ten drowned out by the bombastic spectacles and declarations at commemorative events that present a black and white version of history. The sustained campaign in the right-wing press attacking the efforts to rebuild the monument in Srb has lasted for ten months at the time of this writing. It has featured graphic descrip-tions of atrocities committed against Croats (Ustaša crimes against Serbs, which precipitated the armed uprising, are not mentioned at all) and accusations of a planned genocide from 1941.[36]

Although the virulent polemics over the commemorations and politically di-visive historical interpretations of World War II described in this text still exac-erbate ethnic and ideological tensions, encouraging signs exist from the Croatian and regional political leadership that steps are being taken towards a commemo-rative culture that promotes cooperation and tolerance rather than perpetuating the wounds of the past. Croatia's new president, Ivo Josipović, was widely hailed for his visit in April 2010 to sites of war crimes committed by Croats and Bosniaks in Bosnia-Herzegovina, honoring the victims from both sides of the conflict in

---

36. Nearly every issue of the weekly *Hrvatsko slovo* from July 2009 until April 2010 has featured an article protesting the commemoration in Srb and the restoration of Radauš's monument.

the 1990s while accompanied by Archbishop Vinko Puljić and reis-l-ulema Mustafa Cerić. The following month he visited three sites of memory in the Serb entity (Republika Srpska) of Bosnia-Herzegovina related to the victims of the three main ethnic groups, drawing praise in the region and from the European Union.[37]

This new commemorative culture extended to the memorializations of World War II. Even though the commemoration of the Jasenovac death camp remains divided between the one of the Bosnian Serbs (at Donja Gradina) and the one held at the Stone Flower memorial in Croatia, President Josipović told reporters that a place like Jasenovac is not a place for everyday politics. He also became the first president to visit the mass grave of Partisan victims at Tezno and to visit the monument at Bleiburg (albeit not at the time of the commemoration), where he declared that, as far as Croatian politics is concerned, World War II was over as of that visit, and a chapter of Croatian history was closed so that Croatians could turn to the future while leaving the subject of the war to historians.[38] At Brezovica on 22 June 2010, Josipović reaffirmed many of the same values and motifs of his predecessor Mesić, but this time took an added step by articulating not only that antifascism was the true source of Croatian statehood and identity, but also that Serbs were a part of that antifascism:

> Upravo ovdje, u Brezovici, Hrvatska je ustala i hrvatski je narod zajedno sa Srbima i drugim narodima i narodnostima nekadašnje Jugoslavije, fašizmu, nacizmu, zločinu i izdaji rekao odlučno NE. Narodnooslobodilačka borba, u kojoj su nezaobilaznu ulogu imali i hrvatski komunisti na čelu s Josipom Brozom Titom, ali i ne samo oni, već i svi slobodoljubivi ljudi, bila je dio svjetskog pokreta za slobodu i dostojanstvo čovjeka, pravedna borba u kojoj je dobro nadvladalo zlo […] Antifašizam i borba partizana povijesni su temelj novouspostavljene hrvatske državnosti, čiji je suvremeni nastavak, pravedni i obrambeni Domovinski rat doveo do uspostave samostalne i demokratske Republike Hrvatske.[39]

> Precisely here, in Brezovica, Croatia rose up and the Croatian people, along with Serbs and other nationalities and minorities of the former Yugoslavia, resolutely said "NO" to fascism, Nazism, criminality, and betrayal. The National Liberation Struggle, in which Croatian communists headed by Josip Broz Tito had an irrefutable role, along with other freedom-loving people, was a part of the international movement for freedom and the dignity of mankind, a righteous struggle

---

37. *Novi list*, 31 May 2010: 3.

38. *Večernji list*, 21 June 2010: 6.

39. Josipović, Ivo, "Predsjednik Josipović položio vijenac ispred spomenika Prvom sisačkom partizanskom odredu (HINA)," 22 June, 2010, Brezovica, transcript available at the website of *Ured predsjednika Republike Hrvatske*, http://www.predsjednik.hr/22062010, accessed 29 June 2010.

in which good overcame evil [...] Antifascism and the Partisan struggle are the historic foundations of the newly reestablished Croatian statehood, and whose contemporary continuation was the just and defensive Homeland War, which led to the establishment of the independent and democratic Republic of Croatia.

The speeches held in 2010 emphasized that the tragedies of the past should not be forgotten, but should also not keep the nations of the region trapped in the past or be used to justify new bouts of hatred. It remains to be seen if Croatia's political class is up to the challenge of building a commemorative culture which can reinforce a modern, democratic, and tolerant state aware of, but not perpetually burdened by, the tragedies of the twentieth century.

Primary sources

Čanak, Nikola, interview with author in Srb, Croatia, 25 Nov. 2009.
Declaration of Antifascism [*Deklaracija o antifašizmu*], Apr. 2005.
IPSOS Strategic Marketing Survey, Oct. 2011.
Josipović, Ivo, transcript of speech given in Brezovica, Croatia, 22 June 2010.
Mesić, Stjepan, transcript of speech given in Brezovica, Croatia, 22 June 2008.
Mesić, Stjepan, transcript of speech given in Brezovica, Croatia, 22 June 2009.
Mesić, Stjepan, transcript of speech given in Jasenovac, Croatia, 20 Apr. 2008.
Mesić, Stjepan, transcript of speech given in Jasenovac, Croatia, 26 Apr. 2009.
Pozaić, Valentin, transcript of speech given in Jazovka, Croatia, 22 June 2009.
Pupovac, Milorad, interview with author in Zagreb, Croatia, 1 Oct. 2009.
Rodić, Dragan, interview with author in Srb, Croatia, 25 Nov. 2009.

Newspapers

Borba, Glas antifašista, Hrvatski list, Hrvatsko slovo, Jutarnji list, Novi list, Novosti, Večernji list, and *Vjesnik.*

CHAPTER 7

Commemorating the Warsaw Uprising of 1 August 1944

International relational aspects of commemorative practices

Titus Ensink and Christoph Sauer
University of Groningen
E.F.A.J.Ensink@rug.nl
C.L.A.Sauer@rug.nl

This chapter describes the way Poland repeatedly involved other parties, notably former enemies, in commemorations of the Warsaw Uprising of 1 August 1944, thus turning a national Red Letter Day into a transnational event. The Uprising is ambiguous: it led to defeat, yet Poland is proud of it since it stands for her heroism, and the Uprising was suppressed by the Germans, yet Poland feels that the USSR/Russia bears some responsibility for its failure since the Red Army did not support the Uprising. Following a model proposed by Assmann, it is shown that Poland's repeated efforts to turn a commemorative occasion into a ritual in which both victims and culprits participate are successful: acknowledgement of responsibility leads to forgiveness and reconciliation. A discourse analysis of speeches by speakers from Poland, Germany, and Russia shows that the key to success is the victim's willingness to forgive, and the culprit's willingness to acknowledge guilt.

Keywords: commemorative discourse, discourse analysis, Poland, Germany, Russian Federation, Warsaw Uprising, Katyń, reconciliation, collective narrative, national identity, political speeches, joint commemoration, common ground, metonymy

1. Introduction: 1 August as a key event in Polish history

The Warsaw Uprising (Polish: *Powstanie Warszawskie*) started on 1 August 1944. It led to a two-month battle at the end of which the German occupying forces defeated the Poles. The Poles fought their battle alone. Allied Forces (France, Great Britain, the United States, Australia, New Zealand, South Africa, and Canada) provided some air support, but the Soviet Red Army (also a member of the Allied Forces), which had come close to the Polish capital, did not provide any support.

The uprising's key feature was the revolt of an occupied people (Poland) against their oppressor (Germany). The event's meaning to the Polish identity may thus initially be described as: "we as Poles stand up to regain our independence and sovereignty." At first sight, the meaning of 1 August seems similar to that of 11 November, another Polish national holiday, since Poland became independent on that date in 1918 (Hałas 2002b).

On 1 August 1944, however, the Poles did not regain their independence, since the uprising was suppressed after a fierce battle. German occupying forces were defeated several months later by the Red Army, after which Poland was subjected to Soviet dominance (Davies 2003). From the viewpoint of Polish identity, the meaning of 1 August does not signify independence, but rather the *striving for independence*, ignoring the immediate and concrete result: defeat. Defeat implies humiliation, but striving for independence implies *heroism, courage, pride, restoration of one's self-esteem*, and similar values, which are expressed in the collective narrative built around the event (see Wertsch 2002). Thus, 1 August is an important date in Polish history. (The Warsaw Uprising is to be distinguished from the uprising of the Warsaw ghetto of 1943. It should be noted that Poland pays less attention to the ghetto uprising than to the uprising of 1944.)

Historic events as key moments in the collective history may be restricted to only one community, for instance, concerning the constitution, or a revolution. In many cases, however, historic events pertain to more communities; they are double-sided. At least two perspectives, therefore, are relevant. To realize a public performance, one must choose either to address the event "among ourselves" within one's own collectivity, or to address it jointly. In the first case, the focus is on one's *collective identity*; in the second case, the focus is on managing *mutual relations*. Commemorations always involve some tension between these two approaches.

In this chapter, we focus on the second approach: *jointly realized commemorations*.

From the viewpoint of international relations, the Warsaw Uprising commemoration implies markedly complex relations:

1. Between Poland and Germany: victim – occupier (destroyer). This relation is defined by the Uprising as such. However, on several occasions, German representatives have acknowledged guilt or responsibility toward Poland (Ensink and Sauer 2003b: 88–89).

2. Between Poland and the Allied Forces: (fighting) victim – friends. In 1944, the Allied Forces were united in fighting the common enemy (Germany), but there has been a long intermezzo after 1945: during the Cold War, Poland belonged to the USSR-dominated Eastern Bloc, whereas the other former Allies belonged to the Western Bloc (the Unites States, France, Great Britain, and Canada). At the time of the uprising, the Allied Forces – with the exception of the Soviet Union – were at a great distance. They gave air support, but it was insufficient.

3. Between Poland and Russia: ambiguous between (fighting) victim – friend on the one hand, and victim – occupier on the other. The Poles counted on the Soviets for support, but they did not receive any. Consequently, the Poles see the Red Army now as a betrayer. Moreover, the very moment of the uprising was important because the Poles sought to guarantee Polish independence from Soviet dominance by overthrowing the Germans before the Soviets could do so. The uprising, however, did not prevent Poland from eventually coming under communist rule, within the Soviet sphere of influence. The communist occupation, however, was rather veiled. Officially, Poland was a sovereign independent state, but the majority of Poles felt occupied. Two other factors contribute to the complexity of the Polish-Russian relation: the Molotov-Ribbentrop Pact of August 1939, in which Hitler and Stalin secretly divided the Baltic Region, including Poland, among themselves, and the mass murder of Katyń.

Thus, the Warsaw Uprising is not a bilateral event between Poland and Germany; rather, it is at the very least (if we do not consider the other Allies) a triangular event including also the Soviet Union. In Figure 1, the roles of these involved parties in the event are stressed. The goal of commemorating is to overcome the negative aspects of those roles and to enter new relations.

Figure 1. Main actors involved in the Warsaw Uprising

Assmann (2009) proposed a model for the possible approaches to dealing with the past. The differences between these approaches concern the tension between the needs of one's own community (pertaining to one's identity and the role the past plays in defining that identity) and the need to maintain or redefine the relationship with another community involved in one's past. Assmann refers to the work of the philosopher Avishai Margalit, who proposed two paradigmatic solutions for the problem of dealing with a traumatic past: either remembering or forgetting, either preservation of the past or orientation towards the future. Assmann (2009: 32) argues that Margalit's proposal should be extended to rather four models:

1. dialogic forgetting
2. remembering in order to prevent forgetting
3. remembering in order to forget
4. dialogic remembering.

Assmann describes the fourth model as follows:

> It concerns the memory policy of two or more states that share a common legacy of traumatic violence. Two countries engage in a dialogic memory if they face a shared history of mutual violence by mutually acknowledging their own guilt and empathy with the suffering they have inflicted on others.
>
> As a rule, national memories are not dialogic but monologic. They are constructed in such a way that they are identity-enhancing and self-celebrating; their main function is generally to "enhance and celebrate" a positive collective self image. National memories are self-serving and therein closely aligned to national myths. [...] With respect to traumatic events, these myths provide effective protection shields against events that a nation prefers to forget. When facing negative events in the past, there are only three dignified roles for the national collective to assume: that of the victor who has overcome the evil, that of the resistor who has heroically fought the evil and that of the victim who has passively suffered the evil. Everything else lies outside the scope of these memory perspectives and is conveniently forgotten.   (Assmann 2009: 40–41)

Furthermore, she characterizes the expected outcome of the application of the fourth model as follows:

> Dialogic remembering transforms a traumatic history of violence into an acknowledgement of guilt. On the basis of this shared knowledge the two states can coexist peacefully rather than be exposed to the pressure of periodical eruptions of scandals and renewed violence. For the fourth model, however, there are as yet only few illustrations. It is still best described by its conspicuous absence.
>   (Assmann 2009: 44)

Contrary to Assmann's claim, we will show that the way the Warsaw Uprising is commemorated in Poland (together with the most centrally involved other nations) is at least partly an example of the fourth model. Because Poland has good reasons to feel victimized by the international political and military developments of World War II (the Warsaw Uprising being a key moment in these developments) it might be expected that overcoming her victimhood is an important aspect of Polish identity. Nevertheless, during the past two decades, Poland addressed the past in a much broader perspective. On several commemorative occasions, Poland did not merely dwell upon her own victimhood but also attempted to involve in the commemoration those who victimized Poland. Inviting perpetrators may involve confrontation but also may involve reconciliation. Reconciliation, however, is a goal that cannot be reached immediately. It must be preceded by an admission of guilt. Only after and through the admission of guilt can reconciliation be achieved. Reconciliation fundamentally changes a relationship. Both victimhood and perpetratorhood shift to the past, and the road is open to a perspective on the future which may even be shared by the former victim and perpetrator. Thus, jointly addressing the common past in commemoration may have a clear impact on international relations.

2. The development of the commemoration of 1 August in Poland

During the communist era (1945–1989), 1 August was not celebrated. The date's meaning was downplayed in official life, similar to the downplaying of the other day of independence, 11 November, which was replaced by 22 July, *Rocznica ogłoszenia Manifestu PKWN* (the Day of the Manifest of the Polish Committee of National Liberation). From the communist viewpoint, the uprising was a hazardous and reckless event; moreover, its commemoration would fuel anti-Soviet resentments (Davies 2003: 509) for precisely the reasons shown in Figure 1.

After 1990, 1 August became a calendric public ritual. After the collapse of communism, the Poles felt a *real* independence, regained after forty-four years of communist rule. Therefore, the Poles see a direct link between the Warsaw Uprising and Polish identity. Although the event turned into a defeat, the prevailing Polish narrative is one in which the *intention* is more important than the result. The intention – striving for independence – is paired to the means: the lone proud and courageous hero. Destruction bears the seed of rebirth. Furthermore, as Galasiński (2003) has shown, in official Polish speeches, Catholic Poland sees itself as "the Christ among nations." And similar to the fate of Christ, who gave his life to find a collective salvation, Poland's role in the uprising is conceived of as a willing sacrifice to reach noble results, rather than as that of a mere passive victim.

Since the uprising is an important hallmark of Polish identity, the anniversary is commemorated every year, and it is taken as an occasion to honor the values central to the uprising. In the past two decades, we may distinguish two main developments.

The first is the reinforcement and *conventionalization* of the Poles' own perspective on the event, namely that the Uprising was an act of heroism connected to martyrdom, out of which eventually grew Poland's independence, not only from the German occupation but also from communist rule. The Polish perspective has also been reinforced by the Polish translation in 2004 of Davies (2003), in which an international authority on history adopts the Polish viewpoint.

The second is the commemoration's incorporation in a changing society. New generations grow up: witnesses of the events grow old or die, and the younger generations must be educated about past events and their meaning. In 2004, both the opening of the Museum of the Warsaw Uprising and the launching of its website fit this pattern. Main events in the 2008 commemoration were the incorporation of quasi-entertaining events such as a bike ride along the main sites of fighting, the painting of graffiti, and open air performances in which the uprising was re-enacted.

In July 2009, President Lech Kaczyński proposed[1] to turn 1 August into an official national holiday. Polish society received his proposal favorably. According to a poll, more than 70% of Poles endorsed the proposal. The *Sejm* ratified the proposal on 8 October 2009. Since 2010, 1 August is the *Narodowy Dzień Pamięci Powstania Warszawskiego* (the National Day Commemorating the Uprising of Warsaw). The president's proposal stated that this holiday is meant to honor the heroes of the uprising who "sprzeciwili się okupacji niemieckiej i widmu sowieckiej niewoli zagrażającej następnym pokoleniom Polaków," 'opposed the German occupation and the looming Soviet captivity threatening the next generation of Poles.'

Among Poles, this may have been a readily accepted collective narrative in the sense of Wertsch (2002), in which the own role of the Poles and the associated values are defined. But does the outside world support and acknowledge the Polish conception implied in this narrative? Is it possible to introduce the

---

1. *Projekt ustawy o ustanowieniu Narodowego Dnia Pamięci Powstania Warszawskiego* (Bill to Establish a National Warsaw Uprising Commemoration Day), available on the official website of the President of the Republic of Poland, *prezydent.pl*, July 2009, http://www.prezydent.pl/download/gfx/prezydent/pl/defaultaktualnosci/9/752/1/powstanie-warszawskie_projekt_ustawy.pdf, accessed 20 May 2011.

perspectives of the other involved parties into the commemoration and to find a common ground from which the past may be jointly approached?

To address these questions, we have to turn to 1 August 1994 and 1 August 2004: the fiftieth and sixtieth anniversaries of the Warsaw Uprising, respectively. On these two occasions speeches were held by representatives of the three nations we focus on here: Poland, Germany, and Russia. A discourse analysis of these speeches should focus on the content and interactional aspects. The substantive issues relate to the way the speakers try to resolve some inevitable issues:

–   What is the event, how is it regarded, and – often also – how should it specifically *not* be regarded? These questions may be problematic and contended since the event may be viewed from different perspectives or differently defined (see Blommaert 2005: 142–157).
–   Who are involved, in what role, and in what relationship? These questions are by definition problematic when they concern a perpetrator-victim relationship.
–   What is the rationale for commemorating? Finding present-day meanings as a rationale is related to present-day interests, which may be in conflict or may not suit everybody.

The interactional aspects relate to the actions performed by the speakers. The speaker must solve an inherent tension between the expectation of the host and the reluctance of the home audience to admit guilt or even responsibility. Ideally, representative speakers will perform actions that fit both kinds of expectations.

In the following analysis, we will focus on how these substantive questions are tackled by the respective speakers, particularly in their choice of descriptions, and how they perform their actions. The key question is whether they succeed in finding a common ground, despite the divided past.

3.   The international commemorations of the Warsaw Uprising

3.1   The international commemoration of 1994

The 1994 commemoration of 1 August is particularly important not only for superficial numeric reasons (the fiftieth anniversary), but also for deeper reasons pertaining to the historical development of the communities involved. Poland, Germany, and Russia had gone through internal and external changes. The Berlin Wall fell in 1989, the communist GDR collapsed, and Germany was reunited in 1990. The communist regimes collapsed in both USSR and Poland (as well as in other countries). In 1991, the USSR was dissolved and the Russian Federation became its successor state. In 1990, Poland redefined her state's identity in abolishing the communist "People's Republic."

Thus, in 1994, the former main actors in the Warsaw Uprising had seen recent shifts in their internal and external identities. For that reason, 1 August 1994 is highly interesting because each party must involve itself from a newly gained identity, seeking to distinguish the present position from the past one. Willingness to participate in such a joint ritual implies willingness to do relational work, and not just to stick to one's old cherished view of history.

Therefore, the commemoration organized by Polish president Wałęsa in 1994 shows remarkable and rather unique features (for details, see Ensink and Sauer 2003a: 19–20). Wałęsa invited *all* parties that participated in the battle of the Warsaw Uprising. During the ceremony, representative speakers of Poland, Germany, the United States, Great Britain, France, Russia, South Africa, Canada, New Zealand, and Australia addressed the audience. In all speeches, speakers had to take into consideration several questions: How is the uprising to be looked upon? What was the role played in that event? Why is it relevant now to commemorate?

We will now focus on the Polish, German, and Russian speeches.

The first speaker was Polish president, Lech Wałęsa. He began by offering a factual description of the uprising. He used the description to infer a historical function regarding Poland: the *intention* was to get back its freedom, the *result* was immediate defeat and later a lone fate. Poland made a sacrifice and stood alone. The Warsaw Uprising is linked both to the outbreak of World War II on 1 September 1939 and to the end of World War II, after which Poland still had to strive for complete sovereignty. Thus, the uprising is given a *metonymic* quality: for Poland, the Warsaw Uprising is part of, and stands for, her lost freedom, both under German and under Soviet occupation (Poles see the period of Soviet dominance as directly linked to the Polish fate in World War II). Moreover, the uprising expressed the Polish *attitude* of willingness to make sacrifices for regaining freedom (see Galasiński 1997 and 2003).

After doing his descriptive work, Wałęsa goes on to address the relations. First, he addresses the *Western Allies*. He remembers gratefully what the Allied Forces did. Then he addresses the most complicated relation: *Russia / Soviet Union*. Wałęsa starts by making a distinction between Russia and the Soviet Union, thus implying that the present-day representatives have at least some shield between themselves and the Soviet responsibility. Next, he links the role of the "Soviet Empire" to the Warsaw Uprising:

> Mam świadomość, że historia zrzuciła na Rosję bagaż win, krzywd i zbrodni sowieckiego imperium. Jest w nim również krzywda powstańczej Warszawy. Ten bagaż uwiera i wzajemnie od siebie odpycha.

I am aware that history burdened Russia with the blame and harms done by the
Soviet Empire. In it there is also the harm done to the Warsaw of the Uprising.
The burden causes discomfort and pulls us from each other.

This passage is remarkable since it implies that Wałęsa puts *direct* responsibility
("the harm done to Warsaw") on the Soviet Union. Moreover, the Warsaw Uprising is linked to or at least compared to the mass murder of Katyń: Wałęsa remembers in one sentence Katyń, Poles murdered by the NKVD, and soldiers of the
uprising. Thus, Wałęsa stresses Soviet guilt. He nevertheless offers some counterbalance as compensation: many Russian soldiers died in combat on Polish land,
for "wolność bez przymiotników," 'freedom without adjectives.' The counterbalance offers a perspective: there is a "ziarno przyjaźni," 'seed of friendship' which
can grow "na glebie prawdy i demokracji," 'on the soil of truth and democracy.'

Regarding Germany, Wałęsa starts by stressing German guilt: "Nasze narody
dzieliło morze krwi. Jest w nim takze krew powstańczej Warszawy. Przez to morze
droga do siebie daleka," 'A sea of blood divided our nations. In it there is also the
blood of the insurgent Warsaw. Through this sea, the road to each other is far.'

He then praises the German episcopate and former Chancellor Brandt: they
set an example to follow. Just as he did with Russia, Wałęsa offers some counterbalance as compensation by mentioning examples of German anti-Nazi resistance. Again, the counterbalance offers a perspective: although Wałęsa does not
absolve the *morderców Warszawy*, 'murderers of Warsaw,' these feelings are not
passed onto the German nation. He expresses the belief that the Poles want to and
can live with their German neighbors in friendship.

In sum, Wałęsa offers his audience a coherent view of the Warsaw Uprising.
From the outside, it is a crime committed by others, which turned Poland into a
lone victim. At the same time, the sacrifice made by the Poles seemed a failure but
eventually turned out to be fruitful: not a Pyrrhic victory but a "Pyrrhic defeat,"
so to speak. Based on this viewpoint, Wałęsa addresses the two main culprits (in
Polish eyes) – Germany and the Soviet Union / Russia – confronting them with
their guilt but simultaneously offering a perspective on reconciliation.

How did both addressees, Germany and Russia, react? It must be noted that
in a formalized ritual such as a commemoration, no spontaneous reaction takes
place. In fact, all speeches have been carefully prepared and have been fixed in
writing before they are delivered to the audience. Nevertheless, some interaction
is involved, even on this formalized level, since speakers know each other's expectations and preoccupations, and know they must react to them.

On behalf of Germany, President Roman Herzog spoke. His speech may be
considered a careful and successful balancing act (see Ensink and Sauer 1995 and
2003b): he appears to be careful concerning German interests, but on the other

hand, he acknowledges German responsibility for the core of the commemorated events. Herzog begins his speech interactionally: "Es ist ein bewegender Moment für mich, Ihnen über die Gräber der Toten des Warschauer Aufstandes hinweg heute die Hand zu reichen," 'It is a moving moment for me to be extending my hand to you across the graves of those who died in the Warsaw Uprising.'

Herzog expresses gratitude for the invitation, and understanding for "die Gefühle jener, die meiner Teilnahme kritisch gegenüberstehen," 'the feelings of those who are critical of my presence here.' He stresses the need for reconciliation, understanding, and trust:

> Das kann nur weiterwachsen und gedeihen, wenn unsere Völker sich dem Grauen ihrer jüngsten Geschichte in aller Offenheit stellen. [...] Im Bewusstsein, der Vergebung bedürftig zu sein, aber auch zur Vergebung bereit.
>
> This can only continue to grow and thrive if our peoples openly face the horrors of their recent past. [...] Conscious of being in need of forgiveness, but also willing to forgive.

Thus, Poland and Germany seem to be treated on a par. Next, however, the Warsaw Uprising is described in a way that acknowledges German responsibility: "Der 1. August ruft uns in Erinnerung, welch unermessliches Leid von Deutschen über Polen gebracht wurde," '1 August reminds us of the immeasurable suffering that was brought upon Poland by Germans.' In this formulation, Herzog acknowledges in fact the metonymic relation between the uprising and the general Polish fate, as presupposed in Wałęsa's speech.

In his subsequent wording, Herzog distinguishes between Nazis and Germans, not denying the close link between these categories during the war. The culmination of his speech is to ask for forgiveness, thus repeating Brandt's gesture in verbal form: "Heute aber verneige ich mich vor den Kämpfern des Warschauer Aufstandes wie vor allen polnischen Opfern des Krieges: Ich bitte um Vergebung für das, was ihnen von Deutschen angetan worden ist," 'Today, however, I bow before the fighters of the Warsaw Uprising as well as before all the Polish victims of the war. I ask for forgiveness for what was done to you [them?] by Germans.'

The Russian Federation was represented not by its president, Boris Yeltsin, but by his "personal envoy" Sergei Filatov. Filatov addressed the audience with a speech that was concluded by a letter from Yeltsin. Consequently, his speech is a double message, the second embedded within the first, the first a prelude to the second (see Steinke 2003). Filatov characterizes the Warsaw Uprising as both heroic and tragic. He restricts himself to offering these positive evaluative terms; he refrains from discussing the role played by the Soviet Union. There are, apart from thanking for the invitation and offering best wishes, no direct actions in this speech. Both Filatov and Yeltsin (in the read-aloud letter) stress the parallels between Poland and Russia: both fought against Nazism and totalitarianism, and both peoples are on the road toward democracy. Filatov does not apologize; he merely acknowledges the existence of diverging perspectives, the resolution of which must be found by scholars, by historical research:

> Мы за то, чтобы история Варшавского восстания, советско-польских отношений того периода, была полностью открыта и изучена. Взгляды историков на этот период зачастую не совпадают, но веление времени и мудрость политиков состоит в том, чтобы обращение к прошлому остановилось не барьером между нами, а наоборот взаимно оберегало нас от повторения прошлых ошибок.

> We are in favor of making the history of the Warsaw Uprising, of Soviet-Polish relations at that time, fully open and studied. The views of historians on that time are often divergent, but the imperative of the time and the wisdom of politicians consist in ensuring that references to the past do not put up barriers between us. Quite the opposite that they mutually prevent us from repeating the old-time mistakes.

Shifting the resolution to future historical research makes it clear that the Russians are not prepared to acknowledge the metonymic extension of the Uprising to Poland's loss of freedom under Soviet rule.

In comparing the German and Russian reactions, it is also remarkable that Herzog, Filatov (in his own text), and Yeltsin (in his letter) use the German and Russian equivalents, respectively, of the expression "we bend our head." There is, however, an important difference. Herzog uses the expression humbly, as an introduction to excusing. Filatov and Yeltsin use the expression merely to show respect to the fighters who fought for the same cause they want to stand for. As Germany's representative, Herzog acknowledges the role the Germans played. Filatov and Yeltsin, although they address the Uprising, avoid going into its aftermath and into the long loss of sovereignty it stands for.

3.2   The international commemoration of 2004

Ten years later, in 2004, special attention was again paid to commemorating the Warsaw Uprising, due to its sixtieth anniversary. On 31 July 2004, the mayor of Warsaw, Lech Kaczyński, opened officially the Museum of the Uprising. In his opening speech, he stressed the Warsaw Uprising's meaning for Poland and its history, thus reinforcing the Polish narrative about Polish identity: a victim who heroically refused to be a victim and thus, although defeated, won in the end.

The next day, on the anniversary proper, an international commemoration again took place, on a more modest scale than in 1994. During a ceremony at the Warsaw Insurgents Square, speeches were delivered by German chancellor, Gerhard Schröder, British deputy prime minister, John Prescott, and US secretary of state, Colin Powell. After a gala concert, an address by Polish president, Aleksander Kwaśniewski, closed the commemorative ceremony.

Although the Russians had been invited, they did not participate in the commemoration, thus being "notably absent." Therefore, there was also no possibility for apologizing. In 2004, a nationalist restorative policy was dominant under Putin, which made the Russians even more reluctant to participate if one was expected to apologize.

In his speech, German chancellor Schröder combined a laudatory description of his Polish hosts with an acknowledging and remorseful attitude toward the role of the Germans. At the beginning of his speech Schröder said:

> Wir verneigen uns heute vor dem Opfermut und dem Stolz der Männer und Frauen der polnischen Heimatarmee [...] Wir beugen uns heute in Scham angesichts der Verbrechen der Nazi-Truppen [...] An diesem Ort des polnischen Stolzes und der deutschen Schande hoffen wir auf Versöhnung und Frieden.

> We bow today before the self-sacrifice and the pride of the men and women of the Polish Home Army [...] Today we bow in shame, faced with the crimes of the Nazi troops [...] In this place of Polish pride and German shame, we hope for reconciliation and peace.

Schröder is thus doing the relationship work expected of him. In reference to the past, he reinforces the Polish perspective on Polish identity; as the representative of Germany, Schröder accepts the role of being heir to the Nazi perpetrators, although he does not identify with them, and acknowledges the guilt resulting from Nazi actions. After doing so, Schröder is free in the remainder of his speech, to discuss present-day and future perspectives. The past is acknowledged, and then attention is shifted to the present and the future. Moreover, Schröder reinforces the Polish perspective by acknowledging that Germans are not entitled to make restitution claims:

> Wir Deutschen wissen sehr wohl, wer den Krieg angefangen hat und wer seine ersten Opfer waren. Deshalb darf es heute keinen Raum mehr für Restitutionsansprüche aus Deutschland geben, die die Geschichte auf den Kopf stellen.

> We Germans know very well who started the war and who were its first victims. Therefore, there can be no room anymore for restitution claims by Germany, which put history on its head.

Schröder stresses the importance of a free Poland being a partner in Europe. There is a common market; both nations share core values. These developments were only possible based on reconciliation *that has been achieved already*. In that context, Schröder recalls the gesture of Willy Brandt and of other Poles and Germans who dedicated themselves to reconciliation.

That Schröder recollects Brandt is significant. When Brandt fell down on his knees in Warsaw in 1970 (see Giesen 2004: 132–135), he made a *new* and unexpected gesture, thus putting the German-Polish relationship on a new footing. Schröder's reference to Brandt implies that he wishes to reinforce the new footing of the relationship, as Herzog did ten years before. Indeed, apologies are not *offered* (after which one must wait to see whether they are accepted), but apologies are *repeated*. The speaker anticipates the host's positive reaction, simultaneously turning away from the burdened past toward a positive vision of the present and future.

In his subsequent address, Polish president Kwaśniewski characterized the Warsaw Uprising in descriptive and evaluative terms that are well known by now, repeating and reinforcing the Polish collective narrative. He links the Uprising explicitly to the values of independence, of being rightful, of having a consistent attitude of responsibility and firmness. He does not dwell on the defeat, but rather stresses the patriotic values expressed in the Uprising.

> Powstanie Warszawskie zapisało się w historii jako zew najgłębszego patriotyzmu, jako niezniszczalna legenda. Z tego przesłania wyrasta wolna, suwerenna, demokratyczna Rzeczpospolita […] Z tego przesłania wyrasta też kanon wartości i postaw, które stanowią wzór dla dzisiejszej młodzieży […] Te wartości, te postawy żyją, są obecne wśród młodych […] Sądzę, że warszawscy Powstańcy mogą być dumni, że o to spełnia się ich testament, że polska młodzież chce godnie kontynuować ich dzieło.

> The Warsaw Uprising is written in history as the deepest appeal of patriotism, as an imperishable legend. With this message grows a free, sovereign, democratic Republic […] This message also grows the canon of values and attitudes that constitute a model for today's youth […] These values, these attitudes are alive, they are present among the young […] I think that the Warsaw insurgents can be proud of that; it fulfills their will that the Polish young people want to continue their work with dignity.

Kwaśniewski defines the Uprising as an important part of Polish identity, and he counterbalances its lack of direct success by highlighting its moral virtue, which won after all. Today's youth are carrying these virtues further.

> Ten gest Panie Kanclerzu ma wymowę historyczną. Jest kolejnym i ważnym znakiem pojednania między naszymi narodami. Dzieliła nas otchłań, otchłań pełna bólu i krwi. Dzisiaj – witamy Pana Kanclerz w Warszawie jako przedstawiciela kraju bliskiego i przyjaznego; sojusznika i partnera. W tej symbolice zawarty jest nasz wspólny tryumf – tryumf nad złem. To jest miara dziejowej drogi, jaką odbyli ku sobie Polacy i Niemcy.

> Your gesture, Mr. Chancellor, has historical significance. It is the next and im-
> portant sign of reconciliation between our nations. An abyss divided us, an abyss
> full of pain and blood. Today we welcome Mr. Chancellor in Warsaw as a repre-
> sentative of a close and friendly country, an ally and partner. In this symbolism
> is contained our shared triumph – the triumph over evil. It is a measure of the
> historical path we Poles and Germans have traversed.

In 2004, the Polish-German interaction during the commemoration made a considerable turn. Not only did the order of speakers change, so did their perspective
on what they addressed in their commemorative speeches. In 1994, acknowledgement of guilt was still awaited; in 2004, it is presupposed: note Kwaśniewski's remark *Dzieliła nas otchłań*, 'An abyss divided us,' which is in the past tense. In 1994,
the perspective was on the burden of the past. In 2004, the perspective has shifted
to the present-day relationship, although the burden is still remembered.

A comparably remarkable shift has not yet been realized in the Polish-Russian
relationship. In 1994, the Russians restricted themselves to remarks about defeat-
ing the Nazis. In 2004, the Russians did not even attend the commemoration that
confronted the past. Therefore, important questions remained unresolved.

3.3   Further developments

Strictly speaking, we should leave our discussion of the international aspects of
the Warsaw Uprising commemoration at that. Good reasons exist, however, to
broaden the discussion now by considering two different though related forms of
international commemoration in 2009 and 2010.

On 1 September 2009 – precisely 70 years after the beginning of World
War II – a joint ceremony was held in Gdańsk in *Westerplatte*, the site of the first
fighting of the war. Although the war's outbreak is distinct from the Uprising,
there is of course a connection. The uprising took place in the war's context, and
from the Polish viewpoint, it has a *metonymic* relation to the war, and even a
metonymic relation to the subsequent foreign occupation. Clearly, Polish representatives try to broaden the perspective on the Warsaw Uprising to include other
related events bearing a similar meaning. Although the ceremony in Gdańsk is
outside this chapter's scope, the Polish expectations link Gdańsk to the same general theme, since Gdańsk involves the same main actors. The Gdańsk ceremony
also concerns a *joint* ceremony in which representatives of former enemies and
victims participate, but where room is also made to address the past through new
alliances and relations.

In his opening speech, Polish president Lech Kaczyński analyses the causes of
World War II and its consequences. The aftermath of the Versailles Treaty is cited

as a seed of the war, as well as the dominance of totalitarian ideologies in the thirties. Kaczyński reproaches the pre-war willingness to negotiate with Hitler. Then he focuses on three aspects of the war and its aftermath that are yet unresolved: the Molotov-Ribbentrop Pact, the mass murder of Katyń, and the partitioning of Europe by the Iron Curtain. Both NATO and the European Union are cited as positive steps away from this burdened past. Kaczyński does not mention individual countries, but from the way he reproaches the intentions behind the Molotov-Ribbentrop Pact, and the Katyń massacre, he clearly aims more at the Soviet Union than at Germany: the heirs to the Soviet Union still must acknowledge what Germany has already acknowledged.

German chancellor Angela Merkel follows the pattern that by now has almost become a successful format: acknowledging guilt and responsibility, and neither describing the results of the actions euphemistically nor trying to rank them. Again, she apologizes. She thanks Germany's former enemies for their willingness to reconcile. Having done so, she shifts attention to the present and future, stressing positive post-war developments and expressing the will to accept responsibility for Germany's past.

Russian prime minister Vladimir Putin stresses the importance of the Red Army's sacrifices in the fight against Nazism. He also stresses the huge losses suffered by USSR soldiers and citizens. Regarding responsibility for the war, Putin equates the Molotov-Ribbentrop Pact to other attempts at appeasing Hitler. He does not attribute a singular position to this pact, but rather he describes the war as the result of the combined attempts made between 1934 and 1939 to appease the Nazis.

> Конечно, нужно признать эти ошибки. Наша страна сделала это. Госдума Российской Федерации, Парламент страны осудил пакт Молотова-Риббентропа. Мы вправе ожидать того, чтобы и в других странах, которые пошли на сделку с нацистами, это тоже было сделано. И не на уровне заявлений политических лидеров, а на уровне политических решений.

> Of course, mistakes have to be admitted. Our country has done so. The State Duma of the Russian Federation, our country's Parliament, has condemned the Molotov-Ribbentrop Pact. We are entitled to expect the same from other countries that had made a deal with the Nazis, and not at the level of statements by political leaders, but at the level of political decisions.

If Putin is willing to acknowledge responsibility, other countries, especially Western ones, should do likewise. From the Polish reactions, that Putin appeared at all is clearly positive, but that he remained aloof concerning both the pre-war responsibility and the post-war Soviet dominance did not answer Polish needs and expectations.

Thus, in September 2009 the picture of the international relations between Poland and Germany on one side, and Poland and Russia on the other, remains largely the same as it was at the time of the commemorations in 1994 and 2004.

However, a major change in this picture occurred in April 2010. On 7 April, a joint commemoration took place in Katyń, to mark the seventieth anniversary of the mass murder. On this occasion, Polish and Russian prime ministers, Tusk and Putin, respectively, delivered speeches. From the Polish perspective, Russian willingness to participate in a joint commemoration of Katyń is already a major step. Russian state television broadcast on 2 April Andrzej Wajda's movie *Katyń* for the first time. Furthermore, although he stressed the mutual fate of Poland and Russia as enemies and victims of Nazism, Prime Minister Putin acknowledged Soviet Russian guilt regarding Katyń: "Этим преступлениям не может быть никаких оправданий," 'There is no justification for these crimes,' "Десятилетиями циничной ложью пытались замарать правду о катынских расстрелах," 'For decades, there were attempts to conceal the truth about the Katyń massacre with cynical lies.'

The joint ceremony was intended to be prolonged, but two days later, Polish president Lech Kaczyński and many high-ranking Polish officials died in an airplane crash near Smolensk airport on their way to Katyń. The Russian support during this Polish national tragedy evoked a further Polish-Russian rapprochement. Russia's state news agency, Ria-Novosti, even published the speech that Kaczyński was to have given in Katyń: It contained a poignant appeal for reconciliation.

4. Concluding remarks

The Warsaw Uprising and its commemoration are primarily relevant to Polish society. In general, the event is commemorated only in Poland. It must be noted that in Poland – in contrast to Western Europe where World War II is the most recent collective trauma – the loss of freedom and sovereignty is not limited to only 1939–1945, but concerns the decades from 1945 to 1989 also. Consider the national holidays in Poland. In the two decades between 1989 and 2009, new national holidays have been established, which are concerned with both eras of the Polish past. The newly established holidays on 13 April (commemorating the victims of Katyń), on 28 June (the Revolt of Poznań in 1956), and on 27 September (the *Solidarność* movement) concern the era of communist rule, whereas the holidays on 27 September (the Polish Underground) and on 1 August (Warsaw Uprising) concern World War II. Clearly, from the Polish viewpoint, liberation from communism is equally important as, and is even intricately linked to, liberation from Nazi rule.

Regarding the way the past is dealt with, we noticed a significant difference between the Polish-German and the Polish-Russian relationships. Although the burden of the past is heavy between Germany and Poland, it has been largely relieved already. The past continues to exist; its burden has largely been resolved due to German willingness to acknowledge guilt and to apologize, starting with Willy Brandt's gesture in 1970, the meaning of which was repeated and reinforced by other German representatives (see also Ensink and Sauer 2003b: 86–90). Its burden has been largely resolved due also to Polish willingness to accept these apologies and to turn attention to a relationship of common interests with a perspective on the future. In contrast, the Polish-Russian relationship is characterized by the Russian reluctance to acknowledge guilt and by the resulting Polish frustration.

The difference we noticed may be explained by some other considerations. First, the distance – both in time and in attitude – from the Nazi past in Germany is greater and more radical than is the distance from the communist past in Russia. In Germany, a Nazi is an outcast, whereas in Russia it is possible to be a Stalinist without suffering similar opprobrium. Second, Germany lost the war, whereas the Soviet Union was one of the winners. Third, because of this, Russia sees itself as the one who liberated Poland from Nazism (hence not Poland's occupier), whereas Germany has been willing to acknowledge its role as Poland's wartime occupier.

Assmann's model (especially the fourth form, *dialogic remembering*) that we described in Section 1, is applicable to the Polish-German form of joint commemoration. As we have shown in this chapter, the burden of the past is not only largely relieved, but the present relationship is also reinforced by means of jointly addressing the past. The Polish-German relationship might function as a model for addressing the burdened past for other nations as well.

Regarding the Warsaw Uprising, dialogic remembering hardly applies to the Polish-Russian relationship, as has already been noticed in a more general sense by Assmann:

> Another lack of dialogic memory has become manifest in the relations between Russia and Eastern European nations. While Russian memory is centered around the great patriotic war and Stalin is celebrated today as the national hero, the nations that broke away from Soviet power maintain a strikingly different memory of Stalin that has to do with deportations, forced labor and mass-killings. The triumphalist memory of Russia and the traumatic memory of Eastern European nations clash at the internal borders of Europe and fuel continuous irritations and conflicts. (Assmann 2009: 41)

Nevertheless, we have seen a major turn also in the Polish-Russian relationship in April 2010. In 2014, we may expect another Polish attempt at organizing a joint commemoration of the Warsaw Uprising. If on that occasion the Russian reaction continues the initiative of April 2010, we may finally expect at least some resolution of the historical tension.

Primary sources

Speeches 1 August 1994

Wałęsa, Lech. 1994. Quoted in Titus Ensink and Christoph Sauer, eds. 2003. *The Art of Commemoration. Fifty Years after the Warsaw Uprising*: 53–56. Amsterdam, Philadelphia: John Benjamins Publishing Company. English translation by Dariusz Galasiński.

Herzog, Roman.1994. Quoted in Titus Ensink and Christoph Sauer, eds. 2003. *The Art of Commemoration. Fifty Years after the Warsaw Uprising*: 60–63. Amsterdam, Philadelphia: John Benjamins Publishing Company. English translation by *Presse- und Informationsamt der Bundesregierung* (Press and information service of the Federal Government).

Filatov, Sergei.1994. Quoted in Titus Ensink and Christoph Sauer, eds. 2003. *The Art of Commemoration. Fifty Years after the Warsaw Uprising*: 177–179. Amsterdam, Philadelphia: John Benjamins Publishing Company. English translation by Andrzej Niedzielski and Klaus Steinke.

Speeches 1 August 2004

Schröder, Gerhard. 2004. "Rede von Bundeskanzler Gerhard Schröder bei seinem Besuch zum 60. Jahrestag des Warschauer Aufstandes am 1. August 2004 in Warschau." Bulletin der Bundesregierung 73 (1) (2004). http://archiv.bundesregierung.de/bpaexport/bulletin/35/693635/multi.htm. Accessed 23 Feb. 2010. English translation by Titus Ensink and Christoph Sauer.

Kwaśniewski, Aleksander. 2004. "Udział Prezydenta RP w uroczystościach z okazji 60. rocznicy wybuchu Powstania Warszawskiego." Available on the official website of the President of the Republic of Poland, *prezydent.pl*, 1 Aug. 2004. http://www.prezydent.pl/archiwalne-aktualnosci/rok-2004/art,396,udzial-prezydenta-rp-w-uroczystosciach-z-okazji-60-rocznicy-wybuchu-powstania-warszawskiego.html. Accessed 23 Feb. 2010. English translation by Anna Ensink and Titus Ensink.

Speeches 1 September 2009

Kaczyński, Lech. 2009. "Przemówienie Prezydenta na obchodach 70. rocznicy wybuchu II wojny światowej." Available on the official website of the President of the Republic of Poland, *prezydent.pl*, 1 Sep. 2009. http://www.prezydent.pl/archiwum/archiwum-aktualnosci/

rok-2009/art,14,671,przemowienie-prezydenta-na-obchodach-70-rocznicy-wybuchu-ii-wojny-swiatowej.html. Accessed 25 Feb. 2010.

Merkel, Angela. 2009. "Rede Bundeskanzlerin Merkel bei der Gedenkveranstaltung zum 70. Jahrestag des Ausbruchs des Zweiten Weltkriegs in Danzig." *Die Bundeskanzlerin*, 1 Sep. 2009. http://www.bundeskanzlerin.de/Content/DE/Rede/2009/09/2009-09-01-bkin-danzig.html. Accessed 25 Feb. 2010.

Putin, Vladimir. 2009. "В.В. Путин выступил на состоявшейся в Гданьске церемонии, посвященной 70-ой годовщине начала Второй мировой войны." *Правительство Российской Федерации*, 1 Sep. 2009. http://www.premier.gov.ru/eng/visits/world/130/3541.html and http://www.premier.gov.ru/visits/world/6130/events/8206/. Accessed 25 Feb. 2010. English translation provided by the website premier.gov.ru/eng/.

Speeches 7 April 2010

Putin, Vladimir. 2010. "Председатель Правительства Российской Федерации В.В. Путин совместно с Премьер-министром Польши Д.Туском принял участие в памятной церемонии в мемориальном комплексе 'Катынь.'" *Правительство Российской Федерации*, 7 Apr. 2010. http://www.premier.gov.ru/visits/ru/10106/events/10122/. Accessed 7 July 2010. Version in English available at http://www.premier.gov.ru/eng/visits/ru/10106/events/10128/. Accessed 7 July 2010.

CHAPTER 8

Ilinden

Linking a Macedonian past, present and future

Marko Soldić
University of Oslo
marko.soldic@gmail.com

In the period of transition since independence from Yugoslavia in 1991, Macedonian national identity has been highly contested. The discourse (r)evolving around the commemoration of the Macedonian national day, *Ilinden,* may be viewed as an arena where such challenges are addressed. By analyzing excerpts from the print media, this chapter aspires to show how challenges facing the Macedonian community and their identity are interpreted, and how solutions to them are negotiated through constructions of continuity between past, present, and future in the *Ilinden* discourse. The focus will be on periods during which potential *disruptions* of the *continuity* of the national identity have been especially strong. The notion of continuity with the *Ilinden* past has rendered understandable and acceptable the massive social, economic, and political changes that the Macedonian community has undergone. Although this *Ilinden* matrix appears to be fixed, primarily its resilience and flexibility have ensured its continuing importance.

Keywords: *Ilinden*, national identity, national myth, collective memory

1. Introduction

The disintegration of Yugoslavia in the early 1990s meant a profoundly different reality also for its southernmost entity, the small Republic of Macedonia. Yet, whereas Slovenia and Croatia willingly left a Yugoslav Federation which was now considered a strain on their progress, Macedonia – an ethnically complex, economically underdeveloped, and highly contested political object – was more reluctant to leave a federation which was frequently regarded as a guarantor for stability and progress. However, as the demise of Yugoslavia was soon a *fait accompli,* Macedonia had little choice but to begin rethinking its position in the

Balkans – and in Europe. From the outset, this process met with great challenges. The reconstruction of a Macedonian national identity outside of Yugoslavia came to be viewed by neighboring states as an encroachment on their symbolic property, with immediate political consequences. The so-called "name issue"[1] with Greece, outstanding questions of minorities with Greece and Bulgaria, and a large and often discontented Albanian minority[2] all interplay with the ethnic Macedonian project of identity construction in a tense dynamic of dispute. Meanwhile, the two largest Macedonian political parties – the Internal Macedonian Revolutionary Organization – Democratic Party for Macedonian National Unity (VMRO-DPMNE), and the Social Democratic Union of Macedonia (SDSM) – hold conflicting views on Macedonian history, a core resource of the nation's identity. These conflicting views add complexity, and threaten to undermine the identity project from within. Given the extreme contestation and insecurity over the nation's identity, it is perhaps unsurprising that, according to a relatively recent EU-sponsored census in the Balkan region, Macedonians are most pessimistic about the future, with roughly one-third of them fearing another armed conflict on their territory (Gallup Balkan Monitor 2008).

The reconstruction of a Macedonian national identity must seek to address such challenges. Within an ethno-national rationale, this process must establish *continuity* in the face of potential *disruption*. Two historical events, and the symbolic chain between them, constitute one medium whereby establishing continuity is attempted. These two events are commemorated in the Macedonian national holiday *Ilinden*: the uprising of 2 August 1903 and the first meeting of the Antifascist Council for the Liberation of Macedonia (ASNOM) on 2 August 1944.

1.1   The Ilinden continuum

The uprising against the Ottomans on St. Elijah's Day, 2 August 1903, has become the focal point for "the reproduction of collective representations" that shape today's Macedonians' understanding of their identity and of their relationship to the past and to their land (Roudometof 2002:7). The reading of the so-called Kruševo Manifesto – an allegedly modern, liberal, and tolerant political declaration of an independent republic – from a balcony in the town centre is seen as the point in history when Macedonian statehood aspirations became reality, if only for a

---

1.   For an explanation of the name issue, please see Section 2.1.

2.   According to the 2002 census, ethnic Albanians constituted roughly 25% of the total population of 2.02 million inhabitants. Macedonians, the largest ethnic group, constituted roughly 64% (Republic of Macedonia State Statistical Office 2002).

few days. The 1903 uprising, the Kruševo Manifesto and the short-lived Kruševo Republic provide basic material for identifying revolutionary spirit, suffering, and ancient aspirations towards a free Macedonian state as essential features of "Macedonianness." It was no coincidence that ASNOM, some years later, chose 2 August 1944 as the date for its first meeting and for proclaiming the Socialist Republic of Macedonia. This became the "second *Ilinden*." If true that "every nationalism requires a touchstone of virtue and heroism, to guide and give meaning to the tasks of regeneration" (Smith 1999:65), then the charismatic leader of the new socialist Yugoslavia, Josip Broz Tito, readily used *Ilinden* as a cornerstone in efforts to encourage Macedonian culture. The aspirations of 1903 were adjusted to contemporary Marxist ideals to form a common denominator for socialism and a controlled form of Macedonian nationalism that was instrumental in fending off claims to the republic's territory and identity by surrounding states such as Greece, Albania, and Bulgaria (Palmer and King 1971). The nationalization of the *Ilinden* myth, previously a poorly documented phenomenon, was supported by extensive historiographical research. This nationalization process created tensions not only along the Skopje-Sofia[3] and Skopje-Athens axes, but also between national and local aspects of the Kruševo legend (Brown 2003). However, the process was successful in launching the *Ilinden continuum*: a mythical unbroken symbolic chain of modern Macedonian nationhood inscribed with myths of suffering and revolution (Brown 2000:160–164; Brunnbauer 2005:283–284; Smith 1999).

1.2   Aim, theory, and method

In this chapter, I analyze how the challenges facing the Macedonian community were and are interpreted, and how solutions to them are negotiated through constructions of continuity between past, present, and future in the discourse on the *Ilinden* commemoration. By focusing on lingual representations and interpretations of the *Ilinden* commemoration, one opens several perspectives for analysis – political and/or popular participation, behavior, interpretation, and self-identification may be taken in context and analyzed. The approach is influenced by disciplines such as critical discourse analysis (CDA) (most notably Chilton 2004) and social anthropology (most notably Donald Tuzin's treatment of creation myths (1997)), which builds further on the structuralist approach to myth of Claude Levis-Strauss (1966). Weight is placed on describing the changing

---

3. Bulgaria commemorates the *Илинденско-Преображенско въстание* (St. Elijah's Day-Transfiguration Uprising) (so named because the uprising further east in the Balkans started only two weeks later, on the feast of the Transfiguration) with many organizations and occasionally government officials participating.

historical and political contexts of the commemoration since the breakup of Yugoslavia, while also analyzing how different players have responded to these changing contexts through language, often seeking to adjust or reinvent national myth. As such, this chapter also reads as a historical overview of the development of Macedonian national identity during two crucial decades.

The print media is a fitting channel in this setting. Here, reports, articles, editorials, letters to the editor, and summaries of political speeches merge to form a wide and dynamic spectrum of perspectives. The material analyzed in this chapter consists of excerpts of text from Macedonian mainstream newspapers such as *Nova Makedonija* (New Macedonia), *Večer* (Evening), *Dnevnik* (The Daily), *Utrinski Vesnik* (Morning News), and *Vest* (News).[4] The process of selecting texts for closer analysis, and eventually exclusion from or inclusion in the main analysis here represented, has been organized as follows: All texts on Ilinden from all mentioned newspapers published before, on, and after the national holiday (three issues) have formed the main pool of material.[5] To narrow down this broad base, special attention has been given to three periods: Before and after independence (1990–1995), the armed crisis (around 2001), and the veto on Macedonian NATO membership (2008 and onwards). It is assumed that these are times when the mentioned pressure on Macedonian national identity has peaked because of political and social events. In the final stage of the selection process, the content of the shortlisted texts has been closely scrutinized. The main criteria for inclusion in the final analysis have been the occurrence in the texts of representations of past, present, and future linked together by Ilinden (continuity), and threats of breaks to this link (disruptions).[6]

The dichotomy of *continuity* versus *disruption* is an important analytical tool in this analysis. In the present context, national identity and political legitimacy are closely connected, and are dependent on the precedence established by "imputed aboriginality and continuity with the past" (Eriksen 2002:71; Lowenthal

---

4.   This analysis concentrates on ethnic Macedonian discourse; therefore, ethnic Albanian media have not been analyzed.

5.   One of the excerpts of texts included in the present analysis breaks with the described method for selection. In Section 4, a text from an academic anthology has been analyzed. It has been included in the analysis due to the rather extreme way in which it attempts to project the *Ilinden* myth and Macedonian national consciousness backwards in time. I have concluded that this break with the methodological pattern is justifiable, since the text represents a view on *Ilinden* that is regularly encountered in Macedonia as of the last years.

6.   The prevalence of such representations among the shortlisted texts was rather high. There were no examples of representations of the *Ilinden* myth which directly countered the central argument of this analysis.

1985: 53). The *Ilinden* myth offers a basis for Macedonian collective memory whereby a line of continuity may be projected not only from 1903 until today, but also backwards in time through the dots, as it were, of more peripheral historical myths.[7] The thought here is that, by the ethno-national rationale, construction of such continuity becomes a mode of responding to threats of disruption.

As John R. Gillis has noted, while identities, as "a sense of sameness over space and time [...] sustained by memory," seem fixed, they are rather the opposite, namely flexible interpretive frameworks for experience that are constantly revised to fit changing circumstances (1994: 3). Yet this flexibility has limits. Myth and identity may not simply be handed down from political elites to passive subjects who then form artificial nations in acceptance. Rather they must resonate with the individual's own history, with the individual's need to feel part of a larger community, and finally, with the individual's need to render present events meaningful and understandable by seeing existence as in continuity with the past (Smith 1999).[8]

2.   A third *Ilinden*? (1990–1995)

In 1990, *Ilinden* was commemorated while Yugoslavia was on the brink of collapse. Headlines such as "Силна антимакедонска кампања во соседството," 'Powerful anti-Macedonian campaign in the neighborhood'[9] and "Страв од македонизмот," 'Fear of Macedonanism,'[10] signaled that the waning framework of Yugoslavia caused insecurity in the face of pressure from neighboring states and from internal issues. Heated polemics with Greece and Bulgaria over minorities, as well as a Bulgarian delegation's attempt to travel to Skopje to lay a wreath at the tomb of the "Grand Bulgarian" Goce Delčev, dominated the prelude to that year's

---

7.   In the Macedonian discourse on national identity, attempts are made to draw the continuity of *Ilinden* back to, among other events, the establishment of the VMRO party in 1853 (as described by Troebst 2007: 412–413), the Karpoš uprising of 1689 (see, for instance, *Nova Makedonija,* 28 Oct. 1989: 1, 11), and even, as we shall see, the battle at Chaeronea in 338 BC (Mukoska-Čingo 2005). According to their advocates, all represent the same battle, one inspired by revolutionary zeal and aspirations towards Macedonian nationhood, of which *Ilinden* is the best-known manifestation.

8.   This view is particularly inspired by Smith's historical ethno-symbolism as an alternative approach to the study of nationalism.

9.   *Nova Makedonija,* 1 Aug. 1990: 1, 3. All translations in this chapter are the author's own, unless stated otherwise.

10.   *Večer,* 1 Aug. 1990: 1, 3.

commemoration.[11] Indeed, the commemoration itself would be overshadowed by threatening incidents at the Prohor Pčinjski monastery – site of the legendary ASNOM meeting – when Serb nationalist Vojislav Šešelj and his movement removed and destroyed memorial placards referring to the meeting. Later that day, clashes between Yugoslav militia and Macedonian nationalists occurred, and leaders of the party Movement for Pan-Macedonian Action (MAAK) were prevented from announcing their "Manifesto for a free, independent, and sovereign Macedonian state" at the monastery. These incidents were described as *најголем срам*, 'the greatest shame,'[12] and *најголемото понижување*, 'the greatest humiliation,'[13] in newspaper headlines.

Yet, in addition, metaphors of new times also prevailed. Headlines such as "Македонска пролет," 'Macedonian spring,'[14] "[Крушевската Република:] Прва република на Балканот," '[The Kruševo Republic:] first republic in the Balkans,'[15] "Враќање на Илинденските извиришта," 'A return to the *Ilinden* roots,'[16] and "Историјата во сопствени раце," 'History in our own hands,'[17] clearly spoke of new times, while simultaneously heeding the ostensibly unchanged ideals of *Ilinden*.

Because of the *Ilinden* myth's place in Macedonian self-consciousness, the potential revolution that the Yugoslav Federation's fall represented was, perhaps inevitably, interpreted immediately as a possible "third *Ilinden*." This interpretation was portrayed in the media by such details as the heading band of the 1991 *Ilinden* Special Edition of *Nova Makedonija*, which read "1903–1944–1991," as well as by the printing of the newly created Declaration of Sovereignty of the Republic of Macedonia instead of the usual Kruševo Manifesto and ASNOM declaration reproductions.[18] *Nova Makedonija* also devoted to the issue an entire page headlined "По првиот и вториот – трет Илинден?" 'After the first and second – a third *Ilinden*?' and invited emerging political players of Macedonia to address the turbulent times with the *Ilinden* myth as the framework of their interpretations.

---

11. *Nova Makedonija*, 1 Aug. 1990: 3. Like the *Ilinden* uprising, both Bulgarians and Macedonians claim one of its biggest heroes, Goce Delčev.

12. *Večer*, 3 Aug. 1990: 1, 3.

13. *Nova Makedonija*, 4 Aug. 1990: 3.

14. *Nova Makedonija*, 2 Aug. 1990: 1.

15. Ibid., 2.

16. *Večer*, 2 Aug. 1990: 2.

17. Ibid.

18. *Nova Makedonija*, 2 Aug. 1991: 11.

Kiro Popovski, of the Socialist Union of Macedonia, began by offering a view of a third *Ilinden* as "национална, економска, социјална, културна и политичка ренесанса," 'a national, economic, social, cultural, and political renaissance':

> Историјата не се повторува. Првиот Илинден се обидовме да го оствариме со оружје, но времетраењето на македонската држава беше кусо, меѓутоа, со длабоки траги и силен национален израз. Вториот Илинден го остваривме со Револуцијата и создадовме држава на дел од етничката територија на Македонија. Третиот Илинден може да го оствариме ако ги прифатиме вредностите на новото време. То значи, до Третиот Илинден преку демократија, преку сестран развој, преку обединета Европа!

> History does not repeat itself. We attempted to realize the first *Ilinden* with weapons, yet the duration of the Macedonian state was short, though leaving deep traces and a forceful national expression. We realized the second *Ilinden* with revolution and created a state on one part of the ethnic territory of Macedonia. The third *Ilinden* we will realize if we accept the values of these new times. In other words, towards a third *Ilinden* through democracy, through widespread development, through a unified Europe![19]

Popovski's interpretation not only established the line of continuity from 1903 to 1990, but it also saw the goal of a unified Macedonia within Europe as being in line with the past. His statement may be interpreted as a remarkably early example of aspirations of Europeanization; yet, later in the interview, he also stated that his goal of a unified Europe was really the goal of uniting all Macedonians in the area.[20]

In 1990, most political players in Macedonia agreed upon preserving Yugoslavia in some form. This was also the official view, as confirmed by the *Ilinden* speech of the president of the (still) Socialist Republic of Macedonia, Vladimir Mitkov, at Mečkin Kamen that year.[21] However, forces arguing for Macedonian independence were gaining momentum, with MAAK and VMRO-DPMNE taking the initiative. The interpretation of a hypothetical "third *Ilinden*" provided by the leader of VMRO-DPMNE, Ljupčo Georgievski, clearly conveyed aversion towards the Yugoslav concept and those who advocated its continued existence. While clearly also establishing continuity with the *Ilinden* past, Georgievski did so with different emphasis, launching an alternative view of Macedonian history.

---

19. *Nova Makedonija*, 2 Aug. 1990: 5.

20. Ibid.

21. *Nova Makedonija*, 3 Aug. 1990: 2. Mečkin Kamen, right outside of Kruševo, was the scene of the legendary last battle of the 1903 uprising. Today, the site is the main one for commemorating the "first" *Ilinden*.

In his eyes, *Ilinden* was still an unfulfilled dream. In addition, his parallel between the repression by the Ottomans and that by the Yugoslav communist regime de-emphasized the continuity of battle and revolution, elevating suffering, and martyrdom instead:

> Сосема е разбирливо македонскиот народ да го очекува својот трет Илинден, ако идејата на слободна, независна и обединета Македонија не ја оствари со првиот [...], кога Илинденското востание и Крушевската република беа со крв задушени од Отоманската империја и со вториот [...], [кога] Македонија го доживеа она што сите го знаеме. Стравовлада, чистки, репресии и монтирани судски процеси, со кои заврши и животот на Методија Андонов Ченто. Дали третиот Илинден ќе значи тотален слом на мрачните сили што Македонија ја турнаа во новото васалство [...] тешко е да се рече.

> It is entirely understandable that the Macedonian nation is waiting for its third *Ilinden*, since the idea of a free, independent and united Macedonia was not realized following the first [...], when the *Ilinden* uprising and the Kruševo Republic were drowned in blood by the Ottoman Empire, and following the second [...], [when] Macedonia experienced that which we all are aware of: A terror regime, purges, repression, and show trials, which also ended the life of Metodija Andonov Čento.[22] Whether the third *Ilinden* will mean a total collapse of the dark forces that are pushing Macedonia towards renewed slavery [...] is difficult to say.[23]

Thus, while difficulties with neighboring states constituted the more explicit challenge marking the *Ilinden* discourse in the early 1990s, the emerging political dispute and squabbles over history between the two major political parties of ethnic Macedonians were also noticeable.

Finally, so was the relationship between Macedonians and Albanians. The 1989 constitution of Macedonia clearly defined the Albanians as a minority in a state dominated by Macedonians. This designation reduced the co-existential motivation of an Albanian minority already increasingly radicalized due to the harsh conditions their close brethren endured under Serb rule in neighboring Kosovo. The deterioration was clear in a rare example of an Albanian voice

---

22. Metodija Andonov Čento became the first president of ASNOM in 1944. However, allegedly due to his leaning too far towards Macedonian nationalism, he was tried, sentenced and imprisoned, and was erased from official memory by the communist regime after he died in prison. In later years, he has been hailed by nationalists as a hero, and has come to symbolize the nationalist view of the "second" *Ilinden* as something initially positive, yet soon corrupted by Yugoslav communism.

23. *Nova Makedonija*, 2 Aug. 1990: 5.

surfacing in the overtly Macedonian *Ilinden* discourse; Nevzat Halili, of the Party for Democratic Prosperity of Macedonia (PDP), in rather poetic terms, revealed his view on the "third *Ilinden*":

> Илинден, секако е една поема за вековните ракувања меѓу народите, што исто така вековно го населуваат овој простор. Историјата сакала да бидеме заедно, и таа логика со визионерска антипација воспримила духовен облик, траен и прифатлив за сите во Манифестот на Крушевската република. […] Илинден на народот им влеваше вера и сигурност дека политичките ситуации низ кои помина албанската, турската народност и другите етнички групи во последните десет години […] се преодни и не се пример како да се живее заедно.

> *Ilinden* is indeed a poem for century-old handshakes between nations (*narodite*)[24] who have also lived on these lands for centuries. History wanted us to be together, and with visionary anticipation, that logic received a spiritual form, lasting and understandable to all through the Manifesto of the Kruševo Republic. […] *Ilinden* infuses the nation with faith and persuasion that the political situations that the Albanian, Turkish nationality (*narodnost*) and other ethnic groups have gone through during the last ten years […] are transitional, and not examples of how one should live together.[25]

Halili also used the *Ilinden* myth as a set of common references with which to analyze the changing times. Through it, both the grievances and the visions of a better future for a large social group of the emerging state were projected. The "situations suffered" by minorities for ten years under the Macedonian majority were by Halili constructed as in conflict with the historical continuity represented by the Kruševo Manifesto. Therefore, those situations were considered as a break with the past and, as such, wrong. These excerpts suggest that, even at the birth of Macedonian democracy, *Ilinden* served not only as an interpretive framework, but also as a medium for formulating critique and for offering responses to challenges.

As the September 1991 independence referendum at least theoretically settled Macedonia's relationship to the dying Yugoslav Federation, attention turned to the perceived negation of Macedonian identity. Most prominently, Greece

---

24. The original Macedonian words have been included in the translation to highlight the distinction in status between nations and nationalities of the Yugoslav system. The *narodnost* category was reserved for members of ethnic groups living in Yugoslavia that had a mother country outside the federation. These ranked lower than members of the *narod* category did. The Albanians of Macedonia viewed the Macedonian constitution as a continuation of this system.

25. Ibid.

hampered international recognition of the young state, claiming that the name *Macedonia* implies territorial ambitions towards Greece's northern region bearing the same name. According to the Greek view, the Macedonia of antiquity and its symbols are the property of Greece. Thus, both the name and the Macedonian government's choice to use in the new flag the Star of Vergina, a symbol commonly associated with Philip II (father of Alexander the Great), became sources of bilateral conflict with Greece. Soon, this struggle for international recognition became "another *Ilinden*."

This result was visible in the annual address to the nation by the Macedonian Orthodox Church (MPC) during the 1992 commemoration. While the MPC tends to emphasize the *Ilinden* myth's religious aspect, namely the day of St. Elijah, the MPC also reproduces what it alleges to be strong ties between church, nation, and identity by its contributions to the *Ilinden* discourse. This reproduction is often manifest in *Ilinden*-related elaborations on the role of the Church during the 1903 uprising;[26] yet now, it was combined with perspectives on the current name issue. According to then Archbishop Gavril:

> Нашиот прв Илинден е вистински израз на нашето македонско родољубе. И пред Илинден [...] македонскиот народ, воден од своите црковни и народни предводници, повеќепати востанувал и се борел за својата народна и црковна слобода [...]. Токму така, кога нашите соседи ја разделија Македонија и сметаа дека ја избришале од картата на Балканот, дека засекогаш ги замолкнале македонското име и македонскиот дух – пак востана македонскиот народ [...]. Оваа [...] е нашиот Втор Илинден.
>
> Our first *Ilinden* is a true expression of our Macedonian patriotism. Even before *Ilinden* [...] the Macedonian nation, led by its religious and national leaders, on several occasions rose up and fought for its national and religious freedom [...]. In the same manner, when our neighbors divided Macedonia and believed they had erased her from the map of the Balkans, and that they had silenced the Macedonian name and the Macedonian spirit forever – again the Macedonian nation rose up [...]. This [...] is our second *Ilinden*.[27]

Initially, following the pattern of establishing the link between the two *Ilindens*, Archbishop Gavril also reflected upon the revolutionary zeal, thereby linking the national and the religious dimensions. However, in a new twist, he also linked "name" and "spirit," and saw these as threatened by destructive neighbors already during the disruptions of World War II, with clearly backdated references to current events. This backdating provided a mode of interpreting and responding to

---

26. See, for instance, Pravoslaven bogoslovski fakultet "Sveti Kliment Ohridski" 2006.

27. *Nova Makedonija*, 1 Aug. 1992: 1, 2.

the "present *Ilinden*," namely by a legitimate self-defensive battle for what is "ancient and Macedonian":

> Деновиве Европската заедница донесе Резолуција, со која ни поставува услов за нашето признавање да се откажеме од името на нашата држава – Македонија. Но македонскиот народ не може да ја прифати ваквата одлука и да се откаже од своето вековно име и од сето она што со векови го создал на својата македонска земја. Ние, како Црква и како народ, сме исправени пред еден предизвик, пред една решавачка борба за одбрана на своето име, за името на нашата татковина Македонија, за се што е македонско со векови.

> These days, the European Union has put forth a resolution by which our recognition is conditioned on our renouncing the name of our country – Macedonia. However, the Macedonian nation cannot accept such a decision and renounce its ancient name and all that it has created through the centuries on its Macedonian soil. We, as a church and as a nation, are facing a challenge, a crucial battle in defense of our name, of the name of our Macedonian fatherland, of all that is and has been Macedonian for centuries.[28]

Parallel to the emergence of the mentioned contested symbols in the discourse on Macedonian national identity, tensions between VMRO-DPMNE and SDSM increased. Now, they not only differed about the Yugoslav period, but also increasingly differed about whether today's Macedonians descended from Macedonians of antiquity or from Slav invaders of the sixth and seventh centuries – the latter being the official view during the Yugoslav period. *Nova Makedonija* – then still mainly socialist and SDSM friendly – pointed to the "поткопувајќи ја подмолно најголемата вредност и достоинството на овој народ," 'treacherous undermining [of] the highest value and dignity of this nation' that such alternative historical interpretations represented. Attempts at disrupting the *Илинденскиот континуитет*, 'the *Ilinden* continuity,' were seen as cynical attempts of "антимакедонскиот слој," 'an anti-Macedonian circle,' with assistance from internal enemies such as "политиканти, националистички шпекуланти, смешни имитатори и фалсификатори на светата вмровска идеја," 'dishonest politicians, nationalist speculators, ridiculous imitators, and falsifiers of the holy VMRO idea.'[29]

---

28. Ibid.

29. *Nova Makedonija*, 2–3 Aug. 1994: 1.

3. Ethnic crisis (2001)

In late winter 2001, an armed crisis broke out in Macedonia. Started by ethnic Albanian paramilitaries operating on the border between Kosovo and Macedonia, it seemed to come unexpectedly to Albanians, Macedonians, and international observers alike. True, incidents of violence and unrest along ethnic lines had been numerous during the 1990s. But the fact that Macedonia's Albanian minority was politically represented and generally lived under far better conditions than their brethren in Kosovo contributed to a view both in Europe and in the country itself of Macedonia as a peaceful and tolerant success story of the former Yugoslavia. However, after the outbreak of violence, the rebellion received widespread support from Macedonia's Albanians, and inspired dismay and anger among ethnic Macedonians. The complex reasons for the outbreak were arguably somewhat simplified during the peace process, in which Western mediators, probably partly due to having the Kosovo crisis fresh in mind, were seen as emphasizing addressing the grievances of the Albanian population. In addition, several disarming incidents brokered by international observers were seen by Macedonians as letting Albanian rebels off too easily. Many Macedonians saw the result of the peace talks, the Ohrid Framework Agreement (OFA), as one of a long line of imposed concessions by Western mediators that essentially rewarded what those many Macedonians regarded as Albanian terrorism. The crisis resulted in outbursts of Macedonian nationalist antagonism towards Albanians and the international community, and conditions for ethnic reconciliation and Euro-Atlantic integration were temporarily worsened in multiethnic and allegedly EU- and NATO-orientated Macedonia.

Although some intellectuals and analysts had warned of a conflict, the inhabitants of Macedonia were nevertheless substantially shocked when it occurred. This shocked reaction is especially visible when comparing the *Ilinden* discourses of 2000 and 2001. The message of the commemoration of 2000 was dominated by the seemingly uniting goal of Euro-Atlantic integration, and gave few indications of trouble ahead. A front-page article of *Nova Makedonija* about the 2000 commemoration stated that "идеалите на Илинден коинцидираат со денешниот европски дух," 'the ideals of *Ilinden* coincide with the European spirit of today.'[30] Another front page article was dedicated to the prestigious opening of Macedonia's stand at the Hanover EXPO, during which the German hosts reportedly even "потенцираа значењето на Македонија во решавањето на балканските

---

30. *Nova Makedonija*, 3 Aug. 2000: 1, 2.

воени и политички конфликти," 'stressed the importance of Macedonia in solving Balkan wars and political conflicts.'[31]

The contrast to the radicalized *Ilinden* discourse of 2001 was stark. The *Nova Makedonija* front page of 1 August was dominated by connotations of disruption, such as "Албанските терористи продолжуваат со етничко чистење: Прогонети Македонци од селата кај Групчин," 'Albanian terrorists continue ethnic cleansing: Macedonians fleeing villages in Grupčin area,'[32] and "Военa кризa: Почна ли поделбата на Македонија?" 'Armed crisis: Has the division of Macedonia commenced?'[33] Connotations of disruption were also clear in *Večer*, which published a collection of short interviews with various celebrities, asking them to describe what *Ilinden* meant to them. A journalist described *Ilinden* 2001 as "несреќна проба на издржливоста на Македонецот да опстане со својот национален идентитет," 'an unfortunate test of the endurance of the Macedonian in defending his national identity.' An actor explained how he awaited every *Ilinden* with strong emotions, "особено сега кога како нација се бориме за опстанокот" 'especially now when we, as a nation, are fighting for survival,' while others spoke of "не дај Боже да ја загубиме државата," 'help us God, not to lose our country.' A folk singer called for increased awareness of Macedonia's antique period, "кој некои [без] право го сметаат за свој," 'which some people [without] justification regard as theirs.'[34]

Existential fear intermingled with nationalism and produced rather extreme reactions. In a comment in *Nova Makedonija*, the myth of suffering, with its potent religious connotations, was once again elevated above the myth of revolutionary zeal and above aspirations of nation- and statehood. Yet, confirming the pattern of the previous excerpts reproduced in this analysis, this elevation was done explicitly within the framework of the *Ilinden* continuum:

> Илинден е олицетворение на македонскиот непокор. Се олицетвори во 1903-та, по петвековната вјарменост под отоманската окупација, […] [кога] жртвениците на многувековниот македонски непокор […] со сопствената крв ја преосветија македонската библиска земја […]. Македонската земја имаше и второ илинденско преосветување во крвавиот виор на Втората светска војна […]. Во 1990-та го достигнаме зенитот на својата многувековна борба. Република Македонија стана суверена и независна држава – сонот

---

31. Ibid.

32. *Nova Makedonija*, 1 Aug. 2001: 1, 3.

33. Ibid., 1, 5.

34. *Večer*, 1–5 Aug. 2001: 22–23.

на многу генерации од македонскиот народ, чии најдобри синови и ќерки ги положија своите животи за постигнување на таквата света цел.

(Spiroski 2001)

Ilinden is the manifestation of Macedonian insubordination. It manifested itself in 1903, after the five-centuries-long yoke of Ottoman occupation, [...] [when] the martyrs of the centuries-old Macedonian insubordination [...] sanctified the Macedonian biblical land with their own blood [...]. The Macedonian land also had its second *Ilinden* sanctification, in the bloody whirlwind of World War II [...]. In the 1990s, we reached the zenith of our centuries-old battle. The Republic of Macedonia became a sovereign and independent country – the dream of numerous generations of the Macedonian nation, whose best sons and daughters gave their lives to achieve this holy goal.

In the last, most extreme section, the continuity of "the battle" was redrawn within the new reality of ethnic violence, as the commentator continued to speak of the victimization and suffering of the Macedonian people, while also clearly defining the enemy. As such, the final quote also acts as a form of matrix of the past through which the present should be understood and possibly also acted upon:

На Шара, во Вејце и други места северозападниот дел на Република Македонија најдобрите синови и ќерки на македонскиот непокорен народ повторно ја леат својата крв во одбраната на териториалниот интегритет и на суверенитетот на македонската држава против великоалбанските терористички окупатори и крвожедни зверови и домашните предавници [...]. Слушнете ги, нивниот свет глас го слојува нашите милениуми и од минатото и од иднината.

(ibid.)

In the Šar, in Vejce, and other places in northwestern Macedonia, the best sons and daughters of the Macedonian defiantnation are once again spilling their blood in defense of the territorial integrity and the sovereignty of the Macedonian state against greater-Albanian terrorist occupiers and bloodthirsty beasts and national traitors [...]. Hear how their holy voice is binding together our millenniums of the past and the future.

The content of these extreme passages is highly negative and potentially destructive, especially when considering the political and social circumstances in which they occur. Indeed, these circumstances ("suffering," "martyrdom") are interpreted as legitimizing a fierce act of self-defense against the ethnic Albanians of Macedonia, who are more or less explicitly portrayed as the remnants of Ottoman oppressors and fifth columnists, threatening the Macedonian nation from within. The use of the word "blood" numerous times, often in connection with words with religious connotations ("biblical," "sanctify," "holy," "martyrs"), evokes both the notion of an ancient right to this land as well as the notion of purity and the need for purification so common to extreme nationalist rhetoric. Finally, these passages revolve around the notion of *Ilinden* as something continuous, ancient, and everlasting ("binding together our millenniums of the past and the future," "centuries-old battle"), and thereby not possible to suppress ("defiant"). In sum, these passages stand as no less than a call for just war – a fourth *Ilinden*.

Nevertheless, moderate viewpoints also surfaced. One held that while, unexpectedly, "опасност за опстанок на македонската држава можат да бидат Албанците," 'the Albanians could pose a danger to the persistence of the Macedonian nation,' the armed crisis was a result of internal squabbling and power aspirations of Macedonian politicians, who thereby hindered a clear strategy to defend Macedonian national interests: "денес [...] со право секој од нас си го поставува прашањето дали македонската нација е исправена пред нов Илинден?" 'today [...], with justification, each and every one of us is posing the question: Is the Macedonian nation facing a new *Ilinden*?' (Tomovski 2001).

This viewpoint resonates with increasing attention (in the media and in politicians' addresses) given to the VMRO-DPMNE and SDSM rivalry in the *Ilinden* discourse of 1997 to 2000,[35] and which continued after the 2001 armed crisis had ended. The trend of Mečkin Kamen and Pelince[36] becoming rival sites of commemoration, according to political affiliation and corresponding view on history, crystallized during *Ilinden* in 2002. In the nationalist fervor following the armed crisis in 2001, the gathering at Mečkin Kamen that year saw record attendance of more than a hundred thousand Macedonians (Profiloski 2002). Prime Minister Georgievski had the spotlight by himself, as President Boris Trajkovski and SDSM delegates were absent, which was termed "национален срам," 'a national shame' (ibid.).

The previous example was a relatively moderate attempt at giving a nuanced explanation of the crisis rather than merely blaming it on external enemies. Viewpoints that were even more moderate were emerging. One article referred to examples of cooperation between Albanians and Macedonians during the 1903 uprising, and spoke of traditions of peaceful coexistence strong enough to overcome current difficulties and to form the basis for a common future.[37] However, highlighting the multiculturalism and democratic ideals allegedly represented by

---

35. See, for instance, *Nova Makedonija*, 1 Aug. 1997:2; *Nova Makedonija*, 4 Aug. 1998:1, 2; *Nova Makedonija*, 3 Aug. 1999:1, 2, 3; and *Nova Makedonija*, 1–2 Aug. 2000:1.

36. Pelince, at the outskirts of Kumanovo, was the provisional arena for the ASNOM-related celebrations during the years of Macedonian-Serbian tensions, since Prohor Pčinjski is located in Serbia.

37. *Nova Makedonija*, 1–5 Aug. 2001:5.

the *Ilinden* myth and its Kruševo Manifesto was nothing new. Similar notions had surfaced during the Euro-Atlantic aspirations of Macedonia before 2001. Yet with the events of 2001, a trend of accommodating reconciliation with the Albanian minority through the continuity of *Ilinden* clearly gained momentum. An opinion surfacing in the *Ilinden* discourse of 2002 illustrates this trend:

> Раката на довербата и сожителството секогаш била несебично подавана кон сите оние што живеат на овие простори. Крушевската Република го стори тоа со својот Манифест, повикувајќи ги под ист покрив и Албанците и Турците и сите други националности во Македонија. АСНОМ им ја подаде раката на соживот на сите југословенски народи. И охридскиот рамковен договор, без оглед на сите околности во кои беше создаден, не беше ништо друго освен уште една подадена рака за мир, доверба и соживот.
>
> (Tomovski 2002)

> A hand for trust and co-existence has always unselfishly been stretched out to all those who live on this territory. The Kruševo Republic realizes this with its Manifesto, calling for Albanians and Turks and all the other nationalities of Macedonia under the same roof. ASNOM stretched out a hand of co-existence to all Yugoslav nations. In addition, the Ohrid Framework Agreement, notwithstanding the conditions under which it was signed, is nothing else but another outstretched hand for peace, trust, and co-existence.

The alleged multiculturalism and tolerance of the Kruševo Manifesto, and its ideals, whose timeless validity is realized through the continuity of the *Ilinden* myth, are projected through ASNOM to the OFA. The present inter-ethnic crisis is indirectly understood as a deviation from the norm of peaceful coexistence. However, whereas the excerpt above may clearly be described as a moderate and tolerant contribution to the discourse, it implicitly refrains from putting any blame on the Macedonians themselves, whose hand has always been *подадена за мир*, 'outstretched for peace'.

4. Bucharest and beyond (2008 onwards)

At the NATO summit in Bucharest in April 2008, Greece vetoed Macedonian NATO membership, even though Macedonia was deemed ready by all standards. Obviously, the reason was the unresolved name issue. The veto represented a serious disappointment to a generally EU- and NATO-friendly Macedonia. Shortly after the shock of 2001, the *Ilinden* discourse had once again been dominated by European viewpoints; Kruševo was even, somewhat pretentiously, termed "главен град на европската идеја за демократија на Балканот," 'the capital of the European idea of democracy in the Balkans,' on the front page of *Nova Makedonija* in 2003 in connection with the prestigious one hundredth[38] anniversary of the uprising. By 2008, Macedonians had the friendliest attitude to the EU in all of the Balkans. According to an EU survey, 84% of ethnic Albanians and 57% of ethnic Macedonians had a positive view.[39] The corresponding figure was only 24% of all Croatians in Croatia, the Balkan country then closest to actually realizing EU membership (Gallup Balkan Monitor 2008).

However, with the Greek veto, fertile ground was created for a more overtly nationalist approach. For instance, in an interview published the day before the *Ilinden* commemoration of 2008, Foreign Minister Antonio Milošoski (VMRO-DPMNE) spoke of defending "уставниот, националниот, јазичниот, историскиот идентитет и […] интегритет на Македонија [од] грчката агресија," 'the constitutional, national, linguistic, historical identity and […] the integrity of Macedonia [from] Greek aggression.' The minister also asserted that his country was ready for EU membership talks, but said that he would not be surprised if the prospective membership would also be blocked by a Greek veto, which indeed occurred the following winter.[40] The official reactions to this second veto evoked notions of an adamant, ancient Macedonian nation faced with grave and unjustified threats of disruption. The then new president, Gjorgje Ivanov (VMRO-DPMNE backed), reportedly stated that "Macedonia will continue to exist," and that his country is "a strong country that will not cave in to pressures and possible injustice."[41] Prime Minister Nikola Gruevski followed suit, arguing that Greece cannot challenge Macedonia's name or identity, since Macedonians have existed "ever since Alexander the Great."[42]

That Bucharest represented a turning point regarding more favorable conditions for the somewhat stubborn and defiant form of Macedonian nationalism is reflected by the intensification of the "antiquization" campaign centered on Alexander the Great (Trajanoski 2010). One example of this campaign was a short film consisting of footage from archaeological excavations, sporting the slogan *Македонија: Вечна*, 'Macedonia: Eternal,' which was broadcasted on national

---

38. *Nova Makedonija*, 1 Aug. 2003: 1, 2.

39. The census also established that whereas 69% of ethnic Albanians wanted to change the republic's name to achieve NATO and EU membership, the corresponding figure for ethnic Macedonians was only 3%.

40. *Dnevnik Online*, 1 Aug. 2008, http://www.dnevnik.com.mk/?itemID=94E4F67865D9A 548885BDE9C91CA255A&arc=1.

41. *BalkanInsight.com*, 8 Dec. 2009, http://www.balkaninsight.com/en/main/news/24237.

42. *BalkanInsight.com*, 8 Dec. 2009, http://www.balkaninsight.com/en/main/news/24245.

television. There are numerous other examples of this campaign, which aims to stretch the continuity of Macedonian national consciousness thousands of years back in time: Grandiose plans of urban landscaping, the erecting of numerous statues, and the renaming of stadiums, airports, and highways are but a few.[43]

This campaign has also entered the *Ilinden* discourse, for instance through the works of the Macedonian Academy of Science and Arts (MANU).[44] In 2005, it released an anthology celebrating the one hundredth anniversary of the *Ilinden* uprising, which, among other things, sought to establish a link between *Ilinden* and the ancient battle, allegedly between the Macedonians and Greeks, at Chaeronea in 338 BC:

> Илинден е и 2 август 338 г.п.н.е. битката кај Херонеја како победа на Македонците над Грците, а тоа е исклучено од свеста на нашата македонска меморија […] Илинден 1903 година значи реафирмација, потзетување на митот за минатото на еден народ и неговите корени […]. [Илинден е] победа кај Херонеја, […] континуитет со Јустиниан Прима се до денес со АСНОМ и уставот на Република Македонија од 1991 година со кој се конституира самостојна македонска држава, но за жал само на еден дел од нејзината македонска територија.   (Mukoska-Čingo 2005: 36–37)

> *Ilinden* is also 2 August 338 BC, with the battle at Chaeronea, which stands as the Macedonians' victory over the Greeks, yet which is excluded from our Macedonian collective memory […]. *Ilinden* of 1903 means a reaffirmation, a reminder of the mythical past of a nation and its roots […]. [*Ilinden* is] the victory at Chaeronea, […] continuity with Justinian Prima[45] all up until today, with ASNOM and the Constitution of the Republic of Macedonia of the year 1991, with which an independent Macedonian state was constructed, yet, sadly, only on part of its Macedonian territory.

---

43. In summer of 2007, the Macedonian government even invited representatives of the Pakistani Hunza tribe, reckoned descendants of Alexander the Great, to tour Macedonia in a bizarre publicity stunt.

44. MANU also produced a Macedonian encyclopaedia, which created upheaval in autumn 2009. In addition to claiming Macedonian descent from Alexander the Great, the encyclopaedia also, contrary to established historical theory, claimed that the Albanians of Macedonia were settlers who arrived there only in the sixteenth century. Moreover, the Albanians were termed *Shiptari* in the encyclopaedia – a term perceived as derogatory when used by Slavs. The brouhaha resulted in the withdrawal of the encyclopaedia, and MANU was forced to rewrite controversial sections.

45. The reference here is probably to Emperor Justinian I, claimed by some nationalists to have been ethnic Macedonian, or to the town raised in his name in the fourth century AD, the remains of which lie in what is today southern Serbia.

This excerpt reads as an explicit attempt at linking a relatively recent notion of Macedonia's antique past with the far more consolidated central pillar of Macedonian national identity, namely the *Ilinden* myth. In this longer line of continuity, the uprising of 1903 is seen as a "reaffirmation" and a "reminder" rather than the true starting line of Macedonian history, which, according to this interpretation, lies far back in antiquity. The whole present discourse on Macedonian versus Greek identity is reflected in the notion of a *battle* whose outcome was a *Macedonian* victory over the *Greeks*.

However, the main theme of the 2008 commemoration seemed again to be Europe. At Pelince,[46] Gruevski reaffirmed Euro-Atlantic integration as "одговорноста пред иднината и историјата," 'the responsibility of our future and history.'[47] The prime minister also firmly established the line of continuity from 1903, through 1944, to 1991, stating that "тие успеаја, а нашата битка е пред нас," 'while they were successful, we have our battle in front of us.'[48] The 2009 address, of the new president Ivanov, reproduced the alleged link between the Kruševo Manifesto and European ideals:

Идеалите на Крушевскиот манифест за еднаквост и права на сите, без разлика на нивната етничка и верска припадност, направија Македонија да израсне во пример за регионот и за европската демократија во срцето на Балканот. Овие придобивки, со добрососедските односи и постојаната отвореност на Македонија кон светот, ги оживуваат идеалите на нашите предци. Тие се и гарант за иднината на новите генерации.

The ideals of the Kruševo Manifesto of equality and justice for everyone, regardless of their ethnic and religious affiliation, made Macedonia stand out as an example for the region and for a European democracy in the heart of the Balkans. These achievements, alongside good neighborly relations and the constant openness of Macedonia towards the world, revive the ideals of our predecessors. They are also a guarantee for the future of new generations.[49]

---

46. For the 2008 commemoration of *Ilinden*, the Macedonian government refrained from even bringing up the possibility of marking the event at Prohor Pčinjski with Serbian authorities. Before the 2009 commemoration, however, a deal was brokered which allowed an official Macedonian delegation to visit the monastery.

47. *Dnevnik Online*, 4 Aug. 2008, http://www.dnevnik.com.mk/?itemID=9BA0DEDA756C 39498DB64EF69398A0B1&arc=1.

48. *Utrinski Vesnik Online*, 4 Aug. 2008, http://www.utrinski.com.mk/default.asp?ItemID= B9B79AB67752F541AA5A34C280AAE5FB.

49. *Dnevnik Online*, 4 Aug. 2009, http://www.dnevnik.com.mk/?itemID=15D5F5F720839 141A7144BDD0FE57680&arc=1.

While in such excerpts establishing continuity according to the European quality of the *Ilinden* ideals is obvious, an attempt is also made to create a discursive distance between Europe and Balkan, and also indirectly to criticize Greece's position in the name issue as "Balkan," that is, backwards: "Пред нас се предизвиците за надминување на историските балкански неодоразбирања. Пред нас е стандардизација на европските општества," 'ahead of us there are challenges of historical Balkan misunderstanding to overcome. Ahead of us is the standardization of a European society.'[50]

The deterioration of relations between Macedonia and Greece seemed momentarily to have shifted focus away from the SDSM-VMRO rivalry, which dominated the 2007 commemoration. According to one commentator, the squabbles represented a threat to "континуитет на македонската битка," 'the continuity of the Macedonian battle,' as exemplified by *Ilinden*. According to him, the two *Ilindens* were indivisible and equally dependent upon each other, and together formed a foundation for the continuity and unity of the Macedonian people – a feat which no political party has the right to exploit (Cvetanoski 2007). *Vest* approached the issue from a more tabloid angle by having two female models dress up as a World War II communist guerrilla fighter and a revolutionary of 1903, respectively, before "фрлија дрвените кубури на земја и се гушна во знак на симболично помирување," 'throwing their wooden pistols to the ground and hugging each other in a sign of symbolic reconciliation.'[51] The *Ilinden* speeches of both then President Branko Crvenkovski (SDSM-backed) and Prime Minister Gruevski, reflected awareness of the negative opinions on the political split affecting the *Ilinden* discourse. Crvenkovski, at Pelince, spoke of the need to prevent divisions along both ethnic and political lines,[52] while Gruevski, at Mečkin Kamen, similarly pointed to the importance of "надминеме политичките разлики и да водиме [битка] заедно," 'our overcoming political differences to lead [the battle] together.'[53] However, the two parties remain divided on the right way to handle the name issue, and both seem bent on exploiting the issue to score political points against their rival. Yet the *Ilinden* discourse has also proven an arena for critique *against quarrelling politicians*, rather than simply a fighting ring for

---

50. Ibid.

51. *Vest Online*, 1 Aug. 2007, http://star.vest.com.mk/default.asp?id=138839&idg=7&idb=2136&rubrika=Makedonija.

52. *Dnevnik Online*, 3 Aug. 2007, http://www.dnevnik.com.mk/?itemID=20A2C6050655504E9779BF22BC849FAB&arc=1.

53. Ibid., http://www.dnevnik.com.mk/?itemID=A0C6573181C5F344930EF2ADE95361EA&arc=1.

politicians' battles *against each other*. At the *Ilinden* commemoration of 2009, Aleksandar Damovski, of *Nova Makedonija,* compared the main Macedonian political players after 1991 to the heroes of 1903, with no favorable outcome for those of modern times:

> Што и да напишат денешните хроничари за ликовите и делата на нашите актуелни политичари, војводи и народни претставници, останува впечатокот за недостојноста воопшто да се споредуваат со илинденците, со нивната посветеност, борбеност, пожртвуваност во одбраната на достоинството и на идентитетот.   (Damovski 2009)

> Whatever today's chroniclers may write about the life and work of our contemporary politicians, revolutionary leaders, and national representatives, it would be an indignity to even compare them to the *ilindenci*,[54] to their dedication, fighting spirit, their will to sacrifice for the defense of dignity and identity.

5. Conclusion

The difficult first phases of Macedonia's post-socialist transition have to a considerable extent been reflected in the *Ilinden* discourse. The *Ilinden* continuum, as a set of collective memories sustaining one of the central pillars of Macedonian national identity, has functioned as a matrix for interpreting and responding to the challenges that have faced the Macedonian community. While also being an ingredient in negative competition over power, the notion of continuity with the *Ilinden* past has nevertheless rendered understandable and acceptable the massive social, economic, and political changes this community has undergone. However, though this matrix appears to be fixed, primarily its resilience and flexibility have ensured the continuing importance of the *Ilinden* commemoration to the Macedonian nation. The importance of the *Ilinden* myth and of the *Ilinden* commemoration to Macedonians is reflected in the fact that players with political agendas choose to communicate their ideology through the myth and the commemoration. Yet their targets have not always been receptive, choosing rather to promote their own worldview through the *Ilinden* matrix.

Today, the path towards Euro-Atlantic integration is the main topic of the *Ilinden* commemoration. According to the rationale of the *Ilinden* continuum, Macedonia's path towards Europe started with the fateful events of August 1903, and today represents the main unfulfilled battle of the Macedonian nation.

---

54. Literally, *"the Ilindens"* in this context meaning "the heroes of the *Ilinden* uprising(s)."

Primary sources

Gallup Balkan Monitor. 2008. *Summary of Findings*. Annual report on censuses held in the Western Balkans. Available at *balkan-monitor.eu*. http://www.balkan-monitor.eu/files/BalkanMonitor-2008_Summary_of_Findings.pdf. Accessed 30 May 2011.

Republic of Macedonia state statistical office. 2002. *Book 1: Total Population, Households and Dwellings*. Skopje: The state statistical office. (downloadable at http://www.stat.gov.mk/publikacii/knigaI.pdf)

Editorials and comments

Cvetanoski, Viktor. 2007. "Političarite go delat narodot za Ilinden." *Utrinski Vesnik Online*, 1 Aug. 2007. http://www.utrinski.com.mk/?ItemID=96AFCF1B75B2C746AC4615B442B53A.

Damovski, Aleksandar. 2009. "Heroite pred godini … i denes." *Nova Makedonija Online*, 1 Aug. 2009. http://www.novamakedonija.com.mk/NewsDetal.asp?vest=819958519&id=13&prilog=0&setIzdanie=21753.

Profiloski, Ljube. 2002. "Porakite od Mečkin Kamen," *Nova Makedonija*, 5 Aug. 2002, 1–2.

Spiroski, Miroslav. 2001. "Crvenata linija na nepokorot," *Nova Makedonija*, 1–5 Aug. 2001, 3.

Tomovski, Risto. 2001. "Nov Ilinden?" *Nova Makedonija*, 1–5 Aug. 2001, 2.

———. 2002. "Svetloto na Ilinden," *Nova Makedonija*, 1–4 Aug. 2002, 11.

Trajanoski, Žarko. 2010. "Grčkiot virus," *Dnevnik*, 11 Jan. 2010, 9.

CHAPTER 9

Slovak national identity as articulated in the homilies of a religious holiday

Alexander Bielicki
University of Oslo
alexander.bielicki@ilos.uio.no

Religious and national identity can be linked in various ways. This chapter examines how religious elites in Slovakia shape the parameters of the nation through discourse during their celebration of a religious-themed, state holiday *Sviatok Panny Márie Sedembolestnej* (Our Lady of the Seven Sorrows Day). The scope of this piece deals primarily with one question: How do the bishops and archbishops presiding over these events talk the nation, or more specifically, how do they present national history and represent national solidarity and homogeneity in their discourse? By examining the homilies delivered at the Slovak national pilgrimage, the main religious event of the national holiday, this chapter sheds light on how the Slovak Catholic religious elite discursively constructs ideas of national identity and nationhood.

Keywords: national identity, national holiday, religious holiday, pilgrimage, Slovakia, Šaštín-Stráže, homiletics

1.   Introduction

While Our Lady of Seven Sorrows Day (*Sviatok Panny Márie Sedembolestnej*)[1] has been celebrated as an official state holiday since 1994, the pilgrimage to the National Basilica in Šaštín-Stráže[2] (the object of Marian devotion from which

---

1.   Our Lady of the Seven Sorrows is one of the names given to the Virgin Mary in reference to the sufferings in her life. Mary, in this particular incarnation, as Our Lady of the Seven Sorrows, is considered to be the patron saint of Slovakia.

2.   Formerly, Šaštín and Stráže nad Myjavou were two separate villages, but they are now incorporated into the town Šaštín-Stráže. Often, references to religious events in Šaštín-Stráže will simply list the place as Šaštín, since the basilica is in that section of town.

the holiday stems) has existed in some form for several hundred years. Despite its long history, its designation as the Slovak national pilgrimage is a phenomenon of the twentieth century and its renewed popularity can only be traced to the 1980s. This pilgrimage, celebrated on 15 September, is the national celebration of Mary of the Seven Sorrows, and is not directly connected with any of the international celebrations of the Virgin Mary among Catholics. Celebrations and feasts commemorating the Seven Sorrows of Mary are not specific to Slovakia, and according to the Catholic Church, these commemorations are prescribed to fall on the Friday before Palm Sunday or 15 September – before 1913, the third Sunday in September (Holweck 1912). This particular commemoration, though, corresponds to an established state holiday, thereby increasing the visibility of the event. The Catholic Church in Slovakia seems to be nearly alone in elevating this September commemoration of Our Lady of the Seven Sorrows to such prominence; however, other countries, nations, and regions certainly have their own days devoted to the Sorrowful Mother. Of course, 15 September is not the only celebration devoted to Mary in Slovakia, as the country has a long history of Marian devotion which manifests itself in pilgrimages and celebrations throughout the year, at many different locations.

Thousands of believers flock to the National Basilica every year on 15 September, and several TV channels offer live broadcasts so that audiences can participate in the event from home. In addition, members of the National Council[3] are guests of honor for the pilgrimage event, and even the president of the Slovak Republic often attends. In one sense, Our Lady of Seven Sorrows Day can be said to be a church-supported state holiday; yet in another sense, it is a state-supported church ritual. The event's religious aspects certainly receive primacy over its national aspects; however, some participants do show up with Slovak flags, and the nation may be referenced often throughout the event. Undoubtedly, the event is both religious and national, and these two aspects coincide to form an event of importance for many participants. Religious symbols of the event may be re-appropriated for national purposes, and national discourse is often inserted into the event's religious speeches. How, then, are the *national* elements utilized to reinforce the *religious* elements of the event, or how do the two coincide to strengthen their respective roles? How do the event's main speakers *talk the nation*, and how does this talk resonate with participants?

This chapter deals primarily with one of these questions: How do the event's main speakers talk the nation? Or, more specifically, how do they present national history and represent national continuity and homogeneity in their discourse?

---

3.   The Slovak parliament

Since 1989, questions regarding the connection between Catholicism and nationalist ideology in Slovakia have frequently revolved around nationalist proclamations by church leaders, around commemorations of the World War II Slovak state and its leader Jozef Tiso, and, less frequently, around the lack of Hungarian representation among the clergy in Slovakia. This chapter looks beyond these headlines to some of the more subtle connections between national identity and Catholicism. Instead of looking for nationalist proclamations in the event's speeches, I examine how discourse concerning the nation is constructed by religious elites for the purposes of this national holiday and pilgrimage. In other words, I examine how aspects of national identity and history play out in the discursive performance of this holiday.

This particular pilgrimage event can be characterized as both *national* and *religious* in nature, and the combination of these two aspects is partially responsible for its popularity. In addition, its continued popularity, its ability to draw pilgrims, is partly enhanced by the existence of the national holiday.[4] Our Lady of the Seven Sorrows Day is the only major pilgrimage in Slovakia which has a corresponding non-working state holiday. Šaštín and the pilgrimage to the National Basilica have been invested with large amounts of symbolic capital during certain moments when the Slovak nation has been considered oppressed. When expressing nationalism was utilized as a seemingly legitimate form of protest against the policies and actions of a state over which many inhabitants of the largely Catholic Slovak lands felt they had little control, the symbolic capital created around pilgrimage events throughout Slovakia drew pilgrims for specific reasons, many of which concerned opposition politics. However, in present-day Slovakia, extra-religious symbolic connections with Roman Catholic pilgrimage have somewhat diminished. Often, nationalized events (or events claimed by the government in the name of the nation), fail to enthuse large segments of the populace who do not consider the nation (or the nationalized events) to be threatened, at risk, or otherwise endangered. When popular social movements no longer perceive a symbolic connection between themselves and a certain pilgrimage event, the event's appeal may drop sharply (Frank 2009: 180–181). A significant minority of the population still envisions the Slovak nation as under siege, as a group whose culture, language, and sometimes whose very existence is perceived to be threatened (especially by the Hungarians). Nevertheless, that Our Lady of the Seven Sorrows Day and the pilgrimage celebrated on that day are invested with more religious

---

4.   The popularity of the pilgrimage to Šaštín is encouraged by the existence of the non-working holiday associated with it. The non-working holiday is further protected by the concordat signed between the Holy See and the Slovak government, which forbids the government from removing existing religious holidays from the state calendar.

than national symbolic capital should not be surprising, nor, however, should it be considered self-evident.

In order to access the discursive links between nation and religion represented in this holiday event, I will look to the homilies delivered at the celebration. Homilies are part of the Catholic liturgy, addressed directly to the congregation. Technically speaking, the homily differs from the sermon in that the purpose of a sermon is to provide some form of religious instruction while the purpose of a homily is to apply scripture to real-life situations. "The homily is not a biblical lecture but a biblical interpretation of the life addressed to a particular liturgical assembly in a particular place and time" (Waznak 1998: 18). This viewpoint is particularly instructive for analyzing the homilies of this pilgrimage event, as these speeches should be viewed as proposed bridges between scriptural accounts and the lives of those assembled to participate in the celebration. Homilies express a theology of Catholic social life. They serve as a window into how the clergy believe Catholic religiosity should be lived.

Representations of the nation and of nationhood delivered in homilies during the national pilgrimage to Šaštín-Stráže have undergone certain changes over the past twenty-five years. The genre of homily is without doubt quite a standardized form, so the changes to which I refer are not those concerning style or structure. The changes which have occurred are changes in content and theme, in the choice of the symbols and metaphors used, and in the choice of the historical events referenced. In some cases, the same symbols and events continue to be referenced over time, but those symbols and events undergo significant reinterpretation.

The corpus of homilies delivered at Šaštín over the past twenty-five years serves as a commentary on many issues, but most notably for this study, on the ways in which the nation and national identity are envisioned by Slovakia's Catholic elite. Homilies do not stand alone as individual speech acts separated from other discourse within the Church. The homilies are influenced by myriad political, economic, social, and moral issues, both inside and outside the Slovak Republic. These addresses are shaped by society, just as they are attempts to shape it; they are reflections, and they are suggestions. They are shaped by other discourse within the Church, and through these reflections and suggestions offered within the homilies, they shape the Church's discursive landscape. For this reason, they are important discursive events to study, and while each homily may not be completely representative of the more prominent ideas within the Church at any given moment, they display the multi-vocality of the Church and the possible representations on offer; moreover, in this particular case, they display the possible representations of the nation.

1.1   Methodology

For the purposes of this study, I will employ social anthropologist Richard Handler's notion of nationalism as an "ideology about individuated being" (Handler 1988: 6). According to Handler,

> it is an ideology concerned with boundedness, continuity, and homogeneity encompassing diversity. It is an ideology in which social reality, conceived in terms of nationhood, is endowed with the reality of natural things.   (ibid.)

Both parts of Handler's definition are equally important. First, the nation must be conceived as a real entity, and second, a connection to that entity must have relevance for the beholder. This concept is not unlike that of entitativity, which has developed within social psychology. Entitativity can be described as "the extent to which a group is perceived as having real existence" (Castano 2004: 44). Handler's constituent concepts of national identity – boundedness in space and time, continuity in time and space, and perceived homogeneity – can be viewed as the prerequisites for giving a group identity *real existence*. Second, this real existence must attain real meaning, such that members of the group identify themselves readily with that group identity. Research in social psychology seems to show that the level of entitativity and the group's ability to engender identification among its prospective members are directly correlated. Essentially, there exists the objectification of a subjective group entity, accompanied by a constructed salience of that group identity.

In the selected homilies presented here, I am not looking for proclamations made in the name of the nation; instead, I am looking for the elements of national identity as enumerated by Handler. I am looking for representations of the nation, and how those representations are presented to the event's participants. I am looking for the ways in which this salience is constructed. Although this is the national pilgrimage to the National Basilica on the national holiday dedicated to the national patron, not all homilies delivered for this event are heavily laden with nationalizing language; in fact, some homilies for this event are very light in nationalizing language. For the purposes of this study, I have chosen two homilies which are filled with nationalizing language, the 1984 homily by Bishop Július Gábriš and the 2007 homily by Bishop Štefan Sečka, to more readily demonstrate the representations of the nation offered in the homilies delivered on Our Lady of Seven Sorrows Day. Furthermore, the selection of these two homilies becomes particularly interesting when comparing the nationalizing discourse of the communist era with the nationalizing discourse of the post-communist present. In addition, these two homilies have found audiences beyond the day of the celebration. They have been reprinted on devotional websites, and Bishop Gábriš' 1984 homily has even been published in Slovak Catholic devotional journals.

2. The 1984 homily

After the communist takeover of Czechoslovakia in 1948, many church activities were driven underground by authorities, but still managed to continue in some form despite the pressure. Monastic orders were suppressed, many Church officials were imprisoned, religious activities were confined within church walls, and new clergy had to be approved by the state. The government restricted new vocations and blocked church promotions, essentially attempting to create a situation whereby the old clergy would slowly die off and there would be few new priests to replace them. However, the underground church ensured the continuity of the Catholic Church in Slovakia by clandestinely ordaining new priests, performing sacraments and disseminating religious literature and news through samizdat.[5] The Seven Sorrows homily delivered in 1984, therefore, occurred in an environment where the Catholic Church, especially the underground church, was starting to better organize itself against the communist government's restrictive religious policies. In addition, around this time, pilgrimages generally started gaining momentum as a viable method of social protest against the state's religious policies. This particular pilgrimage was precipitated by a series of events concerning the government's rejection of a papal visit to Velehrad for the 1,100th anniversary of the death of St. Methodius; this rejection mobilized popular support for the Catholic Church and fomented anger against the state even before the pilgrimage. During this period, Slovak bishop Július Gábriš of Trnava delivered his homiliy for the Our Lady of the Seven Sorrows pilgrimage to Šaštín in 1984, in which he details for his audience a very particular Catholic history of the Slovak lands:

> V tej dobe v neďalekých Strážoch mala letné sídlo Mária Terézia. Aj ona počas svojho pobytu takmer každú nedeľu prichádzala ku kaplnke a veľmi zbožne sa modlila pred sochou Panny Márie Sedmbolestnej. A keď videla tie veľké zástupy, ktoré sem prichádzali na púť, dala si zavolať predstavených paulínov a požiadala ich, aby sa dali dostavania tohto veľkého chrámu. Dala im aj veľkú sumu peňazí a sľúbila im, že bude podporovať celú stavbu. Urobila to dosť tajne, veď bola cisárovnou v krajine, kde náboženské pomery neboli ešte usporiadané, kde bolo mnoho šľachticov protestantov, ktorí mali negatívny postoj k úcte k Panne Márii. Robila to teda viac-menej tajne a preto máme málo historických záznamov. Je však pravdou, že tento chrám by neexistoval, keby na jeho výstavbu nebola

---

5. See especially Doellinger (2002).

poskytla Mária Terézia veľkú finančnú pomoc. Roku 1764 bol tento chrám do-
končený. Na slávnostnej posviacke chrámu sa zúčastnila aj Mária Terézia so svo-
jím dvorom. Slávnostne preniesli sochu Piety z trohrannej kaplnky a umiestnili
ju na oltári. Odvtedy sa tento chrám stal pútnickým miestom zasväteným Sedembolestnej – Patrónke Slovenska.   (Gábriš [1984] 2009)

At that time, in nearby Stráže, was the summer residence of Maria Theresa. And
during her time spent there, she came almost every Sunday to the chapel and
prayed very piously before the statue of Our Lady of the Seven Sorrows. And
when she saw the large crowds which came on the pilgrimage, she gave a call
to the Pauline superiors and requested them to begin building this large cathedral. She also gave a large sum of money and promised to support the entire
construction. She did this quite secretly, as she was empress in a country where
the religious situation was still organized such that there were many Protestant
noblemen who had a negative attitude towards devotion to the Virgin Mary. She
did it more or less secretly, and because of that, we have little historical record. Yet
it is true that this cathedral would not exist if its construction had not been aided
by Maria Theresa's large financial contribution. In the year 1764, this cathedral
was completed. The ceremonial consecration of the cathedral was attended by
Maria Theresa and her court. Solemnly they carried the statue of the Pieta from
the triangular chapel and placed it on the altar. From that time, this cathedral
has been a pilgrimage site dedicated to Our Lady of the Seven Sorrows, patron
of Slovakia.

This excerpt, especially the last three sentences, portrays Maria Theresa as a supporter of Slovak Marian devotion. She was an active, very devout, supporter of
Catholicism; however, the images presented in this homily portray the importance of her sponsorship for *Slovak* Catholics, as opposed to the wider Catholic
community. The placement of the adverb *odvtedy*, 'from then' or 'from that time,'
indicates that Maria Theresa is significantly responsible for the institutionalization
of Slovak Marian devotion. Moreover, it legitimizes the humble beginnings of the
pilgrimage by adding historical star power in the person of Maria Theresa. In reality, the Pieta statue in question had been venerated by believers since the sixteenth
century, long before the basilica was constructed; and it had become a popular
object of pilgrimage since the early eighteenth century (Moricová 2007: 21–22).

Furthermore, Bishop Gábriš notes that "solemnly they carried the statue."
While "they" is probably meant in the generic sense of the word, the placement
of the phrase tends to suggest that Maria Theresa and her court carried the statue
to the altar. Given the tenuous situation of Slovak Catholics when this homily
was delivered, these images indicate that in the past, the Slovak nation has had
the support of important rulers, and while the contemporary predicament put
them at odds with the powerful communist powers, they still enjoyed the support

of historical heavyweights like Maria Theresa. Such a connection between Maria Theresa and the Slovak nation might seem out of place in present-day discourse stemming from church sources: now that Slovakia exists as an independent state, references to past periods of perceived subjugation are often unequivocally relegated to the dustbin, without contemplation of the period's relative merits.

Not only Slovakia's Habsburg past is referenced during the homily; there are even positive reflections specifically upon Slovakia's time in the pre-Habsburg Kingdom of Hungary. Hungarian kings Charles Robert and Mathias Corvinus are referenced in positive, even glowing terms as the rulers who, respectively, ended slavery in the Slovak lands and expanded Marian devotion throughout upper Hungary. The 1984 homily offers frequent references to the Slovak nation, but packages them in a Catholic history of the Slovak lands as an integral spiritual cog in the Hungarian Empire. Catholics of Hungary and the Slovak lands are presented in a shared history, whereas in the post-communist political situation, Hungarian and Slovak histories of the land are usually given quite contradictory treatments. In post-communist Slovak Church discourse, we find some examples of fostering a shared history between Hungarians and Slovaks, especially in the instances of Hungarian and Slovak bishops reaching out across the divide; unfortunately, though, these instances are exceptions rather than the norm (Moravčíková 2007). Nevertheless, they illustrate that within the Church, different formulations of the nation exist, and that the Church functions more as a battlefield on which this ethnic strife is played out, than as an actor in the conflict.

> Náš národ, milí bratia a sestry, prežil ťažké časy a zachránil sa iba preto, že sa opieral o mariánsku úctu. Spomenul som iba tri udalosti a to zánik Veľkomoravskej ríše, vpád Tatárov a stopäaťdesiatročné pustošenie Turkov na našom území. V týchto obdobiach boli všetky predpoklady, aby náš slovenský národ bol úplne zničený, vytrhnutý zo zeme. A predsa nezanikol! Prečo nezanikol? Len preto, že sa opieral o Božiu pomoc a o pomoc Matky Božej Bolestnej.
>
> (Gábriš [1984] 2009)

> Our nation, dear brothers and sisters, survived the hard times and was saved only because it relied upon Marian devotion. I mentioned only the three incidents: the extinction of the Great Moravian Empire, the invasion of the Tartars and the 150-year plundering by the Turks on our territory. In these times, all preconditions existed that our Slovak nation would be completely devastated, torn out of the earth. And yet still, it was not extinguished! Why not extinguished? Only because it relied on God's help and on the help of the Mother of God.

These words link the contemporary Catholic Church and the history of the Slovak nation in a chain of suffering. Furthermore, while the history detailed in the homily seeks to present the Slovak nation's suffering and its unwavering devotion to Mary, this version of history also reinforces the continuity of the Slovak nation. Handler notes that a "negative vision of the struggle for survival presupposes the positive vision of collective unity and maturity – for how can an entity that does not in the first place exist run the risk of disintegration?" (Handler 1988: 5). However, this is not merely a simple reification of the nation through building a collection of past sufferings. It not only reifies the nation, but also reifies a contemporary vision of the Slovak nation, imagining it as an unchanged group since the time of the Great Moravian Empire.

Also important to note is that shrines of Marian devotion often contain an element of *ethnic election*. The idea that Mary appeared to "our people" or bestowed blessings or miracles upon "our people," is a common theme. The Virgin "bestows a sense of choseness and specialness upon the persons to whom she appears, and upon the social collectivity – normally the ethnic group of a nation – with which these persons identify" (Skrbiš 2005: 448). So, the Virgin not only recognizes national difference, but selects a nation on which to bestow her blessings. While the specific miracles attributed to Mary (or theologically speaking, the miracles attributed to God through Mary's intercessions) are not directly referenced in the homily, the interwoven strands of national survival and Marian devotion highlight this connection between the Virgin Mary and the nation.

Strengthening the bond between Marian devotion and the Slovak nation, Bishop Gábriš repeatedly connects Mary's life with the life of the Slovak nation. Here is one of the more blatant examples:

> Náš slovenský národ strašne veľa trpel. Keď bolo s národom zle, mohol sa uchádzať len o nadprirodzenú pomoc. Naši veriaci tiež cítili, že nikto na svete netrpel tak, ako Panna Mária, keď držala vo svojom náručí mŕtve telo svojho Syna. Preto nikto na svete neporozumie utrpeniu nášho národa tak, ako práve Ona. Pre túto príčinu sa vytvoril taký teplý vzťah k Bolestnej Matke Božej u našich predkov. Preto si ju zo srdca uctievali a vyvolili za Patrónku.   (Gábriš [1984] 2009)

> Our Slovak nation has suffered terribly. When things were bad for our nation, it could only apply for supernatural aid. Our believers also felt that no one in the world suffered such as Our Lady when she held in her arms the dead body of her son. Therefore, no one in the world understands the suffering of our nation as she does. For this reason was created such a warm relationship to the sorrowful Mother of God among our ancestors. Thus it was from the heart that they worshipped and chose her for a Patron.

Not only does the 1984 homily directly address the history of the pilgrimage to Šaštín, it also provides historical examples which can be directly paralleled to the struggle of that time. Therefore, it not only treats the nation as a highly entitative unit, but also calls for the salience of that unit in response to the contemporary struggles (which are not mentioned directly, but which are referred to by Bishop Gábriš as "dark" or "difficult" times). The parallel between history and present fosters a connection between the vision of the historical Slovak nation and the vision of the contemporary Slovak nation, which can serve to create the illusion of historical legitimacy for such an emotional attachment. Furthermore, as in this excerpt, we often find highly similar vocabularies of struggle and suffering accompanying both the narratives of Our Lady of the Seven Sorrows and the narratives of the Slovak nation; moreover, an event such as this holiday lends itself quite well to joining these highly similar vocabularies. In 1928, one author even went so far as to posit the corresponding seven sorrows of the Slovak nation (Moricová 2007: 25). This type of discourse not only posits the nation as a very real entity with the ability to suffer, but also posits that it has suffered as much as Mary is purported to have suffered.

While history and suffering are thoroughly referenced in this homily, it can still be viewed as a somewhat inclusive representation of the nation in that it refers to a version of history that does not demonize neighboring nations, but instead focuses on oppression from outside forces. Furthermore, it even highlights contributions made by Hungarians to Slovak Catholic society. It is a history of opposition to non-Catholic powers usually beyond the borders of the Kingdom of Hungary, and it was this oppositional statement that was partly responsible for the success of this message.[6] In the mid-to-late 1980s, the Church gained the support of even those individuals who were nominally Catholic because they considered the Church to be the ideological opposition to the state. As for opposition in Slovakia, the Church was nearly the only game in town.[7] After the failure of the communist state, the Church lost its major enemy, and with it lost the unwavering support of the nominally Catholic. A new platform began to develop within the Church against the "imported" ideas of liberalism, cultural relativism, and humanism, all of which were equated with atheism. Moral issues failed to mobilize many of these nominal Catholics in defense of the Church. And although certain elements of the Church obtained indirect access to the state political arena during the 1990s, the Church's overall political influence nevertheless began to wane.

---

6. The 1984 homily by Bishop Gábriš has been reprinted in Catholic magazines several times since then and has also been published online.

7. For information on the environmentalist opposition in the Slovak lands, see Snajdr (2008).

3.   The 2007 homily

> In particular, the Church was very skilled in mobilizing people's energy and activity in a centralized, authoritarian state, ideologically and politically polarized, in which all contributors to debate taking place in the public sphere used the symbolic discourse of a black-and-white, polarized world, picturing opponents as enemies and accumulating categories of value-loaded classifications. The pluralistic world, relativism and tolerance, acceptance of differences and readiness to establish different platforms of interaction with people and groups of different worldviews, was for the Church a new world.   (Mach 2007:128)

The competition of ideas, this free market of thought, proved difficult for the Church to adjust to while it was still using the old formulations; however, in the homilies delivered over the past few years at Šaštín, one sees the face of a changing Slovak Church.

"Naozaj, Liberalizmus nás klame. Ponúkal slobodu, ktorá nás zotročuje," "Really, liberalism deceives us. It offered freedom, which enslaves us" (Tondra 2009). In one sense, not that great a shift has occurred. Under communism, the words coming from the pulpit in the National Basilica pleaded for unity against the prevailing politics of the day. Twenty years later, the plea is very much the same, only now directed towards the "imported ideas" of moral relativism and secular humanism, which have replaced the authoritarian dictates. Homilies from the past several years have concentrated on the evils of pornography, tabloid journalism, and abortion. These perennial issues of the Catholic Church have been discursively transformed into new trials for the Slovak nation, according to the clergy responsible for delivering the homilies at these pilgrimage events. In the following analysis I will use examples from the 2007 homily by Bishop Štefan Sečka.

> Dnes slávime sviatok Sedembolestnej a tu je príležitosť zamyslieť sa nad zmyslom našej národnej existencie a spýtať sa ako to, že my Slováci sme cez dlhé stáročia vedeli odolávať aby nás nepohltili a nepochovali dravé vlny dejín. Sme národom na ktorého hrade nevládla kráľovská dynastia a nemôžeme sa chváliť slávnymi víťazstvami. Predsa však náš národ jedno víťazstvo dosiahol, že po tisícročie mlčania a neslobody prekonal samého seba tak, že sa dnes môže postaviť medzi národy Európy. Z národných dejín vieme, ako ťažko zápasili naši predkovia o svoju existenciu, o svoj životný priestor, o svoju reč, o svoju vieru, o svoju kultúru. Zápasili, zvíťazili, lebo v tomto zápase sa spontánne utiekali k Božej Matke.
> (Sečka 2007)

> Today we celebrate the holiday of Our Lady of the Seven Sorrows and here is an opportunity to reflect on the meaning of our national existence and to ask how it is that we Slovaks, through the long centuries, knew to resist so that the ferocious waves of history would not devour and bury us. We are of a nation who did

not have a kingly dynasty to rule in our castles, and we cannot boast of famous victories. However, our nation reached one victory that, after a thousand years of silence and living without freedom, we were able to overcome, so that today we find ourselves among the nations of Europe. We know from national history how hard our ancestors fought for their existence, for their living space, for their language, for their faith, for their culture. They fought; they won, because in this game they spontaneously took refuge in the Mother of God.

Bishop Sečka offers the holiday as "an opportunity to reflect on the meaning of our national existence." This wording suggests that a salience of nation should exist for Slovak Catholics, and that a salience of Catholic identity should be present in Slovaks. The homily also speaks of a victory for the Slovak nation, a victory that can only be assumed to be the realization of the Slovak state, the ultimate reward for any national project. This type of rhetoric ignores the fact that the creation of the Slovak nation-state resulted from the intractable arguments of a small group of political elites, rather than from any outpouring of popular will or from a plebiscite. Discourse such as this takes the notion that the Slovak nation naturally requires a Slovak state and projects it back in time before the era of nation-building, suggesting that such a process is the unfaltering will and destiny of the nation.

> Drahá Matka, z histórie vieme, že tu už boli národy i kultúry, ktoré tieto otázky riešili podľa svojho úsudku. Dnes sú na nich už len spomienky, sú už históriou, zmizli v toku dejín celé národy a zanikli kultúry. Pomôž aby sme obstáli.
>
> (Sečka 2007)
>
> Dear Mother, from history we know that here were nations and cultures that addressed these questions according to their own judgment. Today, they are only memories, they are already history. Entire nations disappeared in the flow of history and cultures vanished. Help us to withstand.

This small excerpt is interesting for several reasons. One, it presents the life of nations as a constant struggle for survival, thereby using some of the vocabulary of struggle mentioned in regard to the 1984 homily. Also, this plea for national survival is constructed in the form of a prayer to the Virgin Mary, rather than as an invitation to the audience to help ensure the national survival. This plea not only reinforces the idea of "ethnic election" (referred to earlier) by assuming that Mary recognizes national differences and will bestow her blessings upon a particular nation, but it also employs an interesting rhetorical device by constructing this idea in the form of a prayer, which serves to make a statement on the importance of national survival more palatable to audience members who may be uncomfortable with overt nationalist proclamations.

In the following excerpt, Bishop Sečka uses yet another interesting rhetorical device. He extensively quotes an apostolic letter by Pope Paul IV, one written in the 1960s. By doing so, the bishop reengages forty-year-old ideas within a very new social context.

> Veľmi výstižne to napísal pápež Pavol VI. V apoštolskom liste Quam pulchram: "Neochvejnú vieru osvedčil v priebehu storočí aj slovenský ľud, vedený učením a príkladom svätého Cyrila a Metoda, a ani dnes od nej neodpadol. Veľkou útechou mu bola vrúcna úcta k bolestnej Panne čiže k Sedembolestnej, ktorú odpradávna jednomyseľne vzývajú ako Patrónku celého Slovenska. Keď ju potom začali zvlášť uctievať v šaštínskom chráme na území Trnavskej apoštolskej administratúry, náš predchodca blahej pamäti pápež Pius XI. ju roku 1927 svojou autoritou potvrdil za nebeskú ochrankyňu tejto krajiny. Táto svätyňa patrí celému slovenskému ná-rodu, sústreďujú sa tam početné púte veriacich aj zo vzdialenejších krajov: pri-chádzajú pred starodávnu sochu preblahoslavenej Panny Márie Sedembolestnej a vo vrúcnych modlitbách jej vylievajú svoje žiale a strasti". Takto chápali naši predkovia úlohu Matky Panny Márie v Ježišovom i národnom živote.
>
> (Sečka 2007)
>
> Pope Paul IV wrote it very aptly in the apostolic letter Quam Pulchram, "also the Slovak people, directed by the teaching and example of Cyril and Methodius, proved unwavering faith over the course of the centuries and even today have not fallen away from it. A great comfort to the Slovak people was the ardent devotion to the sorrowful Mother, who from time immemorial they unanimously refer to as the Patron of all Slovakia. When they began to worship her especially in the Šaštín cathedral on the territory of the Trnava apostolic administrative unit, our late predecessor Pope Pius XI, in 1927, by his authority, confirmed her as heavenly protector of this country. This shrine belongs to the whole Slovak na-tion; concentrated there are numerous pilgrimages of believers even from distant provinces: they come before the ancient statue of the Blessed Virgin Mary and in their ardent prayers they pour out their grief and sorrow to her." In that matter, our ancestors understood the role of Mary in Jesus's and in our national life.

Although most of the words from the last excerpt are not the bishop's own, his invocation of Pope Paul IV's message serves two functions: one, it reinforces the connection between Our Lady of the Seven Sorrows and the Slovak nation, and two, it contextualizes this message within the societal framework of 2007, one markedly different from that of 1967, when the Pope issued these words. It may be banal to point out, but this difference is especially important in the sense of na-tional politics. In 1967, the Slovak nation is perceived to be oppressed by the state; whereas in 2007, the Slovak nation is perceived to have a monopoly on state power within the Slovak Republic. When it was written, this apostolic letter was meant to encourage the Slovak nation (perceived almost as a singularly Catholic group) in its struggles for religious freedom. The battle for religious freedom in the Slovak lands has of course ended, thus these words must be understood in a new, vastly different context. When the Pope officially named Our Lady of the Seven Sorrows as Patron of Slovakia, obviously, no Slovak state existed. In the perception of some, the Slovak nation has gone from *oppressed* minority in the Czechoslovak state to *oppressive* majority in the new Slovak state. These words in their new context reinforce a vision wherein the Slovak Catholic voice speaks for Slovakia.

Handler's conception of nation becomes especially relevant in analyzing the excerpts presented above. The Slovak nation, in this last excerpt, is said to have had a connection with the Virgin Mary since "time immemorial." In Handler's terms, this phrase speaks to the continuity and homogeneity of the nation. Marian devotion is tagged as a defining characteristic of Slovak national identity; and therefore, "ownership" of this Marian shrine is vested in the "whole Slovak nation." Furthermore, continuity is also referenced, not only through phrases such as "time immemorial," but also through direct references to "our ancestors." These phrases project present conceptions of the nation into the past, giving distant ancestors certain qualities that are considered important in the present, insinuating the boundedness and salience of the nation even before the national projects of the last two hundred years. The passage stating that the Slovak people, "proved unwavering faith over the course of the centuries and even today have not fallen away from it," speaks even more to the concept of continuity, highlighting longstanding adherence to Cyril and Methodius's message and to the belief that this adherence exists unchanged until the present (until the issuance of the Pope's message).

Boundedness in space is referenced indirectly. The Slovak nation is said to correspond to the territory where these "numerous pilgrimages" take place. This small passage indicates a link between the nation and the territory. First, the shrine at Šaštín is dedicated to the Slovaks, and then the Pope's message connects all pilgrimage sites in the territory with the Slovak nation, thus reifying the territorial integrity of the Slovak lands and implying a national ownership of those lands. Pilgrimage can be considered a politically provocative act when the connection to territory is introduced. Pilgrims mark off territory when they cross it on their journey. Not only the sacred site, but often also the path to the sacred site can be claimed by the group attending the pilgrimage, a group which today is often considered in national terms rather than in other terms.

One common theme between the 1984 homily and the 2007 homily is that of Marian devotion as the method by which the Slovak nation can triumph over perceived evils of the time; how the representatives of the Church hierarchy conceive of the nation has changed, but the perception of its power to overcome adversity has not. The 1984 homily describes the nation's overcoming of Turkish and Tartar invasions as a parallel to the nation's possibility to overcome the imposed communist government, a type of rule considered by many to be an alien concept in the devoutly religious Slovak lands.

One fundamental difference between the homilies, insofar as the building of a past history is concerned, is the relative expanding or contracting of the national narrative, what is included and what is excluded from the narrative. The 1984 homily can be envisioned as the representation of a nation whose subordinate position is endemic. Within this frame, the possibility for positive reflection on some of the better aspects of past "outside rule" seems to exist, at least in this particular case. In this homily, we see an expanded view of Slovak national history from the end of the Great Moravian Empire to the present, a national history where positive aspects are possible even while the nation is under the control of "foreign rule." This view is in direct opposition to that concerning the one thousand years of oppression as proposed in the 2007 homily. The framework created by the "one thousand years" viewpoint makes a positive evaluation of any Hungarian connection, whether past or present, quite difficult.

4. Conclusion

As the content of a homily is inevitably contingent on the socio-political environment of the moment, the impetus of the messages delivered at the national pilgrimage has changed. The impetus has transformed in reaction to changing relationships within the Church, as well as in reaction to the Church's changing relationship with the state, with state political structures and with political parties within those structures.

The nationalizing language of the 1984 homily demonstrates an inclusive representation of the nation, a representation that invites people to join the opposition body politic referred to as the nation, a nation that, while Slovak in ethnicity, corresponds to the goals of other ethnic nations, most notably the Hungarian nation. Under communism, it was possible to envision certain nations as similarly subjugated; thus, in some situations they could be considered as brothers against government oppression. In certain circles, the nation became almost synonymous with opposition to the state, in that it evokes a dichotomy wherein the communist state is regarded as illegitimate, and the idea of "the people," in its incarnation as "the nation," is inserted into the legitimate counter position. Such a position allows for discourse which posits the histories of perceived ethnic nations as a common struggle. This language, and this vision, quickly faded after the end of the communist regimes.

Political culture in the early years of post-communist Slovakia was characterized by political moves based almost solely upon three things: contingency, parties with no clear platforms, and upon the resulting confusion (Cohen 1999). Parallels can undoubtedly be made to the case of the Slovak Catholic Church. During the final years of Czechoslovakia, in the Slovak lands the Church became synonymous with opposition, with the nation. Furthermore, the cause of the Church was aided by its connection to the West. Since the Church became the diametrically opposed opposite to communism (in Slovakia), once that battle was won, the discourse of political elites and the discourse of religious elites were no longer constrained to follow the same paths. Moral relativism and secular humanism became the new enemies of the day. These ideals are envisioned to come directly from Europe, specifically Western Europe. The dichotomy of two distinctly different Europes (Eastern and Western) still exists in the recent discourse of the Slovak Church. Whereas the West previously represented the freedom to practice religion and the freedom of open ties with the Vatican, now it represents hedonism, consumerism, relativism, and secularism.

I would argue that other factors, in addition to the prominent place of the Catholic Church in post-communist Slovak society, influence the Church's exclusionary language as well, especially the lack of a clear enemy, the Church's new attack on specific moral issues, and the trend towards a higher degree of conservatism within the Slovak Church. Yet, despite the inclusionary and exclusionary ends to which the nation may be utilized in the homilies of this religious holiday, the ways in which the nation is discursively represented are not drastically different. Bishops Gábriš and Sečka both make appeals to the boundedness, continuity, and homogeneity of the Slovak nation; and while they both demonstrate a similar continuity and both tag Marian devotion as a defining characteristic of the Slovak nation, they offer some different conceptions of boundaries concerning who is included and who is excluded. These implicit boundaries between inclusion and exclusion define their differences in representing the nation.

The homilies analyzed here exhibit a discursive framework through which the nation is treated as a highly entitative unit, not only through explicit declarations but also through implicit framing. This framing demonstrates the malleability of the representations of the nation, even while the subject of those representations is perceived to exist unchanged. Talking the nation does not only occur in *explicit* ways, and Handler's formulation of nation helps us to view some more *implicit* ways of representing the nation in discourse. The ideas of boundedness, continuity, and homogeneity are used in the national representations presented in these homilies, and that use not only reifies the nation, but creates a dynamic wherein the national and the religious are mutually reinforcing.

In the homilies discussed here, we find different representations of what the idea of the nation should mean for Slovak Catholics. We find constructions which serve to not only reify, but also to reinvigorate the nation. In the former, we find a triumphant history of Catholics in the Slovak lands punctuated by periods of national suffering; while in the latter, we are told the story of an unbroken millennium of suffering. These examples help to highlight the variety of ways in which the nation has been, and continues to be imagined by the Slovak religious elites over the past twenty-five years. These examples of elite discourse may not tell us how participants actually live these concepts, but they certainly give an insight into how the life of the nation is discursively constructed in regard to religious identity.

Primary sources

Gábriš, Bishop Július. [1984] 2009. "Beda národu, ktorý sa zriekol náboženstva!" Homily presented at the National Basilica in Šaštín-Stráže, Slovakia on 16 Sep. 1984. Quoted from *Christ-net.sk*, http://blog.christ-net.sk/?q=node/340.

Sečka, Bishop Štefan. 2007. "Homília zo šaštína na sviatok Sedembolestnej." Homily presented at the National Basilica in Šaštín-Stráže, Slovakia on 15 Sep. 2007. Quoted from *Magnificat Slovakia: Mariánske spravodajstvo a vydavateľstvo*. http://www.magnificat.sk/htm02/homsas.htm.

Tondra, Bishop František. 2009. "Homília Mons. Františka Tondru na pontifikálnej svätej omši na slávnosť Sedembolestnej Panny Márie, patrónky Slovenska, v Šaštíne." Homily presented at the National Basilica in Šaštín-Stráže, Slovakia on 15 Sep. 2009. Quoted from *Tlačová kancelária: Konferencie biskupov Slovenska*. http://www.tkkbs.sk/view.php?cisloclanku=20090918019.

CHAPTER 10

The Czech and Czechoslovak 28 October
Stability and change in four presidential addresses 1988–2008

Karen Gammelgaard
University of Oslo
karen.gammelgaard@ilos.uio.no

Presidential addresses given about the most prominent Czech and Czechoslovak secular holiday, 28 October, contribute noticeably to articulating collective identity. In this chapter, four 28 October addresses are analyzed: one by Czechoslovakia's last communist president, Gustáv Husák (1988); two by Czech president Václav Havel (1993, 1998); and one by Czech president Václav Klaus (2008). The addresses' contexts are described and their "staging" is analyzed. The main analysis concerns the presidents' selections of past events, their communication of their worldviews, and how their selected events and communicated worldviews tallied with how they categorized "us" and "them": Husák excluded most Czechoslovak citizens from the "us" category. Havel broadened the "us" category so much that he almost failed to delimit his audience from other collectives. Klaus clearly delimited the Czechs as a national collective. Yet he also came close to depicting the Czech nation as being under threat.

Keywords: secular holidays, Czech Republic, Czechoslovakia, genres, collective identity, Gustáv Husák, Václav Havel, Václav Klaus, presidential addresses, self-designation, genre sets, categorization analysis, modality

1. Introduction

When on the evening of 28 October 2008, Czech Republic viewers switched on their TVs to follow live the celebration in Prague Castle, they heard the announcer say that the celebration took place "tak jako každý rok," 'in the same way as every year.' However, during the next 90 minutes, the announcer repeatedly mentioned celebratory components occurring for the first time. A celebration, consequently, may be "the same" while simultaneously absorbing something new.

This chapter deals with stability and change in a central component of celebrating the *Den vzniku samostatného československého státu* (Day of the Establishment of the Independent Czechoslovak State) on 28 October, namely the president's address. I analyze four addresses: the address by Czechoslovakia's last communist president, Gustáv Husák in 1988 (Husák 1988), the two addresses by Czech president Václav Havel in 1993 and in 1998 (Havel 1993, 1998), and the address by Czech president Václav Klaus in 2008 (Klaus 2008). For analysis here, the address by Husák was accessed in its printed form. The addresses by Havel and Klaus were accessed on Havel's and Klaus' websites. When the addresses were originally given, in addition to their spoken versions, all appeared in newspapers. Three addresses, those given in 1988, 1998, and 2008, marked decennials of the establishment of the independent Czechoslovak Republic in 1918. The fourth address, Havel's in 1993, is included because it was the first 28 October address given by the independent Czech Republic's president. Following the breakup of Czechoslovakia, the Czech Republic came into being on 1 January 1993. Speaking on 28 October 1993, President Havel addressed a collective that now lived in fundamentally altered constitutional circumstances.

Yet 1993 was not the first year that 28 October was used to rearticulate identity. The day was first celebrated in 1919 after the Parliament of the Czechoslovak Republic pronounced 28 October as a state holiday.[1] Until 1938, the holiday was variously celebrated: celebratory addresses, military parades, concerts, and the unveiling of monuments (Hájková et al. 2008). Many celebrations included adoration of Tomáš Garrigue Masaryk, who had headed endeavors to establish an independent Czechoslovakia and who served as the new state's president from 1918 to 1937. After the Munich Agreement in September 1938, and during German occupation, 28 October could not be celebrated. Celebrations resumed in 1945, but soon after World War II, Czechoslovak communists attempted to appropriate 28 October for their political goals (Abrams 2005: 141). When they seized power in 1948, denial of continuity with the Masaryk interwar republic became a significant feature in their construction of "people's democratic Czechoslovakia." In 1951, the communist parliament renamed 28 October *Den znárodnění* (Nationalization Day), thereby linking it with nationalization decrees proclaimed on 24 October 1945.[2] Yet another symbolic value appeared after the 1968 Warsaw Pact invasion. The Soviet-backed communist leadership added the name *Den*

---

1. *Zákon ze dne 14. října 1919, jímž se prohlašuje 28. říjen za svátek státní* (Law of 14 October 1919 Proclaiming 28 October a State Holiday), *Sbírka zákonů a nařízení státu Československého*, no. 115 (1919): 123.

2. *Zákon ze dne 2. listopadu 1951 o státním svátku, o dnech pracovního klidu a o památných a významných dnech* (Law of 2 November 1951 on a State Holiday, Non-Working Days, and

prohlášení o československé federaci (Day of the Declaration of the Czechoslovak Federation).[3] Thereby, they connected 28 October with the only popular reform surviving from the liberal Prague Spring. Accordingly, specific commemoration of Masaryk's Czechoslovakia on 28 October was further undermined. In 1975, 28 October ceased to be a non-working holiday.

The genre of 28 October presidential address dates from 1919, when Masaryk spoke to Parliament on the first anniversary of the 1918 events (see reprint of his speech in Masaryk 2003).[4] His successor, Edvard Beneš, continued the tradition of speaking about 28 October, even while exiled in London during World War II.[5] The addresses given sporadically by political leaders on 28 October during communist rule (1948–1989) closely agreed with the communist interpretation of the day. For instance, in 1958, the main celebration occurred under the slogan *1919–1958 – Bez Velké říjnové socialistické revoluce by nebylo samostatného Československa*, '1919–1958 – Without the Great October Socialist Revolution there would have been no independent Czechoslovakia' (*Rudé právo*, 29 Oct. 1958). And in 1978, President Husák addressed "60. výročí vzniku Československé republiky a 10. výročí přijetí zákonu o Československé federaci," 'the sixtieth anniversary of the establishment of Czechoslovakia and the tenth anniversary of the passage of the bill on the Czechoslovak federation' (Husák 1979).

As of 2010, 28 October is the Czech Republic's most prominent secular holiday.[6] Politicians and citizens give comparable attention only to 17 November, *Den boje za svobodu a demokracii* (The Day of Struggle for Freedom and Democracy), marking communism's fall in 1989, and to 8 May, *Den vítězství* (Victory Day), marking World War II's end. On these two days, both non-working holidays, celebrations focus on the fight against totalitarianism. *Den českého státnosti* (The Day of Czech Statehood), 28 September, receives little interest. For instance, it has not sparked any tradition of presidential address. In the official calendar, 1 January is called *Den obnovy samostatného českého státu* (The Day of the Recovery of the Independent Czech State). This holiday marks the materialization of the

---

Days of Remembrance and Significance), *Sbírka zákonů republiky Československé*, no. 47 (1951):250–251.

3.   The federalization law was ratified on 27 October 1968.

4.   See also Masaryk's 1928 address (Masaryk 1994).

5.   See for instance reprint of Beneš's 1940 address in Beneš (1947).

6.   In 2000, parliamentarians passed the law on the set of holidays. See *Zákon ze dne 29. června 2000 o státních svátcích, o ostatních svátcích, významných dnech a o dnech pracovního klidu* (Law of 29 June 2000 on State Holidays, Other Holidays, Days of Significance, and Non-Working Days), *Sbírka zákonů Česká republika*, no. 73 (2000):3526.

independent Czech Republic in 1993. Because it falls on New Year's Day and because many Czechs regret Czechoslovakia's breakup, its symbolism is generally ignored. The president's address on 1 January resembles New Year's addresses by other European heads of state.

2.   Method

The four selected presidential addresses about 28 October will be analyzed on the basis of genre. Genre is a dynamic response to and construction of a recurring situation (Devitt 2004: 13). In other words, in the concept of genre, stability and change meet. Stability stems from texts of a particular genre displaying similar features. For instance, same-genre texts are created by people in similar positions, they concern a recurring event, they disseminate similarly, and they include similar sets of recognizable discursive devices. On the other hand, when preparing a new text in a particular genre, those involved use their individual ability and creativity. These individual contributions provide the genre with change.

For analytical purposes, genres can be viewed both as typified social practices and as discourse structure types (van Dijk 2008). As typified social practices, genres represent what people do in recurrent situations. As discourse structure types, genres explain how people recognize typified social practices. Analyzing a genre's typified social practice and discourse structure type, we should remember that they are two sides of the same coin. Changes in discursive structure equal changes in social practice and vice versa.

Paradoxically, a genre's relative stability enables us to study both social and discursive change. In our case, because the social practice of giving the presidential address remained relatively stable, we may detect changed ways of using discursive means. Similarly, because the discourse structure type of the addresses remained relatively stable, we may uncover changes regarding the speakers' priorities and stances, and regarding the circumstances under which the presidents gave the addresses. This chapter's descriptions of the presidential addresses contribute to characterizing the genre as it has evolved since 1988 and to characterizing it as being different from related genres, such as commemorative speeches on other occasions.

Overall, as discursive structure types, the 28 October presidential addresses are characterized by reference to the addressed community and by use of linguistic means that position it in time and space. This positioning conditions delimitation of the addressed collective. Regarding stylistics, speaking about the most prestigious secular holiday, presidents will use formal to bookish language. All addresses analyzed here were read aloud by middle-aged, male presidents standing before an audience in Prague Castle. Mass media broadcasted the addresses live and newspapers reprinted them.

As social practices, the state holiday addresses are, in general, used by the presidents to articulate the identity of the community they serve and of which they are members. They "self-designate" the addressed community (Megill 1998). In doing so, they reflect upon the community's past, present, and future. Presumably, their reflections rise above day-to-day concerns and deal with the long course of history, particularly on decennials such as those analyzed here – the seventieth, eightieth, and ninetieth anniversaries of the 1918 events – and on the first state holiday celebrated in the Czech Republic, in 1993.

When in their addresses the presidents articulated identity, their articulating had a performative function: By giving the addresses, they re-established the community. All articulations of identity have this performative function. However, presidents "talk community" from a particularly forceful position. As the symbol of the state and as its head, a president speaks as a member of that state community and simultaneously addresses other members from above. Additionally, the systems of collective memory, which cultivate, for instance, the institution of secular holidays, strengthen the position of the president's state holiday address. The public will consider the 28 October address important and relevant even before the president delivers it. Finally, the president's personal achievement and public standing, his *ethos*, may reinforce his address's performative power. In these respects, Presidents Husák, Havel, and Klaus differed profoundly. When Husák spoke in 1988, he personified a state in an economic, moral, and political morass. Havel, the former dissident and acclaimed hero of the 1989 Velvet Revolution, enjoyed unrivaled popularity, although some, including Klaus, continually criticized his allegedly naïve conception of politics. A right-wing liberal, Klaus provoked affinity as well as antipathy.

Analysis of the presidential addresses' verbal means forms the bulk of this chapter. However, the addresses are interrelated with other genres sharing the overarching purpose of celebrating 28 October. They are also interwoven with co-occurring non-verbal symbolic components and events. I will describe these contexts first.

3.   Contexts

The presidents gave their addresses in specific political, social, and cultural contexts. These contexts changed thoroughly in Czechoslovakia and later in the Czech Republic in the 1988–2008 period. I recapitulate only the major constitutional changes. The end of communist one-party rule occurred as a "negotiated collapse" (Civín 2005): Mass rallies began on 17 November 1989, Husák resigned as president on 10 December, and Havel was elected his successor on 29 December. Czechoslovakia's breakup, prepared during 1992, occurred peacefully. Havel, then Czechoslovak president, resigned in July 1992, but became the Czech Republic's president in February 1993. In 1999, the Czech Republic joined NATO. Klaus was elected president in February 2003. In 2004, following a referendum, the Czech Republic joined the EU. A well-known Euro-skeptic, Klaus blocked the Lisbon Treaty ratification process by delaying the Czech Republic's ratification until November 2009.

Prior to 1988, public discourse on 28 October was almost non-existent. The state-controlled media largely ignored the day and no celebrations occurred. Surprisingly, in late September 1988, via a statutory measure, communist authorities proclaimed 28 October *Den vzniku samostatného československého státu* (The Day of the Establishment of the Independent Czechoslovak State) and re-launched it as a non-working holiday.[7] Perhaps via this maneuver, they hoped to calm growing social unrest. Recently, on 21 August 1988, large demonstrations had commemorated the 1968 Soviet invasion.

The reemergence of 28 October as a state holiday called for new ways of celebrating. A new set of genres with that overarching purpose emerged. Genres initiated and controlled by the authorities included speeches by communist leaders, editorials, interviews, opinion articles, reportages, the president's decision on amnesty, a television play, historical commentaries, and congratulatory telegrams – that from the Central Committee of the Soviet Union's Communist Party was given prominence. Additionally, on 27 October, a delegation of state echelons laid wreaths on Masaryk's grave, a mass rally took place, and salutes were fired in Prague and Bratislava. On 28 October, recruits swore their military oath and the National Theatre gave a festive performance (Bedřich Smetana's opera *Libuše*). Moreover, the opposition took action. The dissident Charter 77 movement issued what its spokespersons termed a "meditation for the anniversary of the republic" (Devátý et al. 1990). Also, a new generation of protesters organized a rally to celebrate the state holiday. They managed to read aloud a declaration before riot police intervened. Seemingly, President Husák's address failed to stand out amongst

---

7.   *Zákonné opatření předsednictva Federálního shromáždění ze dne 21. září 1988, kterým se mění a doplňuje zákon č. 93/1951 Sb. o státním svátku, o dnech pracovního klidu a o památných a významných dnech* (Statutory Measure of the Presidency of the Federal Assembly of 21 September 1988 Amending Law No. 93/1951 Sb. concerning a State Holiday, Non-Working Days, and Days of Remembrance and Significance), *Sbírka zákonů Československá socialistická republika*, no. 30 (1988): 830.

this eruption of state holiday activities. Contemporaneous newspapers show no resonance of his address.

Genre variety is difficult to compare across 1989 because public life changed fundamentally after communism's fall. Clearly, however, the years 1990–1992 saw only ephemeral genres relating to 28 October, such as an "anniversary congratulation," a "declaration on the establishment of the republic" by former dissidents, and addresses by various politicians, including one by President Havel during tumult in Bratislava on 28 October 1991. In sum, in these years, instability characterized 28 October celebrations. The list of laureates appointed on the day (first used in 1991) seems the most lasting state holiday genre from the years when Czechoslovakia disintegrated.

Since then, the situation has stabilized so that a relatively stable set of genres reappears every year. Typical genres include: the presidential address, the list of laureates, addresses by intellectuals, artists, and politicians (including those from extremist parties), round-table discussions, reports from celebrations, and newspaper comments (editorials occur rarely). Regarding dissemination and resonance, the presidential address surpasses all other genres. Broadcast live on all major television channels and on radio, and reprinted or reported in all major newspapers, it is often commented upon by political observers.

The presidential address has its fixed place in the sequence of the president's activities on 28 October. At Prague Castle, the president names new generals and soldiers swear the military oath. The president also visits monuments. Havel put flowers at the statue of Saint Wenceslas in Wenceslas Square in downtown Prague, whereas Klaus has laid wreaths at the statue of Masaryk near Prague Castle. Furthermore, the presidential address connects to local celebrations throughout the country. In recent years, on 28 October, citizens enjoy free entrance to museums and other cultural institutions, and they may visit central political institutions, such as Parliament.

In a narrow perspective, the presidential address interrelates with celebratory components occurring on the same spot immediately before, during, and just after the address. Using a theatrical term, I call the composition of these components the address's *staging*.[8]

In 1988, Husák gave his address on 27 October in the Spanish Hall at Prague Castle (Figure 1).

The address's staging imitated a Party meeting. Indeed, the address was given as the main component of the "festive meeting of the Central Committee of The Czechoslovak Communist Party." The Spanish Hall was decorated with the

---

8. Staging is described based on newspaper reportages, photos, and multimedia.

Figure 1. Husák delivering his address on 27 October 1988. Photo: CTK

Czechoslovak and the Red flags, a large number "70," and a red banner with the slogan *V pevné jednotě lidu, národů a národností ČSSR za další rozkvět socialistické vlasti*, 'In firm unity of the people, the nations and the ethnic groups of CSSR for the purpose of further flourishing of the socialist fatherland,'[9] Prominent Central Committee members sat facing the audience in the hall, literally backing up Husák. Party members and diplomats made up the audience. Before Husák spoke, the Czechoslovak state anthem was played and the Party's first secretary opened the meeting. After Husák finished his address, the *Internationale* resounded throughout the hall.

Since 1991, the presidential address has been delivered at a fixed time (evening, 28 October) and in a fixed place (Vladislav Hall in Prague Castle). Also, the linkage between the address and the laureate medal presentation stems from 1991. After Czechoslovakia's breakup, the presentation was interrupted until 1995 because the Czech Parliament had to first adopt a new law on medals. Since then,

---

9.   The slogan was used also on banners in the mass rally organized by authorities in Wenceslas Square on 27 October 1988; it appeared at the top of the front page of the communist daily *Rudé právo* on 28 October 1988, and as the heading of Husák's address in that issue. Also, Husák quoted the slogan in closing his address. Such verbatim re-use of texts and sequences across genres characterizes communist new-speak.

Figure 2. Havel delivering his address on 28 October 1993. Photo: CTK

the presentation has been a poignant component of the celebration. The presentation follows immediately after the presidential address. The laureates, often tearfully, listen attentively as the chancellor reads aloud each medal commendation before the president presents each medal. Often the commendations tell stories of endured hardships. Because the laureates are rewarded for past deeds, the medal presentation links the past and the present. The names of each year's laureates are kept secret until the presentation. Disclosure of the laureates' names works as a dramatic tool, attracting the citizens' attention. Consequently, the presidential address is situated immediately before the day's emotional culmination.

Whereas the medal presentation has remained relatively stable, other staging components have changed. As Figure 2 shows, the staging of Havel's 1993 address featured symphony musicians. Most likely, pieces played included the national anthem. (Sources do not specify the musical pieces.) Flowers predominated amongst decorations in Vladislav Hall. In addition, Speaker of Parliament Milan Uhde and (then premier) Václav Klaus gave addresses at the evening celebration. President Havel and guests wore dark suits. Commentators characterized the celebrations as modest.

The staging of Havel's address in 1998 (Figure 3) did not change much from that of 1993, whether due to Havel's general lack of interest in pomp or due to his poor health that, in the last years of his presidency, limited his public appearances.

Figure 3. Havel delivering his address on 28 October 1998. Photo: CTK, Judita Thomová-Mauerová and Tomáš Železný

Figure 4. Klaus delivering his address on 28 October 2008. Photo: CTK, Michal Doležal

The low-key celebrations on Czechoslovakia's eightieth anniversary were criticized by right-wing politicians, who found that they lacked dignity and wide public attention.

After Klaus took office, staging of the 28 October address changed again (Figure 4). On 28 October 2008, the audience in Vladislav Hall consisted of the political elite and high-ranking state officials accompanied by spouses. Women wore evening gowns and many men wore black tie. Many wore uniforms or other official dresses. A large Czech flag hung from the renaissance ceiling. The Czech coat of arms decorated the president's lectern. Behind the president at the lectern, that year's laureates were seated; members of the presidential guard held flags and banners.

The celebration proceeded as follows:

1. Entrance of president's spouse, heads of the Senate and the Parliament, former President Havel, and spouses accompanied by fanfare
2. Entrance of banners from World War I accompanied by fifteenth century Hussite chorale[10]
3. Entrance of the national flag and the president's flag
4. Entrance of the president to fanfare from Bedřich Smetana's opera *Libuše*
5. National anthem
6. Presidential address
7. Presentation of medals

In sum, the staging accumulated symbols of Czechness. It pointed to an ancient, cultured national collective with military traditions. The staging of Klaus's address differed not only from the pronounced communist staging of Husák's address in 1988, but also from the relatively low-key staging during Havel's presidency. Most importantly, the staging of Klaus's address was heavily endowed with national Czech symbols.

4. Verbal means

In their addresses, the presidents articulated their selections of past events and their worldviews. The verbal means used for these purposes often express other things simultaneously. I analyze only how the presidents articulated (1) Fixed points, (2) "Us" versus "them" categorization, and (3) Modality.[11] Fixed points are

---

10. The musical pieces referred to several historical layers. For instance, the Hussite chorale referred to the fifteenth century and to Masaryk's interwar Czechoslovakia, when the chorale was played at most state and military celebrations.

11. The delivery of the addresses (the presidents' voice quality, tempo, eye movements etc.) is not analyzed here. Also, the media design is not analyzed (see Sauer 2007 for an analysis of media design of addresses by heads of state). In the TV broadcast, the camera's movements, distance and positioning, and the cuts participate in the complex semiotic construction of the address. Other semiotic resources participate when the address is reprinted in newspapers.

those "fateful events from the past" (Assman 1995) that the presidents chose to include in their addresses. The fixed points form the backbone of the presidents' interpretation of the past. Thus, it is useful to analyze them first. "Us"/"them" categorization is analyzed because "us" and "them" are the most general categories that presidents may use when they delimit the addressed community. Analyzing modality reveals both the presidents' stances concerning the fixed points and their beliefs that caused their "us"/"them" categorization. I analyze these facets across the four selected presidential addresses, although also regarding verbal means, Husák's address differed fundamentally from Havel's and Klaus's. For instance, using numerous clichés typical of communist language, Husák spoke far longer than his successors did.[12]

4.1   Fixed points

In Tables 1–3, each president's selected past events are listed by giving their approximate years. I include the original wording since, in the actual addresses, form is inseparable from the different ways of conceiving the same event.

For his address, Husák chose fixed points typical of the Czechoslovak communist party's general narrative. The past begins about the time of industrialization. The Russian October Revolution is a seminal event. The 1918 events are but new circumstances in class struggle. The Party's founding, its seizing power, and its allegedly many successes and only few mistakes on the road towards socialism constitute the events to be memorized.

In addition to the many clichés used to express the fixed points, a common feature of all fixed points concerns the agency of the Communist Party and of the Soviet Union. Husák's narrative of the past left little room for other agents.

Unsurprisingly, Havel chose different fixed points. In both his addresses, 1918 functioned as the focal point, depicted as a watershed in the community's past. He referred to the more distant past only generally. In the 1993 address, he also included the first era of international constitutionalism. Inevitably, in 1993 he had to refer to the recent events leading to the Czech Republic's establishment. He did not repeat those events as a fixed point in 1998, however. Instead, the fixed points included general experiences with twentieth century totalitarianism.

Havel's narrative of the past, thereby, included continuity of the Czech Republic's territory. Yet its main emphasis concerned those events where the Czechs had participated in the general successes and failures of Western liberal democracies.

---

12. Husák used approximately 4200 words. Havel in 1993 used 730 words and in 1998 used only 675 words. Klaus used 1234 words.

Table 1. Husák's fixed points

1918	"celkově však společenské poměry v novém státu určoval třídní charakter jeho politického systému," 'overall, however, the class character of its political system determined social conditions in the new state.'
1921	"Rok 1921 se vytvořila revoluční strana – Komunistická strana Československa," 'In 1921, a revolutionary party emerged – The Communist Party of Czechoslovakia.'
1945	"Nikdy nezapomeneme, že rozhodující sílou, která rozdrtila hitlerovský fašismus a přinesla svobodu Československu i jiným národům, byl sovětský lid a jeho slavná Rudá armáda." 'We will never forget that the crucial force that devastated Hitlerian fascism and that brought freedom to Czechoslovakia and to other nations was the Soviet people and its [sic] glorious Red Army.'
1948	"Díky revolučnímu postupu Komunistické strany Československa, která mobilizovala široké vrstvy pracujícího lidu, mohla dělnická třída definitivně převzít do svých rukou politickou moc." 'Thanks to the revolutionary policy of the Communist Party of Czechoslovakia, who mobilized the broad classes of the working people, the working class could conclusively take political power.'
1969–1971	"V poměrné krátké době a přitom politickými prostředky se podařilo zvládnout konsolidační proces ve straně a společnosti, obnovit hodnoty socialismu v naší zemi." 'In a relatively short time, and simultaneously by political means, it turned out well to manage the consolidation process in the Party and in society, it turned out well to revive socialist values in our country.'
1986	"Na neodkladné potřeby naší společnosti, na nové podmínky a tendence ve světovém vývoji reagoval XVII. sjezd Komunistické strany Československa." 'The seventeen Congress of the Communist Party of Czechoslovakia responded to our society's urgent needs and to the new conditions and tendencies of international events.'

The totalitarian past as a fixed point occurred also in Klaus's address, but Klaus more concretely mentioned the Nazi occupation and the Communist takeover; that is, he took a more narrowly Czech perspective. In contrast to Havel, Klaus highlighted World War I. He also highlighted those periods when the Czechs had been part of large empires, periods he implicitly compared to that of Czech EU membership.

Far more self-assuredly than Havel, Klaus referred to Czech nationhood and to Czech statehood as congruent entities. Yet he did not depict the Czech nation as monolithic: Many of his fixed points had provoked public disputes over their interpretation, and Klaus almost seemed pleased to accentuate these disputes.

In sum, regarding fixed points, the presidents coincided only in selecting Czechoslovakia's establishment in 1918. Their selections of all other fixed points differed. Husák selected those typical of the communist narrative. Havel selected those where the Czechs' history exemplified general trends of European and Western democracies. Klaus selected those showing dispute and the dangers to

Table 2. Havel's fixed points

Prior to 1000	"České země – se svou rozmanitě se proměňující státností – existují přes tisíc let." 'The Czech lands, their statehood changing in different ways, have existed more than one thousand years' (1993).
1775– 1789	"Tvůrci nové republiky vycházeli z naděje, že ideály francouzské a americké revoluce o občanské rovnosti se stanou základem nových vztahů mezi evropskými státy a národy" (1993). 'The new republic's creators proceeded in the hope that the ideals of civil equality of the French and American revolutions would become the fundament of new relationships between European states and nations.'
1918	"dnes je tomu sedmdesát pět let, co povstal lid českých zemí, aby v souladu s mnoha-letým úsilím svých politických vůdců vyhlásil samostatný stat," 'today, seventy-five years have passed since, in agreement with its political leaders' long-standing efforts, the people of the Czech lands rose to declare the independent state' (1993).
	"Když před osmdesáti lety vrcholil boj za naši nezávislost," 'When eighty years ago the struggle for our independence culminated' (1998).
1933– 1989	"Evropu zasáhl mor různých fašismů a posléze nacismu, jemuž evropské demokracie nedokázaly včas čelit […]. Desítiletími komunismu a rozdělené Evropy byla tato trpká éra dovršena" (1998). 'The plague of various fascisms and then of Nazism inflicted on Europe a plague that European democracies could not face in time […]. Decades of communism and of a divided Europe completed this bitter era.'
1992	"Nezanedbatelná část slovenské společnosti podpořila ve volbách politickou repre-zentaci, která dala po složitých státoprávních jednáních přednost samostatnému stá-tu před další existencí federace. Češi tuto vůli respektovali" (1993). 'A not insignifi-cant part of Slovak society supported in the elections political representatives who, after complicated constitutional negotiations, gave priority to an independent state rather than to the federation's continued existence. The Czechs respected this wish.'

a small nation. In their highly different narratives, also their interpretations of Czechoslovakia's establishment differed. Husák interpreted it as a rather irrele-vant step on the road towards communist victory. Havel interpreted it as a culmi-nation of meticulous work. And Klaus interpreted it as the Czech elite's victory in a conflict of interests.

4.2   "Us" versus "them" categorization

In everyday life, usually, people categorize while accomplishing something other than merely categorizing. In contrast, in state holiday addresses, presidents are expected to articulate the addressed collective's identity. Articulating identity entails categorizing as a central discursive activity. I loosely base the analysis of how the presidents categorized "us" and "them" on membership categorization

Table 3. Klaus's fixed points

About 900	"Česká státnost však za sebou v té chvíli měla již téměř tisíc let své existence," 'Yet in that moment, Czech statehood had already passed nearly one thousand years of existence.'
1620–1918	"kdy jsme byli součástí široce založeného rakousko-uherského integračního projektu," 'when we were components in the broad Austrian-Hungarian integration project.'
1914–1918	"První světová válka nebyla naší válkou, ale počet jejích obětí byl i u nás nesmírně vysoký," 'World War I was not our war, but the number of its victims was extremely high also in our country.'
1918	"je tomu přesně devadesát let, kdy byla obnovena naše suverenita," 'exactly ninety years have passed since our sovereignty was renewed.'
1939–1945	"I během nacistické okupace jsme měli v Londýně exilovou vládu," 'Also during Nazi occupation, we had an exile government in London.'
1948	"Když byla v únoru 1948 zlikvidována i ona okleštěná poválečná demokracie," 'When in February 1948, even that curtailed post-war democracy was eliminated.'
1968	"To se projevilo i v srpnu 1968. Tehdy šlo spíše o zásah impéria do svého neposlušného regionu než o okupaci jednoho suverénního státu druhým," 'This appeared also in August 1968. Then it was rather about an empire encroaching upon its disobedient region than about the occupation of one sovereign state by another.'
2004	"Jsou tomu čtyři roky, kdy jsme se většinovou demokratickou volbou občanů stali členy Evropské unie a dobrovolně jí předali značnou část své suverenity," 'Four years have passed since, via a citizens' majority democratic referendum, we joined the EU and voluntarily passed to the EU a considerable part of our sovereignty.'

analysis (Lepper 2000; Leudar, Marsland, and Nekvapil 2004). This methodology adds category-bound activities to the basic categories of "us" and "them."

Husák's category of "us" narrowed as he coordinated this category with his fixed points of the past. "Us" came to subsume the contemporary communist leadership only: *Marxisticko-leninské síly v Komunistické straně Československa*, 'The Marxist-Leninist driving forces in the Czechoslovak Communist Party.' In a parallel move, he gradually increased the scope of "them." "Them" subsumed not only capitalists, Nazis, and those who misunderstood national, social, and economic matters in Czechoslovakia. "Them" included also, for example, the mass media, *značnou část veřejnosti*, 'a considerable part of the public,' and those lacking discipline and showing indifference. "Us" acted according to knowledge and logic, whereas "them" lacked problem-solving abilities. Moreover, "them" acted with malicious motives. For instance, they *rozdmýchávaly nacionalismus a šovinismu*, 'were fomenting nationalism and chauvinism.'

Havel in 1993 faced the problem of categorizing the community left in the Czech Republic after Czechoslovakia's breakup. He referred to the addressed community both as *Češi*, 'the Czechs' and as *lid českých zemí*, 'the people of the Czech lands.' In addition, Slovaks were included in "us," namely those Slovaks who participated in establishing Czechoslovakia in 1918. Throughout the 1993 and 1998 addresses, Havel categorized Czech values as subsumed in general ones: parliamentarian democracy, the idea of the state governed by law, and the orientation towards Western liberal civilization (1993 address), and the ideals of freedom for citizens, equality between people, and the democratic Europe (1998 address). "Us," characteristically, *tuto vůli respektovali*, 'respected this wish' of the Slovak majority.

Both Havel and Klaus ascribed several negative qualities to "us": self-confinement, sentimental patriotism, mistrust, reactionary behavior (Havel), and frivolity (Klaus). Those negative qualities exceeded the negative qualities of the presidents' "them" category. In other words, both presidents saw Czechs as their own worst enemies. Havel and Klaus differed in how they ascribed those qualities to subgroups. Havel ascribed all qualities to all category members. Also, he mentioned Czechs' negative qualities only as possibilities of all Czechs. Klaus frequently referred to conflicting values and views within the "us" category, and he assigned those values and views to specific groups: people for or against remaining in the Habsburg Empire, people disagreeing over interpreting 1968 events, and people for or against more power to the EU. In many cases, his sub-categorizing constituted an opposition between elites and the common people. Masaryk and his supporters, emigrants fleeing totalitarianism, and resistance fighters in World War II, belonged to the elite. Also, Klaus's opening, in which he addressed explicitly TV viewers and radio listeners in addition to the audience in Vladislav Hall, fits this pattern.

In contrast to Husák, who magnified characterizing "them," both post-1989 presidents almost ignored "them." In 1993, Havel characterized carefully those who had opted for the independent Slovak state the previous year as "[n]ezanedbatelná část slovenské společnosti," 'a not insignificant part of the Slovak society.' He did not mention other non-Czech "them." In 1998, he mentioned no external "them" at all. When in 2008 Klaus included external "them," he portrayed "them," too, as an internally differentiated category. For instance, he underlined the conflict between the ideals and the *Realpolitik* of European powers:

> Važme si spojeneckých svazků se zeměmi, které stojí na stejných civilizačních hodnotách, na jakých před devadesáti lety vznikla novodobá republikánská podoba našeho státu. Nedělejme si však přehnané iluze o míře jejich altruismu. Mají své vlastní přirozené a srozumitelné státní a národní zájmy, tak jako je měly vždycky.

Let us appreciate alliances with countries maintaining the same values of civilization on which ninety years ago the modern republican form of our state emerged.
But let us not have any illusions about the extent of their altruism. They have their
own natural and understandable state and national interests as they always had.

4.3   Modality

I use the complex concept of modality to summarize various verbal means that
the presidents used to give their perspectives when, in their addresses, they articulated their audience's identity. Modality has been defined as "the space between
'yes' and 'no'" (Halliday and Matthiessen 2004: 147). Yet definitions of modality
differ; therefore, I apply rather roughly the notion and some generally acknowledged modality types (alethic, deontic, epistemic, and root).

Husák's address was governed by the alethic modality; that is, he expressed
necessities and possibilities from the standpoint of objective conditions: "Pře-
svědčivě se potvrdila životnost a pevnost spojení Čechů a Slováků ve společném
československém státu," 'The vitality and the firmness of joining the Czechs and
the Slovaks in the shared Czechoslovak state have been convincingly affirmed.'
The alethic modality correlated with the near absence of agency. Husák's address teemed with passive constructions and other constructions without human
agents: "Stále silněji se projevovala vyčerpanost možnost expanzívního vývoje,"
'The exhaustion of the possibilty of expansive development showed up in an
increasingly powerful manner.' Verbalizing himself as the possessor of objective
truths, Husák in his address showed no willingness to discuss. His address was
also entirely impersonal. He never used the first person singular. Similarly, he addressed the audience only once, when in the opening, he used the communist address: "Vážené soudružky a soudruzi, vážené hosté," 'Honored female comrades
and comrades, honored guests.'

Havel's 1993 address was strongly marked by the deontic modality; that is, he
expressed necessities and possibilities from the standpoint of social norms and
ethical principles: *I na to bychom neměli zapomínat*, 'We should not forget that
either'; *Stát se [...] těšil obecné úctě*, 'The state [...] enjoyed general esteem.' In
addition to a few instances of the epistemic modality (the degree of certainty),
instances occurred of the so-called *thetic* modality, a variant of the epistemic modality (Daneš 2000: 90). Havel presented his thoughts, arguments, and findings
as if saying, "That is how things are": "Dějiny se však neřídí a nemohou řídit jen
logikou citů," 'Yet history is not and cannot be governed just by the logic of feelings.' The teacher-like thetic modality occurred particularly clearly when Havel
assumed the interpreter's role: *Chtěl tím říct*, 'By that he wanted to say'; *Znamená
to, že*, 'This means that.'

Also Havel's 1998 address based on the deontic modality: *Dovolíte-li*, 'If you allow me,' *podle mého názoru*, 'in my opinion.' Again, the co-occurring epistemic modality suggested that Havel was not sure of his interpretation and that he was open to discussing it: *Myslím, že*, 'I believe that.'

In Klaus's address, modality took no prominent place. He avoided the intermediate space between "yes" and "no," between positive and negative polarity. Only a subtype of the so-called *root modality* occurred, namely the modality concerned with intention and willingness (Papafragou 2000): *Chci připomenout*, 'I will remind'; *Važme si spojeneckých svazků*, 'Let us appreciate allied covenants.' Polarity and root modality fitted Klaus's frequent mention of conflicting stances and his frequent use of confrontational means to link sentences: *Není to pravda, ale*, 'This is not true, but'; *ač je to minulost*, 'though it is the past'; *Zvítězila však koncepce jiná*, 'However, a different concept won.' If Husák articulated collective identity as a detached scientist, and Havel as a learned discussant, then Klaus articulated collective identity as a politician amid a fight.

5.   Conclusions

The four presidential addresses given about 28 October in 1988, 1993, 1998, and 2008 show few stable features. These concern the age and sex of the presidents, the script-bound oral delivery occurring at Prague Castle and being broadcast, and the inclusion of 1918 as a fixed point.

Changes appear more clearly. Most evidently, Husák's address differs so much from the post-1989 addresses that continuity of the genre may be questioned. Fundamental differences concern how his address was positioned against other events and public genres, staging, fixed points, "us"/"them" categorization, and modality.

Obviously, problems arise when we compare Husák's address, given in still existing Czechoslovakia, with those of the presidents of the successive Czech Republic. From 1988 to 2008, thorough constitutional changes and changes in public life altered the general context of the 28 October presidential addresses. However, throughout the period, the cause for celebration on 28 October remained Czechoslovakia's establishment, not the Czech Republic's. Therefore, in a sense, Husák had an easier task. He spoke from a position of clear continuity of the state established in 1918. Nonetheless, he failed to address precisely that continuity. His narrative of the state's seventy-year existence became a narrative of the narrow group of Party echelons who derived their legality from the 1968 Soviet invasion. The address scarcely differed from countless other addresses given by Party leaders in the last years of communist rule. To make things worse, Husák, a Slovak, spoke Czech. By shunning his mother tongue in favor of broken Czech, Husák failed to use language as a national symbol – for Czechs as well as for Slovaks.

Havel and Klaus, on the other hand, have earned praise as sophisticated users of the Czech language (Kraus 2003). Their linguistic sophistication becomes all the more important as sociological research has showed that Czech Republic inhabitants consider the ability to speak Czech as the main element in Czechness (Vláchová and Řeháková 2009).

More similarities between the Czech presidents' addresses should be emphasized, such as their references to the ancient past of the addressed community. The choice of Vladislav Hall, the coronation hall of Czech kings, as the place of delivery constitutes a salient reference to ancient nationhood. Another important similarity was established in 1991 when the presidential address became linked with the presentation of medals.

Nonetheless, the addresses of the two Czech presidents also differed remarkably. Regarding "us"/"them" categorization, Havel's addresses may be characterized as abstract and general, at times perhaps even vague. Klaus's address, on the other hand, may be described as concrete insofar as conflicts are pinpointed. Provided nationhood is also about precisely delimiting a nation's individuated being (Handler 1988), then Havel's 1993 address almost failed to delimit the Czechs as different from any other (democratic, Western) nation. The differentiating component was essentially the centuries-long existence of the Czech lands. Yet, in both his addresses, Havel's means of modality signaled that his interpretation was open to discussion. Klaus delimited the Czechs as a national entity, particularly as opposed to supra-national polities. Simultaneously, he pinpointed conflicts within the Czech nation. This pinpointing may indicate that Klaus considered the Czech nation self-aware enough to endure open conflicts. Since he assigned conflicting stances to groups of people (however loosely characterized), he came close to using the discursive strategy of national identity that has been characterized as justification (Wodak 2006). He articulated national identity as being under threat from groups within and outside the Czech Republic. In the 1988–2008 period, 28 October has turned no less political, but clearly has turned more national.

Primary sources

Addresses

Beneš, Edvard. 1947. "Nepovolujte nátlaku! Projev k národnímu svátku r. 1940." In *Edvard Beneš: Šest let exilu a druhé světové války. Řeči, projevy a dokumenty z r. 1938–45*: 95–100. Prague: Orbis.

Havel, Václav. 1993. "Projev prezidenta republiky Václava Havla ke státnímu svátku České republiky." *Václav Havel's net site: http://www.vaclavhavel.cz/*, 28 Oct. 1993. http://www.vaclavhavel.cz/showtrans.php?cat=projevy&val=229_projevy.html&typ=HTML. 12 May 2009.

Havel, Václav. 1998. "Projev prezidenta republiky Václava Havla ke státnímu svátku České republiky." *Václav Havel's net site: http://www.vaclavhavel.cz/*, 28 Oct. 1998. http://www.vaclavhavel.cz/showtrans.php?cat=projevy&val=121_projevy.html&typ=HTML. 23 Oct. 2009.

Husák, Gustáv. 1979. "Úvodní projev na slavnostním shromáždění k 60. výročí vzniku Československé republiky a k 10. výročí příjetí zákona o československé federaci. 27. října 1978." In *Gustáv Husák: Projevy a stati. Květen 1976–prosinec 1978*: 97–105. Prague: Svoboda.

Husák, Gustáv. 1988. "V pevné jednotě lidu, národů a národností ČSSR za další rozkvět socialistické vlasti. Projev soudruha Gustáva Husáka na počest 70. výročí vzniku Československé republiky." In *Rudé právo,* 28 October 1988: 3.

Klaus, Václav. 2008. "Projev prezidenta republiky k 28. říjnu 2008." *http://www.hrad.cz/*, 28 Oct. 2008. http://www.hrad.cz/cs/prezident-cr/soucasny-prezident-cr-vaclav-klaus/vybrane-projevy-a-rozhovory/5.shtml. 5 Oct. 2009.

Masaryk, Tomáš Garrigue. 1994. "Prezident Masaryk k desátému výročí republiky." In *T. G. Masaryk: Cesta demokracie III. projevy, články, rozhovory 1924–1928*: 322–335. V. Fejlek (ed.). Prague: Ústav T.G. Masaryka.

Masaryk, Tomáš Garrigue. 2003. "Poselství prezidenta Republiky československé." In *T. G. Masaryk: Cesta demokracie I. Projevy, články, rozhovory 1918–1920*: 171–178. V. Fejlek and R. Vašek (eds). Prague: Masarykův ústav AV ČR.

Multimedia

"Předávání státních vyznamenání prezidentem republiky 2008." Česká televise video, 67: 44. 28. October 2008. *Czech television's net site.* http://www.ceskatelevize.cz/ivysilani/10205970779-predavani-statnich-vyznamenani-prezidentem-republiky-2008/?streamtype=WM3. 9 Oct. 2009.

Newspapers

Issues from 28, 29, and 30 October of the following titles:

Dnes 2000–2009
Mladá fronta 1986–1996
Lidové noviny 1987–2009
Právo 1995–2005
Rudé právo 1985–1992

CHAPTER 11

Disputes over national holidays

Bosnia and Herzegovina 2000–2010

Svein Mønnesland
University of Oslo
svein.monnesland@ilos.uio.no

This chapter analyzes the discourse of leading politicians in Bosnia and Herzegovina on the occasion of national holidays from 2000 to 2010. Fifteen years after the Dayton Agreement, Bosnia and Herzegovina has no common law on national holidays at the state level. This lack is due to varying concepts of history and how the state should be organized, and reveals deep-rooted conflicts in a society consisting of Bosniaks, Serbs, and Croats. Each of the two administrative parts of Bosnia and Herzegovina, referred to as entities, has its own holidays that are contested by the other entity. Within the Bosniak-Croat entity, there is a conflict between the two groups that constitute it. The discourse used to mark holidays is usually aimed at legitimizing one's own holidays and delegitimizing others' holidays. The analysis shows how the (de)legitimization strategies relate to time, space, and modality.

Keywords: Bosnia and Herzegovina, national holidays, political discourse, legitimization strategies, delegitimization strategies, discourse world, disputed history, Bosnian newspapers

1. Introduction

1.1 A state with no common national holiday

Bosnia and Herzegovina is an example of a state with no commonly accepted holiday related to state formation. A country normally needs symbols such as a flag, coat of arms, and national anthem. Many countries add a national holiday celebrating state formation to these symbols. All of the Yugoslav successor states have one or more national holidays (e.g., statehood days and/or independence days) regulated by laws that commemorate recent or older historical events significant for state formation. Taking into consideration the political context of Bosnia and Herzegovina, one can interpret the absence of an officially recognized national holiday referring to a significant event in the country's history as yet another indication of diversity and conflict in Bosnia and Herzegovina.

Because Bosnia and Herzegovina still lacks a common law on national holidays, the question of holidays arises frequently in political discourse. This chapter analyzes the rhetoric used by Bosnian politicians to mark disputed holidays.[1] The theoretical framework is that of Paul Chilton's (2004) approach to political discourse. The material consists of political speeches and other public utterances by leading politicians in the Bosnian media.[2] The focus is on late postwar Bosnia, 2000 to 2010. All major media were systematically investigated in connection with the holidays in question.

1.2   Analyzing political speeches

Political discourse, defined as politicians' use of language, always has a purpose expressed through specific linguistic means. Politicians use certain strategies to attain their aims. Chilton (2004: 45) postulates three strategies. The first strategy concerns coercion (setting an agenda and using power). The second strategy concerns legitimization (positive presentation of oneself and boasting) and delegitimization (negative presentation of others). Delegitimization includes differentiation ("us" vs. "them"), accusations, insults, and so on. The third strategy concerns representation (control of information, secrecy, and censorship) and misrepresentation (lies, omissions, denial, and euphemisms).

Through discourse, a politician explicitly or unconsciously reveals his "discourse world" (Chilton 2004: 54), which can be described by analyzing features such as time, space, and modality. Politicians are by definition concerned with time (past, present, and future), space (territory), and deontic modality (right and wrong regarding how the world should be). According to Chilton, positive entities of space and modality can be said to be "close" to the speaker, whereas negative ones are more "distant" (Chilton 2004: 58). The terms "close" and "distant" are

---

1.   "Bosnian" will be used throughout this chapter hereafter as a short term for "Bosnian and Herzegovinian."

2.   The material is taken from the newspapers: *Oslobođenje* (Liberation), a prestigious and independent newspaper; *Dnevni avaz* (Daily Voice), a popular Bosniak-oriented newspaper; and the two popular dailies *Dan* (Day) and *Nezavisne novine* (Independent News), the second published in Banja Luka, Republika Srpska. Online news is cited from FENA (the Federal News Agency), 24sata.info, and BH RAJA. See the list of primary sources at the end of this chapter. All translations are made by the author.

to be understood in the deictic sense, connected to the speaker (first person, *I*, *we*) or more distant (third person, *they*). The modal axis expresses beliefs and values, ranging from positive to negative. Politicians mostly connect positive words with themselves, their own party, or collaborators. The positive features typically belong to "us" and the negative ones to "them." A time axis is relevant in order to determine which historical period is important in the mind of the politician.

The following discussion analyzes the linguistic means of legitimization and delegitimization used by leading Bosnian politicians, and how they relate to time, space, and deontic modality.

1.3   The political framework

Bosnia and Herzegovina was one of the six republics of the Socialist Federal Republic of Yugoslavia. In 1991, when Yugoslavia broke apart, the ethnic structure of Bosnia and Herzegovina was 43% (Muslim) Bosniaks, 31% (Orthodox) Serbs, and 17% (Catholic) Croats. As a consequence of the breakup of Yugoslavia, Bosnia and Herzegovina was drawn into a war that lasted from 1992 to 1995. The result of the war and ethnic cleansing was a division of the territory based on ethnic affiliation.

The Dayton Agreement, signed on 14 December 1995, ended the war and was also the constitution of the postwar state. The Dayton Agreement made Bosnia and Herzegovina into a de facto federation of two administrative units called "entities" – the *Republika Srpska* (Serb Republic) and *Federacija Bosne i Hercegovine* (Federation of Bosnia and Herzegovina, hereafter the Federation), the latter consisting of mainly Bosniaks and Croats.[3] The two entities have their own assemblies and other political bodies. Above these entities is the state level. According to the Dayton Agreement, Bosnia and Herzegovina is one state with a central presidency, parliament, and other common institutions, such as the constitutional court. It remained unclear after Dayton how independent the two entities should be. The Dayton Agreement established the Office of the High Representative (OHR) to supervise implementation of the agreement. The High Representative was given authority to impose laws, dismiss politicians, and so on. The OHR's efforts to strengthen the central authorities were opposed, especially by the Serbian side. The growing independence of the Republika Srpska made it difficult to carry out unifying efforts (on post-Dayton development, see Chandler 1999; Bose 2002). On the Croatian side, there were efforts to establish a specific Croatian

---

3.   The administrative levels in the political structure of Bosnia and Herzegovina are state, entity, canton (only in the Federation), and municipality.

community, called *Herceg-Bosna*, but no such administrative unit was included in the Dayton Agreement and was not allowed by the OHR.

In addition to the two entities, there is a third administrative unit, the small District of Brčko in northeast Bosnia. During the peace talks, the municipality of Brčko was contested by Serbs and Bosniaks, and its status was not solved at Dayton in 1995. An arbitration agreement in 1999 established a district under international supervision. The District of Brčko, with about eighty thousand inhabitants (consisting of Serbs, Bosniaks, and a minority of Croats), has its own assembly and its own laws. It does not belong to either of the entities.

The post-Dayton period has witnessed a growing split between politicians of the three ethnic groups. Not only has it been impossible to introduce laws at the state level in essential fields of society, but state symbols are also contested. The leading politicians from 2000 to 2010 are briefly presented below.

The Bosniak Sulejman Tihić (*Stranka demokratske akcije* [SDA] [Party of Democratic Action], a nationalist Muslim party) was a member of the three-member Presidency from 2002 to 2006. He was replaced by the Bosniak Haris Silajdžić from 2006 to 2010 (*Stranka za Bosnu i Hercegovinu* [SBiH], [Party for Bosnia and Herzegovina], an alternative Muslim party, earlier a member of the SDA). In the Republika Srpska, the Serb Milorad Dodik was prime minister from 2006 to 2010, when he was elected president of the Republika Srpska, succeeding Rajko Kuzmanović (2007–2010). The Croat member of the Presidency, Željko Komšić (since 2006, re-elected in 2010), belonging to the Social Democratic Party, is considered a moderate politician. Dragan Čović, leader of the nationalist Bosnian-Croatian party *Hrvatska demokratska zajednica* (HDZ) (Croatian Democratic Union), was the Croat member of the presidency from 2002 until he was dismissed by the OHR in 2005. The discourse of these politicians reveals fundamental differences in the Bosnian political landscape.

1.4 Many holidays, none in common

Even fifteen years after Dayton, no agreement on holidays exists at the state level. Politicians have not been able to agree on which historical event(s) should be chosen to celebrate. The parliament has rejected proposed laws on holidays five times.

In the Federation, an amendment to the 1994 *Zakon o praznicima*[4] (Law on Holidays) was adopted in 1995, *Zakon o državnim praznicima Republike Bosne i*

---

4. *Službeni list Republike BiH* 13 (1994).

Hercegovine (Law on State Holidays in the Republic of Bosnia and Herzegovina).[5] Official secular holidays were to be 25 November, *Dan državnosti* (Statehood Day), and 1 March, *Dan nezavisnosti* (Independence Day).[6]

July 11 is commemorated in the Federation as *Dan sjećanja na žrtve genocida u Srebrenici* (Day of Commemoration of the Srebrenica Genocide Victims), in accordance with the European Parliament resolution of 15 January 2009.[7] This resolution calls upon all EU countries and the western Balkan countries to introduce a commemoration day on the anniversary of the Srebrenica genocide. Many countries have done so, but proposals to proclaim the date an official commemoration day in Bosnia and Herzegovina have not been passed in the parliament due to Serbian objections. In 2010, 11 July was proclaimed *Dan žalosti* (Day of Mourning) in the Federation.

The Bosnian Serbs have introduced their own public holidays. In 2005, the Assembly of the Republika Srpska adopted a law on holidays, *Zakon o praznicima Republike Srpske*[8] (Law on Holidays of the Republika Srpska): 9 January as *Dan republike* (Republic Day) and 21 November as *Dan uspostave Opšteg okvirnog sporazuma za mir u Bosni i Hercegovini* (Day of the Establishment of the General Agreement on Peace in Bosnia and Herzegovina); that is, the signing of the Dayton Agreement. The law imposes penalties for working on these days. Both holidays are connected to the establishment of a separate Serb entity within Bosnia and Herzegovina. A revised law was adopted in 2007[9] that keeps these two holidays.

The District of Brčko received its law on holidays, *Zakon o praznicima Brčko Distrikta BiH*[10] (Law on Holidays in the District of Brčko, Bosnia and Herzegovina), in 2002, imposed by the OHR. In the District of Brčko, the international

---

5.   *Službeni list Republike BiH* 9 (1995).

6.   The variant *Dan neovisnosti* occurs in some texts.

7.   European Parliament, RSP/2009/2502, "Resolution on Srebrenica," 15 January 2009, http://www.europarl.europa.eu/oeil/FindByProcnum.do?lang=en&procnum=RSP/2009/2502, 7 May 2011.

8.   Published in *Službeni glasnik Republike Srpske*, 27 July, 2005. Available at the website of *Privredna komora Republike Srpske*, www.komorars.ba/bbm_azzuro/dokument.php?id=667, 8 May 2011.

9.   *Zakon o praznicima Republike Srpske* (Law on Holidays in the Republika Srpska), *Službeni glasnik Republike Srpske* 43 (2007). http://www.narodnaskupstinars.net/lat/zakoni/zakon.php?id_zakona=231, 8 May 2011.

10. *Službeni glasnik Brčko Distrikta BiH* 19 (2002). http://skupstinabd.ba/ba/zakoni/ba/zakon-o-praznicima-br-distrikta-bih.html, 8 May 2011.

community, through the OHR, supervises everything that may be interpreted as expressions of nationalism, in schoolbooks and so on, and no holidays with a national affiliation are allowed. In addition to New Year's Day and 1 May, 8 March, *Dan uspostavljanja Brčko Distrikta* (Day of Establishment of the Brčko District), was introduced.

Regarding religious holidays, a great number exist in Bosnia and Herzegovina because the population consists of followers of various faiths: Muslims, Orthodox Christians, and Catholics. So far, no law has been passed at the state level to regulate religious holidays, only at the entity level. This chapter discusses only secular holidays.

Leading politicians' discourse on the occasion of holidays is analyzed below; first the holidays in the Federation and then those in the Republika Srpska. The utterances are not selected chronologically because the same rhetoric is repeated more or less in the same way from year to year after 2000. Typical utterances are quoted, not entire speeches.

2.   Holidays in the Federation of Bosnia and Herzegovina

2.1   Statehood Day: 25 November

In the Bosniak-Croat Federation, 25 November is celebrated as Statehood Day because in 1943 the Antifascist Council of Bosnia and Herzegovina (ZAVNO-BIH) adopted a resolution stating that Serbs, Muslims, and Croats should have equal status in the future in Bosnia and Herzegovina.[11] The Bosnian Council was part of Josip Broz Tito's Yugoslav Antifascist Council (AVNOJ), which functioned as a provisional wartime parliament dominated by the communists. Only a few days after the Bosnian resolution, on 29 November 1943, the Yugoslav Antifascist Council made its historical decisions on the future organization of Yugoslavia, and that date was celebrated as Republic Day in communist Yugoslavia. When the Federation of Bosnia and Herzegovina celebrates 25 November, that date thus has a very close connection to partisan warfare and Tito.

To mark the celebration of Statehood Day in 2007, the Bosniak politician Sulejman Tihić explained:

> Za svakog Bosanca i Hercegovca ovaj dan je najvažniji praznik u državi. Ovo je samo potvrda državnosti BiH i potvrda da je BiH bila na strani koalicije koja se

---

11. The Muslims, later named Bosniaks, were not recognized as a nation in prewar Yugoslavia.

borila protiv fašizma. Oni koji ne slave i ne priznaju ovaj praznik, ne priznaju Dejtonski sporazum i Aneks IV.   (*Dnevni avaz*, 26 Nov. 2007)

For every Bosnian and Herzegovinian, this day is the most important holiday in the state. This is only a confirmation of the statehood of Bosnia and Herzegovina and a confirmation that Bosnia and Herzegovina was on the side of the coalition that fought fascism. Those that do not celebrate and recognize this holiday do not recognize the Dayton Agreement and Annex IV.

On the time axis, for Tihić the most important event in the history of his country is the World War II. On the modal axis, it is a "confirmation"; that is, a legitimization of both statehood and participation in the antifascist struggle. The spatial axis comprises the entire country ("every Bosnian and Herzegovinian"). The opponents are accused of not recognizing the Dayton Agreement – a strong accusation because the international community considers this agreement to be the foundation of the state. The accusation may be felt to be insulting because the opponents, the Serbs, celebrate the signing of the Dayton Agreement (21 November). The Bosniak Haris Silajdžić stated in 2007: "Neki političari u BiH ne obilježavaju ovaj bitan datum i ja bih to nazvao političkom i ljudskom nepristojnošću," 'Some politicians in Bosnia and Herzegovina do not mark this essential date, which I would call political and human rudeness' (*Nezavisne novine*, 25 Nov. 2007). "Some politicians" refers, of course, to Serbian politicians in the Republika Srpska, and especially Dodik, Silajdžić's main opponent. Silajdžić's expression *nepristojnost*, 'rudeness' is quite a strong delegitimization of his opponents.

The Serbs deny the historical importance of 25 November 1943 because they claim that the Bosniak or Muslim nation did not exist at the time, and they therefore see the date as having no historical significance.[12] The underlying reason is that the leaders of the Republika Srpska do not want a united country and they see 25 November as a symbol of unity. To mark 25 November 2008, the Serb leader Milorad Dodik issued a statement criticizing representatives of international organizations and foreign embassies for supporting the celebration of 25 November. According to him, in doing so they disdain the institutions of Bosnia and Herzegovina. He concluded: "Proslava 25. novembra je vještačko forsiranje priče o nekom navodnom kontinuitetu državnosti, koji nije ni postojao," 'The celebration of 25 November is an artificial imposition of a story about an alleged continuity of statehood, which did not exist' (*Dnevni avaz*, 26 Nov. 2008).

---

12. The Bosniaks (then referred to as Muslims) were recognized as a nation by the Tito regime only around 1970. Earlier they had to declare themselves as Serbs, Croats, or Yugoslavs. It is interesting that the Communist Party introduced "Muslim" as an ethnic denotation. Only in the early 1990s was the historical term "Bosniak" reintroduced.

His delegitimization of others consists of negative expressions such as *vještačko*, 'artificial', *forsiranje priče*, 'imposing a story', and *navodni*, 'alleged'. His time axis does not go back to the World War II. He rejects historical continuity and thereby the legitimacy of the state based on the Communist Party. In observing 25 November 2010, Dodik was even more explicit:

> Onima, koji slaveći ovaj dan, pokušavaju da podvale istorijske neistine i svojoj i međunarodnoj javnosti, preporučujemo da još jednom pregledaju službene glasnike, pročitaju istorijske čitanke i svakako pogledaju Dejtonski sporazum. Svi predstavnici međunarodne zajednice koji pridaju značaj ovom nepostojećem prazniku ustvari doprinose podjeli BiH.
>
> (FENA, the Federal News Agency, 25 Nov. 2010)

> To those that celebrate this day, trying to deceive both their own public and the international community through historical lies, I recommend that they once again read official gazettes and history textbooks, and study the Dayton Agreement. All international representatives that convey any importance to this non-existing holiday are in fact contributing to the division of Bosnia and Herzegovina.

Because attack is the best form of defense, here Dodik accuses the international representatives of exactly what they accuse him of: division of Bosnia and Herzegovina. By calling the day "non-existent," in 2010 he used rhetoric that is more aggressive than that of his earlier discourse.

However, there is also disagreement within the Federation. Because of the connection to the Yugoslav Communist Party, 25 November is mostly celebrated by politicians from the Social Democratic Party, who have a historical link to the communists.

In 2008, the sixty-fifth anniversaries of both AVNOJ and ZAVNOBIH were celebrated. The Social Democrat Komšić participated at both celebrations. His speeches on these occasions are typical of his interpretation of Statehood Day. He argues that 25 November is celebrated as a commemoration of the World War II, of the establishment of ZAVNOBIH, and of Bosnians that gave their lives in the antifascist struggle. ZAVNOBIH is considered a symbol of a united Bosnia and Herzegovina, "kamen temeljac na kojem počiva moderna i demokratska BiH," 'a cornerstone upon which modern, democratic Bosnia rests,' "događaj koji potvrđuje kontinuitet državnosti BiH," 'an event that confirms the continuity of Bosnian statehood' (Komšić 2008). Although Dodik uses this date as an argument against historical continuity, Komšić sees it as strong support of exactly that. Arguing against the Serbs that do not recognize 25 November, but instead celebrate the signing of the Dayton Agreement, Komšić stated:

Dan potpisivanja Daytonskog mirovnog sporazuma smatram važnim datumom u novijoj istoriji BiH, koji treba obilježavati na dostojanstven način, ali 25. novembar – dan održavanja ZAVNOBIH-a i donošenja njegovih odluka – lično smatram neprikosnovenim, nedodirljivim i jedinim Danom državnosti Bosne i Hercegovine.[13]

I consider the day of the signing of the Dayton Agreement an important date in the recent history of Bosnia, which should be marked in a dignified manner, but 25 November – the date of ZAVNOBIH, and the decisions reached there – I personally find sacrosanct, inviolable, and the sole Statehood Day of Bosnia and Herzegovina.

The strategy used by Komšić is not to blame the others for celebrating the day. He expresses respect towards the others' day, but in a more modest way than when praising his own day. The others' day is *važan*, 'important' and deserves *dostojanstven*, 'dignified' celebration. This is not an open delegitimization of the others. However, regarding his own day he uses the terms *neprikosnoven*, 'sacrosanct' and *nedodirljiv*, 'inviolable,' both very positively loaded. By overloading his positive terms, he delegitimizes the viewpoints of the others. This is clearly stated in his final statement, that his day is *jedinim Danom državnosti*, 'the sole Statehood Day.' This is an example of how delegitimization may be expressed in a "polite" way (Chilton 2004: 39–40), avoiding direct accusations.

2.2   Independence Day: 1 March

Within the Federation, there is a split between Croats and Bosniaks regarding the celebration of 1 March, *Dan nezavisnosti* (Independence Day). In general, it is celebrated only in areas with a Bosniak majority. In areas with a Croat majority, as in western Herzegovina, 1 March is an ordinary working day, despite its status as an official holiday. The town of Mostar is divided: on the eastern (Bosniak) side, 1 March is celebrated and schools are closed, and on the western (Croat) side schools and other institutions operate normally.

This difference is due to a conflicting interpretation of the historical event underlying the holiday, the referendum on 1 March 1992. The Bosniaks see the referendum as the crucial step towards independence. In 2004, the Bosniak Sulejman Tihić stated:

Prvog marta 1992. godine, građani BiH opredijelili su se za nezavisnu, suverenu, samostalnu i cjelovitu Bosnu i Hercegovinu, državu ravnopravnih naroda i

---

13. http://www.zeljkokomsic.ba/index.php?lang=ba&sel=13&view=84, 7 May 2011.

građana. BiH je proglasila nezavisnost i samostalnost u svojim historijskim i međunarodno priznatim granicama. (*Dnevni avaz*, 1 Mar. 2004)

On 1 March 1992, the citizens of Bosnia and Herzegovina committed themselves to an independent, sovereign, autonomous and integral Bosnia and Herzegovina, a state of equal nations and citizens. Bosnia and Herzegovina proclaimed its independence within its historical and internationally recognized borders.

Tihić's discourse world is "citizens of Bosnia and Herzegovina," implying that he is speaking on behalf of the entire population. The "we" dimension is thus also extended to include the "others." Repeating three adjectives denoting the same quality, *nezavisan*, 'independent,' *suveren*, 'sovereign,' and *samostalan*, 'autonomous,' and in addition the adjectives *cjelovit*, 'integral,' and *ravnopravan*, 'equal,' Tihić's discourse is overloaded with positive words, perhaps because the historical event is contested. He has a time dimension that goes further back than 1992, mentioning Bosnia's "historical borders," which usually implies the Ottoman period (which, after more than four hundred years, ended in 1878). The entire text has a legitimizing function.

Not only politicians use 1 March to emphasize the celebration's historic dimension. At the solemn commemoration of 1 March in 2003, the Bosniak historian Omer Ibrahimagić declared that 1 March is one of the four most important dates in Bosnian history, the others being the first mention of Bosnia in written sources in 955, Ban Kulin's letter to Dubrovnik in 1189, and the antifascist resolution in 1943 (*Oslobođenje*, 1 Mar. 2003). Moreover, the well-known Bosniak intellectual, Muhamed Filipović, stated: "1. mart, kao najznačajniji dan u političkoj i državnoj povijesti BiH, jeste i dan ispunjenja snova generacija velikih ljudi," 'March first, as the most important day in the political and national history of Bosnia and Herzegovina, is the day of fulfillment of the dreams of generations of great people' (*Oslobođenje*, 1 Mar. 2001). Filipović's spatial world here seems to include all Bosnians, but "the dreams of generations" obviously belong to only one part of the population, the Bosniaks.

The Croats do not consider 1 March to be of any significance. Although the Croats participated in the referendum and voted for independence in 1992, they later came into conflict with the Bosniaks, accusing them of domination. Many Croats wanted a separate Croatian community, *Herceg-Bosna*, or even union with Croatia. *Dan Hrvatske zajednice Herceg-Bosne* (Day of the Croatian Community of *Herceg-Bosna*), 18 November, is celebrated among the Croats, and, although it is not an official holiday, it is a non-working day in the West Herzegovina Canton, which has a Croat majority. An extreme statement by the leader of the nationalist Croatian party HDZ, Dragan Čović, is the following:

HDZ BiH ima vrlo jasan plan, te smo jasno definirali što želimo oko uređenja BiH. Želimo poručiti kako je BiH prije svega hrvatska zemlja, te pripada prije svega Hrvatima koji žive u njoj.   (24sata.info, 20 Sept. 2010)[14]

The political party HDZ BiH has a very clear plan, and we have clearly defined what we want in connection with the constitution of Bosnia and Herzegovina. We want to convey that Bosnia and Herzegovina is first and foremost Croatian land, and belongs primarily to the Croats living there.

To state that Bosnia and Herzegovina is *prije svega*, 'primarily' Croatian land is tantamount to negating the right of the others to the country. Although this statement was not given on the occasion of a holiday related to state formation, it explains why nationalist Croats do not consider 1 March their holiday.

The main opponents of 1 March are nevertheless the Serbs. In 2008, Milorad Dodik, the prime minister of the Republika Srpska, stated:

RS je protiv Dana nezavisnosti BiH koji je samoproglašen od samo nekoliko njih i podržan od samo dijela međunarodne zajednice. To nije dan nezavisnosti BiH i ne može biti, jer tada je preglašen jedan narod i donesena odluka koja je uvukla narod BiH u rat. Ako oni žele slaviti ratne datume, to je njihova stvar.

(*Nezavisne novine*, 1 Mar. 2008)

The Republika Srpska is against the Independence Day of Bosnia and Herzegovina because it was declared unilaterally by only some of the inhabitants and supported by only a part of the international community. It is not, and cannot be, an independence day of Bosnia and Herzegovina because one nation was outvoted and a decision was made that drew Bosnia and Herzegovina into war. If they want to celebrate war dates, that is their business.

Dodik's spatial world is, implicitly, the majority of the population because he claims that "only some of the inhabitants" voted for independence.[15] In addition, his international spatial world is a supposed majority because the others' international support is restricted to "only a part." These two expressions, although not explicitly, imply that Dodik speaks on behalf of the majority, both domestic and foreign. In reality, most countries did recognize the independence of Bosnia and Herzegovina in 1992. The "we" dimension is, however, in the next sentence explicitly "one nation"; that is, his own, the Serbs. Moreover, "we" were exposed to an injustice, being "outvoted." The expression *preglašen*, 'outvoted' is clearly

---

14. http://www.24sata.info/vijesti/politika/43585-FOTO-Dragan-Covic-BiH-prije-svega-hrvatska-zemlja.html, 10 May 2011.

15. Here he is partly right because only 63.4% of the population voted in 1992. The Serbs largely boycotted the referendum, and the majority favoring independence, 99.4%, consisted of Bosniaks and Croats (Pirjevec 2001: 125).

negative, although in a democracy it is the rule that the majority decides. The culmination of delegitimization strategies is the claim that the decision "drew the country into war." For Dodik, the others' independence day is "a war date." In other years as well, in his comments marking 1 March, Dodik has repeated the same: that the day is a day celebrating war.

3.   Holidays in the Republika Srpska

3.1   Republic Day: 9 January

Dan republike (Republic Day), 9 January, is celebrated because on that day in 1992 the Bosnian Serb authorities declared the creation of the *Srpska Republika Bosne i Hercegovine* (the Serbian Republic of Bosnia and Herzegovina), which declared independence in April from Bosnia and Herzegovina. In July the same year, the name was changed to the Republika Srpska, which was later accepted in Dayton. Because this declaration meant the early breakup of Bosnia and Herzegovina, even before the war broke out, it is understandable that the other ethnic groups do not see this declaration as anything but a provocation. Today this day is called the *Krsna slava Republike Srpske* (Republika Srpska's Patron Saint's Day). The *krsna slava* is the traditional Serbian Patron Saint's Day, each family celebrating their *slava*, 'feast' at home, with a visiting priest. Because of this religious connotation – 9 January is *Sveti prvomučenik i arhiđakon Stefan* (the feast of St. Archdeacon Stephen) on the Serbian Orthodox calendar – representatives of the Serbian Orthodox Church participate, together with politicians, in celebrating this day.[16]

On this occasion, Bosnian Serb politicians resort to a panegyric discourse, emphasizing the independence of their entity, intermingled with religious rhetoric. On 9 January 2009, the president of the Republika Srpska, Rajko Kuzmanović, stated in his speech given at the official celebration:

> Malo je u svijetu država, državotvornih i federalnih jedinica ili druge vrste entiteta, koji imaju tako snažan oslonac u svjetovnosti i duhovnosti, pravu i pravdi, legalnosti i legitimnosti, kao što ga ima Srpska. [...] Ona je miroljubiva i narodna, odana ideji prava i pravde, ideji humanosti i ravnopravnosti.
>
> (*Dan*, 11 Jan. 2009)

> There are few states in the world, state-building entities, federal entities, or other kinds of entities that have such a strong basis in secularity and spirituality, law

---

16. On the merging of religious and national commemorations in the Balkans, see Roudometof (2005).

and justice, legality and legitimacy, as the Republika Srpska. [...] It is peace-loving and patriotic, devoted to the idea of law and justice, the idea of humanity and equality.

Nouns emphasizing the state's legal basis are repeated: *pravo*, 'law,' *Pravda*, 'justice,' *legalnost*, 'legality,' and *legitimnost*, 'legitimacy.' Other positive words dominate the discourse, including adjectives (*miroljubiva*, 'peace-loving,' *narodna*, 'patriotic,') and nouns (*humanost*, 'humanity,' *ravnopravnost*, 'equality'). In addition, elements from religious discourse are evident because Kuzmanović claims that the state's legitimacy is also based on *duhovnost*, 'spirituality.' Although the Republika Srpska is considered by many to be a para-state, Kuzmanović claims that few other countries in the world have a more solid basis for their statehood. The need to legitimize Republic Day, and thereby the state, is obviously so great that it is necessary to resort to grave exaggerations.

Representatives of the other two ethnic groups in Bosnia and Herzegovina, Bosniaks and Croats, consider 9 January a date connected to preparation for war. In 2010, Haris Silajdžić officially denounced 9 January in a press release distributed from his presidential cabinet. Commenting on the Serb declaration in 1992, he stated:

> Deklaraciju je potpisao osuđeni ratni zločinac Momčilo Krajišnik, a u njenom usvajanju učestvovali su i drugi zločinci, kao Radovan Karadžić i Biljana Plavšić. Svečano obilježavajući dan kada su ozvaničeni planovi za genocid, etničko čišćenje i druge zločine, dužnosnici RS entiteta šalju jasnu poruku da se zalažu za očuvanje tekovina Karadžićeve Republike Srpske, a ne entiteta koji je prema odredbama Daytonskog sporazuma trebao dovesti do povratka izbjeglica i konstitutivnosti svih naroda.   (24sata.info, 10 Jan. 2010)[17]

> The declaration was signed by the sentenced war criminal Momčilo Krajišnik, and other war criminals participated, such as Radovan Karadžić and Biljana Plavšić. By solemnly celebrating the day when plans for genocide, ethnic cleansing, and other crimes were made official, the politicians of the Republika Srpska are sending a clear message that they are dedicated to the preservation of Karadžić's Republika Srpska, and not an entity that according to the regulations of the Dayton Agreement should allow refugees to return and allow all nations to be constitutive.

In this text, the delegitimization of the others is brought to a climax. The three leading Bosnian-Serb politicians of the 1990s are characterized as *ratni zločinci*, 'war criminals,' which, by the way, is in compliance with the decision of the

---

17. http://www.24sata.info/vijesti/politika/23860-Silajdzic-Osuda-proslave-januara-dana-Tadicevo-prisustvo.html, 10 May 2011.

International Criminal Tribunal for the Former Yugoslavia in The Hague. The expressions used in this text include the most serious accusations possible, *genocid*, 'genocide,' *etničko čišćenje*, 'ethnic cleansing,' and *drugi zločini*, 'other crimes.' The present Serbian leaders are described as followers of Karadžić, the indicted war criminal, implying that the actual politicians are following a policy of genocide. The temporal dimension encompasses the past – the planning of genocide ahead of the war – and the future, the expected return of refugees.

3.2   Day of Establishment of the General Agreement on Peace: 21 November[18]

The day of the signing of the Dayton Agreement, 21 November 1995, ending the war, had the potential to become a day to collectively remember through common celebration. Originally, this date was proclaimed by the presidency in 1999 as a common national day, *Dan potpisivanja Dejtonskog sporazuma* (Day of the Signing of the Dayton Agreement). This proclamation caused President Clinton to deliver this statement on 1 September 1999:

> Today the Joint Presidents of Bosnia and Herzegovina announced that the national day of their country will henceforth be celebrated on November 21, the anniversary of the Dayton peace accords of 1995. In so doing, the leaders of every ethnic community in Bosnia and Herzegovina have made clear that Dayton marked not merely the end of a war but the beginning of a new country and a blueprint for its future. I am pleased that the date November 21 will be honored as a symbol of multi-ethnic democracy and solidarity between the people of the United States and the people of Bosnia and Herzegovina. (Clinton 1999, 2:1482)

However, Clinton's vision did not come true. This date was not accepted by the parliament of Bosnia and Herzegovina; that is, by the non-Serbs.

Since 2007, 21 November, Dayton Agreement Day, has been an official holiday in the Republika Srpska. By coincidence, this date is celebrated in the Serbian Orthodox Church as *Dan Svetoga Arhangela Mihaila* (Feast of the Archangel Michael), although this coincidence is usually not mentioned by politicians. The focus is on the fact that the Republika Srpska was recognized. Milorad Dodik stated in a press release in 2007:

---

18. This is a translation of the official name of this holiday as given in the Law on Holidays of the Republika Srpska *Dan potpisivanja Opšteg okvirnog sporazuma za mir u BiH*. The shorter term "Dayton Agreement Day" will be used hereafter.

Mi obilježavamo potpisivanje Daytonskog sporazuma jer je to odluka naših najvećih tijela. To je važan dan, jer je uspostavljen mir na osnovi kreacije političkog sustava u BiH koji se bazira na dva entiteta.   (FENA, 21 Nov. 2007)

We mark the signing of the Dayton Agreement because it was decided by our highest bodies. It is an important day because peace was founded on creating a political system in Bosnia and Herzegovina based on two entities.

Dodik sees the Dayton Agreement not primarily as a symbol of a peace settlement – that is, not as a symbol of peace – but as an international agreement that consolidated the creation of the Serb entity within Bosnia and Herzegovina. When he emphasizes the "political system [...] based on two entities," what is important for him is the fact that the Republika Srpska received international recognition through the Dayton Agreement.

Bosniak politicians see the signing of the Dayton Agreement as important, but for different reasons. In 2007, Silajdžić explained:

Ideja je bila da 25. novembar ostane Dan državnosti, a da 21. novembar bude praznik mira. Nadam se da ćemo postići dogovor, jer ovo nije dobro za nas u BiH, ni za sliku naše države u svijetu da imamo praznik kojem ne prisustvuju svi predstavnici BiH.   (*Dnevni avaz*, 25 Nov. 2007)

The idea was that 25 November should remain Statehood Day, and that 21 November should be a holiday of peace. I hope that we will reach an agreement because it is not good for us in Bosnia and Herzegovina, nor for the image of our state in the world, that we have a holiday that is not attended by all representatives of the state.

Here, Silajdžić's legitimizing strategy is to appeal to the Serbs' patriotism, that Bosnia and Herzegovina's image in the world is being damaged by their not observing a common holiday. It is not very likely, however, that such an appeal will have any impact in the Republika Srpska. For Silajdžić, the crucial symbolic meaning of 21 November is peace. These different interpretations are possible because the Dayton Agreement had two aspects: it was both a peace treaty and a new constitution for the country. Moreover, the constitutional framework had a dual aspect: a country that was both united and divided. This duality made it possible for politicians to emphasize one of the two aspects, unity or division.

Silajdžić has strongly opposed the Dayton Agreement's division of Bosnia and Herzegovina into two halves, demanding that the two entities be abolished as administrative units and replaced by several regions with less autonomy. In his speech for 25 November 2009, he said:

Dayton jeste bio kompromis ali to ne znači da bilo ko smije vršiti kompromise sa samim tekstom Daytona. Precizan balans koji je sadržan u Daytonu je i omogućio njegovo potpisivanje. [...] Dayton je predvidio entitetsko glasanje u kojem učestvuju sva tri naroda. Također je predvidio vlasništvo Bosne i Hercegovine, a ne entiteta, nad svom imovinom njenih prethodnica. Dayton je, uostalom, predvidio i obilježavanje ovog Dana državnosti u cijeloj Bosni i Hercegovini. Umjesto toga, danas imamo etničko glasanje, nelegalno raspolaganje državnom imovinom, i ignorisanje i negiranje ovog praznika.   (Silajdžić, 25 Nov. 2009)

Dayton was a compromise, but that does not mean that anyone can compromise with the very text of the Dayton Agreement. The precise balance contained in the Dayton Agreement actually enabled its signing. [...] Dayton provided for voting in the entities with the participation of all three nations. It also provided for Bosnia and Herzegovina's, and not the entities', ownership over the property of its predecessors. Dayton, after all, provided for the marking of this Statehood Day on the entire territory of Bosnia and Herzegovina. Instead, today we have ethnic voting, illegal disposition of state property, and disrespect for and negation of this holiday.

According to Silajdžić, the Dayton Agreement, although a *kompromis*, 'compromise,' was inherently a positive event, showing *balans*, 'balance.' It should secure equal rights for citizens of all three constituent ethnic groups. His negative term 'ethnic voting' refers to the fact that the Dayton Agreement contained rules that, according to him, could undermine the formal political equality of all citizens of Bosnia and Herzegovina. In the parliament, one entity, the Republika Srpska, could block decisions based on their constitutional right to secure the interests of their ethnic group. Further, Silajdžić claims that state property should belong to the entire state, not to the entities. His spatial world thus includes the entire republic of Bosnia and Herzegovina, and is not confined to one entity. He is against the extensive autonomy of the entities, and he calls for more centralization. According to Silajdžić, the Serbs have distorted Dayton by confining voting and state property to the entity level. The expressions *nelegalno raspolaganje*, 'illegal disposition' and *ignorisanje i negiranje*, 'disrespect and negation' convey a clear delegitimization of the others.

Dayton Agreement Day is thus an example of how a historical event can be interpreted differently. In their discourse, both sides refer to the Dayton Agreement as a positive event, as an important point on the time axis. The historical narratives connected with the day differ, however, according to national affiliation. Politicians emphasize different aspects of the Dayton Agreement according to their interests. Bosniak politicians see it as a peace treaty and Serb politicians as a confirmation of their Serb Republic within Bosnia and Herzegovina.

4. A neutral discourse – imposed from outside?

Bosnia-Herzegovina was not totally dominated by nationalist discourse in this period. Because of the international presence, especially the surveillance by the High Representative, efforts are sometimes made by local politicians to use a neutral discourse when discussing sensitive topics.

Many efforts have been made to establish a common holiday related to the state formation in Bosnia and Herzegovina. In 2005, representatives from the Social Democratic Party, proposed a law in the parliament including 1 March and 25 November, but the proposal was not passed due to resistance from the Serbian side (*Nezavisne novine*, 1 Mar. 2005). Any attempt to establish a common holiday would therefore have to exclude contested dates. This view was supported by the international community. In January 2009, the Ministry of Civil Affairs proposed a law on holidays that would not include the specific holidays celebrated in the two entities (Šegrt 2009).[19] None of the proposed holidays would have any explicit connection to Bosnian affairs: *Nova godina* (New Year's Day); 1–2 May, *Međunarodni praznik rada* (International Labor Day); 9 May, *Dan pobjede nad fašizmom* (Day of Victory over Fascism); and 26 June, *Dan podrške žrtvama nasilja* (Day of Support for Victims of Violence). The discourse on this proposal was, consequently, neutral, without nationalist overtones. However, the ministry's proposal was rejected by Bosniak representatives, who argued against the abolition of Independence Day and Statehood Day.

On 15 July 2009, the Commission for Internal Politics of the Council of Ministers (Government of Bosnia and Herzegovina) proposed additional official holidays: Independence Day, 1 March; Statehood Day, 25 November; and 21 November as the Day of the signing of the Dayton Agreement. Moreover, instead of 26 June, the Day of Support for Victims of Violence, they proposed 11 July (the date of the Srebrenica massacre) as a *Dan sjećanja na žrtve genocida* (Commemoration Day of Victims of Genocide) (24sata.info, 15 July, 2009).[20] These proposals were met with vehement protests from the Serbs.

On 16 July 2009, the Council of Ministers made their final decision: Bosnia and Herzegovina shall have only the "international" holidays proposed earlier (*Dnevni avaz* 4974 [17 July, 2009]: 14). No day connected with the past of Bosnia and Herzegovina was included. This decision was met with mixed reactions. Most

---

19. http://www.nezavisne.com/novosti/bih/Nesporni-Nova-godina-i-1-maj-35120.
html?modul=stampano-izdanje&poziv=dogadjaji&naslov=Nesporni-Nova-godina-i-1-
maj&idv=35120, 30 May 2011.

20. http://www.24sata.info/vijesti/bosna-i-hercegovina/11440-Jedinstven-stav-novembar-
kao-dan-drzavnosti-Bosne-Hercegovine.html, 31 May 2011.

critical were the Bosniaks because their holidays were not included, and the Bosniak members abstained from voting. The Serbian and Croatian members of the government accepted this proposal. A Croatian member of parliament called this decision *napredak*, 'a progress,' and *dobro*, 'good.'[21] In April 2010, the parliament of Bosnia and Herzegovina discussed the proposed law on holidays for the fifth time, but reached no agreement (FENA, 21 Apr. 2010). The Serbs would not accept 1 March, 25 November, and 11 July, characterizing them as "political." Thus, Bosnia and Herzegovina remained a country with several competing national holidays.

Other state symbols have also been contested in Bosnia and Herzegovina. Due to disagreement in the parliament about the flag, High Representative Carlos Westendorp imposed his solution in 1998, a new design without any specific symbols connected to Bosnia and Herzegovina (Jedlicki 1999; Kolstø 2006). In 2001, the parliament adopted a law on the flag, accepting Westendorp's solution. Another example is the anthem. In 1999, the High Representative imposed a law on the music of the anthem. For years, the text of the anthem was discussed, but no agreement was reached. In 2009, a parliamentary commission accepted the lyrics, later supported by the Ministry of Justice in 2010, but the lyrics have not yet been adopted by the parliament.

No similar international intervention by the High Representative has been made regarding a common national holiday. Of all the issues concerning national symbols in Bosnia and Herzegovina, common national holidays at the state level remain the most politically sensitive. The discourse on occasions of holidays continues to be highly nationalistic. All attempts to impose neutral holidays, and a neutral discourse, have failed.

5. Conclusion

Chilton (2004) postulates a multidimensional model of political discourse, involving space, time, and modality. These are essentially what politics is about: space (territory), time (past, present, and future), and modality (about values, opinions, and being right).

As indicated in this analysis, in Bosnia and Herzegovina the question of space permeates all discourse on national holidays because this question relates to the division or non-division of the country. The discourse of Bosniak politicians explicitly or implicitly concerns the entire population of Bosnia and Herzegovina;

---

21. "Koji će biti državni praznici?" *BH RAJA*, 20 July 2009. Statement by Velimir Jukić, HDZ. http://www.bhraja.ca/index.php?option=com_content&task=view&id=5548.

that is, the entire country. For Serbian politicians, particularly those of the Republika Srpska, their explicit concern is their own entity; that is, half of Bosnia and Herzegovina.

On the time axis, the question of the state's past is disputed. The Bosniaks go back to the World War II, whereas the Serbs begin in 1992. Their concepts of what was important in 1992 differ because the Serbs see the declaration of a Serbian entity, the Republika Srpska, as crucial, whereas the Bosniaks see the referendum on independence as the most important event. The authors of the political discourse analyzed lack a common understanding of history and how the state should be constituted.

On the modal axis, the analysis of politicians' discourse in Bosnia and Herzegovina has revealed a fundamental division between the various "us" and "them" groups. This discourse is extremely positive when celebrating one's own holidays and extremely negative when condemning the celebration of the others' holidays. Extreme accusations are used about the others' celebrations, connecting the date, if possible, to the preparation for war and war crimes. The discourse is exaggeratedly positive about one's own commemorations. Only exceptionally does a moderate, inclusive, discourse occur. This chapter analyzes the linguistic means of legitimization and delegitimization used by leading Bosnian politicians.

The disputes between the ruling elites of the three ethnic groups gives a clear indication of how the political climate has developed after the Dayton Agreement in 1995. The period from 2000 to 2010 reveals that relations between the ethnic groups have deteriorated. Bosnia and Herzegovina still lacks a common law on holidays. When leading politicians characterize a national holiday of the others as a "war date," one realizes how far they are from reaching any agreement. The observance or non-observance of a holiday serves as an outward sign of deep-rooted discord in society.

Because Statehood Day and Independence Day are connected to the very establishment and legitimization of the state, these days serve as the perfect occasion for politicians to either defend the state or deny the legitimate basis of the state. A discourse of legitimization and delegitimization is therefore the rule when marking holidays in Bosnia and Herzegovina.

Primary sources

European Parliament, RSP/2009/2502, "Resolution on Srebrenica." January 15, 2009. Accessed 30 Mar. 2011. http://www.europarl.europa.eu/oeil/FindByProcnum.do?lang=en&procnum=RSP/2009/2502.

Clinton, William J. 1999. "Statement on Announcement of the Bosnia-Herzegovina National Day, September 1, 1999." *Public Papers of the Presidents of the United States: William J. Clinton 1999*, Vol. 2: 1482. Washington: United States Government Printing Office. Accessed 8 Apr. 2011. http://frwebgate2.access.gpo.gov/cgi-bin/PDFgate.cgi?WAISdocID= 98bpON/0/2/0&WAISaction=retrieve.

Komšić, Željko. 2008. "Govor člana Predsjedništva BiH Željka Komšića u povodu obilježavanja 25. novembra, Dana državnosti Bosne i Hercegovine, 25.11.2008." *Željko Komšić: Član Predsjedništva Bosne i Hercegovine iz reda hrvatskog naroda.* Accessed 31 Mar. 2011. http:// www.zeljkokomsic.ba/index.php?lang=ba&sel=13&view=84.

Silajdžić, Haris. 2009. "Govor člana Predsjedništva BiH dr. Harisa Silajdžića u povodu obilježavanja 25. novembra, Dana državnosti Bosne i Hercegovine." *Predsjedništvo Bosne i Hercegovine: Govori. 25. November 2009.* Accessed 7 May, 2011. http://www.predsjednistvobih.ba/gov/1/?cid=14165,2,1.

Šegrt, R. 2009. "Nesporni Nova godina i 1. maj." *Nezavisne novine,* 4 Jan. 2009. Accessed 30 May, 2011. http://www.nezavisne.com/novosti/bih/Nesporni-Nova-godina-i-1-maj-35120. html?modul=stampano-izdanje&poziv=dogadjaji&naslov=Nesporni-Nova-godina-i-1-maj&idv=35120.

CHAPTER 12

What Europe means for Poland

The front-page coverage of Independence Day
in *Gazeta Wyborcza* 1989–2009

Knut Andreas Grimstad
University of Oslo
k.a.grimstad@ilos.uio.no

This chapter examines one of Poland's most influential newspapers, *Gazeta Wyborcza,* and its front-page coverage of what is arguably the country's most popular national holiday, Independence Day. Specific attention is given to how *Gazeta*'s writers discursively constructed a Polishness compatible with European values, both before and after the country's EU admission. Within the newspaper's Euro-Polish identity project, they reinforced the idea of a common past, present, and future, while introducing a concept of European supranationalism that, however, did not replace but instead served to complement Polish nationalism. Insofar as *Gazeta* gives space to many different voices, including those of its Euro-skeptic adversaries, its predominant strategy is one of inclusion.

Keywords: Polish Independence Day, Polish newspapers, Polish online newspapers, *Gazeta Wyborcza*, newspaper front pages, national identity construction, discourse analysis, topoi

1. Introduction

Narodowe Święto Niepodległości (the National Holiday of Independence), or *11 Listopada* (11 November), has become firmly established in Poles' national consciousness.[1] Restored in 1989 as one of the basic symbols of interwar Poland, it refers to the attainment of independence in 1918, when the partitioned country

---

1. According to an opinion poll of 2008, 48 percent of Poles say that attaining independence in 1918 is worth celebrating. See "11 Listopada najważniejszy," '11 November is the most important,' *Gazeta Wyborcza* (Kraj edition) from 10–11 Nov. 2008.

became an independent state, the "Second Republic."[2] A recurring celebration, 11 November is laden with ceremonies such as laying wreaths at the Tomb of the Unknown Soldier in Warsaw and at the Tomb of Marshal Piłsudski at Wawel Castle in Cracow, solemn high masses held in churches nationwide, reenactments of historical events, festive parades, open-air concerts, and a gala performance at the National Theater. On 1 May 2004, Poland – now constitutionally known as the Third Republic – joined the European Union, a major step in its postcommunist transition to democracy. Ever since the admission process had been finalized a year earlier, many treated the development as proof that the transition was complete, that democracy was stable and secure. However, the Poles had not finished debating their Europeanness or their participation in Europe; with the ongoing process of Europeanization, national themes continued to be vigorously discussed in academic literature and in the media (Godzic 2009; Hałas 2002b; Krzyżanowski 2008; Kutter 2007; Main 2003). *Gazeta Wyborcza* (the Electoral Gazette) stands out in this regard: under Adam Michnik's editorship, this high-quality daily has become a very successful business enterprise that not only continues to dominate the Polish newspaper market in terms of influence and circulation, but also appears to have consolidated its position as the "most often bought and read opinion-making newspaper in Poland and the most popular daily title among advertisers" (Agora S.A., co-owner of *Gazeta Wyborcza*, 2012).

1.1   Method and terminology

This chapter focuses on how *Gazeta*'s writers argue in favor of a Polishness that is compatible with European values, understood as liberal democracy. According to this argument, the political process in Poland should be competitive, and pluralism should allow for the presence of multiple political parties and ethnic minority groups. In considering the interplay between text and layout in *Gazeta*'s national identity project, I posit the newspaper's front page as a separate unit whose items (e.g., photographs, illustrations, headlines, and blocks of texts) seize the reader's attention to varying degrees and through a variety of means, depending mainly on their salience and information value. As outlined by Gunter Kress and Theo van Leeuwen, if an item is prominently placed above the fold and on the left of the page, it is presented as the idealized or generalized essence of the information, and as something that is well established or familiar to the reader, respectively. Conversely, if an item is less prominently placed below the fold and on the right, it is presented to the reader as more specific or practical information often

---

2. See Norman Davies (2005: 291–321).

accompanied by directions for actions, and as something that is new or unknown (Kress and van Leeuwen 1998: 189–195). By indicating the interrelationship between the events represented on the page (e.g., between the splash, the lead story, and an adjacent sidebar story), and in the newspaper as a whole (e.g., in inside follow-up articles), the front page is a well-thought-out extension of the values and themes that the newspaper wishes to communicate to its readers.

Here I draw on the understanding of topoi presented in *The Discursive Construction of National Identity* by Ruth Wodak et al. (2009): they are "obligatory elements of argumentation," whether explicit or inferable, "the content-related warrants or 'conclusion rules' which connect the argument or arguments to the conclusion of the central claim" (Wodak et al. 2009: 34–35). From this vantage point, I examine five of *Gazeta*'s most frequently used topoi by tracing its pro-European front-page coverage of 11 November since 1989:

1. the topos of comparison: to emphasize Poland's positive political continuity, notably by establishing a link to the model character of the "founding fathers"
2. the topos of history as a teacher: to emphasize the difference between Poland then and now, to justify integration
3. the topos of consequence: to declare Polish isolationism as obsolete and disastrous
4. the topos of terrible place: to emphasize negative features of Poland's national uniqueness (xenophobia, isolationism)
5. the topos of idyllic place: to emphasize positive features of Poland's national uniqueness (the multicultural heritage, pluralism) and to placate Euroskeptics.

Particularly interesting is whether certain themes and actors are foregrounded and, if so, how they are named, specified, and assigned to something or someone. However, having studied the holiday editions from this period, I discovered that 11 November was not always featured as a lead story. Notably, throughout the 1990s, when a liberal-democratic consensus dominated Polish politics (Pankowski 2010: 70–74), it received little more than the required coverage of historical and commemorative events, and was seldom linked to issues of European participation. Hence I concentrate on texts from the period 2002 to 2009 that explored the thematics of Europeanization and Polish independence, and that featured on the front page of the editions of 10, 11, or 12 November. When relevant, I also discuss follow-up pieces published inside the main section of a given holiday edition.[3]

1.2   The historical and political context

To better understand *Gazeta*'s discursive strategies, one can consider the Polish nonviolent revolution of 1989 and the intellectuals in the political opposition. Among these were such well-known Solidarity members as Adam Michnik, Jacek Kuroń, and Tadeusz Mazowiecki, all of whom played a crucial role in round-table discussions between the opposition and the communist regime, which facilitated the peaceful transition to democracy in Poland. Having rejected the revolutionary rhetoric of all or nothing, Michnik then decided to launch a new, above-ground daily, an outcome of the roundtable contract: *Gazeta Wyborcza*.[4] The first edition, on 8 May 1989, meant that Poland now had its first independent newspaper since 1940. Small wonder that, while evolving into the Polish newspaper of responsible record *and* the chief forum for intellectual discussion, it became closely linked to the country's long history of struggling for independence.[5] Significantly, through-out the 1990s, when the dividing line in Polish politics was initially between the postcommunist and post-Solidarity camps, then increasingly in the first years of the twenty-first century between nationalism and left-wing liberalism, *Gazeta* supported pluralist values and sought to reorient Polish national identity in Euro-pean-style, liberal democratic terms (Śpiewak 2000). Briefly stated, *Gazeta*'s writ-ers have drawn on the following definitions: Poland as poor and backward, the sovereignty of the nation-state as outdated because of globalization, and integra-tion as a just compromise between the powerful and weak states of the EU.

---

3.   *Gazeta*'s themes, language, and rhetoric have been subject to a considerable amount of research. Among the most recent studies are: Sebastian Wierny, "To samo, a inne. Wstęp do porównawczej analizy zawartości Gazety Wyborczej," in: *Zeszyty Prasoznawcze* 3–4, Cracow, 2003, 26–34; Edyta Pałuszyńska, *Nagłówki w "Gazecie Wyborczej": (ekspresywna leksyka, fraze-matyka, metaforyka)*, Łódź, 2006, 52–70; and Artur Wierzbicki, "Językowe środki perswazji w 'Gazecie Wyborczej,'" in: *Studia Medioznawcze* 1, Warsaw, 2006, 11–25. To my knowledge, however, no attention has been paid to how the newspaper treated discursively the topic of European integration in relation to Independence Day, notably on the holiday front-pages from the period 2002 to 2009.

4.   Although controversial and often criticized for both his business acumen and his political stance, Adam Michnik (b. 1946) has had, it seems fair to say, enormous influence and "stands out in any consideration of postcommunist journalism" (Wachtel 2006:159).

5.   Rafal Pankowski (2010:94) calls *Gazeta Wyborcza* "the most powerful voice of the 1990s zeitgeist."

During the decade from 2000 to 2010, Polish Euro-skeptics and anti-Europe-anists contributed to an ideologization of the Polish state that introduced a wide spectrum of activities aiming to preserve traditional values, especially Catholic ones, in the face of modernization. Consequently, the nationalist-conservative media have not only covered the Euro-skeptic arguments of the right-wing party *Prawo i Sprawiedliwość* (Law and Justice, PiS), but have also promoted the claims of far-right groups such as *Samoobrona Rzeczypospolitej Polskiej* (Self-Defense of the Republic of Poland, SRP) and *Liga Polskich Rodzin* (League of Polish Fami-lies, LPR) against further immersion in the EU. Most opponents of the idea of adopting, or readopting, the values and institutions of liberal democracy intend to eradicate the liberal, pro-European policies of the Third Republic; that is, of a Poland that in their view has spoiled the social and political life of the country. In so doing, they speak of a wished-for *Fourth Republic*, which is markedly Euro-skeptic. On the other hand, there are the center-left *Sojusz Lewicy Demokratyc-znej* (Democratic Left Alliance, SLD) and the center-right *Platforma Obywatelska* (Civic Platform, PO), both of which conceive of the readoption of the values and institutions of Western civilization in a positive manner (Koczanowicz 2008:80). The pro-European media convey these values but are also split into strongly sov-ereignist and integrationist camps, with *Gazeta* leading the latter.

This polarization is not tearing today's Poland apart, but it does, in part, cause an incompatibility of discourses and a low level of consensus (Czyżewski, Kowalski, and Piotrowski 2010). Judging from what he writes, Michnik sees himself as a defender of those dialogic values that permitted the peaceful break-through of 1989, and thus advocates a patient and tolerant approach to the politi-cal and moral tensions of postcommunism (Michnik 1998, 2005, 2007). Hence his negative attitude towards restricting the participation of former communists in the successor political appointee positions and in the civil service. Indeed, this approach has made his newspaper the target of critical attacks from various quar-ters, especially the ultra-conservatives and neo-fundamentalists (Matynia 2009).[6] Increasingly, *Gazeta* has been perceived as a biased, Jewish-controlled publication aimed at liberal readers that generally support the European values of the new

---

6. Suffice it to mention here the response of the Polish media to *Rywingate* (2002–2003), a cor-ruption scandal involving both an attempt to bribe *Gazeta* and a possible government cover-up. Not only did this event turn into a major political watershed and result in the first televised par-liamentary investigations in postcommunist Poland, it also led to a sharpening of the criticism of Michnik, who became the main target of attacks from the right.

left, and Michnik himself has become a symbol of everything that is dangerous and detrimental to Poland (Głowiński 2009: 176).[7]

As mentioned, not every front page of the holiday editions from 1989 to 2009 featured 11 November as a lead story, nor did they treat the topic of "Poland and Europe." Consequently, I have selected texts and figures from eight editions from the period 2002 to 2009 that not only thematize Poland's place in Europe, but also highlight the main characteristics and the development of *Gazeta*'s discursive construction of national identity. Before proceeding, however, it may be useful to take an initial look at the edition of 1989, the year when Independence Day was restored and Poland's first post-war independent newspaper established.

2. Streamlining freedom stories: 1989

Above the fold on the right of *Gazeta*'s first holiday edition on 10 November 1989, Michnik declared that 11 November belongs to various generations, political camps, and ideological orientations, to all compatriots that died for an independent Poland. In his article headlined "Niepodległość dzisiaj," 'Independence today,' Michnik evoked the interwar Second Republic and legendary freedom fighters Józef Piłsudski and Roman Dmowski, who, despite their different political stances – civic federalism versus ethnic nationalism, respectively – found sufficient agreement to create a cultural common ground for the discussion of Poland's future. Significantly, Michnik used the topos of comparison to establish a link to the "founding fathers," while perpetuating Poland's positive political continuity (see Figure 1).[8]

This point is amplified twofold: first, by the accompanying illustration of a Polish soldier of 1918 standing under a cross, a motif that alludes to the country's

---

7. As pointed out by Michał Głowiński (2009: 257), Michnik's opponents were provoked by everything from his Jewish origin and heroic past to his opinions and successes. For criticism of Michnik and his newspaper, see Ost (2005), Ziemkiewicz (2006), Naylor (2010), and numerous articles written by journalists Piotr Semka and Cezary Michalski, contributors to *Rzeczpospolita* (The Republic) and *Dziennik Polska-Europa-Świat* (The Poland-Europe-World Daily), respectively.

8. Józef Piłsudski (1867–1935) was the first chief of state of the newly independent Poland established in November 1918. Although more a rogue and a conspirator than a seasoned statesman, he was expected to cooperate with the leading politicians from the opposition. Above all he had to reckon with Roman Dmowski (1864–1939), his lifelong rival and detractor, who himself never took the reins of power. When Dmowski's *Obóz Wielkej Polskiej* (the Camp of Great Poland) suffered a definitive blow in 1926, it had sunk deep into nationalist xenophobia (see Norman Davies 2005: 39, 41, 314).

Figure 1. *Gazeta Wyborcza* front page 10–12 November 1989

patriotic and Christian heritage, and, second, by the large headline positioned immediately underneath Michnik's article, "Europa bez muru," 'Europe without walls,' introducing a piece on the historical significance of the events that took place in Berlin on 9 November 1989, only two days before the revival of Poland's own independence holiday.

In the follow-up piece inside the newspaper, Michnik left Polish history aside and addressed the here-and-now:

> Jakiej Polski pragniemy? Opartej na chrześcijańskich wartościach i demokratycz-
> nej, pluralistycznej i europejskiej? Czy też zaściankowej i wiecznie prowincjonal-
> nej, ciasnej i kultywującej własne kompleksy? [...] Co to znaczy dzisiaj chcieć
> niepodległości? Znaczy to konsekwentnie, krok po kroku, przebudować Polskę
> [...] Sytuacja Polski polega na tym, że proces demokratycznych przeobrażeń
> opiera się na kompromisie i wymaga konsekwencji działań – każdy z partnerów
> kompromisu potrzebny jest w politycznym kontrakcie.
>
> (*Gazeta Wyborcza*, 12 Nov. 1989)

> What kind of Poland are we longing for? A Poland that relies on Christian values, that is democratic, pluralist, and European? Or a Poland that is a country bumpkin, forever provincial, narrow-minded, cultivating its complexes? [...] What does "to want independence" mean today? It means to rebuild Poland consistently, step by step [...] Poland's situation depends on the process of democratic transformation being founded on compromise and requires consequences to actions – every one of the partners of the compromise is needed in the political contract.

This quotation was emblematic of the *Gazeta* editorial staff's phrasing insofar as they used 11 November and the independence theme to equate state with nation. In so doing, they took control of the nation as a legitimizing symbol of an integrated Poland that is neither politically nor culturally backward, but instead is "democratic, pluralist, and European" – and resting on Christian values. Central to the editor's thinking, however, was a position that allowed the newspaper to make moral claims in politics while remaining receptive to the necessity of a meeting of minds, the striking of a balance. The argumentative frame was formed by defining ("independence" today) and comparing (two Polands, one of which is civic-pluralistic and outward-looking, the other of which is ethnocentric and hostile to foreign influences). Here, too, the pro-European argument was enhanced by linking the present-day democratic process to the topos of comparison, and by extension, of the "founding fathers" (Piłsudski and Dmowski), their will to unify, to cooperate, and to feel and show solidarity. Moreover, "11 listopada jest dniem, kiedy warto myśleć o tym wszystkim," '11 November is the day when it is worth thinking about all this' (*Gazeta Wyborcza*, 12 Nov. 1989). Thus, the unifying gestures of the front page of the 1989 edition anticipate *Gazeta*'s discursive strategy as it was further developed into the twenty-first century.

2.1   Agonism transformed: 2002–2003

Thirteen years later (2002), after a series of temporary slumps in Polish democratic and political standards, *Gazeta* was again updating the independence theme, trying to keep the path of Europeanness constantly open and free of significant turbulence. In the post-holiday edition of 2002, the entire left half of the front page was dedicated to 11 November, the top featuring a photograph of a Piłsudski look-alike, while the main two-column piece was entitled "Apel wawelski," 'The Wawel appeal' (see Figure 2). Opening with the plea "Powiedz 'Tak' Unii Europejskiej," 'Say "Yes" to the European Union,' this piece informed readers that more than two hundred politicians, intellectuals, and artists had rallied at Wawel Castle in support of Poland's integration into Europe. In an adjacent sidebar on the left, Michnik delivered his own one-column address, "Dzwon Zygmunta," 'The bell of

Figure 2. *Gazeta Wyborcza* front page 12 November 2002

King Zygmunt,' referring to the largest bell hanging in the Sigismund Tower of the Wawel Cathedral, which tolls on special occasions, notably on religious and national holidays. Here, Michnik spoke of 11 November in light of the approaching EU referendum, while comparing the glories of Poland's pluralist past to the shortcomings of its chaotic present. Subsequently, he encouraged fellow Poles to settle permanently "w rodzinie demokratycznej Europy," 'in the family of a democratic Europe,' and then wrote:

> To już nie dzwonek, lecz alarmowy "dzwon Zygmunta". Czy polskie elity go usłyszą? Czy dostrzegą potrzebę przekroczenia podziałów, by utworzyć polski front demokratyczny i patriotyczny na rzecz integracji europejskiej?
>
> (*Gazeta Wyborcza*, 12 Nov. 2002)

> This is no small bell, but the warning "bell of King Zygmunt." Will the Polish elites hear it? Will they perceive the need to overcome divisions in order to create a Polish democratic and patriotic front in favor of European integration?

Again, Michnik stressed the need to cooperate ("to overcome divisions"). Continuing, he concurred with Roman Dmowski's view that the Polish nation does not belong to any particular party or generation, indicating that national identity is a matter for compromise, in which both insiders and outsiders have a place. The message was that Poland as part of Europe is *not* something alien, but is the realization of what is and has always been considered to be Polish. Using the topos of terrible place, Michnik also took issue with rhetoric that he termed "populistyczna, ksenofobiczna, antysemicka," 'populist, xenophobic, antisemitic,' thus emphasizing a distinction between a Euro-skeptic isolationist present and a Euro-enthusiastic integrationist future.

The page's layout reflected its compromising tone. Michnik's prominently positioned address was juxtaposed with an equally high-profile, two-column piece ("W prawo zwrot," 'A Turn to the Right') on the right-wing politician Lech Kaczyński (PiS), whose victory as the newly elected mayor of Warsaw marked the end of the eight-year rule of a center-left coalition (headed by the SLD). With this balanced piece ("Niedzielna dogrywka potwierdziła ogromne poparcie warszawiaków dla kandydata PiS [...] SLD będzie musiał prejść do oppozycji," 'Sunday's runoff confirmed Warsaw residents' enormous support for the PiS candidate [...] the SLD will have to go into opposition'), the editor and his staff may be said to have encouraged a tacit consensus between the political camps as to the rules of procedure, and also encouraged a common standpoint.

Similarly, on the front page of the holiday edition of 2003, *Gazeta* seemed to recognize the need to transform agonism (i.e., struggle or contention) into a more civilized form of democratic engagement. Above the fold, two adjacent sidebars in the left position of the splash, or the lead story (a critical piece on the poor quality of textbooks in Polish elementary schools), thematized Polish independence and Europeanization, respectively. Under the headline "Święto Niepodległości. Powrót do Sulejówki," 'Holiday of Independence. Return to Sulejówek,' the first piece reported from the town where Piłsudski lived before he led the coup d'état that turned Poland into a parliamentary republic (see Figure 3): readers learned that "tu pierwszy obywatel II Rzeczypospolitej [...] uprawiał ogródek, hodował pszczoły, czytał," 'here the first citizen of the Second Republic [...] cultivated his garden, raised bees, and read.' In the follow-up article inside the newspaper, the well-known World War II resistance fighter Zdzisław Jeziorański (a.k.a. Jan Nowak, 1914–2005) reflected on the lessons to be learned from mistaking nationalism for patriotism in recent Polish history. Having referred in particular to the anti-Semitism of the 1930s, he stated that

Patriotyzm jest wysoką wartością moralną, bo uczucie przywiązania do własnego kraju nie idzie w parze z nienawiścią czy wrogością do innych [...] w przeciwień-stwie do nacjonalizmu nie jest konfliktogenny.

(Gazeta Wyborcza, 10–11 Nov. 2003)

Patriotism is a high moral value because attachment to one's own country does not go hand in hand with hatred or enmity towards others [...] unlike national-ism, it does not generate conflict.

Thus, the pro-European argument was enhanced by linking it positively to the topos of comparison (the "founding father," the federalist Piłsudski), and nega-tively to the topos of history as teacher (Poland's legacy of anti-Semitism). At the same time, however, *Gazeta* pointed to the many challenges that faced Poland as a new EU member: below the fold, the other sidebar on the front page was entitled "Przedunijna akcja *Gazety*. Jedzmy do Unii," '*Gazeta*'s pre-union action. Let us eat our way to the Union.' Addressing the producers of local, traditional food, the

Figure 3. *Gazeta Wyborcza* front page 10–11 November 2003

newspaper started a campaign "żeby przed wejściem do UE zastrzec sobie nazwy i receptury polskich przysmaków: kindziuk, kołacza, miodu pitnego," 'to reserve the names and recipes of Polish specialties before entering the EU: *kindziuk* sausage, cream-cheese wedding cake, and traditional Polish mead.' By dealing with the protection of national culinary trademarks in an earnest manner, *Gazeta* acknowledged, as it were, the Euro-skeptic segments in Polish society.

Summing up, it is tempting to say that *Gazeta's* discourse on 11 November in the period from 1989 to 2003 revealed an imperative that overrode almost everything else – the imperative of a civilizing mission aimed at securing a transition to liberal democracy for newly independent Poland under the metaphorical banner of the "return to Europe." In the texts examined so far, definition and comparison were used to establish a modern Polish identity by promoting unification, identification, and solidarity. Simultaneously, however, the topos of comparison, the topos of terrible place, and the topos of history as teacher were used to transform a relatively well-established ethnic national identity and its components into another identity, a civic identity, the contours of which the editor had already conceptualized. Seemingly, this process marked the beginnings of *Gazeta's* attempt to indigenize a vision of a Euro-Polish nation, by appealing to glorious historical precedents and to the prospect of a promising future.

Concerning the ensuing decade in Polish politics, however, postcommunism eventually yielded not only liberal Euro-enthusiasts such as Michnik. Support for Euro-skeptic and anti-Europeanist parties increased, while *Gazeta's* raison d'être as the civic institution that creates reasoning and reasonable citizens waned. Especially from 2002 onwards, as national populist parties increasingly gained control over the understanding of Polish identity (Pankowski 2010: 151–190), the newspaper had to work harder to retain its opinion-forming status among the media and to remain relevant to its formerly more or less unified public (Kochanowicz 2008; Matynia 2009). This raises the following question: after Poland officially joined the EU on 4 May 2004, how did *Gazeta* treat the topic "Poland and Europe" on its front pages in the days immediately before and after 11 November each year?

2.2   Projecting Euro-Polishness: 2004–2006

Whether *Gazeta's* rhetoric is one of compromise and dialogue depends on how *Gazeta* relates as a polemicist to its adversary. With this in mind, I examined the front-page coverage in the days immediately before and after 11 November from 2004 to 2006. In the post-holiday edition of 2004, when Poland entered the EU, the main headline read "III RP – to sukces czy patologia," 'The Third Republic –

Figure 4. *Gazeta Wyborcza* front page 12 November 2004

success or pathology' (see Figure 4). Displayed below the masthead, the corresponding splash featured a large photograph of the president in office. As indicated in the subhead ("Polska to nie wyłącznie sensacja, afery, notatki służb i spiski," 'Poland is not only about sensations, scandals, secret police reports, and conspiracies'), Kwaśniewski (SLD) highlighted his government's successes: economic growth and NATO and EU membership; however, he also blamed the opposition for its "próba zawrócenia kraju z europejskiej drogi," 'trying to turn the country away from the European road.' Subsequently, PiS leader Jarosław Kaczyński was quoted to have proclaimed "My chcemy IV Rzeczypospolitej," 'We want the Fourth Republic,' while comparing the present government's manner of ruling to the "propaganda z okresu stanu wojennego," 'the propaganda during martial law' (*Gazeta Wyborcza*, 12 Nov. 2004). A sidebar above the fold pointed out that the president "w Dniu Niepodległości mówił o najważniejszych dla kraju sprawach," 'spoke about matters on Independence Day that are most important for the

Figure 5. *Gazeta Wyborcza* front page 12–13 November 2005

country,' notably the lack of consensus and cooperation. Characteristically, *Gazeta*'s post-holiday front page portrayed Poland's political scene as a still ongoing battle between the pro-European Third and the anti-European Fourth Republic.

The fall of 2005 marked the beginning of a period of political instability and of mainly ill-starred coalitions. After the parliamentary election on 9 October 2005, the PiS, one of the successful parties, formed a minority coalition led by Kazimierz Marcinkiewicz. The headline of that year's post-holiday splash read "Do brydża z Lepperem," 'Playing bridge with Lepper' (*Gazeta Wyborcza*, 12–13 Nov. 2005; see Figure 5). As readers were informed by the subhead, the PiS could consolidate its government owing to the support of the far-right party LPR and the populist party SRP (whose leader Andrzej Lepper was foregrounded in the headlined metaphor). In the corresponding text, the PiS compared the Third Republic's policies to a card game, linking its liberal followers to activities that are negative or even criminal. In turn, PO leader Donald Tusk was quoted as

Figure 6. *Gazeta Wyborcza* front page 10–12 November 2006

using the jocular phrase "moherowa koalicja," 'mohair coalition' to describe the increasing cooperation between the PiS, LPR, and SRP.[9] In a sidebar on the upper right side, senior journalist Marek Beylin criticized the Fourth Republic's nationalist project for being too centralized and controlled, adding that Prime Minister Marcinkiewicz said little about foreign policy, freedom, or civil self-government.

As expected, on 10 July 2006, the PiS formed a coalition government with the two parties, after which Jarosław Kaczyński was appointed prime minister by his brother, President Lech Kaczyński. In *Gazeta's* holiday edition, the splash covered the government's controversial method of dealing with the failure of a pharmaceutical factory to deliver (see Figure 6):

9. Tusk's phrase connotes "mohair berets," standing for simple-minded people that support the views expressed by Poland's conservative Catholic movement, notably the ultra-nationalist Father Rydzyk.

Za błąd w fabryce leków
Premier wini III RP
Premier Kaczyński zarządził wczoraj wstrzymanie aż do odwołania produkcji w
fabryce leków Jelfa w Jeleniej Górze. – Zawiedli ci, którzy stworzyli porządek
prawny III powiedział.   (*Gazeta Wyborcza*, 10–12 Nov. 2006)

Blunder at the drug factory
Prime minister blames the Third Republic
Yesterday Prime Minister Kaczyński ordered that production at the Jelfa drugs
factory in Jelenia Góra be discontinued until further notice. "The creators of the
Third Republic's legal order have failed," he said.

As expressed in the headline, Kaczyński's attack on the Third Republic may be
interpreted as a negation of the civic-pluralistic vision of Poland as an outward-
looking, European state. More importantly, however, the corresponding text
(which provided a fairly balanced account of the story) was juxtaposed with two
prominently positioned sidebars thematizing the weaknesses of Polish democracy and the dangers of the Fourth Republic, respectively. First, there was a moral
summons above the fold on the left, entitled "Trzeba głosować!" 'You must vote!'
which was mainly aimed at the younger generations; the writer was the well-
known Solidarity member Tadeusz Mazowiecki, Poland's latter-day "founding father" and first freely elected president after independence was regained. Second,
below the fold on the right, a commentary appeared entitled "A ja się boję IV RP,"
'I fear the Fourth Republic,' in which in-house journalist Elżbieta Cichocka – using the topos of terrible place to emphasize cultural and political backwardness –
admitted to having been afraid of the nationalist conservatives and "ich pochopne
decyzje," 'their rash decisions,' since the elections.

Gazeta's front-page coverage of Independence Day 2006 brought the conflict
between the notions of the Third and Fourth Republics out into the open, thus
reflecting the tension between civic-pluralists and Euro-enthusiastic on the one
hand, and ethnic-nationalists and Euro-skeptics on the other. The pro-European
writers employed the technique of juxtaposition when emphasizing the difference
between these stances, and the topos of consequence when presenting Polish right-
wing policies as counterproductive and disastrous. Considering that the writers
also used ad hominem comments when portraying their adversaries in black-
and-white terms, these devices amounted to a double strategy of dismantling and
justification. However, insofar as Euro-skeptic actors (Kaczyński, Marcinkiewicz,
Lepper) and Euro-enthusiastic actors (Kwaśniewski, Tusk, Mazowiecki) were
foregrounded and, as it were, given reliable voices, *Gazeta* treated the themes of
Europe and independence in an open, dialogue-based, and compromise-oriented
fashion.

2.3   Europeanization: 2007–2009

After the parliamentary elections of October 2007, PO leader Donald Tusk took over as prime minister. That year's post-holiday edition of *Gazeta* contained an article below the masthead (headlined "Wyjątkowe Święto Niepodległości. Prosimy dotykać eksponatów," 'An Exceptional Independence Holiday. Please Touch the Exhibited Items'), featuring a photograph of smiling young men dressed as soldiers from Piłsudski's legion (*Gazeta Wyborcza*, 12 Nov. 2007; see Figure 7).

Figure 7. *Gazeta Wyborcza* front page 12 November 2007

Reporting a record interest in 11 November, the text informed readers that, after years of being associated with boring run-of-the-mill commonplace features, celebrations were completely different in 2007: "tak ogromnego zainteresowania świętem 11 Listopada stolica dawno nie widziała," 'such an enormous interest in 11 November has not been seen in the capital for a long time.' Here the writers attributed positive connotations to the Third Republic by using the topos of the idyllic place, emphasizing Poland's positive national uniqueness as reflected in the multicultural heritage of the Polish-Lithuanian Commonwealth (1572–1795), the so-called First Republic. In addition, in his speech at the Tomb of the Unknown Soldier, President Kaczyński declared that the Polish independence of 1918 was the result of a favorable international coincidence, as well as of the work of Polish soldiers and politicians. However, this seemingly well-balanced post-holiday text takes on greater significance when considered together with the splash:

> O co się kłócą w Europie
> Wielka wyprawa 21 reporterów "Gazety". Wysłaliśmy ich do 21 miast Unii Europejskiej, by podpatryzli, czym żyją nasi sąsiedzi. Dziś pierwsza relacja – o co Europa się awanturuje i jak się godzi.　　　　(*Gazeta Wyborcza*, 12 Nov. 2007)

> What they quarrel about in Europe
> The great expedition of twenty-one *Gazeta* reporters. We sent them to twenty-one cities in the European Union so that they could see how our neighbors live. Today's edition offers the first report – on what Europeans argue about and how they are reconciled.

This headline introduced a European story on ethnic discrimination in Oslo, the point being that the parties involved in a protracted dispute reach an understanding through dialogue. Below the fold on the right, a self-promotional plug entitled "Mój kawałek Europy," 'My piece of Europe' continued in a similar vein: "Nasi reporterzy […] popatrywali, jak władza rozmawia z mieszkańcami […] Sprawdźcie, co oni odkryli," 'Our reporters […] observed how the people in power talk with the citizens […] Find out what they discovered.' The association of the independence theme with that of Europe, including the description of *Gazeta*'s junior reporters that are out communicating with their fellow Europeans, underscored the newspaper's project of Euro-Polish identity construction. This is especially so because the Norwegians were portrayed as being capable of ending a quarrel, thus serving as an inspiration for how to deal with conflicting politics in Poland. Again, the writers used the topos of the idyllic place to evoke the multicultural or pluralist heritage of the Polish-Lithuanian Commonwealth. In so doing, they emphasized the positive aspect of their superordinate aim: Poles were encouraged to immerse themselves further in the EU and to embrace their own Europeanness.

Figure 8. *Gazeta Wyborcza* front page 10–11 November 2008

The spirit of compromise also permeated the 11 November coverage of 2008. A month earlier, the PO had formed a coalition majority government with the pro-EU but socially conservative *Polskie Stronnictwo Ludowe* (Polish People's Party, PSL). On the front page of *Gazeta* on 10–11 November 2008, this political event formed the background for a self-promotional plug which was positioned just below the masthead (see Figure 8). Having thematized the government's first year in power, it then introduced a series of assessment activities:

> Rok rządu Tuska
> Premier zaskoczył tych, który uważali, że jedynym jego celem jest utrzymanie wysokiego poparcia w sondażach. Koalicja przegłosowała właśnie ważne i społecznie delikatne ustawy – pisze Witold Gadomski. Przez cały tydzień publicyści "Gazety" oceniają rok rządu Donalda Tuska i stawiają mu oceny. W środę Mirosław Czech podsumuje rozliczanie rządów PiS. W piątek Donald Tusk sam oceni swój rząd Ty też możesz go ocenić – na Wyborcza.pl.
>
> (*Gazeta Wyborcza*, 10–11 Nov. 2008)

One year of Tusk government
The prime minister has surprised those that believed his only goal was to maintain a high level of support in the opinion polls. "The coalition has actually voted
down important and socially sensitive bills," Witold Gadomski writes today. All
week *Gazeta*'s writers will evaluate the first year of Donald Tusk's government
and give him grades. On Wednesday Mirosław Czech will give an account of PiS
rule. On Friday Donald Tusk evaluates his own government. You too can evaluate
him – on Wyborcza.pl.

In addition to presenting Poland's pro-European government as being able and
effective, the plug involved voices from various political parties (consider the liberal-democratic Czech and the centrist-conservative Gadomski) and encouraged
readers to participate in the democratic process ("You too can evaluate him").
At the bottom of the page on the right, a smaller piece informed readers that
today's newspaper would contain a retrospective of the historical events of 1918.
Below the fold, another supplementary item revealed that "11 listopada na to-
pie," '11 November is at the top': almost 43 percent of people asked say that this
anniversary is the most important in Poland's history. Thus, by literally framing
the front page with Independence Day texts, an interrelationship was established
between Polishness and Europeanness, which was underscored in turn by the
splash titled "W NBP Euro jest be," 'In the National Bank of Poland the euro is a
no-no': a critical piece on Polish politicians, mainly from the PiS, who were ob-
structing the introduction of the official currency of the eurozone. The writer of
this piece emphasized the negative common features of President Kaczyński and
his populist radical associates, the SRP and LPR. Given that the text conveyed a
positive connotation of gradual, Europeanist change, it reinforced the division
between integrationists and isolationists. This argumentation was underscored by
a follow-up piece inside the newspaper: a sociological survey, the results of which
indicated that many Poles disliked the way politicians exploited history in relation to the various anniversaries. An adjacent article on the same page informed
readers that the president had not invited the Solidarity legend and former prime
minister, Lech Wałęsa, to the commemorative gala at Warsaw's National Theatre.

The front page of the post-holiday edition displayed the same story with
the headline "11 listopada bez Wałęsy," '11 November without Wałęsa' (*Gazeta
Wyborcza*, 12 Nov. 2008). Placed in the central position below the masthead,
this splash featured a large photograph of an actor dressed as Piłsudski, waving
to spectators from a horse-drawn carriage (see Figure 9). Although the celebrations in Warsaw were covered as usual, President Kaczyński was quoted as criticizing the Third Republic: "Polskę niepodległą należy naprawiać," 'Independent
Poland must be repaired.' The text reiterated the story about Wałęsa's absence

Figure 9. *Gazeta Wyborcza*, 10–11 November 2009

from the presidential gala. In this connection, parliamentary leader Bronisław Komorowski (PO) was quoted as having stated that it was "jakby przed wojną Piłsudskiego nie zaprosić na święto 11 Listopada," 'like not inviting Piłsudski to the 11 November holiday before the war.' Highlighting that the German chancellor, and the presidents of Ukraine, Georgia, and Afghanistan were also absent, here the writer presented the Polish president in negative terms. Moreover, by citing Komorowski's reference to the civic federalist and "founding father" Piłsudski, he – using the topos of comparison – added further weight to the pro-European notion of Polish democracy.

A note on the page's overall design, beginning with a small item positioned on the bottom-left side foregrounding the pro-European Prime Minister Tusk: it is pointed out here that, although the PO and PiS strongly disagreed in their appraisal of the latter's government from 2005 to 2007, "krzywdy sobie nie robią," 'they do not harm each other.' Moreover, the two parties were described as formerly having been joined in "współsprawstwo," 'complicity' and together promoted "hasło IV RP i 'rewolucji moralnej'," 'the slogan of the Fourth Republic and of "moral revolution." ' Again, the readers were encouraged to participate in the democratic process ("Ty też możesz ocenić rząd!" 'You too can evaluate the government!'), while a rather jarring link was established between a Euro-enthusiastic party (the PO) and another that was Euro-skeptic (the PiS). In other words, this inconspicuous item on *Gazeta*'s post-holiday front page reflected discursive strategies that are not aimed one-sidedly at any political party as such.

Finally, on the front page of *Gazeta*'s holiday edition of 2009, the splash positioned immediately underneath the masthead was headlined as follows:

> Berlin jednej Europy
> Niemcy z wielką pompą obchodzili wczoraj 20. rocznicę upadku muru berlińskiego. To święto całej Europy – mówiła pod Bramą Brandenburską Angela Merkel. Lech Wałęsa przypomniał Niemcom, że to ludzie, a nie politycy obalili mur. (*Gazeta Wyborcza*, 10–11 Nov. 2009)

> Berlin of one Europe
> With great pomp, yesterday the Germans celebrated the twentieth anniversary of the fall of the Berlin Wall. "This holiday belongs to all of Europe," said Angela Merkel beneath the Brandenburg Gate. Lech Wałęsa reminded the Germans that it was the people that tore down the wall, not politicians.

By reporting on the German anniversary of 9 November (commemorating the fall of the Berlin Wall) in the holiday edition of 11 November, the front page foregrounded Europeanization and Polish independence (see Figure 10). This effect is matched by that caused by the juxtaposition of two photographs above the fold: one from 1962, depicting West Germans looking across to the East German side of the wall, and the other contemporary, foregrounding Wałęsa, who, present at the anniversary celebrations, was making the victory sign – embodying, as it were, Poles in Europe. Given the centuries-long history of hostility between Poland and Germany, this salient gesture may be interpreted positively within the framework of *Gazeta*'s compromise-oriented identity project. Using the topos of idyllic place both to emphasize Poland's pluralist heritage and to placate *Gazeta*'s Euroskeptical readers, the journalist wrote, "Niemcy […] stały się przyjacielem Polski i naszym rzecznikiem w Europie […] budujemy mosty pojednania," 'Germany […] has become Poland's friend and our spokesman in Europe […] together we build bridges of reconciliation.' In addition, the splash was framed by a double headline at the top of the page: "11 listopada w rocznicę odzyskania niepodległości | Od dziś w gazecie: Kalicki opowiada," '11 November, on the anniversary of the attainment of independence | From today every day: Kalicki narrates.' By announcing three consecutive articles (by former Solidarity member Włodzimierz Kalicki) on

Figure 10. *Gazeta Wyborcza*, 10–11 November 2009

Piłsudski's struggle for Polish independence before and after 11 November 1918, the front page became pro-European, as it were, through and through. Already with his post-holiday piece ("Wygrał Polskę, przegrał wizję," 'Poland won, the vision lost'), the writer interconnected the country's political life past, present, and future, the focal phrase of the independence narrative being the name of the compromise-seeking statesman Piłsudski, who did not altogether succeed (*Gazeta Wyborcza*, 12 Nov. 2009).[10]

In summary, *Gazeta*'s front-page coverage of Independence Day from 2004 to 2009 was "Europeanized" to such an extent that any Euro-skeptic or anti-EU sentiment was, if not neutralized, then seriously challenged. Especially after 2007, when Tusk took office as prime minister, the writers of the front-page texts addressed the thematics of Europe and Polish independence according to the "topos" of changed internal and external circumstances, upon which they based their discursive (re)construction of national identity. Simultaneously, different ideological voices were almost always given some space.

3. Concluding remarks

This chapter on Polish Independence Day has facilitated an understanding of how *Gazeta Wyborcza* would like Poles to act in "being European" and in "being independent." My overarching aim has been to show how the newspaper used 11 November to reinforce a Euro-Polish identity. From the newspaper's first holiday edition of 1989 onwards, its front-page coverage of 11 November reflected the social and political changes in postcommunist Poland, interpreting the challenges of the Polish community's identity. As shown in my examination of *Gazeta*'s rhetorical devices, notably the topos of comparison (the "founding fathers"), the topos of history as teacher, and the topos of the idyllic place, the writers' argumentation schemes served to obtain a specific effect that has been the aim of their discursive strategy: to promote unification and gradual change. The newspaper's identity project was threefold: first, it encompassed the ideas of Polishness and a common culture; second, it reinforced the idea of a past, present, and future common to Poland and Europe; and, third, it introduced a new concept of European supranationalism that, however, did not replace but instead served to complement Polish nationalism. *Gazeta*'s writers may have aimed at disparaging parts of the existing Kaczyński-style construct of Polish identity, but did not provide a new model in its place. The newspaper gave space to many different voices, including those of its ideological adversaries, and allowed them to speak, be they the Euro-enthusiastic actors such as Kwaśniewski, Tusk, and Komorowski, or Euro-skeptic actors such as Lepper, Marcinkiewicz, and the Kaczyński brothers. Moreover, *Gazeta*

---

10. In this connection, *Gazeta* scrutinizes the Piłsudski mythology: in Kalicki's concluding piece ("Dyskretny dictator," 'A discrete dictator'), the model founding father is portrayed as a Pole that has a bent for dialogue, but is human and fallible, as a pluralist whose contribution to independent Poland is significant, but not uncontested (*Gazeta Wyborcza*, 13 Nov. 2009).

emerged as an independent newspaper in the sense that it did not fully subscribe to any political orientation. Rather, it leaned towards achieving consensus. Thus, Michnik and his staff never ceased to encourage politics as coherent as possible among those that differ: realistic compromise, not idealistic polarization, was the line they tried to stick to.

During the 1990s, *Gazeta* was a forum for major debates and was instrumental in crafting a language for grasping the new reality. In the following decade, especially after 2004, when Poland entered the EU, the newspaper was criticized for maintaining its role as a pro-European curator of the young democratic state. In so doing, it had allegedly downplayed the tension between the nation-state and the supranational community, as well as the fears this tension engenders regarding a threatened Polish identity. Here, however, Editor-in-Chief Michnik might be viewed as a steadfast continuer of earlier Polish nation-building programs, notably those promoted by the interwar followers of Piłsudski. This is because Michnik has also urged his compatriots to remember the fates of the neighboring countries; he too believed that in the future these nations would become independent and democratic states, and that a union with them would strengthen the position of Poland. As evidenced in the front pages examined here, 11 November took on meaning as a recurring reminder that *Poles are independent as well as European*. Nevertheless, could it be that a stable democracy in Poland now requires more than one civic-institution-cum-newspaper and more than one inspired editor to serve its reading public? If so, this is not a bad thing, insofar as *Gazeta* – with its project of a modern Euro-Polish identity – has become a normal newspaper, one among several in today's Polish media landscape.

Primary sources

Gazeta Wyborcza 1989–2009
Website: http://archiwum.wyborcza.pl/Archiwum/0,107006.html. 21 May 2012.

References

Aarts, Bas. [1997] 2001. *English Syntax and Argumentation*. Basingstoke, Hampshire: Palgrave.

Abrams, Bradley F. 2005. *The Struggle for the Soul of the Nation. Czech Culture and the Rise of Communism*. Lanham, Maryland: Rowman & Littlefield.

Achugar, Mariane. 2008. *What We Remember: The Construction of Memory in Military Discourse*. Amsterdam: John Benjamins.

Agora S.A. (co-owner of *Gazeta Wyborcza*). 2012. http://www.agora.pl/agora/0,110780.html. Accessed 17 Sept. 2012.

Andrijašević, M. Živko. 2004. *Nacija s greškom (Istorijski eseji)*. Cetinje: Centralna narodna biblioteka Crne Gore "Đurđe Crnojević."

Andrijašević, M. Živko, and Šerbo Rastoder. 2006. *Istorija Crne Gore od najstarijih vremena do 2003*. Podgorica: CICG.

Anić, Nikola. 2005. *Narodnooslobodilačka vojska Hrvatske, 1941–1945*. Zagreb: Savez antifašističkih boraca i antifašista Republike Hrvatske.

Anthonissen, Christine, and Jan Blommaert. 2007. *Discourse and Human Rights Violations*. Amsterdam: John Benjamins.

Assmann, Aleida. 2009. "From Collective Violence to a Common Future: Four Models for Dealing with a Traumatic Past." In *Justice and Memory: Confronting Traumatic Pasts: An International Comparison*, edited by Ruth Wodak and Gertraud Auer Borea. Wien: Passagen Verlag, pp. 31–48.

Assmann, Jan. 1995. "Collective Memory and Cultural Identity." *New German Critique* 65, pp. 125–133.

———. 2005. *Kulturno pamćenje*. Zenica: Vrijeme.

Baldry, Anthony, and Paul J. Thibault. 2006. *Multimodal Transcription and Text Analysis London*. Oakville: Equinox.

Bangerter, Adrian, Mario von Cranach, and Christoph Arn. 1997. "Collective Remembering in the Communicative Regulation of Group Action: A Functional Approach." *Journal of Language and Social Psychology* 16, pp. 365–388.

Barić, Nikica. 2008. "The Rise and Fall of the Republic of Serb Krajina (1990–1995)." In *Croatia since Independence*, edited by S. P. Ramet, K. Clewing, and R. Lukić. Munich: R. Oldenbourg, pp. 89–106.

Bell, Allan. 1991. *The Language of News Media*. Oxford: Blackwell.

Berger, Peter Ludwig, and Thomas Luckman. 1967. *The Social Construction of Reality: A Treatise in the Sociology of Knowledge*. New York: Doubleday.

Billig, Michael. 1995. *Banal Nationalism*. London: Sage.

———.1996. *Arguing and Thinking: A Rhetorical Approach to Social Psychology*, second edition. Cambridge: Cambridge University Press.

———. 1999. *Freudian Repression*. Cambridge: Cambridge University Press.

Biondich, Mark. 2009. "Kontroverze u vezi s Katoličkom crkvom u Hrvatskoj u vrijeme rata 1941.–1945." In *Nezavisna Država Hrvatska*, edited by Sabrina P. Ramet, Zagreb: Alinea, pp. 131–166.

Blommaert, Jan. 2005. *Discourse: A Critical Introduction*. Cambridge: Cambridge University Press.

Bose, Sumantra. 2002. *Bosnia after Dayton. Nationalist Partition and International Intervention*. London: Hurst & Company.

Brkljačić, Maja, and Holm Sundhaussen. 2003. "Symbolwandel und symbolischer Wandel. Kroatiens 'Erinnerungskulturen.'" *Osteuropa* 53, pp. 933–948.

Brković, Milko. 2001. "Diplomatička analiza papinskih pisama druge polovice IX. stoljeća destinatarima u Hrvatskoj." *Rad Zavoda povijesnih znanosti HAZU* 43, pp. 29–44.

Brown, Keith. 2000. "A Rising to Count On: Ilinden between Politics and History in Post-Yugoslav Macedonia." In *East European Monographs: The Macedonian Question*, edited by Victor Roudometof. New York: Columbia University Press, pp. 143–172.

———. 2003. *The Past in Question: Modern Macedonia and the Uncertainties of Nation*. Princeton and Woodstock: Princeton University Press.

Brunnbauer, Ulf. 2005. "Ancient Nationhood and the Struggle for Statehood: Historiographic Myths in the Republic of Macedonia." In *Myths and Boundaries in South East Europe*, edited by Pål Kolstø. London: Hurst & Company, pp. 262–296.

Bunce, Valerie. 1995. "Should Transitologists Be Grounded?" *Slavic Review* 54 (1), pp. 111–127.

Burke, Kenneth. 1989. *On Symbols and Society*. Chicago: The University of Chicago Press.

Castano, Emanuele. 2004. "European Identity: A Socio-Psychological Perspective." In *Identities in Europe and the Institutions of the European Union*, edited by Richard Herrmann, Thomas Risse, and Marilynn Brewer. London: Rowman and Littlefield, pp. 40–58.

Castoriadis, Cornelius. 1987. *The Imaginary Institution of Society*. Cambridge, Massachusetts: MIT University Press.

Chandler, David. 1999. *Faking Democracy after Dayton*. London: Pluto.

Chilton, Paul. 2004. *Analysing Political Discourse: Theory and Practice*. London, New York: Routledge.

Ćirković, Sima. 2004. *The Serbs*, translated by Vuk Tošić. Malden, Mass.: Blackwell.

Civín, Jan. 2005. "Československý komunistický režim v letech 1985–1989." *Středoevropské politické studie* 6 (2–3), pp. 207–227.

Cohen, Shari J. 1999. *Politics without a Past: The Absence of History in Postcommunist Nationalism*. Durham and London: Duke University Press.

Connerton, Paul. 1989. *How Societies Remember*. Cambridge: Cambridge University Press.

Cornis-Pope, Marcel, John Neubauer (eds.). 2004. *A Comparative History of Literatures in European Languages*. Vol. 1 of *History of the Literary Cultures of East-Central Europe: Junctures and Disjunctures in the Nineteenth and Twentieth Centuries*. Amsterdam: John Benjamins.

Czyżewski, Marek, Sergiusz Kowalski, and Andrzej Piotrowski (eds.). 2010. *Rytualny chaos. Studium dyskursu publicznego*. Warsaw: Wydawnictwa Akademickie i Profesjonalne.

Daneš, František. 2000. "Jakou řečí mluví věda. Modalizace vědeckého diskurzu." *Slovo a slovesnost* 61 (2), pp. 81–92.

David, Lea. 2009. "Sećam se, dakle, postojim: Identitet Srba kao refleksija kulture sećanja." In *Pamćenje i nostalgija*, edited by Gordana Đerić. Belgrade: Institut za filozofiju i društvenu teoriju "Filip Višnjić," pp. 139–170.

Davies, Norman. 2003. *Rising '44: "The Battle for Warsaw."* London: Macmillan.

———. 2005. *God's Playground: A History of Poland in Two Volumes. Volume II: 1795 to the Present*. Oxford: Oxford University Press.

De Cillia, Rudolf, Martin Reisigl, and Ruth Wodak. 1999. "The Discursive Construction of National Identities." *Discourse and Society* 10 (2), pp. 149–171.

Detchev, Stefan. 2003. "Mapping Russia in the Bulgarian Press (1886–1894)." *Echinox Journal (Caietele Echinox)* 5, pp. 135–155.

Devátý, Stanislav, Miloš Hájek, and Bohumír Janát. 1990. "Zamyšlení k jubileu republiky." In *Charta 77 1977–1989*, edited by V. Prečan. Scheinfeld-Schwarzenberg: Čs. středisko nezávislé literatury, pp. 348–350.

Devitt, Amy J. 2004. *Writing Genres*. Carbondale: Southern Illinois University Press.

Doellinger, David. 2002. "Prayers, Pilgrimages and Petitions: The Secret Church and the Growth of Civil Society in Slovakia." *Nationalities Papers* 30 (2), pp. 215–240.

Edwards, Derek. 2003. "Analyzing Racial Discourse: The Discursive Psychology of Mind–World Relationships." In *Analyzing Race Talk: Multidisciplinary Perspectives on the Research Interview*, edited by Harry van den Berg, Margaret Wetherell, and Hanneke Houtkoop-Steenstra. Cambridge: Cambridge University Press, pp. 31–48.

Edwards, Derek, and Jonathan Potter. 2001. "Discursive Psychology." In *How to Analyse Talk in Institutional Settings*, edited by Alec McHoul, and Mark Rapley. New York: Continuum, pp. 12–24.

Eger, György, and Josef Langer. 1996. *Border, Region and Ethnicity in Central Europe: Results of an International Comparative Research*. Klagenfurt: Norea, pp. 69–92.

Ejdus, Filip. 2007. "Security, Culture and Identity in Serbia." *Security and Identity* 7–8, pp. 38–64.

Ensink, Titus. 1996. "The Footing of a Royal Address: An Analysis of Representativeness in Political Speech, Exemplified in Queen Beatrix' Address to the Knesset on March 28, 1995." *Current Issues in Language and Society* 3, pp. 205–232.

———. 2009. "Resolving Antagonistic Tensions. Some Discourse Analytic Reflections on Verbal Commemorative Practices." In *Justice and Memory Confronting Traumatic Pasts. An International Comparison*, edited by Ruth Wodak and Gertraud Auer Borea d'Olmo. Wien: Passagen Verlag, pp. 169–193.

Ensink, Titus, and Christoph Sauer. 1995. "Political Communication as Tightrope Walking: German President Roman Herzog's Commemorative Address in Warsaw, August 1 1994." *Politics, Groups, and the Individual* 5, pp. 37–50.

——— (eds.). 2003a. *The Art of Commemoration. Fifty Years after the Warsaw Uprising*. Amsterdam: John Benjamins.

———. 2003b. "A Discourse Analytic Approach to the Commemorative Speeches about the Warsaw Uprising." In *The Art of Commemoration: Fifty Years after the Warsaw Uprising*, edited by Titus Ensink and Christopher Sauer. Amsterdam: John Benjamins, pp. 19–40.

———. 2003c. "The Search for Acceptable Perspectives. German President Roman Herzog Commemorates the Warsaw Uprising." In *The Art of Commemoration. Fifty Years after the Warsaw Uprising*, edited by Titus Ensink and Christoph Sauer. Amsterdam: John Benjamins, pp. 57–94.

Eriksen, Thomas Hylland. 2002. *Ethnicity and Nationalism: Anthropological Perspectives*. London and Sterling: Pluto Press.

Erjavec, Karmen. 2001. "Media Representation of the Discrimination against the Roma in Eastern Europe: The Case of Slovenia." *Discourse and Society* 12 (6), pp. 699–727.

Erjavec, Karmen, and Zala Volčič. 2007. "The Kosovo Battle: Media's Recontextualization of the Serbian Nationalistic Discourses." *Press/ Politics* 12 (3), pp. 67–86.

Fairclough, Norman. 2001. "The Dialectics of Discourse." *Textus* 14 (2), pp. 231–242.

Fairclough, Norman, and Ruth Wodak. 1997. "Critical Discourse Analysis: An Overview." In *Discourse as Social Interaction. Discourse Studies: A Multidisciplinary Introduction* 2, edited by Theun Andrianus van Dijk. London: Sage, pp. 258–284.

Felberg, Tatjana R. 2008. *Brothers in Arms? Discourse Analysis of Serbian and Montenegrin Identities and Relations as Constructed in Politika and Pobjeda Front Page Articles during the NATO Bombing of Yugoslavia in 1999.* Ph.D dissertation. Oslo: University of Oslo.

Fillmore, Charles. 1968. "The Case for Case." In *Universals in Linguistic Theory*, edited by Emmon Bach, and R. T. Harms. New York: Holt, Rinehart and Winston, pp. 1–88.

Fox, Jon. E., and Cynthia Miller-Idriss. 2008. "Everyday Nationhood." *Ethnicities* 8 (4), pp. 536–563.

Frank, Alison. 2009. "The Pleasant and the Useful: Pilgrimage and Tourism in Habsburg Mariazell." *Austrian History Yearbook* 40, pp. 157–182.

Fuller, Linda K. 2004. *National Days/National Ways: Historical, Political and Religious. Celebrations around the World.* London: Praeger Publishers.

Galasiński, Dariusz. 1997. "The making of history. Some remarks on politicians' presentation of historical events. " *Pragmatics* 7, pp. 55–68.

Galasiński, Dariusz. 2003. "The Messianic Warsaw. Mythological Framings of Political Discourse in the Address by Lech Wałęsa." In *The Art of Commemoration. Fifty Years after the Warsaw Uprising*, edited by Titus Ensink and Christoph Sauer. Amsterdam: John Benjamins, pp. 41–56.

Gallagher, Tom. 2003. "Identity in Flux, Destination Unknown: Montenegro During and After the Yugoslav Wars." *International Journal of Politics, Culture and Society* 17 (1), pp. 53–71.

Gee, James Paul. 2005. *An Introduction to Discourse Analysis: Theory and Method.* New York: Routledge.

Geisler, Michael E. 2005. *National Symbols, Fractured Identities: Contesting the National Narrative.* Middlebury, VT: Middlebury College Press.

———. 2009. "The Calendar Conundrum: National Days as Unstable Signifiers." In *National Days. Constructing and Mobilizing National Identity*, edited by David McCrone, and Gayle McPherson. Basingstoke: Palgrave Macmillan, pp. 10 –25.

Giesen, Bernhard. 2004. *Triumph and Trauma.* Boulder, London: Paradigm.

Gillis, John R. 1994. "Introduction." In *Commemorations: The Politics of National Identity*, edited by John R. Gillis. Princeton: Princeton University Press, pp. 3–24.

Głowiński, Michał. 2009. *Nowomowa i ciągi dalsze. Szkice dawne i nowe.* Cracow: Universitas.

Godzic, Wiesław. 2009. "Polskie media a demokracja." In *Demokracja w Polsce 2007–2009*, edited by Lena Kolarska-Bobińska and Jacek Kucharczyk. Warsaw: Obserwatorium demokracji, pp. 233–259.

Goldstein, Ivo. 2008. *Hrvatska 1918–2008.* Zagreb: EPH.

Goldstein, Slavko. 2007. *1941. Godina koja se vraća.* Zagreb: Novi liber.

Greenberg, Robert D. 2008. *Language and Identity in the Balkans: Serbo-Croatian and Its Disintegration.* Oxford: Oxford University Press.

Gross, Peter. 2002. *Entangled Revolutions. Media and Democratization in Eastern Europe.* Washington, D.C.: Woodrow Wilson Center Press.

Hájková, Dagmar, Zdenko Maršálek, Vlasta Quagliatová, Stanislav Slavík, and Richard Vašek. 2008. "28. říjen: proměny jednoho výročí." Cited from http://www.mua.cas.cz/vystavy/wpvpjv-01.html. Accessed 1 Mar. 2010.

Hałas, Elżbieta. 2000. "Transformation in Collective Imagination." *Polish Sociological Review* 3, pp. 309–322.

———. 2002a. "Public Symbols and Polish Identity. Change and Ambiguity of Meaning in State Holidays Calendar of the Third Republic of Poland." In *Symbols, Power and Politics*, edited by Elżbieta Hałas. Frankfurt am Main: Peter Lang, pp. 81–100.

———. 2002b. "Symbolic Politics of Public Time and Collective Memory. The Polish Case." *European Review* 10 (1), pp. 115–129.

———. 2005. "Constructing the Identity of a Nation-State. Symbolic Conflict over the Preamble to the Constitution of the Third Republic of Poland." *Polish Sociological Review* 1 (149), pp. 49–67.

———. 2008. "Social Symbolism: Forms and Functions: A Pragmatist Perspective." *Studies in Symbolic Interaction* 30, edited by Norman K. Denzin, pp. 131–149.

Halbwachs, Maurice. 1992. *On Collective Memory*. Chicago: University of Chicago Press.

Halliday, Michael Alexander Kirkwood, and Christian M. I. M. Matthiessen. 2004. *An Introduction to Functional Grammar*. London: Arnold.

Halliday, Michael Alexander Kirkwood, and Ruqaiya Hasan. 1989. *Language, Context, and Text: Aspects of Language in a Social-Semiotic Perspective*. Oxford: Oxford University Press.

Handler, Richard. 1988. *Nationalism and the Politics of Culture in Quebec*. Madison: University of Wisconsin Press.

Hedetoft, Ulf (ed.). 1998. *Political Symbols, Symbolic Politics: European Identities in Transformation*. Aldershot: Ashgate.

Heer, Hannes, and Ruth Wodak. 2008. "Introduction: Collective Memory, National Narratives and The Politics of the Past." In *The Discursive Construction of History Remembering the Wehrmacht's War of Annihilation*, edited by Hannes Heer, Walter Manoschek, Alexander Pollak, and Ruth Wodak. Basingstoke: Palgrave Macmillan, pp. 1–13.

Heer, Hannes, Walter Manoschek, Alexander Pollak, and Ruth Wodak (eds.). 2008. *The Discursive Construction of History Remembering the Wehrmacht's War of Annihilation*. Basingstoke: Palgrave Macmillan.

Hinckley, Barbara. 1990. *The Symbolic Presidency. How Presidents Portray Themselves*. New York: Routledge.

Hobsbawm, Eric J., and Terence O. Ranger. 1983. *The Invention of Tradition*. Cambridge: Cambridge University Press.

Hoepken, Wolfgang. 1999. "War, Memory, and Education in a Fragmented Society: The Case of Yugoslavia." *East European Politics and Societies* 13 (1), pp. 190–227.

Holweck, Frederick. [1912] 2009. "Feasts of the Seven Sorrows of the Blessed Virgin Mary." *The Catholic Encyclopedia*. New York: Robert Appleton Company. Quoted from *New Advent*. http://www.newadvent.org/cathen/14151b.htm.

Hrženjak, Juraj. 2002. *Rušenje antifašističkih spomenika u Hrvatskoj 1990–2000*. Zagreb: Savez antifašističkih boraca i antifašista Republike Hrvatske.

Huszka, Beáta. 2003. "The Dispute over Montenegrin Independence." In *Montenegro in Transition*, edited by Florian Bieber. Baden-Baden: Nomos Verlagsgesellschaft, pp. 43–62.

Jakubowicz, Karol. 2007. *Rude Awakening: Social and Media Change in Central and Eastern Europe*. Cresskilll, New Jersey: Hampton Press.

Jedlicki, Jerzy. 1999. "Historical Memory as a Source of Conflicts in Eastern Europe." *Communist and Post-Communist Studies* 32, pp. 225–232.

———. 2005. "East-European Historical Bequest en Route to an Integrated Europe." In *Collective Memory and European Identity: The Effects of Integration and Enlargement*, edited by Klaus Eder, and Willfried Spohn. Aldershot, Hampshire: Ashgate, pp. 37–48.

Johnson-Cartee, Karen S. 2005. *News Narratives and News Framing*. Lanham, Md.: Rowman & Littlefield Publishers.

KhosraviNik, Majid. 2009. "The Representation of Refugees, Asylum Seekers and Immigrants in British Newspapers during the Balkan Conflict (1999) and the British General Election (2005)." *Discourse and Society* 19 (3), pp. 477–498.

Koczanowicz, Leszek. 2008. *Politics of Time: Dynamics of Identity in Post-Communist Poland*. New York: Berghahn Books.

Koleva, Daniela. 2007. "The Memory of Socialist Public Holidays: Between Colonization and Autonomy." In *Zwischen Amnesie und Nostalgie: Die Erinnerung an den Kommunismus in Südosteuropa*, edited by Ulf Brunnbauer and Stefan Troebst. Cologne: Böhlau Verlag, pp. 185–198.

Kolstø, Pål. 2006. "National Symbols as Signs of Unity and Division." *Ethnic and Racial Studies* 29 (4), pp. 676–701.

——— (ed.). 2009. *Media Discourse and the Yugoslav Conflicts, Representation of Self and Other*. Farnham, Burlington: Ashgate.

Kordić, Snježana. 2010. *Jezik i nacionalizam*. Zagreb: Durieux.

Koz'menko, I. V. 1952. *Sbornik dogovorov Rossii s drugimi gosudarstvami, 1856–1917*. Moscow: Gospolitizdat. Cited from http://www.hist.msu.ru/ER/Etext/FOREIGN/stefano.htm. Accessed 27 May 2011.

Kraus, Jiří. 2003. "Vyjádření polemičnosti a významových opozic v politickém diskurzu." In *Jazyk, média, politika*, edited by S. Čmejrková and J. Hoffmannová. Prague: Academia, pp. 13–39.

Kress, Gunther. 2003. "Multimodality, Multimedia and Genre." *Literacy in the New Media* 106. London: Routledge, pp. 106–121.

Kress, Gunther, and Theo van Leeuwen. 1998. *Front Pages: (The Critical) Analysis of Newspaper Layout*. In *Approaches to Media Discourse*, edited by Allan Bell, and Peter Garrett. Oxford: Blackwell, pp. 186–219.

———. 1996. *Reading Images: The Grammar of Visual Design*. London and New York: Routledge.

———. 2001. *Multimodal Discourse Analysis: The Modes and Media of Contemporary Communication*. London: Edward Arnold.

Krzyżanowski, Michał. 2008. "On the 'Europeanization' of Identity Constructions in Polish Political Discourse after 1989." In *Discourse and Transformation in Central and Eastern Europe*, edited by Aleksandra Galasińska and Michał Krzyżanowski. London: Palgrave, pp. 95–113.

Krzyżanowski, Michał, Anna Triandafyllidou, and Ruth Wodak. 2009. "Conclusions: Europe, Media, Crisis and the European Public Sphere." In *The European Public Sphere and the Media. Europe in Crisis*, edited by Anna Triandafyllidou, Ruth Wodak, and Michał Krzyżanowski. Basingstoke: Palgrave Macmillan, pp. 261–269.

Krzyżanowski, Michał, and Aleksandra Galasińska. 2009. "Introduction. Discourses of Social and Political Transformation in the 'New Europe'." In *Discourse and Transformation in Central and Eastern Europe*, edited by Michał Krzyżanowski and Aleksandra Galasińska. Basingstoke: Palgrave Macmillan, pp. 1–16.

Krzyżanowski, Michał, and Ruth Wodak. 2009. "Theorising and Analysing Social Change in Central and Eastern Europe: The Contribution of Critical Discourse Analysis." In *Discourse and Transformation in Central and Eastern Europe*, edited by Michał Krzyżanowski and Aleksandra Galasińska. Basingstoke: Palgrave Macmillan, pp. 17–39.

Kubiš, Karel. 2005. "Troublesome Anniversary: The Rise of the Czechoslovak Republic and its European Fellows in Czech Collective Memory." In *Collective Memory and European Identity: The Effects of Integration and Enlargement*, edited by Klaus Eder, and Willfried Spohn. Aldershot, Hampshire: Ashgate, pp. 151–178.

Kusovac, Zoran. 2000. "The Prospects for Change in Post-Tudjman Croatia." *East European Constitutional Review* 9 (3), pp. 57–62.

Kutter, Amelie. 2007. "Re-drawing the Boundaries of the Demos: The Construction of Political Projects in Polish Public Discourse 1989/90 and 2003." Paper presented at the *Changing Europe Summer School II "Crises and Conflicts in Eastern European States and Societies: Stumbling Blocks or Stepping Stones for Democratisation?"* Warsaw, 2–8 Sept. 2007. Cited from http://www.changing-europe.org/download/Summer_School_2007/Kutter.pdf. Accessed 7 Jan. 2011.

Kuzio, Taras. 2001. "Transition in Post-Communist States: Triple or Quadruple?" *Politics* 21, pp. 168–177.

Kuzmanić, Marja. 2008. "Collective Memory and Social Identity: A Social Psychological Exploration of the Memories of the Disintegration of Former Yugoslavia." *Psihološka obzorja* 17 (2), pp. 5–26.

Lakić, Igor. 2005. *Diskurs, mediji, rat*. PhD dissertation. Belgrade: University of Belgrade.

Langer, Josef. 1999. "Towards a Conceptualization of Border: The Central European Experience." In: *Curtains of Iron and Gold: Reconstructing Borders and Scales of Interaction*, edited by Heikki Eskelinen, Ilkka Liikanen, and Jukka Oksa. Aldershot: Ashgate, pp. 25–42.

Lepper, Georgia. 2000. *Categories in Text and Talk: A Practical Introduction to Categorization Analysis*. London: Sage.

Leudar, Ivan, Victoria Marsland, and Jiří Nekvapil. 2004. "On Membership Categorization: 'Us', 'Them' and 'Doing Violence' in Political Discourse." *Discourse and Society* 15 (2–3), pp. 243–266.

Levi-Strauss, Claude. 1966. *The Savage Mind*. Chicago: The University of Chicago Press.

Linz, Juan J., and Alfred Stepan. 1996. *Problems of Democratic Transition and Consolidation. Southern Europe, South America and Post-Communist Europe*. Baltimore and London: John Hopkins.

Ljušić, Radoš. 1995. "The Centuries under Turkish Rule and the Revival of Statehood." In *The History of Serbian Culture*, edited by Pavle Ivić, translated by Randall A. Major. Edgware: Porthill Publishers.

Ljušić, Radoš. 2008. "Ilija Garašanin on Serbia's Statehood." *Balcanica* 39, pp. 131–174.

Lowenthal, David. 1985. *The Past is a Foreign Country*. Cambridge and New York: Cambridge University Press.

Luczynski, Jan. 1997. "The Multivoicedness of Historical Representations in a Changing Sociocultural Context: Young Polish Adults' Representations of World War II." *Culture and
Psychology* 3, pp. 21–40.

Mach, Zdzisław. 2007. "The Roman Catholic Church in Poland and the Dynamics of Social
Identity in Polish Society." In *The Religious Roots of Contemporary European Identity*, edited by Lucia Faltin and Melanie Wright. London: Continuum, pp. 117–133.

Main, Izabella. 2003. *Political Rituals and Symbols in Poland, 1944–2002: A Research Report.*
Leipzig: Leipziger Universitätsverlag.

Makaryk, Irena R. 1993. *Encyclopedia of Contemporary Literary Theory: Approaches, Scholars,
Terms.* Toronto: University of Toronto Press.

Malović, Stjepan, and Gary W. Selnow. 2001. *The People, Press, and Politics of Croatia.* London:
Praeger Publishers.

Martin, James R., and Ruth Wodak. 2003. *Re/Reading the Past: Critical and Functional Perspectives on Time and Value.* Amsterdam: John Benjamins.

Matynia, Elżbieta. 2009. *Performative Democracy.* Boulder, CO: Paradigm Publishers.

McCrone, David, and Gayle McPherson. 2009. *National Days: Constructing and Mobilising National Identity.* Basingstoke: Palgrave.

Megill, Allan. 1998. "History, Memory, Identity." *History of the Human Sciences* 11 (3),
pp. 37–62.

Melegh, Attila. 2006. *On the East-West Slope: Globalization, Nationalism, Racism and Discourses on Central and Eastern Europe.* Budapest and New York: Central European University
Press.

Michnik, Adam. 1998. *Letters from Freedom. Post-Cold War Realities and Perspectives.* Berkeley:
University of California Press.

———. 2005. *Wściekłość i wstyd.* Warsaw: Zeszyty Literackie.

———. 2007. *W posukiwaniu utraconego sensu.* Warsaw: Zeszyty Literackie.

Middleton, David, and Derek Edwards. 1990. *Collective Remembering.* London: Sage.

Mihelj, Sabina. 2011. *Media Nations. Communicating Belonging and Exclusion in the Modern
World.* Basingstoke: Palgrave Macmillan.

Milošević, Saša. 2007. *Srbi u Hrvatskoj 2007.* Zagreb: Vijeće srpske nacionalne manjine grada
Zagreba.

Misztal, Barbara A. 2003. *Theories of Social Remembering.* Philadelphia: Open University
Press.

Moravčíková, Michaela. 2007. "Slovak-Hungarian Relations, Catholicism and Christian Democracy." *Politics and Religion* 2, pp. 5–28.

Moricová, Jana (ed.). 2007. "Šaštínska Sedembolestná patronka Slovenska." *Mariánske pútnické
miesta na Slovensku.* Ružomberok: Katolícka Univerzita v Ružomberok, Filozofická fakul-
ta, pp. 20–26.

Morrison, Kenneth. 2009. *Montenegro, A Modern History.* London, New York: I.B.Tauris.

Mukoska-Čingo, Vesela. 2005. "Ilinden 1903 – koncept na država na makedonskata nacija." In
100 godini Ilinden 1903-2003: Prilozi od naučniot sobir održan na 6–8 maj 2003, edited by
Makedonska akademija na naukite i umetnostite (MANU). Skopje: MANU, pp. 23–38.

Mønnesland, Svein. 1997. *Land ohne Wiederkehr.* Klagenfurt: Wieser.

Naylor, Karl. 2009. "Post-Communism's Useful Idiots." *Central and Eastern Europe Watch*
(blog), 15 Aug. http://easterneuropewatch.blogspot.com/2009/08/post-communisms-
useful-idiots.html. Accessed 7 Jan. 2011.

Nizich, Ivana, Željka Markić, and Jeri Laber. 1995. *Civil and Political Rights in Croatia*. Helsinki: Human Rights Watch.

Offe, Claus. 1997. "Cultural Aspects of Consolidation: A Note on the Peculiarities of Postcommunist Transformation." *East European Constitutional Review* 6 (4), pp. 64–68.

O'Halloran, Kay L. 2008. "Systemic Functional-Multimodal Discourse Analysis (SF-MDA): Constructing Ideational Meaning Using Language and Visual Imagery." *Visual Communication* 7, pp. 443–475.

Oktar, Lütfiye. 2001. "The Ideological Organization of Representational Processes in the Presentation of Us and Them." *Discourse and Society* 12 (3), pp. 313–347.

Ormandžijan, Agop (ed.). 1984. *Čuždi pătepisi za Balkanite, vol. 5, Armenski pătepisi za Balkanite XVII–XIX vek*. Sofia: Nauka i izkustvo.

Ost, David. 2005. *The Defeat of Solidarity: Anger and Politics in Post-Communist Europe*. Itacha: Cornell University Press.

Osteuropa. 2003. "Staatssymbolik und Geschichtskultur." *Osteuropa* 7 (53).

Palmer, Jr., Stephen E., and Robert R. King. 1971. *Yugoslav Communism and the Macedonian Question*. Hamden, Connecticut: The Shoe String Press, Inc.

Pałuszyńska, Edyta. 2006. *Nagłówki w Gazecie Wyborczej(ekspresywna leksyka, frazematyka, metaforyka)*. Łódź: Drukarnia Cyfrowa i Wydawnictwo Piktor.

Pankowski, Rafal. 2010. *The Populist Radical Right in Poland. The Patriots*. London: Routledge.

Papafragou, Anna. 2000. *Modality: Issues in the Semantics-Pragmatics Interface*. Amsterdam: Elsevier.

Pappas, Nicholas C. J. 1994. "Between Two Empires: Serbian Survival in the Years after Kosovo." In *Serbia's Historical Heritage*, edited by Alex N. Draginich. Columbia University Press, pp. 39–51.

Pauković, Davor. 2005. *Uspon i pad "Republike Srpske Krajine": Dokumenti*. Zagreb: CPI.

———. 2009. "Politička tranzicija i Srbi u Hrvatskoj." In *Serbo-Croat Relations: Political Cooperation and National Minorities*, edited by Darko Gavrilović. Sremska Kamenica: CHDR, pp. 133–141.

Pavićević, Đorđe, and Srđan Đurović. 2009. "Relations between Montenegro and Serbia from 1991 to 2006: An Analysis of Media Discourse." In *Media Discourse and the Yugoslav Conflict*, edited by Pål Kolstø. Farnham, Burlington: Ashgate, pp. 129–152.

Pavlaković, Vjeran. 2007. "Eye of the Storm: The ICTY, Commemorations and Contested Histories of Croatia's Homeland War." Cited from www.wilsoncenter.org/topics/pubs/MR347Pavlakovic.doc. Accessed 26. Feb. 2010.

Pavličević, Dragutin. 1996. "A Review of the Historical Development of the Republic of Croatia." *GeoJournal* 38, pp. 381–391.

Pavlowitch, Stevan K. 2002. *Serbia. The History behind the Name*. London: Hurs & Company.

Pennebaker, James W., and Becky L. Banasik. 1997. "On the Creation and Maintenance of Collective Memories: History as Social Psychology." In *Collective Memory of Political Events: Social Psychological Perspectives*, edited by James W. Pennenbaker, Dario Paez, and Bernard Rimé. Mahwah, New Jersey: Lawrence Erlbaum, pp. 3–20.

Péteri, György. 2010. *Imagining the West in Eastern Europe and the Soviet Union*. Pittsburgh: University of Pittsburgh Press.

Peruško, Zrinjka. 2007. "Media and Civic Values." In *Democratic Transition in Croatia*, edited by Sabrina P. Ramet, and Davorka Matić. College Station: Texas A&M University Press, pp. 224–244.

Petričušić, Antonija. 2008. "Nation-Building in Croatia and the Treatment of Minorities: Rights and Wrongs." *L'Europe en formation* 349–350, pp. 135–145.

Petrović, Tanja. 2009. *A Long Way Home: Representations of the Western Balkans in Political and Media Discourses*. http://mediawatch.mirovni-institut.si/eng/a_long_way_home.pdf

Pirjevec, Jože. 2001. *Jugoslovanske vojne 1991–2001*. Ljubljana: Cankarjeva založba.

Potter, Jonathan. 2003. *Representing Reality; Discourse, Rhetoric and Social Construction*. London, New Delhi: Thousand Oaks, Sage Publications.

Pravoslavni bogoslovski fakultet "Sveti Kliment Ohridski" Skopje. 2006. *Jubileen zbornik: 100 godini Ilinden*. Skopje: "Sveti Kliment Ohridski."

Ramet, Sabrina P. 2006. "Introduction." In *The Three Yugoslavias: State-building and Legitimation, 1918–2005*. Washington, DC and Bloomington: Woodrow Wilson Center Press and Indiana University Press, pp. 1–11.

———. 2008. "Politics in Croatia since 1990." In *Croatia since Independence*, edited by Sabrina P. Ramet, Konrad Clewing, and Reneo Lukić. Munich: R. Oldenbourg, pp. 31–58.

Ramet, Sabrina P., and Vjeran Pavlaković. 2005. *Serbia since 1989*. Seattle: Univ. of Washington Press.

Redden, Joanna, and Tamara Witschge. 2010. "A New News Order? Online News Content Examined." In *New Media, Old News*, edited by Natalie Fenton. London: Sage, pp. 171–186.

Reisigl, Martin. 2009. "Spoken Silences Bridging Breaks. The Discursive Construction of Historical Continuities and Turning Points in Austrian Commemorative Speeches by Employing Rhetorical Tropes." In *Justice and Memory Confronting Traumatic Pasts: An International Comparison*, edited by Ruth Wodak, and Gertraud Auer Borea d'Olmo. Wien: Passagen Verlag, pp. 213–240.

Reisigl, Martin, and Ruth Wodak. 2001. *Discourse and Discrimination: Rhetorics of Racism and Anti-Semitism*. London and New York: Routledge.

Rihtman-Avguštin, Dunja. 2000. *Ulice moga grada: Antropologija domaćeg terena*. Zemun, Belgrade: Biblioteka XX vek, Čigoja štampa.

Roberts, Elizabeth. 2007. *Realm of the Black Mountain, A History of Montenegro*. London: Hurst & Company.

Roksandić, Drago. 1995. "Shifting References: Celebrations of Uprisings in Croatia, 1945–1991." *East European Politics and Society* 9 (2), pp. 256–271.

Roth, Klaus, and Juliane Roth. 1990. "The System of Socialist Holidays and Rituals in Bulgaria." *Ethnologia Europaea* 20, pp. 107–120.

Roudometof, Victor. 2002. *Collective Memory, National Identity, and Ethnic Conflict: Greece, Bulgaria, and the Macedonian Question*. Westport, Connecticut: Praeger.

———. 2005. "Toward an Archaeology of National Commemorations in the Balkans." In *National Symbols, Fractured Identities. Contesting the National Narrative*, edited by Michael E. Geisler. Middlebury, Vermont: Middlebury College Press, pp. 35–57.

Šarić, Ljiljana, Andreas Musolff, Stefan Manz, and Ingrid Hudabiunigg. 2010. *Contesting Europe's Eastern Rim. Cultural Identities in Public Discourse*. Clevedon: Multilingual Matters.

Šarkić, Srdjan. 2006. "Constitutional and Legal History of Serbia 1804–1918." In *Modernisierung durch Transfer im 19. und frühen 20. Jahrhundert*, edited by Tomasz Giaro, Frankfurt am Main: Klostermann, pp. 201–222.

Sauer, Christoph. 1996. "Echoes from Abroad – Speeches for the Domestic Audience: Queen Beatrix' Address to the Israeli Parliament." *Current Issues In Language and Society* 3, pp. 233–267.

———. 2007. "Christmas Messages by Heads of State: Multimodality and Media Adaptations." In *Political Discourse in the Media*, edited by A. Fetzer and G. Lauerbach. Amsterdam: John Benjamins, pp. 227–273.

Schluchter, Wolfgang. 1990. "The Future of Religion." In *Culture and Society. Contemporary Debates*, edited by Jeffrey C. Alexander and Steven Seidman. Cambridge: Cambridge University Press, pp. 249–261.

Schutz, Alfred. 1982. *Collected Papers I. The Problem of Social Reality*, edited by Maurice Natanson. The Hague: Martinus Nijhoff.

Schäffner, Christina. 1996. "Political Speeches and Discourse Analysis." *Current Issues In Language and Society* 3, pp. 201–204.

Singleton, Frederick B. 1985. *A Short History of the Yugoslav Peoples*. Cambridge: Cambridge University Press.

Skrbiš, Zlatko. 2005. "The Apparitions of the Virgin Mary of Medjugorje: The Convergence of Croatian Nationalism and her Apparitions." *Nations and Nationalism* 11 (3), pp. 443–461.

Slavnić Ninković, Danka. 2010. "Celebrating Yugoslavia: The Visual Representation of State Holidays." In *Remembering Utopia: The Culture of Everyday Life in Socialist Yugoslavia*, edited by Breda Luthar and Maruša Pušnik. Washington: New Academia Publishing, pp. 65–91.

Smith, Anthony D. 1999. *Myths and Memories of the Nation*. Oxford: Oxford University Press.

Snajdr, Edward. 2008. *Nature Protests: The End of Ecology in Slovakia*. Seattle: University of Washington Press.

Śpiewak, Paweł, (ed.). 2000. *Spór o Polskę 1989–1999. Wybór tekstów prasowych*. Warsaw: Wydawnictwo Naukowe.

Splichal, Slavko. 1994. *Media Beyond Socialism: Theory and Practice in East-Central Europe*. Boulder, Colorado: Westview Press.

Steinke, Klaus. 2003. "How the Russians Handled a Problem. The Warsaw Uprising in Sergey Filatov's Address." In *The Art of Commemoration. Fifty Years after the Warsaw Uprising*, edited by Titus Ensink and Christoph Sauer. Amsterdam: John Benjamins, pp. 173–192.

Stråth, Bo. 2000. "Introduction. Myth, Memory and History in the Construction of Community." In *Myth and Memory in the Construction of Community. Historical Patterns in Europe and Beyond*, edited by Bo Stråth. Frankfurt am Main: P.I.E.-Peter Lang, pp. 19–46.

Sundhaussen, Holm. 2003. "Die 'Genozidnation': Serbische Kriegs- und Nachkriegsbilder." In *Der Krieg in den Gründungsmythen europäischer Nationen und der USA*, edited by Nikolaus Buschmann, and Dieter Langewiesche. Frankfurt am Main: Campus, pp. 351–371.

Sussex, Roland, and Paul Cubberley. 2006. *The Slavic Languages*. Cambridge: Cambridge University Press.

Sygkelos, Yannis. 2009. "The National Discourse of the Bulgarian Communist Party on National Anniversaries and Commemorations (1944–1948)." *Nationalities Papers* 37 (4), pp. 425–442.

Szacka, Barbara. 1997. "Systemtic Transformation and Memory of the Past." *Polish Sociological Review* 36 (2), pp. 119 –131.

Søberg, Marius. 2007. "Croatia since 1989. The HDZ and the Politics of Transition." In *Democratic Transition in Croatia*, edited by Sabrina P. Ramet and Davorka Matić. College Station: Texas A & M University, pp. 31–62.

Teubert, Wolfgang. 2010. *Meaning, Discourse and Society*. Cambridge: Cambridge University Press.

Thompson, T. B. 1990. *Ideology and Modern Society*. Cambridge: Polity Press.

Thorsen, Arve. 2000. "Foundation Myths at Work – National Day Celebrations in France, Germany and Norway in a Comparative Perspective." In *Myth and Memory in the Construction of Community Historical Patterns in Europe and Beyond*, edited by Bo Stråth. Frankfurt am Main: Peter Lang, pp. 331–350.

Tileagă, Cristian. 2008. "What is a 'Revolution'? National Commemoration, Collective Memory and Managing Authenticity in the Representation of a Political Event." *Discourse and Society* 19 (3), pp. 359–382.

Todorova, Maria. 2005. "The Trap of Backwardness: Modernity, Temporality, and the Study of Eastern European Nationalism." *Slavic Review* 64 (1), pp. 140–164.

Trbovich, Ana S. 2006. "Nation-Building under the Austro-Hungarian Sceptre. Croato-Serb Antagonism and Cooperation." *Balcanica* 37, pp. 195–220.

Troebst, Stefan. 2007. *Das makedonische Jahrhundert: Von den Anfängen der nationalrevolutionären Bewegung zum Abkommen von Ohrid 1893-2001*. Munich: R. Oldenburg Verlag.

Tulviste, Peeter, and James V. Wertsch. 1994. "Official and Unofficial Histories: The Case of Estonia." *Journal of Narrative and Life History* 4, pp. 311–329.

Turner, Charles. 2006. "Nation and Commemoration." In *The Sage Handbook of Nations and Nationalism*, edited by Gerard Delanty and Krishan Kumar. London: Sage, pp. 205–213.

Tuzin, Donald. 1997. *The Cassowary's Revenge: The Life and Death of Masculinity in a New Guinea Society*. Chicago and London: The University of Chicago Press.

van Dijk, Theun Andrianus. 1989. "Mediating Racism: The Role of the Media in the Reproduction of Racism." In *Language, Power and Ideology: Studies in Political Discourse*, edited by Ruth Wodak. Amsterdam: John Benjamins, pp. 199–226.

———. 1991. *Racism and the Press: Critical Studies in Racism and Migration*. London and New York: Routledge.

———. 2005. "Contextual Knowledge Management in Discourse Production: A CDA Prospective." In *A New Agenda in (Critical) Discourse Analysis*, edited by Ruth Wodak, and Paul Chilton. Amsterdam: John Benjamins, pp. 71–100.

———. 2008. *Discourse and Context. A Sociocognitive Approach*. Cambridge: Cambridge University Press.

van Leeuwen, Theo. 2005a. *Introducing Social Semiotics*. London and New York: Routledge.

———. 2005b. "Multimodality, Genre and Design." In *Discourse in Action: Introducing Mediated Discourse Analysis*, edited by Sigrid Norris, and Rodney H. Jones. New York: Routledge, pp. 73–94.

Vláchová, Klara, and Blanka Řeháková. 2009. "Identity of Non-self-evident Nation: Czech National Identity after the Break-up of Czechoslovakia and before Accession to the European Union." *Nations and Nationalism* 15 (2), pp. 254–279.

Wachtel, Andrew Baruch. 2006. *Remaining Relevant After Communism: The Role of the Writer in Eastern Europe*. Chicago: The University of Chicago Press.

Walton, John. 2001. *Storied Land: Community and Memory in Monterey*. Berkeley: University of California Press.

Waznak, Robert P. 1998. *An Introduction to the Homily*. Collegeville, Minnesota: The Liturgical Press.

Weber, Claudia. 2006. *Auf der Suche der Nation: Erinnerungskultur in Bulgarien von 1878–1944*. Berlin: LIT Verlag.

Weber, Max. 2004. "The Religions of Civilization and Their Attitude to the World." In *The Essential Weber. A Reader*, edited by Sam Whimster. London: Routledge, pp. 81–100.

Weiss, Gilbert, and Ruth Wodak. 2003. *Critical Discourse Analysis: Theory and Interdisciplinarity*. London: Palgrave Macmillan.

——. 2003. "Introduction: Theory, Interdisciplinarity and Critical Discourse Analysis." In *Critical Discourse Analysis: Theory and Interdisciplin-arity*, edited by Gilbert Weiss, and Ruth Wodak. Basingstoke, New York: Palgrave Macmillan, pp. 1–32.

Wertsch, James V. 2002. *Voices of Collective Remembering*. Cambridge: Cambridge University Press.

Wertsch, James V. 2008. "Narrative Organization of Collective Memory." *Ethos* 36 (1), pp. 120–135.

White, Geoffrey M. 1997. "Mythic History and National Memory: The Pearl Harbor Anniversary." *Culture and Psychology* 3 (1), pp. 63–88.

White, P.R.R. 2006. "Evaluative Semantics and Ideological Positioning in Journalistic Discourse: A New Framework for Analysis." In *Mediating Ideology in Text and Image*, edited by Inger Lassen, Jeanne Strunck, and Torben Vestergaard. Amsterdam: John Benjamins, pp. 37–68.

Wierny, Sebastian. 2003. "To samo, a inne. Wstęp do porównawczej analizy zawartości Gazety Wyborczej." *Zeszyty Prasoznawcze* 3–4, pp. 52–70.

Wierzbicki, Artur. 2006. "Językowe środki perswazji w 'Gazecie Wyborczej'." *Studia Medioznawcze* 1, pp. 11–25.

Wodak, Ruth. 2006. "Discourse-Analytic and Socio-Linguistic Approaches to the Study of Nation(alism)." In *The SAGE Handbook of Nations and Nationalism*, edited by G. Delanty, and K. Kumar. London: Sage Publications, pp. 104–117.

Wodak, Ruth. 2007. "History in the Making/The Making of History: The 'German Wehrmacht' in Collective and Individual Memories in Austria." In *Discourse and Human Rights Violations*, edited by Christine Anthonissen and Jan Blommaert. Amsterdam: John Benjamins, pp. 115–142.

Wodak, Ruth, and Gertraud Auer Borea d'Olmo. 2009. "Introduction." In *Justice and Memory Confronting Traumatic Pasts. An International Comparison*, edited by Ruth Wodak and Gertraud Auer Borea d'Olmo. Wien: Passagen Verlag, pp. 1–6.

Wodak, Ruth, and Norman Fairclough. 2010. "Recontextualizing European Higher Education Policies: The Cases of Austria and Romania." *Critical Discourse Studies* 7 (1), pp. 19–40.

Wodak, Ruth, and Theo van Leeuwen. 1999. "Politische, rechtliche und bürokratische Legitimation von Einwanderungskontrolle: Eine diskurs-historische Analyse." In *Gegen-Rassismen. Konstruktionen-Interaktionen-Interventionen*, edited by Brigitte Kossek. Hamburg, Berlin: Argument Verlag, pp. 100–129.

Wodak, Ruth, Rudolf de Cillia, Martin Reisigl, and Karin Liebhart (eds.). 2009. *The Discursive Construction of National Identity*. Edinburgh: Edinburgh University Press.

Wolff, Larry. 1994. *Inventing Eastern Europe: The Map of Civilization on the Mind of the Enlightenment*. Stanford, California: Stanford.

Wuthnow, Robert. 2001. "Spirituality and Spiritual Practice." In *The Blackwell Companion to Sociology of Religion*, edited by Richard K. Fenn. Oxford: Blackwell, pp. 306–320.

Ziemkiewicz, Rafał. 2006. *Michnikowszczyzna. Zapis choroby*. Warsaw: Wydawnictwo Red Horse.

APPENDIX

List of current laws on national holidays in West and South Slavic countries

Bosnia and Herzegovina

Zakon o državnim praznicima Republike Bosne i Hercegovine (Law on State Holidays in the Republic of Bosnia and Herzegovina). *Službeni list Republike BiH* 9 (1995).

Brčko District

Zakon o praznicima Brčko Distrikta BiH (Law on Holidays in the District of Brčko, Bosnia and Herzegovina). *Službeni glasnik Brčko Distrikta BiH* 19 (2002). Available online at http://skupstinabd.ba/ba/zakoni/ba/zakon-o-praznicima-br-distrikta-bih.html. Accessed 8 May 2011.

Republika Srpska

Zakon o praznicima Republike Srpske (Law on Holidays in the Republika Srpska). *Službeni glasnik Republike Srpske* 43 (2007). Available online at http://www.narodnaskupstinars.net/lat/zakoni/zakon.php?id_zakona=231. Accessed 8 May 2011.

Bulgaria

Kodeks na truda (Labor Code). Available at the website of *Ministerstvo na truda i socialnata politika na Republika Bulgaria*, http://www.mlsp.government.bg/bg/law/law/. Accessed 27 May 2011.

Croatia

Zakon o blagdanima, spomendanima i neradnim danima u Republici Hrvatskoj (Law on Holidays, Memorial Days, and Non-Working Days in the Republic of Croatia). *Narodne novine* 136 (2002). Available online at http://narodne-novine.nn.hr/clanci/sluzbeni/309949.html. Accessed 3 May 2010.

Czech Republic

Zákon o státních svátcích, o ostatních svátcích, o významných dnech a o dnech pracovního klidu (Law on State Holidays, Other Holidays, Days of Significance, Non-Working Days). *Sbírka zákonů Česká republika* 245 (2000). Available at the website of *Ministerstvo vnitra České republiky*, http://www.mpsv.cz/cs/75. Accessed 15 June 2011.

Macedonia

Zakonot za praznicite na Republika Makedonija (Law on Holidays in the Republic of Macedonia). Available at the website of *Ministerstvoto za trud i socijalna politika*, http://www.mtsp.gov.mk/WBStorage/Files/zakon_praznici.pdf. Accessed 15 June 2011.

Zakon za izmenuvanja na zakonot za praznicite na Republika Makedonija (Law on Amendments to the Law on Holidays in the Republic of Macedonia). *Služben vesnik na Republika Makedonija* 18 (2 Feb. 2007). Available at the website of *Sojuzot na stopanski komori na Makedonija: Vodečka makedonska delovna mreža*, http://arhiva.sojuzkomori.org.mk/images/Image/ID_praznicite_18_15022007.pdf. Accessed 15 June 2011.

Montenegro

Zakon o državnim i drugim praznicima (Law on State and Other Holidays). Available at the website of *Skupština Crne Gore,* http://www.skupstina.me/index.php?strana=zakoni&id=498. Accessed 15 June 2011.

Zakon o svetkovanju vjerskih praznika (Law on Celebrating Religious Holidays). *Službeni list Republike Crne Gore* 56 (1993), 27 (1994). Available at http://www.regulativa.me/naslovi/30127-Zakon-o-svetkovanju-vjerskih-praznika. Accessed 15 June 2011.

Poland

Ustawa z dnia 18 stycznia 1951 r. o dniach wolnych od pracy (Law of 18 January 1951 on Non-Working Days). *Dziennik Ustaw Rzeczypospolitej Polskiej* 4 (28) (1951). Available at http://isap.sejm.gov.pl/DetailsServlet?id=WDU19510040028. Accessed 15 June 2011.

Serbia

Zakon o državnim i drugim praznicima u Republici Srbiji (Law on State and Other Holidays in the Republic of Serbia). *Službeni glasnik RS* 43 (2001), 101 (2007). Available online at *propisi.com.* http://www.propisi.com/zakon-o-drzavnim-i-drugim-praznicima-u-republici-srbiji.html. Accessed 30 June 2010.

Slovakia

Zákon z 20. októbra 1993 o štátnych sviatkoch, dňoch pracovného pokoja a pamätných dňoch (Law of 20 October 1993 on State Holidays, Non-Working Days, and Memorable Days). *Zbierka zákonov* 241 (1993). Available online at website of *Ministerstvo kultúry Slovenskej republiky,* http://www.culture.gov.sk/ministerstvo/legislatva2/prvne-predpisy-v-oblasti-kultry/zkony/241/1993. Accessed 20 June 2011.

Slovenia

Zakon o praznikih in dela prostih dnevih v Republiki Sloveniji (Law on Holidays and Non-Working Days in the Republic of Slovenia). *Uradni list Republike Slovenije* 26 (1991). Available online at http://www.uradni-list.si/1/objava.jsp?urlid=199126&stevilka=1091. Accessed 20 June 2011.

Index